SUPERMAN

VOL. 3 THE TRUTH REVEALED

SUPERMAN
VOL. 3 THE TRUTH REVEALED

BRIAN MICHAEL BENDIS

MATT FRACTION | GREG RUCKA | JODY HOUSER
writers

IVAN REIS | KEVIN MAGUIRE | DAVID LAFUENTE | JOE PRADO
OCLAIR ALBERT | JULIO FERREIRA | MICHAEL GAYDOS
SCOTT GODLEWSKI | CULLY HAMNER | BRYAN HITCH
STEVE LIEBER | JIM MAHFOOD | DANNY MIKI
MIKE NORTON | MIKE PERKINS | RILEY ROSSMO
artists

PAUL MOUNTS | ALEX SINCLAIR
IVAN PLASCENCIA | NATHAN FAIRBAIRN | GABE ELTAEB | DAVE McCAIG
ANDY TROY | MICHAEL GAYDOS | JIM MAHFOOD
colorists

DAVE SHARPE
ANDWORLD DESIGN | TROY PETERI | CLAYTON COWLES
SIMON BOWLAND | TOM NAPOLITANO | JOSH REED
letterers

IVAN REIS, JOE PRADO & ALEX SINCLAIR
collection cover artists

SUPERMAN created by **JERRY SIEGEL** and **JOE SHUSTER**
SUPERBOY created by **JERRY SIEGEL**
SUPERGIRL based on characters created by **JERRY SIEGEL**
By special arrangement with the **JERRY SIEGEL** family

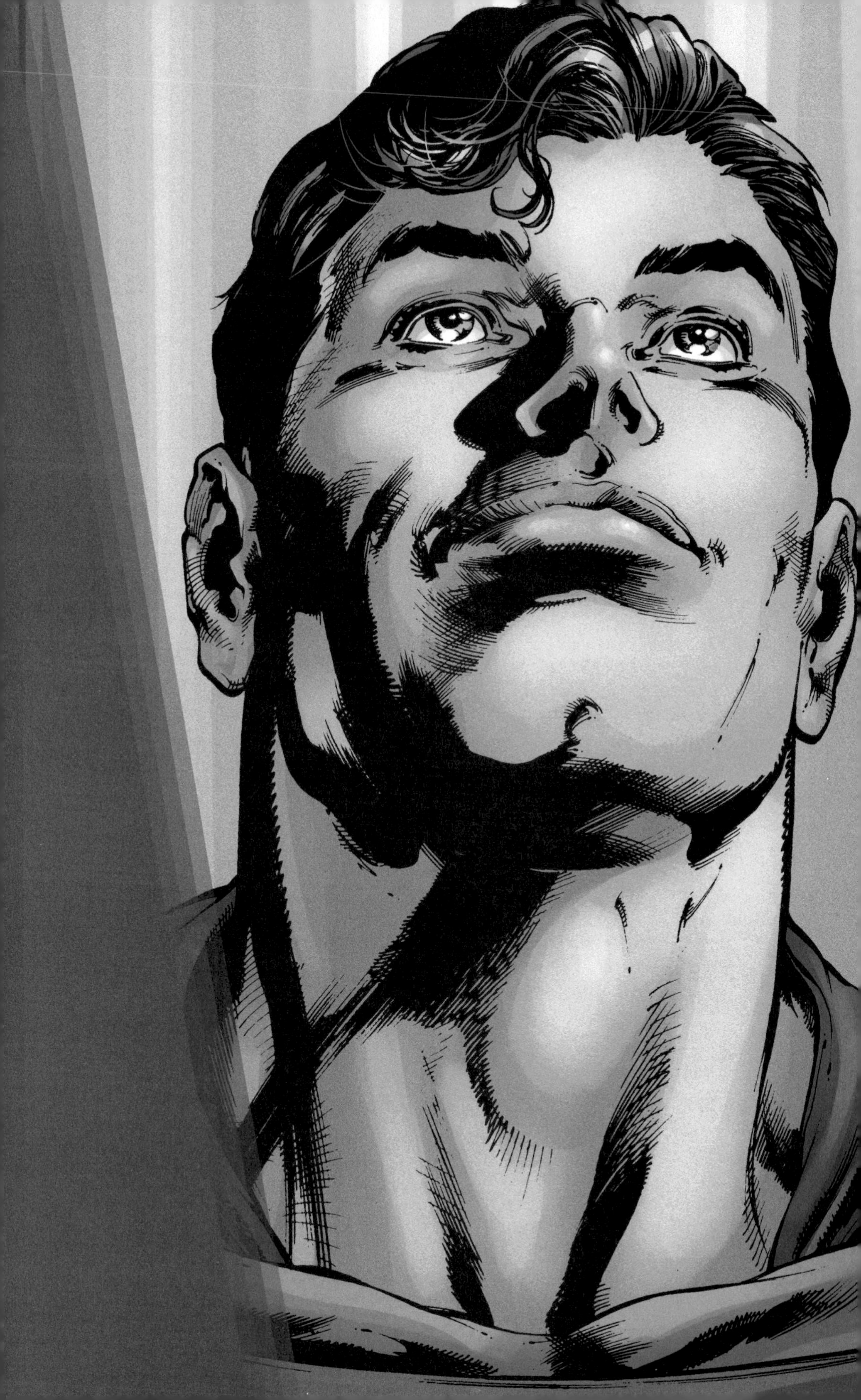

MIKE COTTON
JAMIE S. RICH Editors – Original Series
JESSICA CHEN
BRITTANY HOLZHERR Associate Editors – Original Series
JEB WOODARD Group Editor – Collected Editions
ROBIN WILDMAN Editor – Collected Edition
STEVE COOK Design Director – Books
MONIQUE NARBONETA Publication Design
SUZANNAH ROWNTREE Publication Production

MARIE JAVINS Editor-in-Chief, DC Comics

DANIEL CHERRY III Senior VP – General Manager
JIM LEE Publisher & Chief Creative Officer
DON FALLETTI VP – Manufacturing Operations & Workflow Management
LAWRENCE GANEM VP – Talent Services
ALISON GILL Senior VP – Manufacturing & Operations
NICK J. NAPOLITANO VP – Manufacturing Administration & Design
NANCY SPEARS VP – Revenue
MICHELE R. WELLS VP & Executive Editor, Young Reader

SUPERMAN VOL. 3: THE TRUTH REVEALED

DC Comics, 2900 West Alameda Ave., Burbank, CA 91505
Printed by LSC Communications, Owensville, MO, USA. 1/29/21. First Printing.
ISBN: 978-1-77950-571-2

Library of Congress Cataloging-in-Publication Data is available.

PEFC Certified
This product is from sustainably managed forests and controlled sources
PEFC
PEFC/29-31-337
www.pefc.org

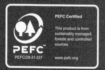

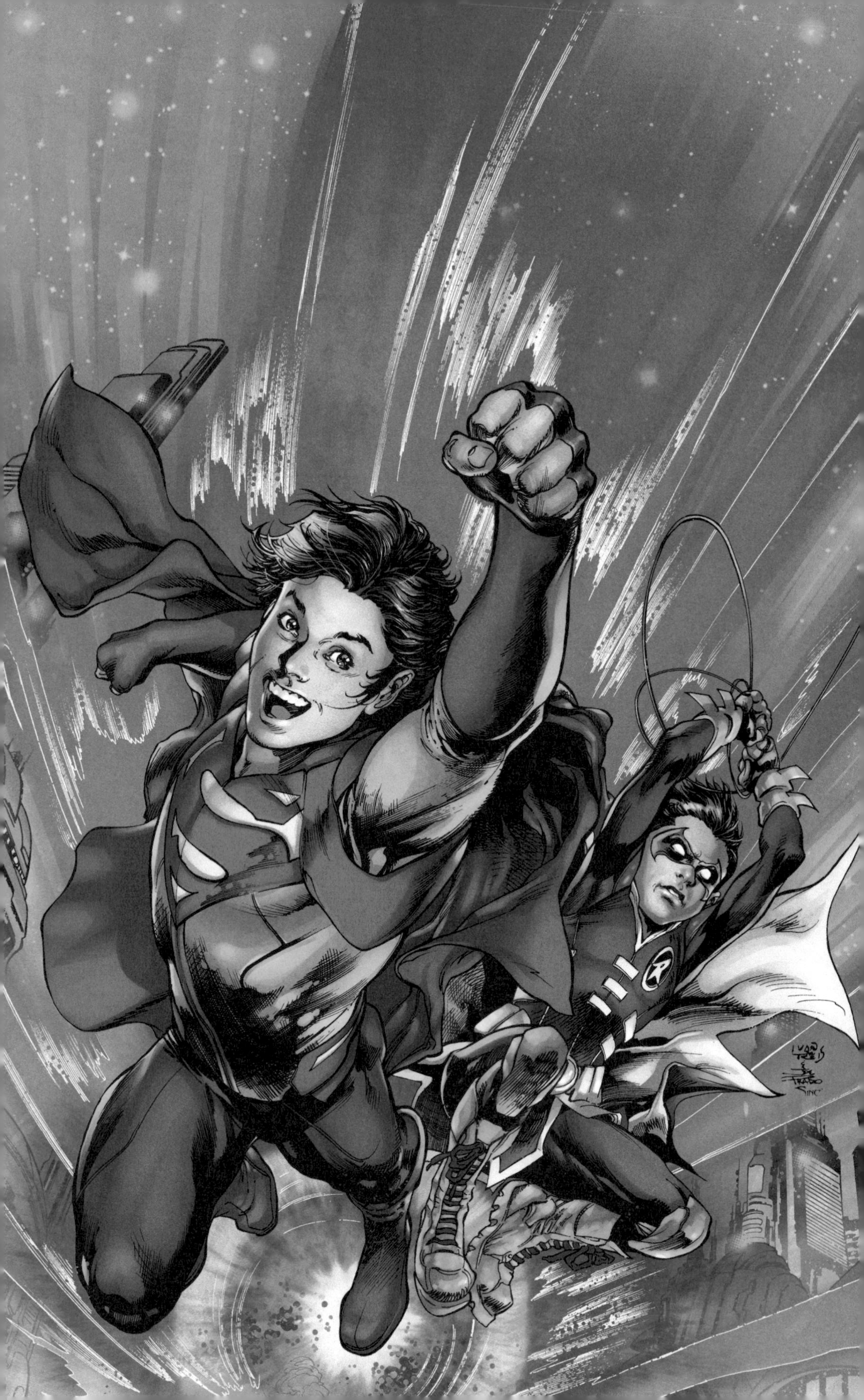

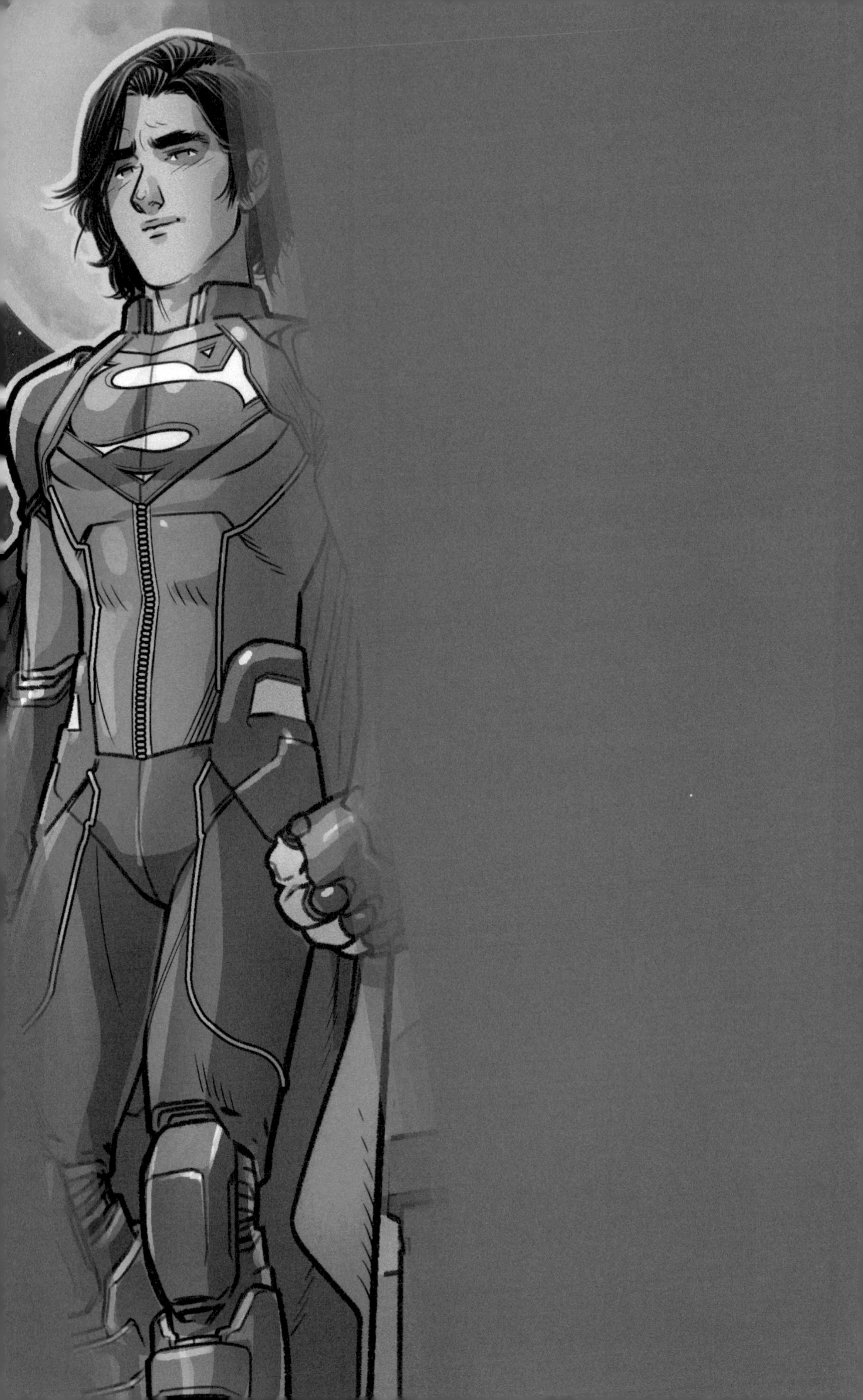

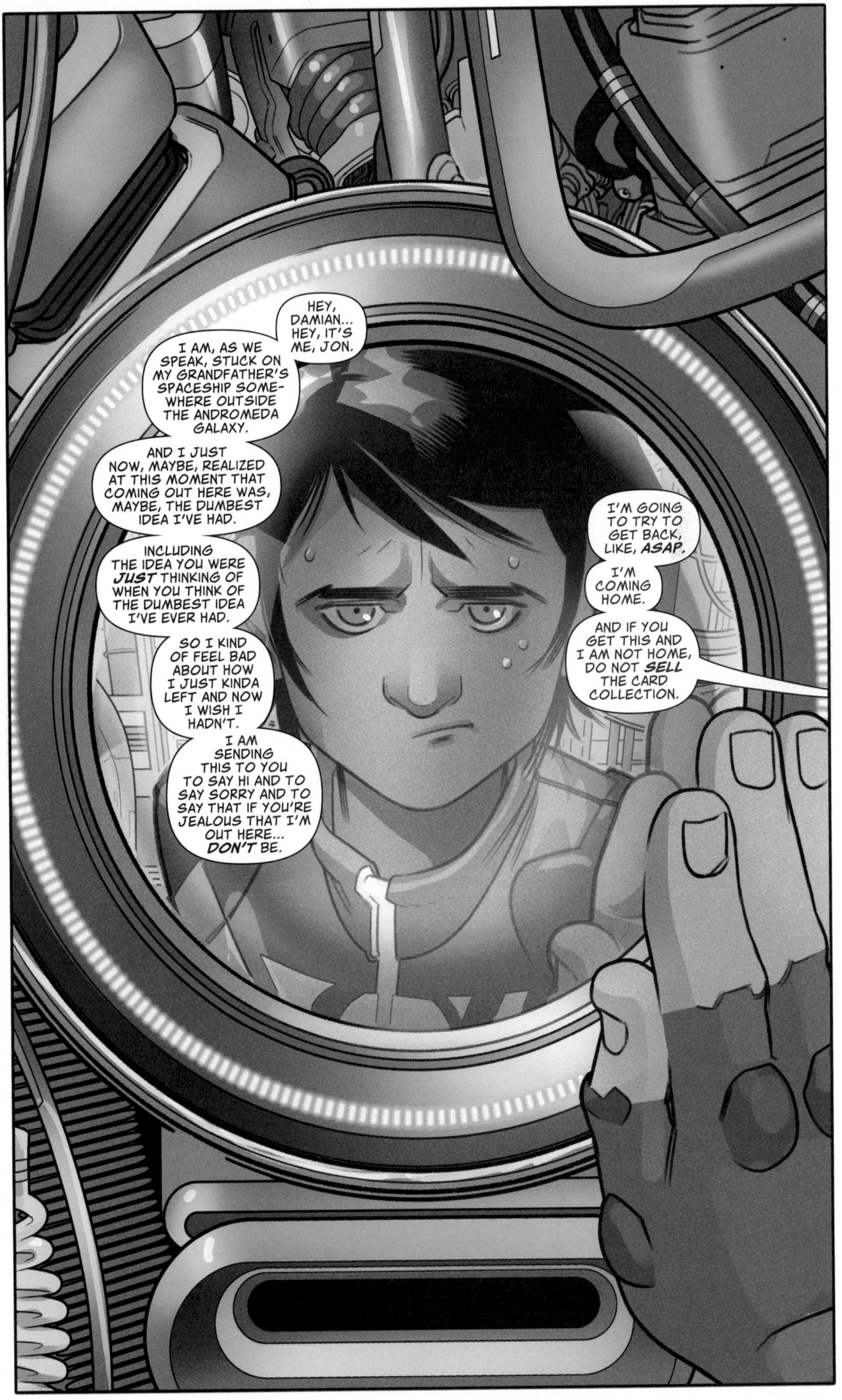
HEY, DAMIAN... HEY, IT'S ME, JON.
I AM, AS WE SPEAK, STUCK ON MY GRANDFATHER'S SPACESHIP SOMEWHERE OUTSIDE THE ANDROMEDA GALAXY.
AND I JUST NOW, MAYBE, REALIZED AT THIS MOMENT THAT COMING OUT HERE WAS, MAYBE, THE DUMBEST IDEA I'VE HAD.
INCLUDING THE IDEA YOU WERE JUST THINKING OF WHEN YOU THINK OF THE DUMBEST IDEA I'VE EVER HAD.
SO I KIND OF FEEL BAD ABOUT HOW I JUST KINDA LEFT AND NOW I WISH I HADN'T.
I AM SENDING THIS TO YOU TO SAY HI AND TO SAY SORRY AND TO SAY THAT IF YOU'RE JEALOUS THAT I'M OUT HERE... DON'T BE.
I'M GOING TO TRY TO GET BACK, LIKE, ASAP.
I'M COMING HOME.
AND IF YOU GET THIS AND I AM NOT HOME, DO NOT SELL THE CARD COLLECTION.

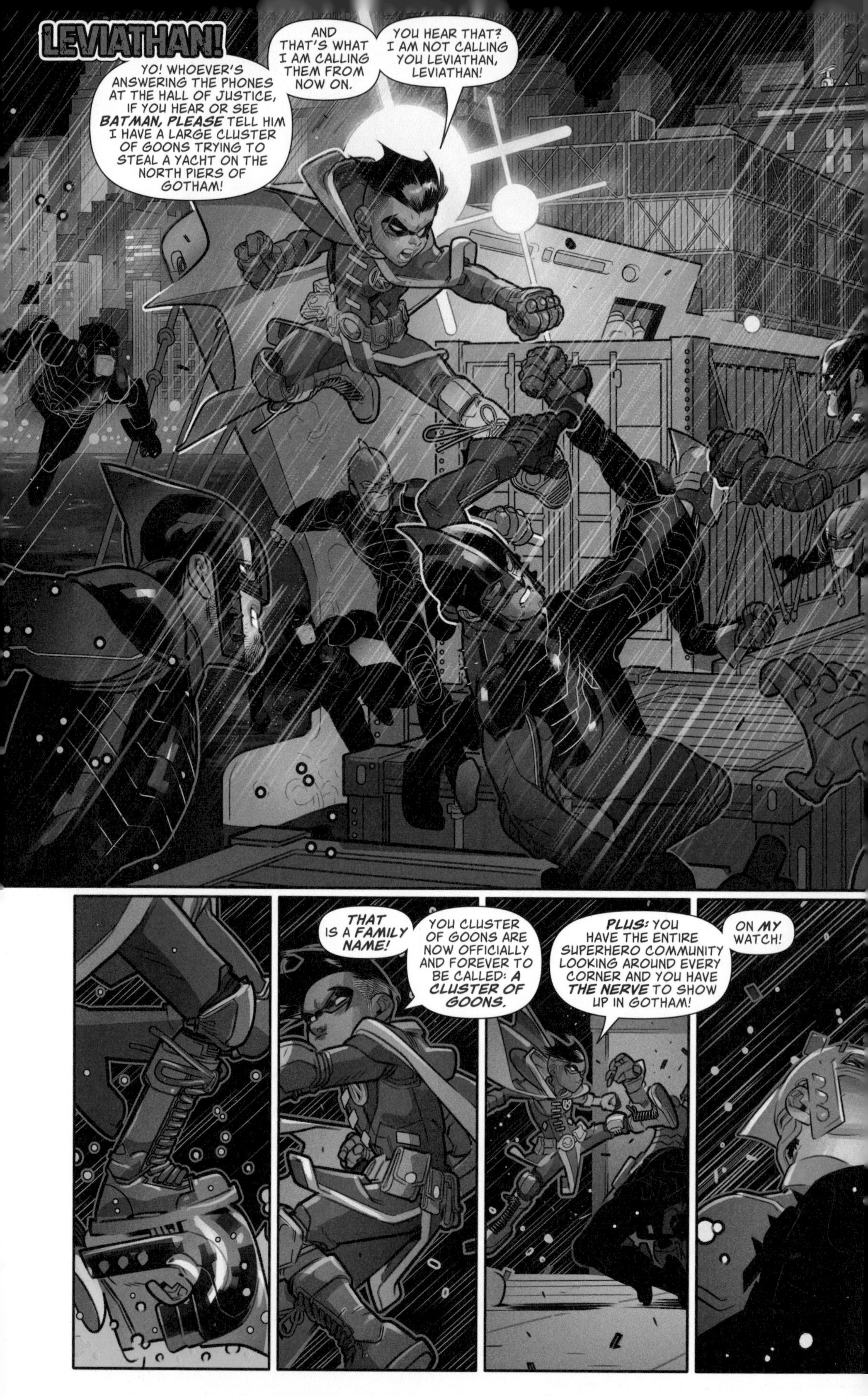
LEVIATHAN!
YO! WHOEVER'S ANSWERING THE PHONES AT THE HALL OF JUSTICE, IF YOU HEAR OR SEE BATMAN, PLEASE TELL HIM I HAVE A LARGE CLUSTER OF GOONS TRYING TO STEAL A YACHT ON THE NORTH PIERS OF GOTHAM!
AND THAT'S WHAT I AM CALLING THEM FROM NOW ON.
YOU HEAR THAT? I AM NOT CALLING YOU LEVIATHAN, LEVIATHAN!
THAT IS A FAMILY NAME!
YOU CLUSTER OF GOONS ARE NOW OFFICIALLY AND FOREVER TO BE CALLED: A CLUSTER OF GOONS.
PLUS: YOU HAVE THE ENTIRE SUPERHERO COMMUNITY LOOKING AROUND EVERY CORNER AND YOU HAVE THE NERVE TO SHOW UP IN GOTHAM!
ON MY WATCH!

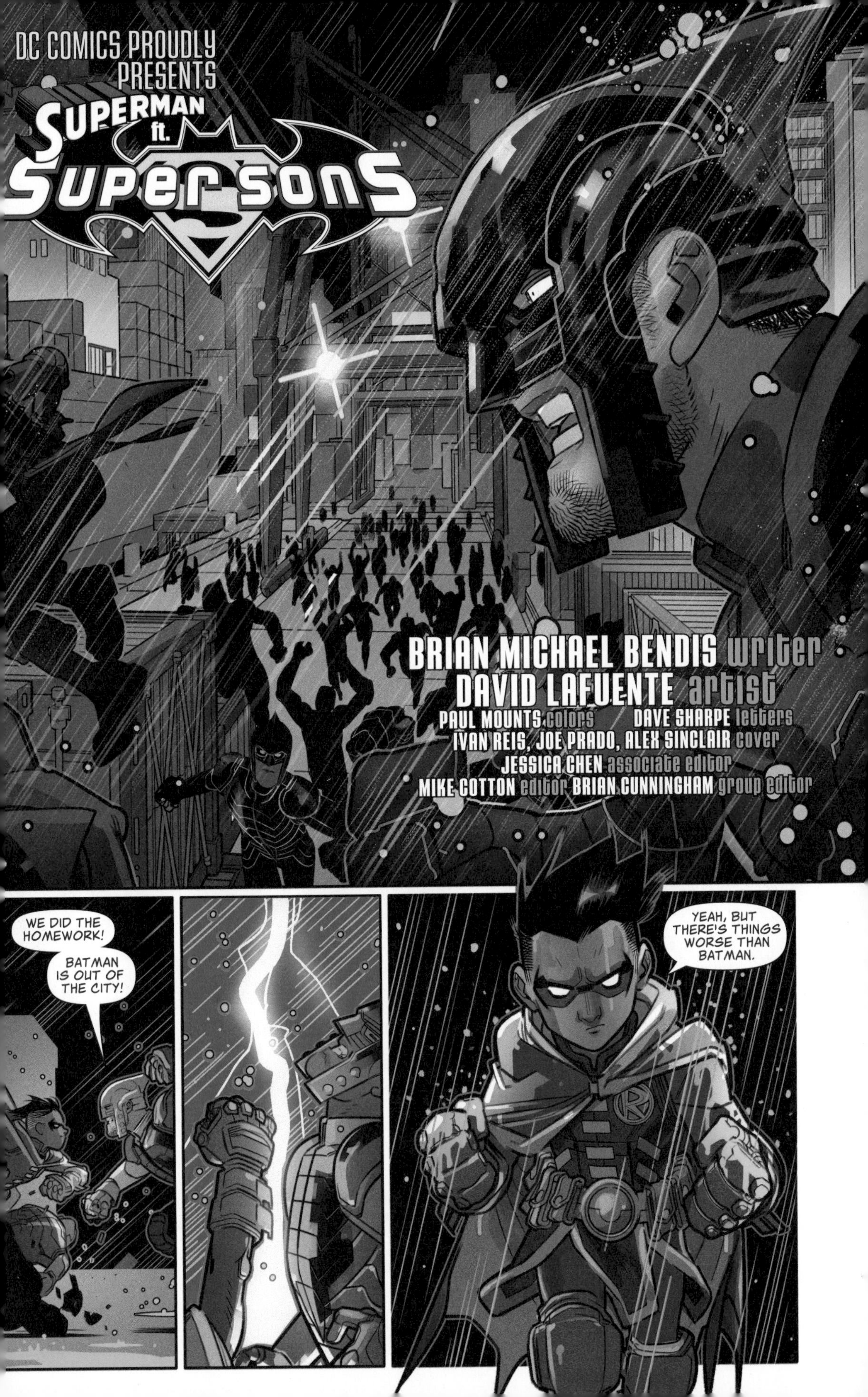
DC COMICS PROUDLY PRESENTS
SUPERMAN ft. SUPER SONS
BRIAN MICHAEL BENDIS writer
DAVID LAFUENTE artist
PAUL MOUNTS colors DAVE SHARPE letters
IVAN REIS, JOE PRADO, ALEX SINCLAIR cover
JESSICA CHEN associate editor
MIKE COTTON editor BRIAN CUNNINGHAM group editor
WE DID THE HOMEWORK!
BATMAN IS OUT OF THE CITY!
YEAH, BUT THERE'S THINGS WORSE THAN BATMAN.

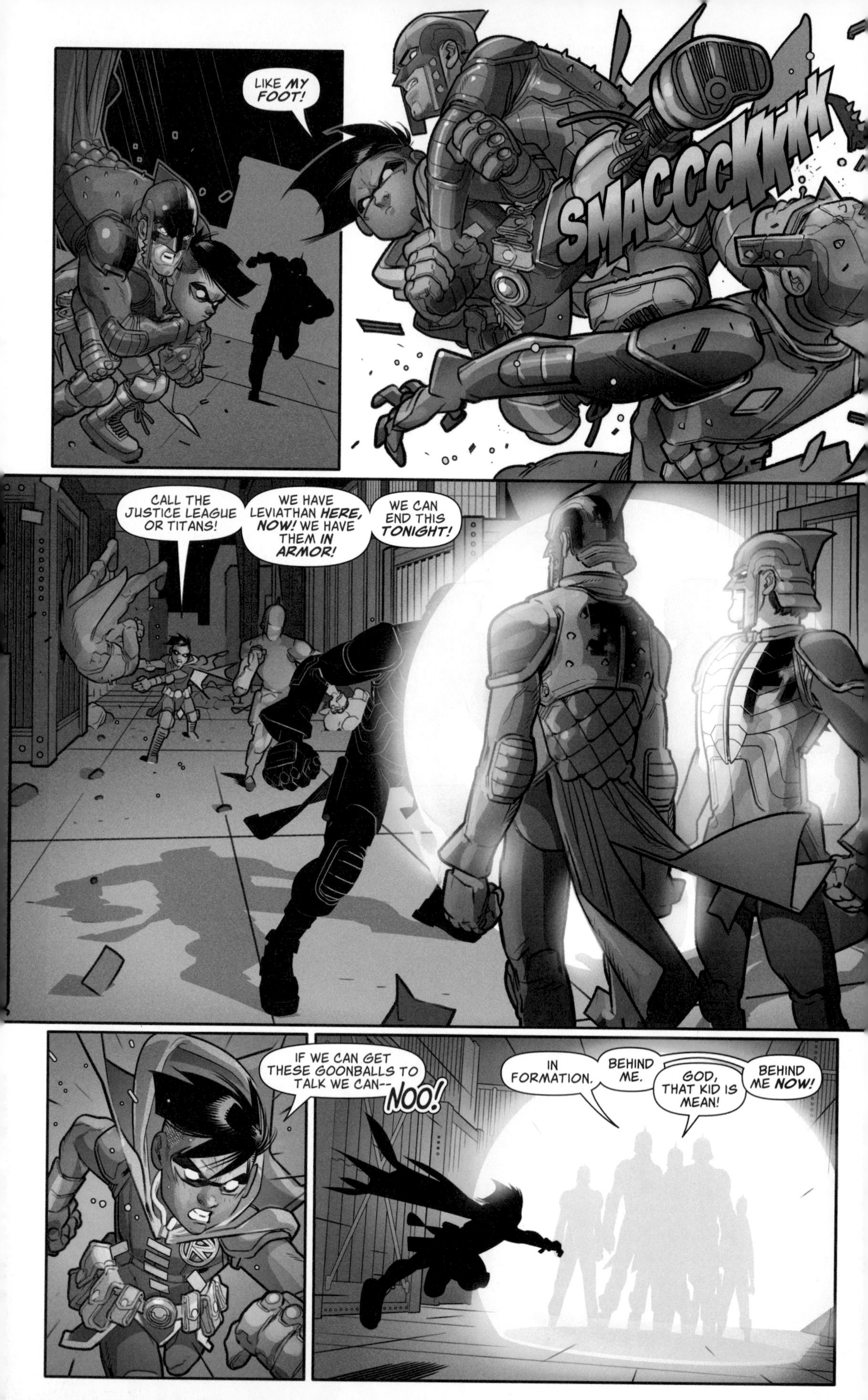
LIKE MY FOOT!
SMACCCKKKK
CALL THE JUSTICE LEAGUE OR TITANS!
WE HAVE LEVIATHAN HERE, NOW! WE HAVE THEM IN ARMOR!
WE CAN END THIS TONIGHT!
IF WE CAN GET THESE GOONBALLS TO TALK WE CAN--
NOO!
IN FORMATION.
BEHIND ME.
GOD, THAT KID IS MEAN!
BEHIND ME NOW!

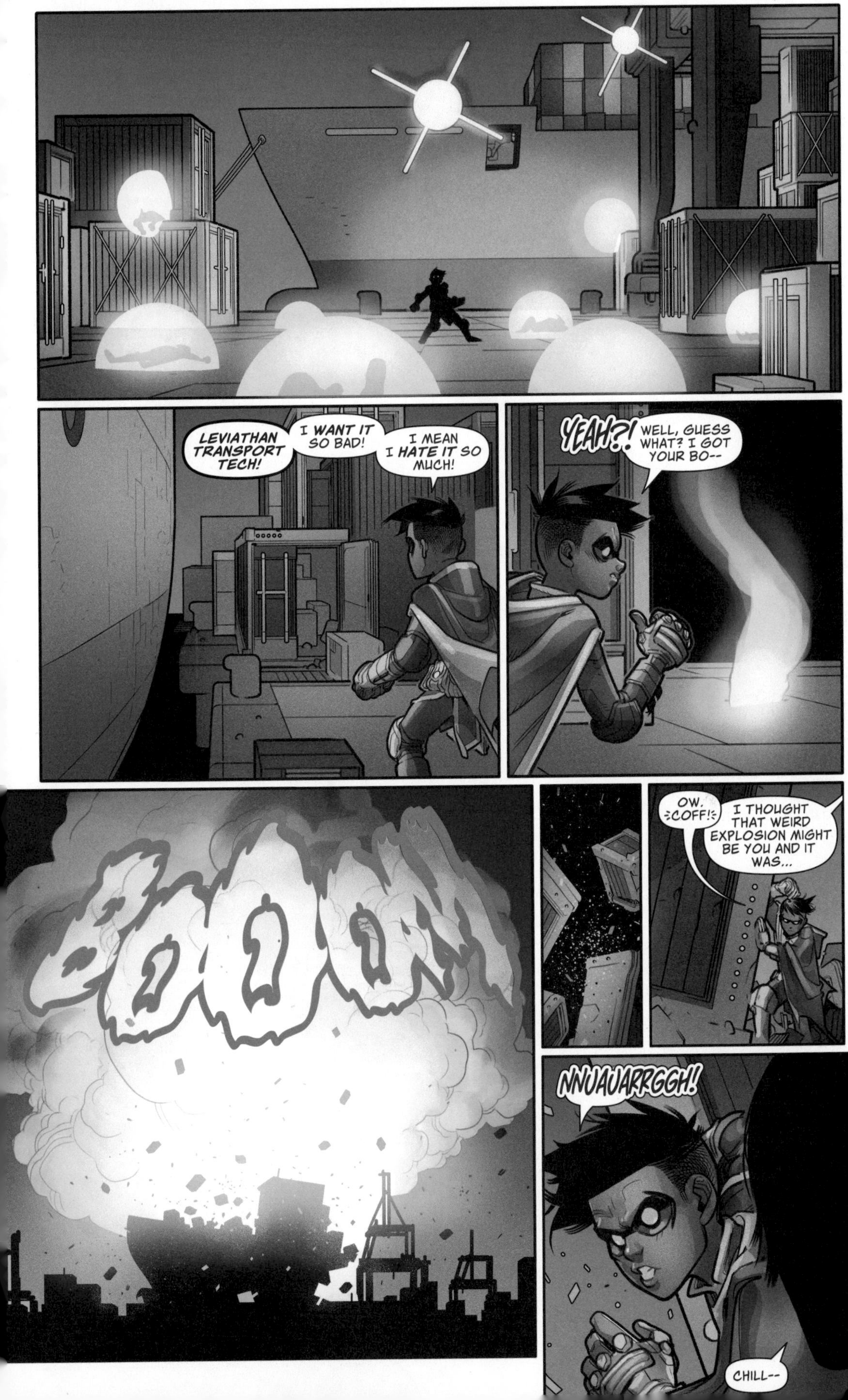
LEVIATHAN TRANSPORT TECH!
I WANT IT SO BAD!
I MEAN I HATE IT SO MUCH!
YEAH?!
WELL, GUESS WHAT? I GOT YOUR BO--
BOOOM
OW. COFF!
I THOUGHT THAT WEIRD EXPLOSION MIGHT BE YOU AND IT WAS...
NNUAUARRGGH!
CHILL--

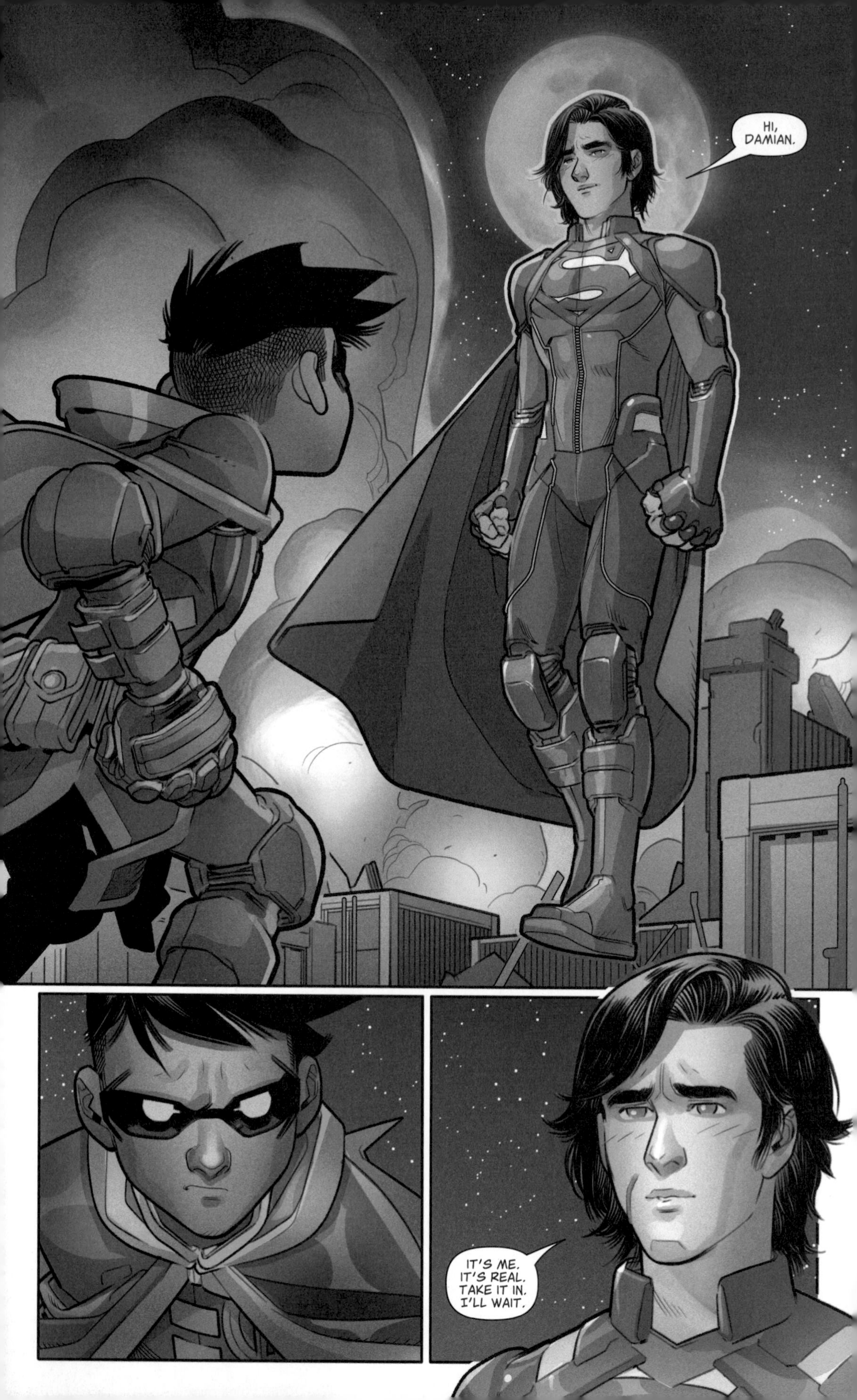
HI, DAMIAN.
IT'S ME. IT'S REAL. TAKE IT IN. I'LL WAIT.

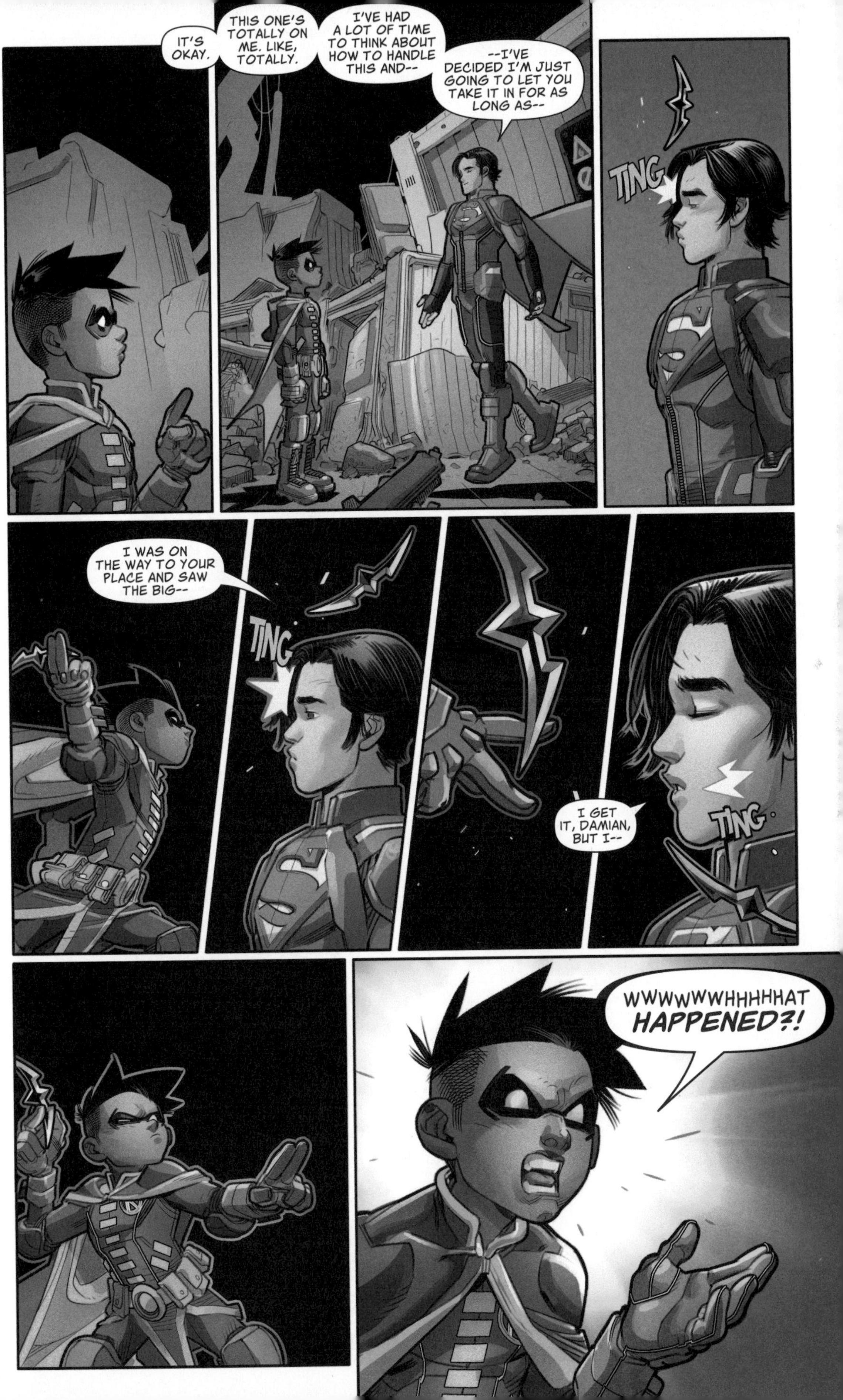
IT'S OKAY.
THIS ONE'S TOTALLY ON ME. LIKE, TOTALLY.
I'VE HAD A LOT OF TIME TO THINK ABOUT HOW TO HANDLE THIS AND--
--I'VE DECIDED I'M JUST GOING TO LET YOU TAKE IT IN FOR AS LONG AS--
TING
I WAS ON THE WAY TO YOUR PLACE AND SAW THE BIG--
TING
I GET IT, DAMIAN, BUT I--
TING
WWWWWWHHHHHAT HAPPENED?!

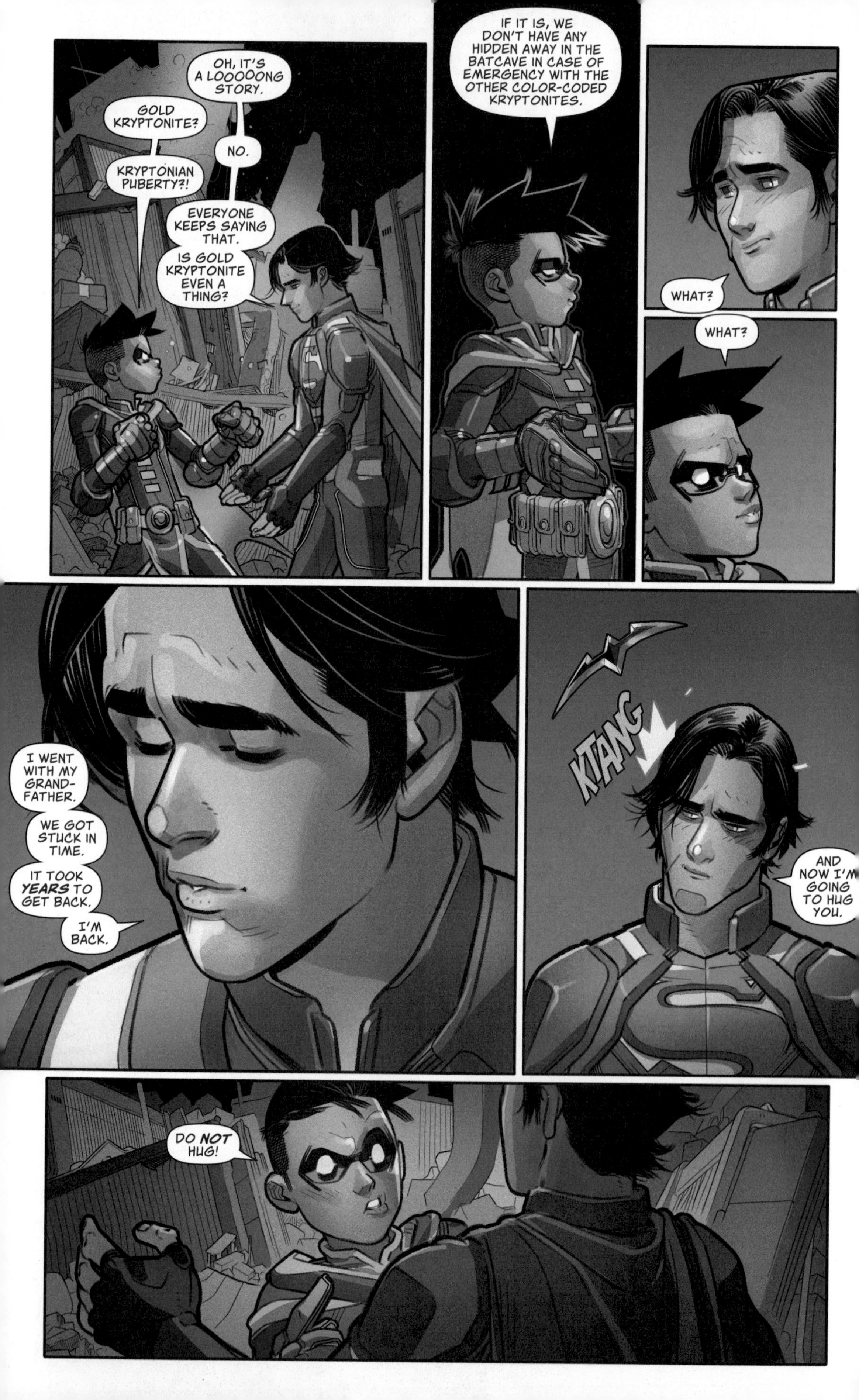
GOLD KRYPTONITE?
OH, IT'S A LOOOOONG STORY.
NO.
KRYPTONIAN PUBERTY?!
EVERYONE KEEPS SAYING THAT.
IS GOLD KRYPTONITE EVEN A THING?
IF IT IS, WE DON'T HAVE ANY HIDDEN AWAY IN THE BATCAVE IN CASE OF EMERGENCY WITH THE OTHER COLOR-CODED KRYPTONITES.
WHAT?
WHAT?
I WENT WITH MY GRAND-FATHER.
WE GOT STUCK IN TIME.
IT TOOK ***YEARS*** TO GET BACK.
I'M BACK.
KTANG
AND NOW I'M GOING TO HUG YOU.
DO ***NOT*** HUG!

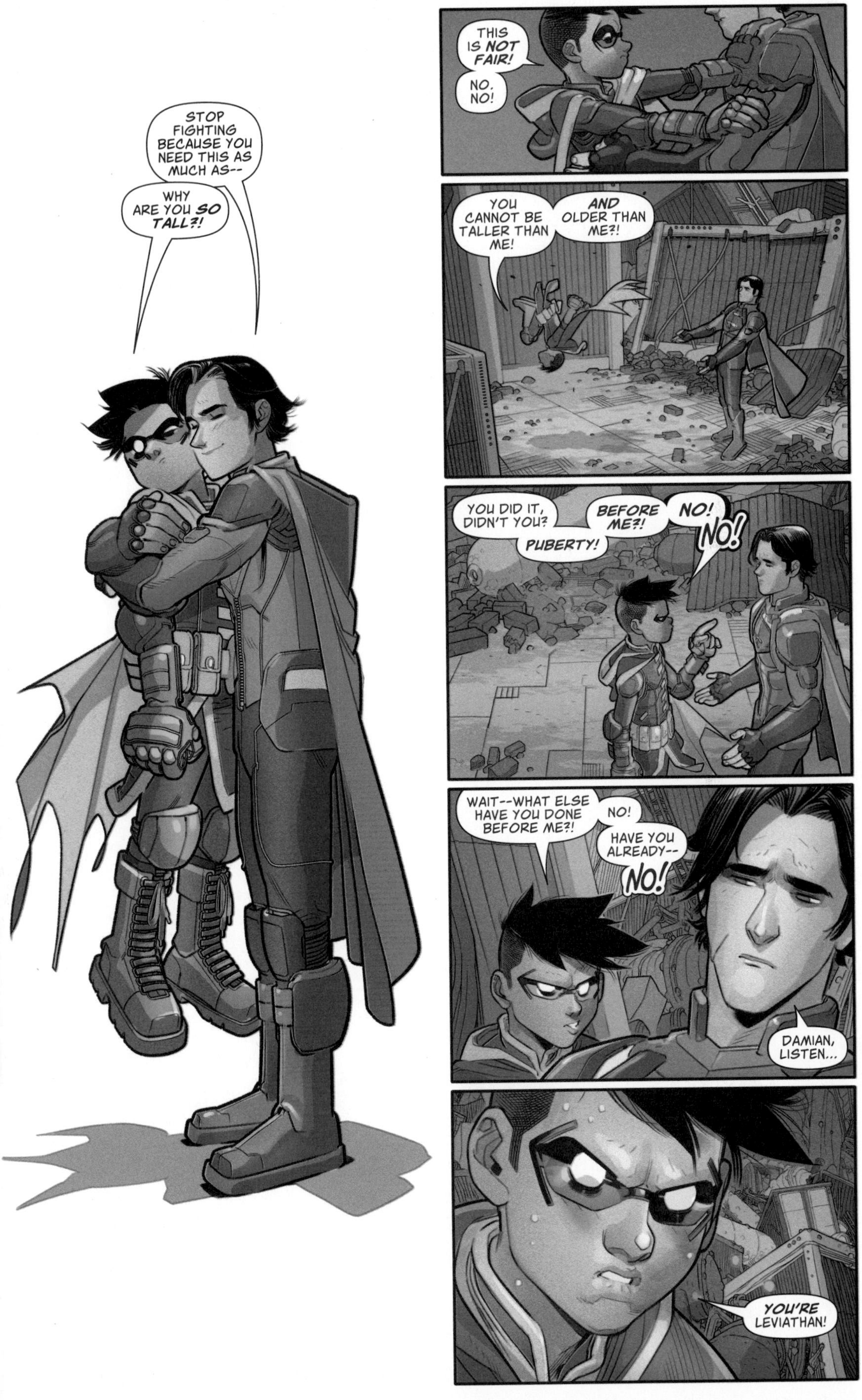

STOP FIGHTING BECAUSE YOU NEED THIS AS MUCH AS--
WHY ARE YOU SO TALL?!
THIS IS NOT FAIR!
NO. NO!
YOU CANNOT BE TALLER THAN ME!
AND OLDER THAN ME?!
YOU DID IT, DIDN'T YOU?
PUBERTY!
BEFORE ME?!
NO!
NO!
WAIT--WHAT ELSE HAVE YOU DONE BEFORE ME?!
NO!
HAVE YOU ALREADY--
NO!
DAMIAN, LISTEN...
YOU'RE LEVIATHAN!

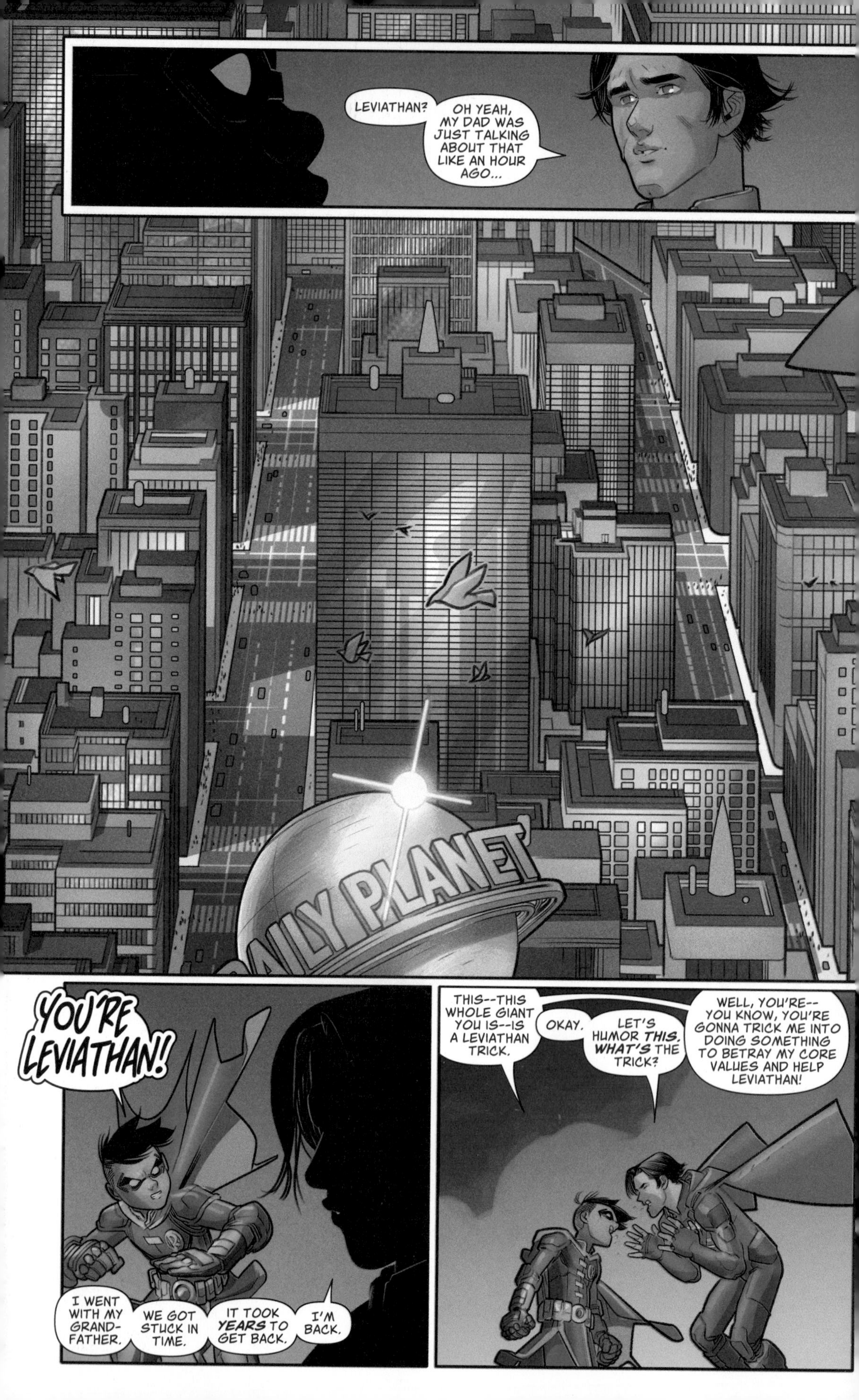
LEVIATHAN?
OH YEAH, MY DAD WAS JUST TALKING ABOUT THAT LIKE AN HOUR AGO...
DAILY PLANET
YOU'RE LEVIATHAN!
I WENT WITH MY GRAND-FATHER.
WE GOT STUCK IN TIME.
IT TOOK YEARS TO GET BACK.
I'M BACK.
THIS--THIS WHOLE GIANT YOU IS--IS A LEVIATHAN TRICK.
OKAY.
LET'S HUMOR THIS. WHAT'S THE TRICK?
WELL, YOU'RE-- YOU KNOW, YOU'RE GONNA TRICK ME INTO DOING SOMETHING TO BETRAY MY CORE VALUES AND HELP LEVIATHAN!

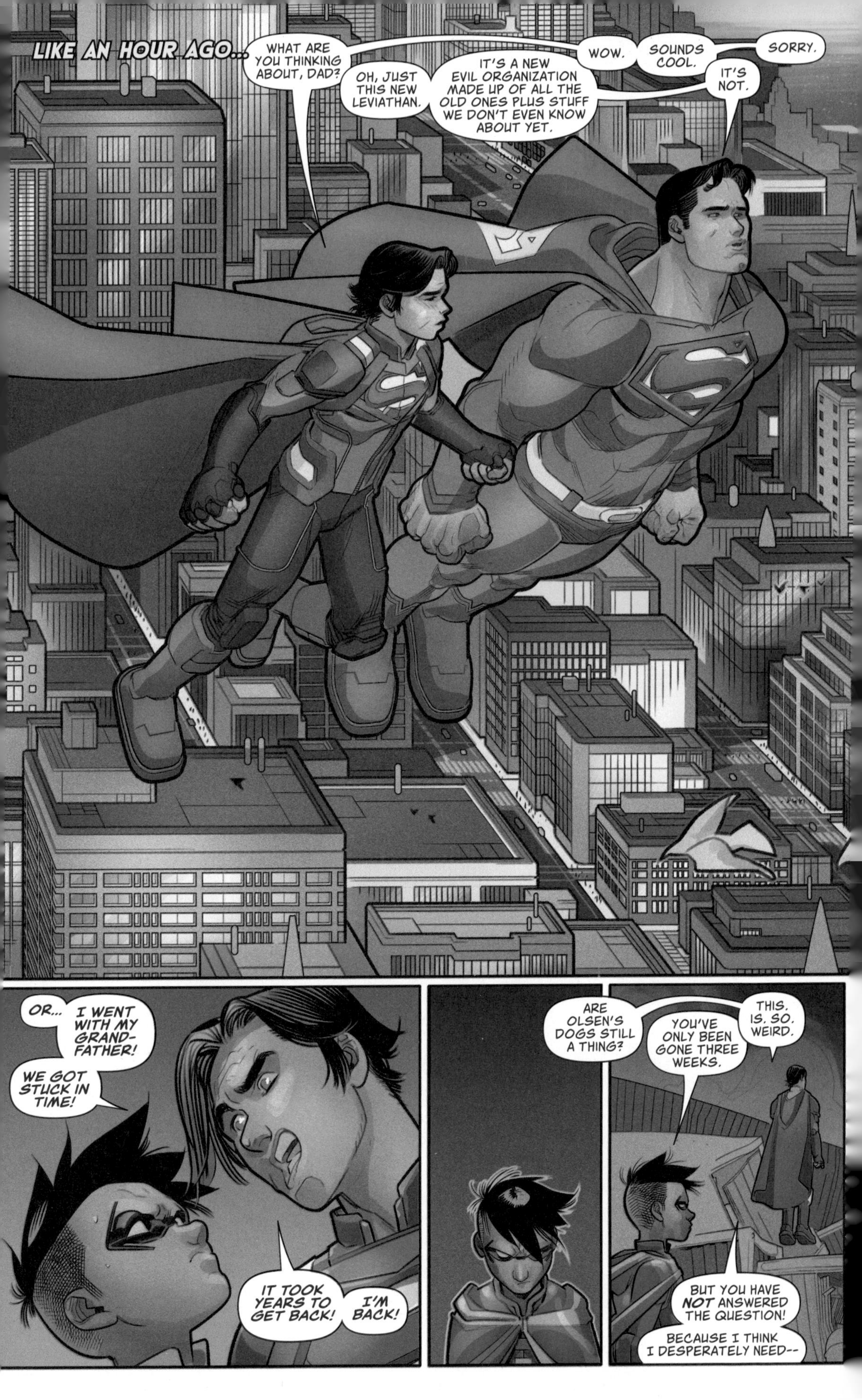
LIKE AN HOUR AGO...
WHAT ARE YOU THINKING ABOUT, DAD?
OH, JUST THIS NEW LEVIATHAN.
IT'S A NEW EVIL ORGANIZATION MADE UP OF ALL THE OLD ONES PLUS STUFF WE DON'T EVEN KNOW ABOUT YET.
WOW.
SOUNDS COOL.
IT'S NOT.
SORRY.
OR... I WENT WITH MY GRAND-FATHER!
WE GOT STUCK IN TIME!
IT TOOK YEARS TO GET BACK!
I'M BACK!
ARE OLSEN'S DOGS STILL A THING?
YOU'VE ONLY BEEN GONE THREE WEEKS.
THIS. IS. SO. WEIRD.
BUT YOU HAVE NOT ANSWERED THE QUESTION!
BECAUSE I THINK I DESPERATELY NEED--

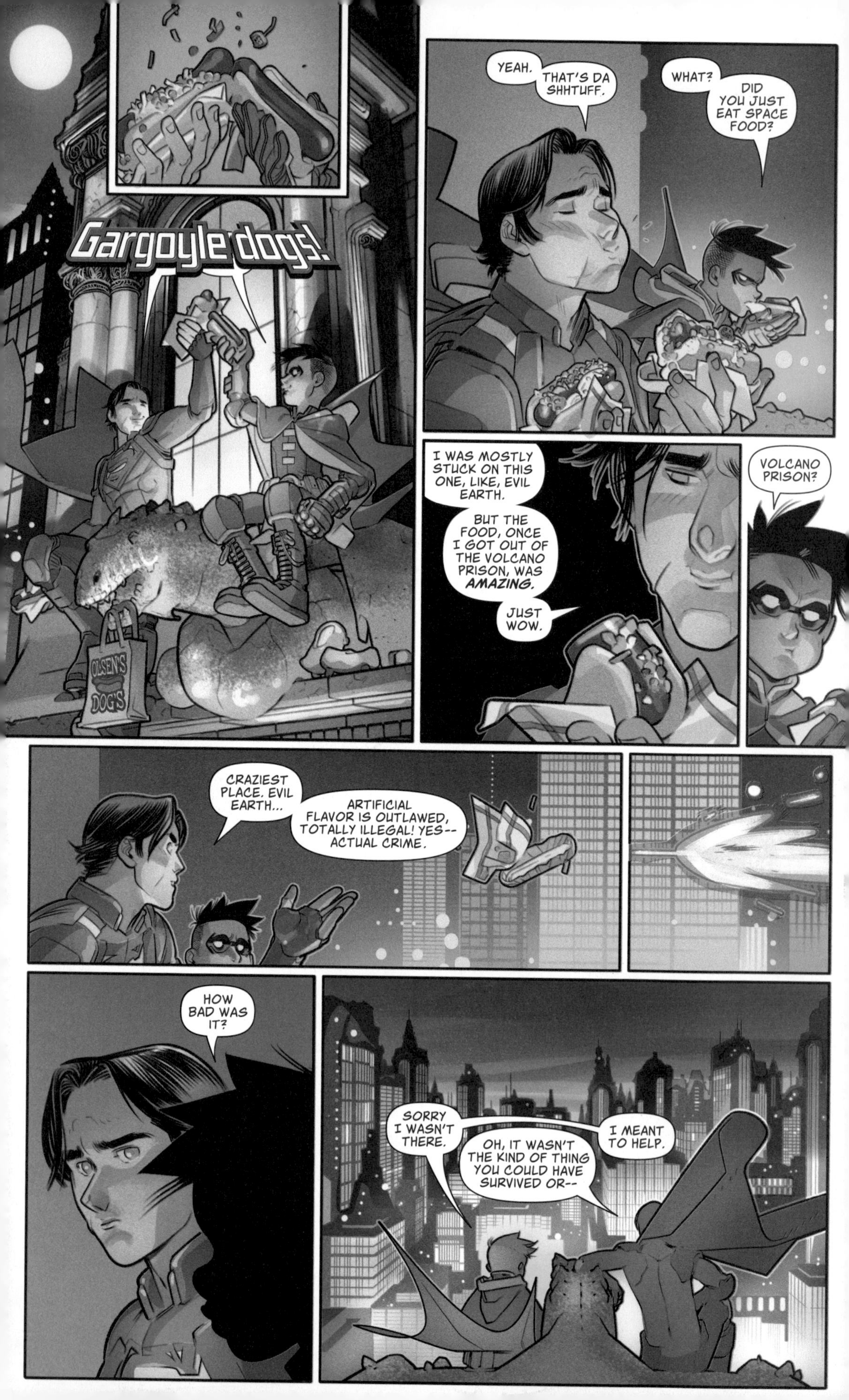

Gargoyle dogs!
YEAH.
THAT'S DA SHHTUFF.
WHAT?
DID YOU JUST EAT SPACE FOOD?
I WAS MOSTLY STUCK ON THIS ONE, LIKE, EVIL EARTH.
BUT THE FOOD, ONCE I GOT OUT OF THE VOLCANO PRISON, WAS AMAZING.
JUST WOW.
VOLCANO PRISON?
CRAZIEST PLACE. EVIL EARTH...
ARTIFICIAL FLAVOR IS OUTLAWED, TOTALLY ILLEGAL! YES-- ACTUAL CRIME.
HOW BAD WAS IT?
SORRY I WASN'T THERE.
I MEANT TO HELP.
OH, IT WASN'T THE KIND OF THING YOU COULD HAVE SURVIVED OR--

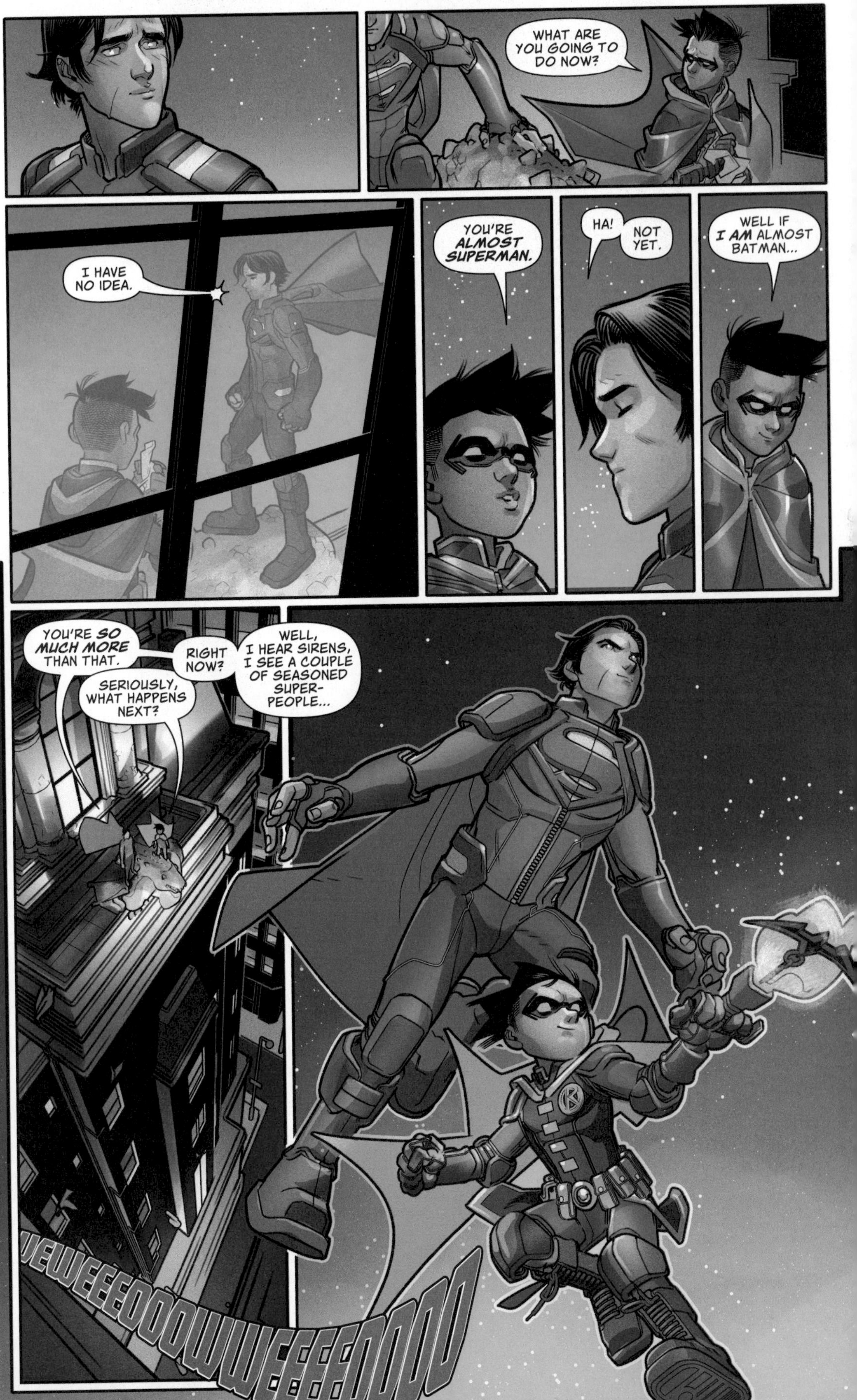
WHAT ARE YOU GOING TO DO NOW?
I HAVE NO IDEA.
YOU'RE ALMOST SUPERMAN.
HA!
NOT YET.
WELL IF I AM ALMOST BATMAN...
YOU'RE SO MUCH MORE THAN THAT.
RIGHT NOW?
SERIOUSLY, WHAT HAPPENS NEXT?
WELL, I HEAR SIRENS, I SEE A COUPLE OF SEASONED SUPER-PEOPLE...
WEWEEEOOOWWEEEEOOOO

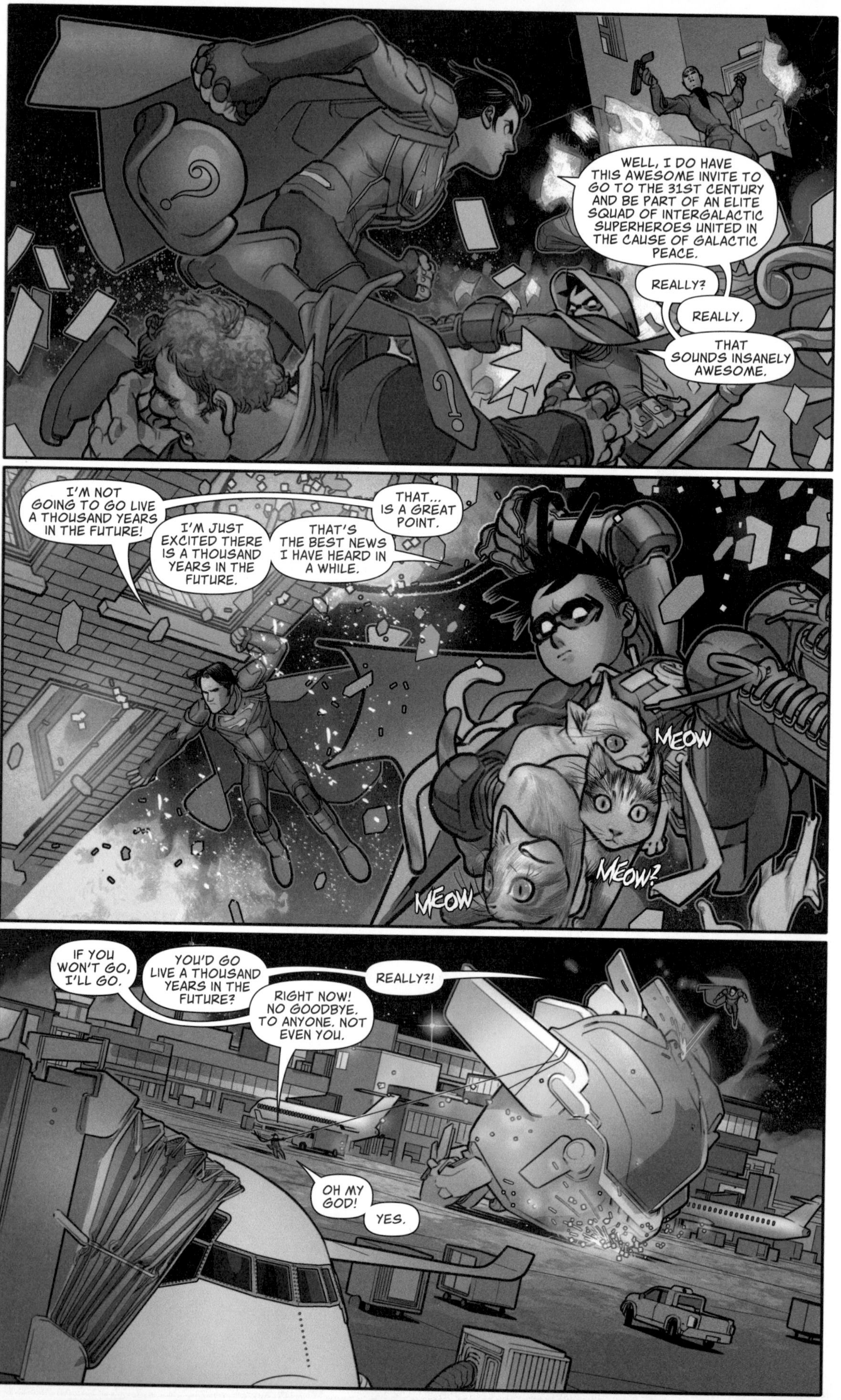
WELL, I DO HAVE THIS AWESOME INVITE TO GO TO THE 31ST CENTURY AND BE PART OF AN ELITE SQUAD OF INTERGALACTIC SUPERHEROES UNITED IN THE CAUSE OF GALACTIC PEACE.
REALLY?
REALLY.
THAT SOUNDS INSANELY AWESOME.
I'M NOT GOING TO GO LIVE A THOUSAND YEARS IN THE FUTURE!
THAT... IS A GREAT POINT.
I'M JUST EXCITED THERE IS A THOUSAND YEARS IN THE FUTURE.
THAT'S THE BEST NEWS I HAVE HEARD IN A WHILE.
MEOW
MEOW?
MEOW
IF YOU WON'T GO, I'LL GO.
YOU'D GO LIVE A THOUSAND YEARS IN THE FUTURE?
REALLY?!
RIGHT NOW! NO GOODBYE. TO ANYONE. NOT EVEN YOU.
OH MY GOD!
YES.

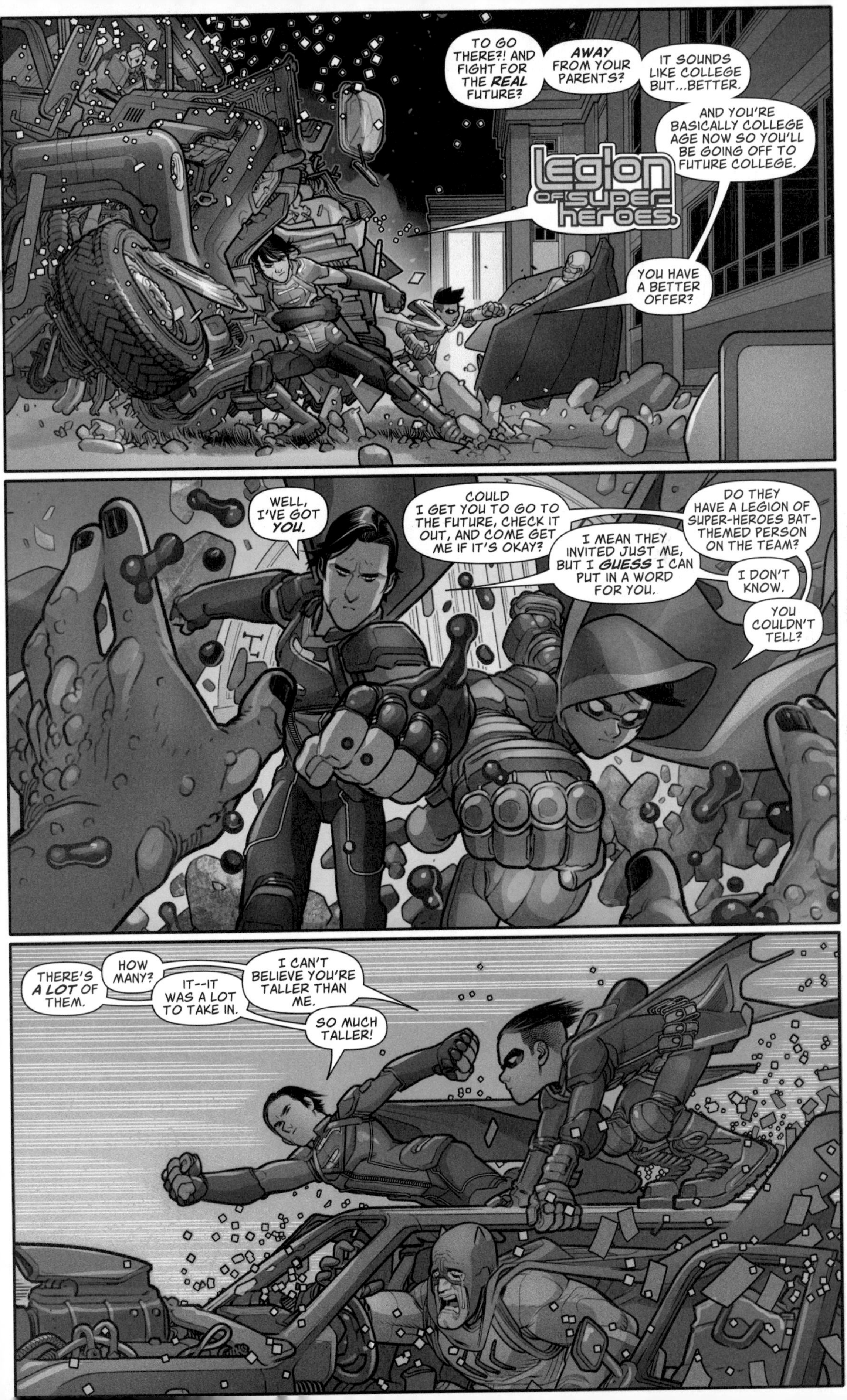

TO GO THERE?! AND FIGHT FOR THE *REAL* FUTURE?
AWAY FROM YOUR PARENTS?
IT SOUNDS LIKE COLLEGE BUT...BETTER.
AND YOU'RE BASICALLY COLLEGE AGE NOW SO YOU'LL BE GOING OFF TO FUTURE COLLEGE.
Legion of Super-Heroes.
YOU HAVE A BETTER OFFER?
WELL, I'VE GOT *YOU.*
COULD I GET YOU TO GO TO THE FUTURE, CHECK IT OUT, AND COME GET ME IF IT'S OKAY?
I MEAN THEY INVITED JUST ME, BUT I *GUESS* I CAN PUT IN A WORD FOR YOU.
DO THEY HAVE A LEGION OF SUPER-HEROES BAT-THEMED PERSON ON THE TEAM?
I DON'T KNOW.
YOU COULDN'T TELL?
THERE'S *A LOT* OF THEM.
HOW MANY?
IT--IT WAS A LOT TO TAKE IN.
I CAN'T BELIEVE YOU'RE TALLER THAN ME.
SO MUCH TALLER!

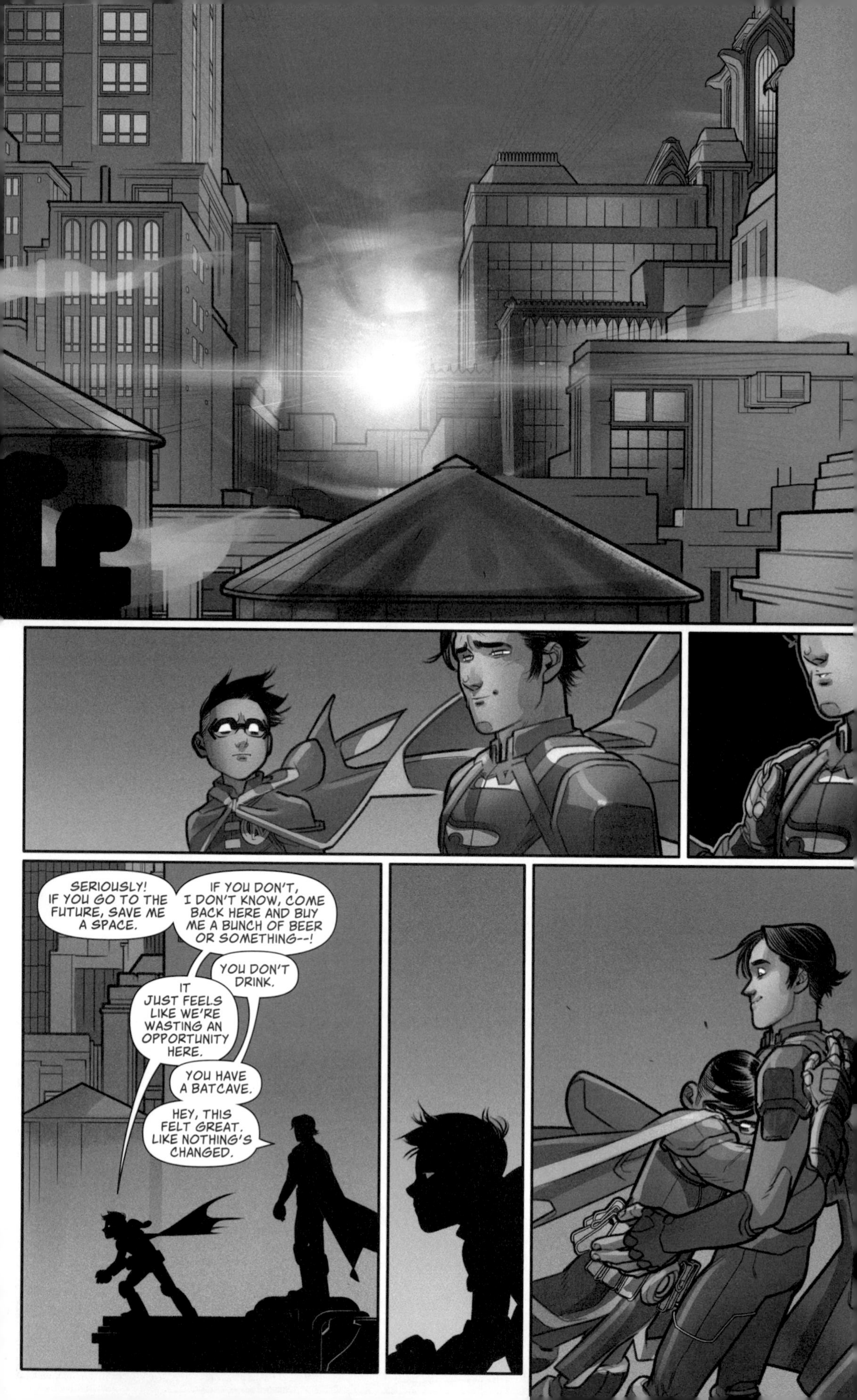
SERIOUSLY! IF YOU GO TO THE FUTURE, SAVE ME A SPACE.
IF YOU DON'T, I DON'T KNOW, COME BACK HERE AND BUY ME A BUNCH OF BEER OR SOMETHING--!
YOU DON'T DRINK.
IT JUST FEELS LIKE WE'RE WASTING AN OPPORTUNITY HERE.
YOU HAVE A BATCAVE.
HEY, THIS FELT GREAT. LIKE NOTHING'S CHANGED.

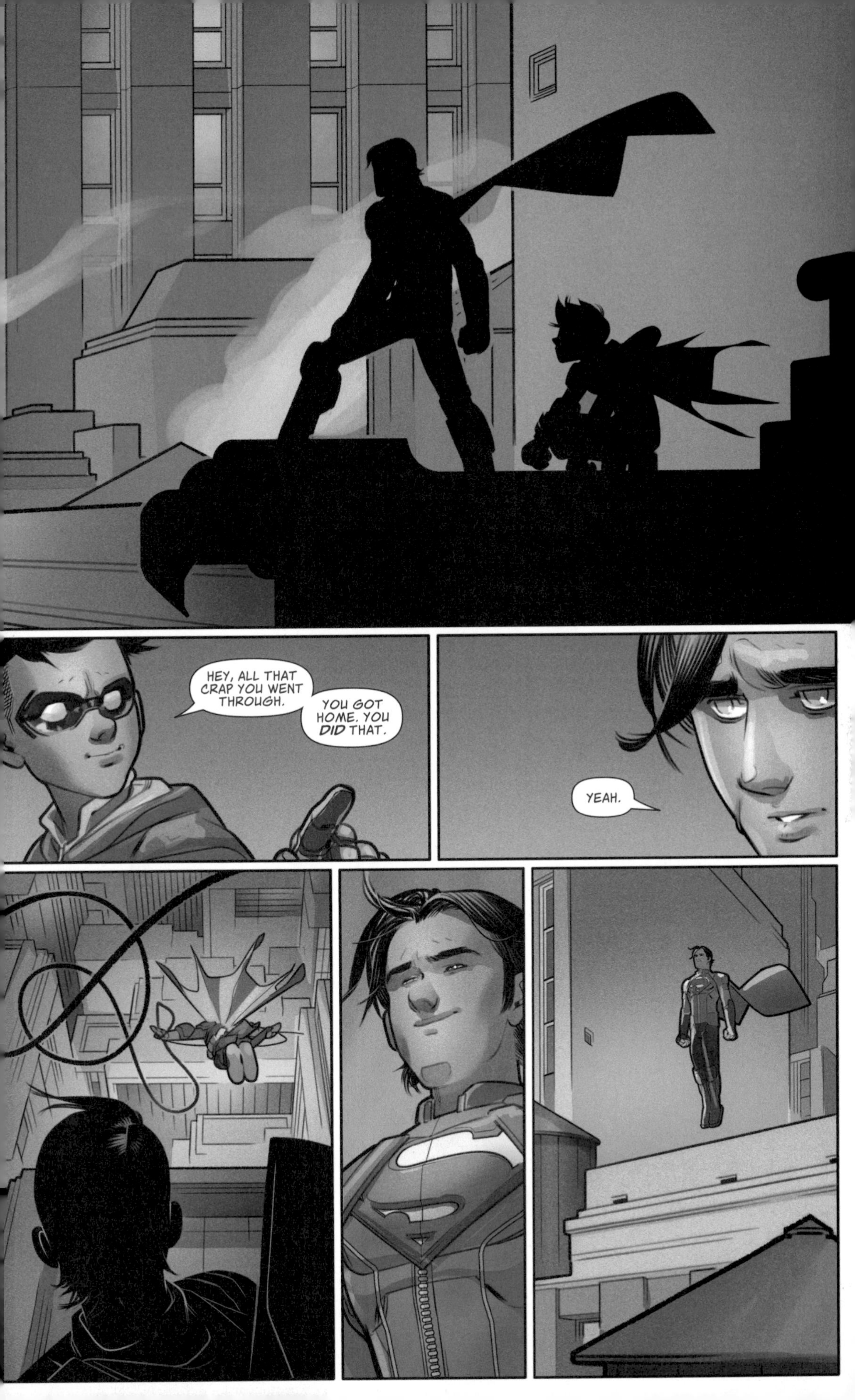
HEY, ALL THAT CRAP YOU WENT THROUGH.
YOU GOT HOME. YOU *DID* THAT.
YEAH.

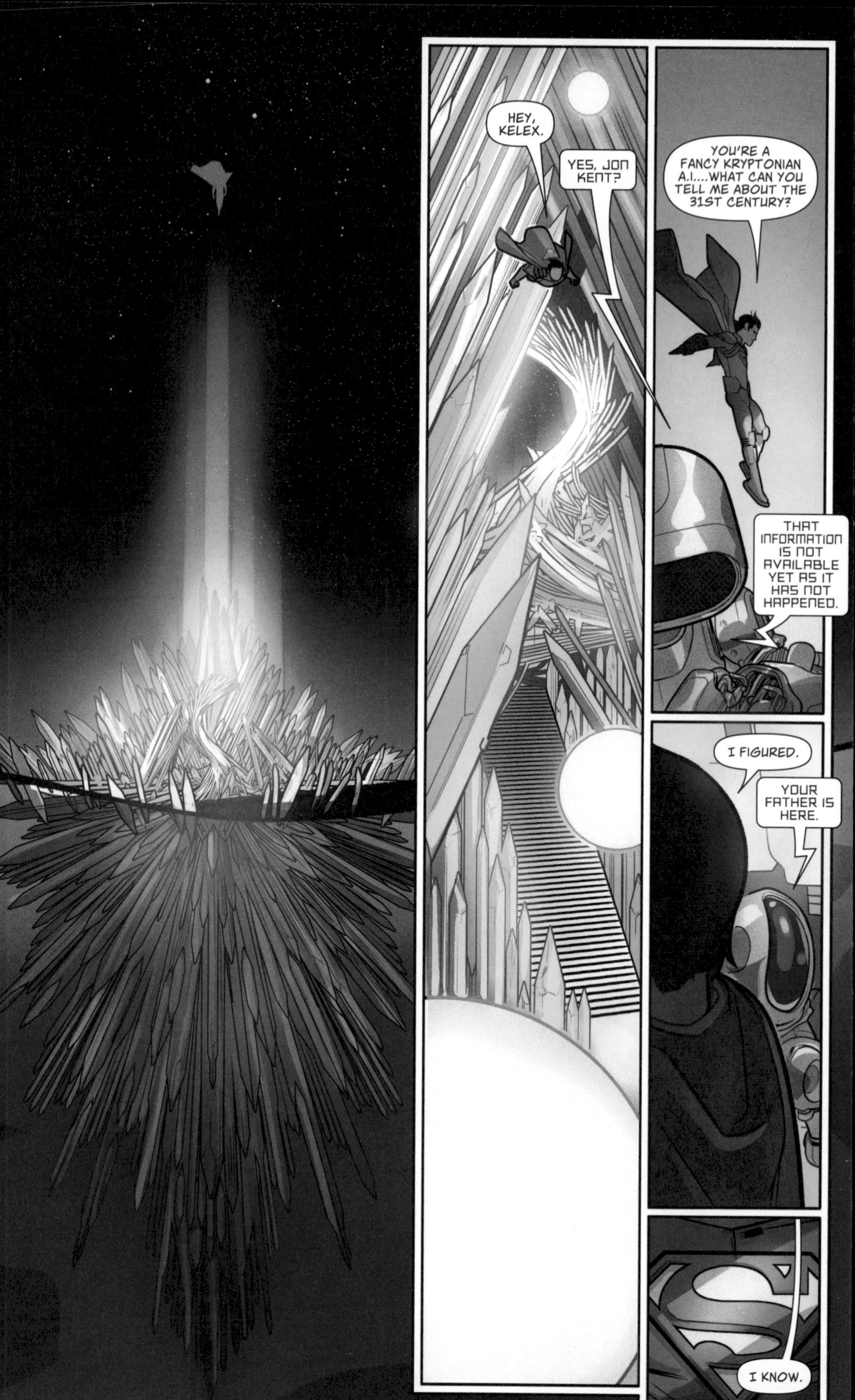
HEY, KELEX.
YES, JON KENT?
YOU'RE A FANCY KRYPTONIAN A.I....WHAT CAN YOU TELL ME ABOUT THE 31ST CENTURY?
THAT INFORMATION IS NOT AVAILABLE YET AS IT HAS NOT HAPPENED.
I FIGURED.
YOUR FATHER IS HERE.
I KNOW.

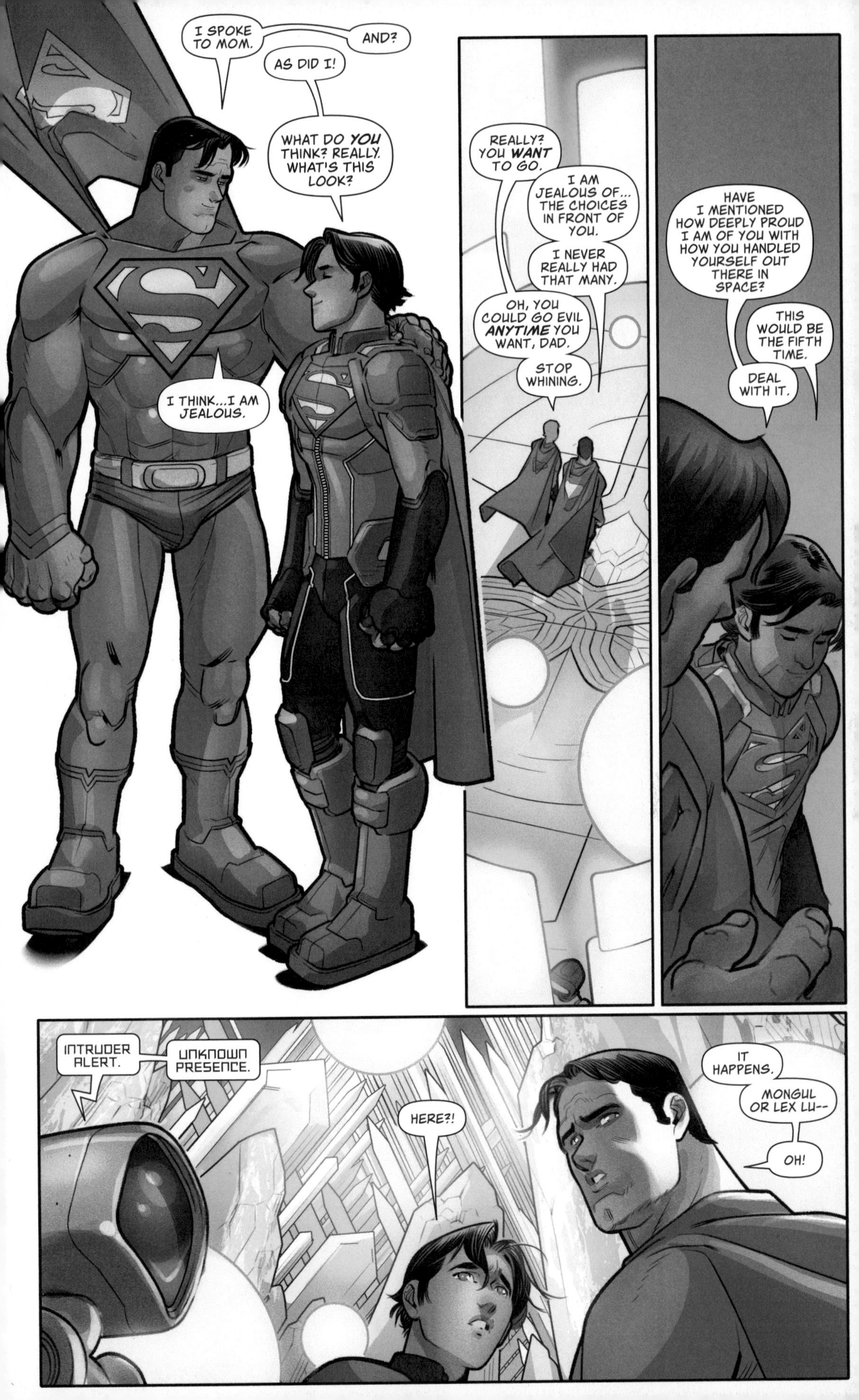

I SPOKE TO MOM.
AND?
AS DID I!
WHAT DO YOU THINK? REALLY. WHAT'S THIS LOOK?
I THINK...I AM JEALOUS.
REALLY? YOU WANT TO GO.
I AM JEALOUS OF... THE CHOICES IN FRONT OF YOU.
I NEVER REALLY HAD THAT MANY.
OH, YOU COULD GO EVIL ANYTIME YOU WANT, DAD.
STOP WHINING.
HAVE I MENTIONED HOW DEEPLY PROUD I AM OF YOU WITH HOW YOU HANDLED YOURSELF OUT THERE IN SPACE?
THIS WOULD BE THE FIFTH TIME.
DEAL WITH IT.
INTRUDER ALERT.
UNKNOWN PRESENCE.
HERE?!
IT HAPPENS.
MONGUL OR LEX LU--
OH!

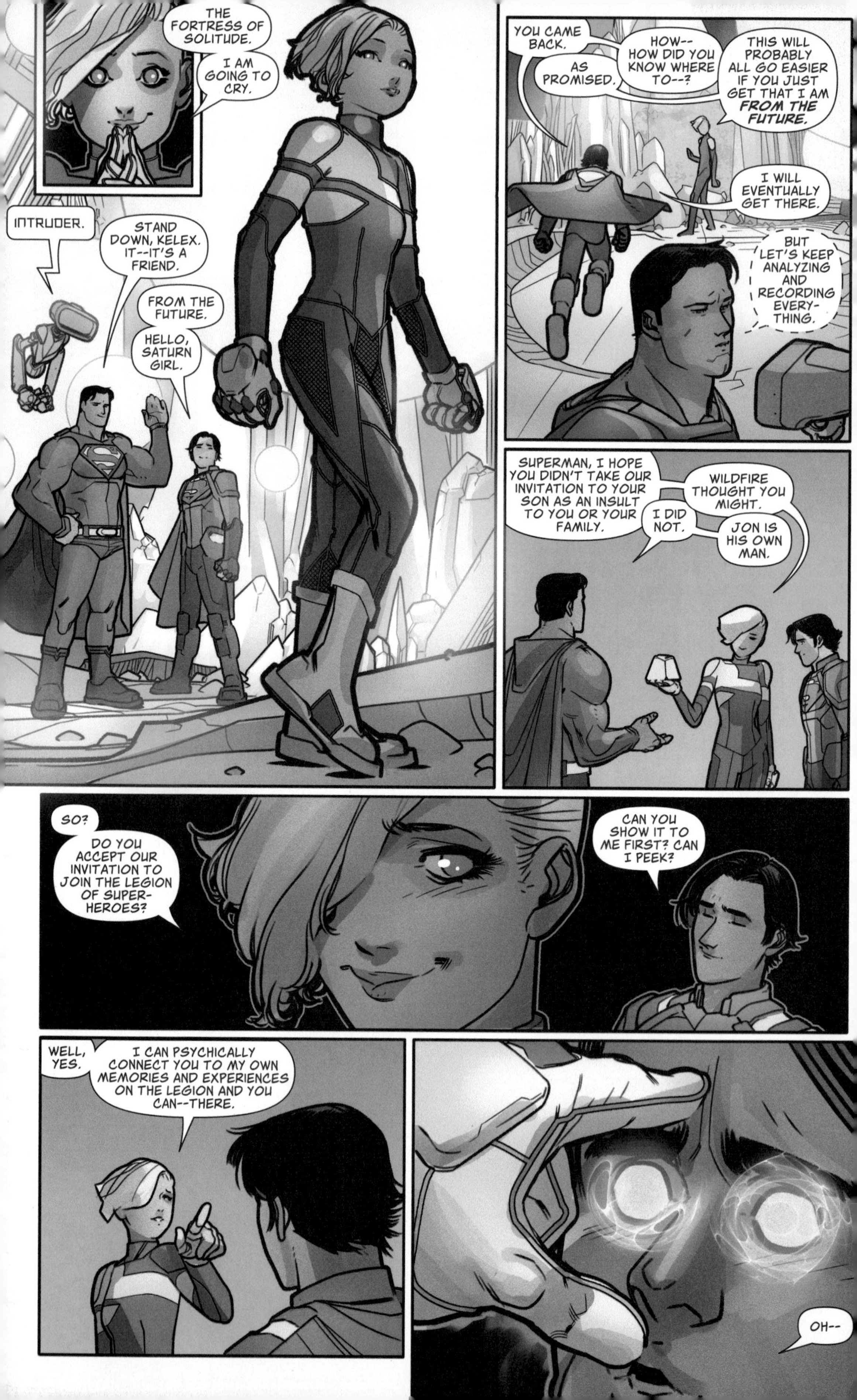

THE FORTRESS OF SOLITUDE.
I AM GOING TO CRY.
INTRUDER.
STAND DOWN, KELEX. IT--IT'S A FRIEND.
FROM THE FUTURE.
HELLO, SATURN GIRL.
YOU CAME BACK.
AS PROMISED.
HOW--HOW DID YOU KNOW WHERE TO--?
THIS WILL PROBABLY ALL GO EASIER IF YOU JUST GET THAT I AM FROM THE FUTURE.
I WILL EVENTUALLY GET THERE.
BUT LET'S KEEP ANALYZING AND RECORDING EVERY-THING.
SUPERMAN, I HOPE YOU DIDN'T TAKE OUR INVITATION TO YOUR SON AS AN INSULT TO YOU OR YOUR FAMILY.
WILDFIRE THOUGHT YOU MIGHT.
I DID NOT.
JON IS HIS OWN MAN.
SO?
DO YOU ACCEPT OUR INVITATION TO JOIN THE LEGION OF SUPER-HEROES?
CAN YOU SHOW IT TO ME FIRST? CAN I PEEK?
WELL, YES.
I CAN PSYCHICALLY CONNECT YOU TO MY OWN MEMORIES AND EXPERIENCES ON THE LEGION AND YOU CAN--THERE.
OH--

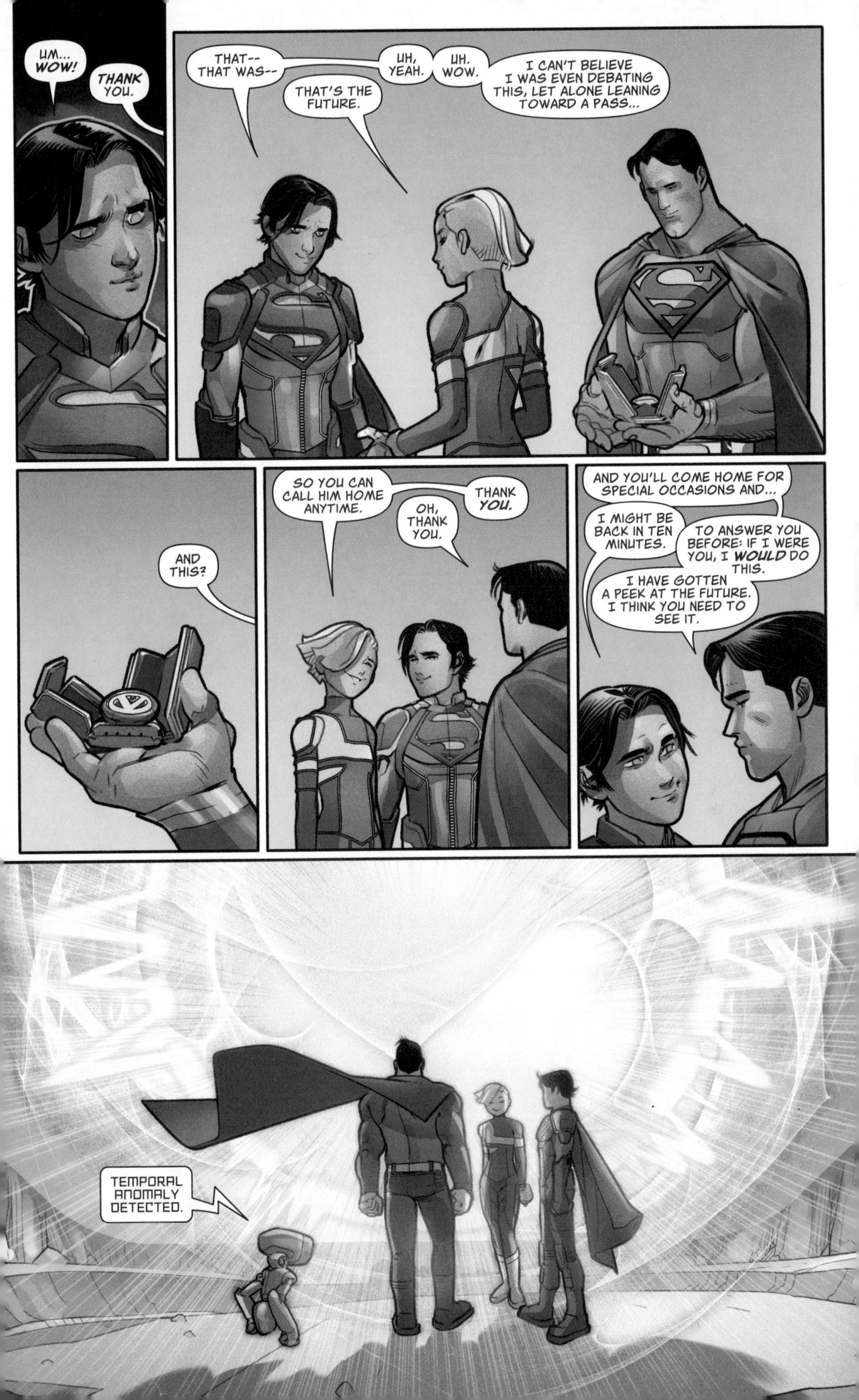

UM... **WOW!**
THANK YOU.
THAT-- THAT WAS--
UH, YEAH.
UH. WOW.
THAT'S THE FUTURE.
I CAN'T BELIEVE I WAS EVEN DEBATING THIS, LET ALONE LEANING TOWARD A PASS...
AND THIS?
SO YOU CAN CALL HIM HOME ANYTIME.
THANK ***YOU.***
OH, THANK YOU.
AND YOU'LL COME HOME FOR SPECIAL OCCASIONS AND...
I MIGHT BE BACK IN TEN MINUTES.
TO ANSWER YOU BEFORE: IF I WERE YOU, I ***WOULD*** DO THIS.
I HAVE GOTTEN A PEEK AT THE FUTURE. I THINK YOU NEED TO SEE IT.
TEMPORAL ANOMALY DETECTED.

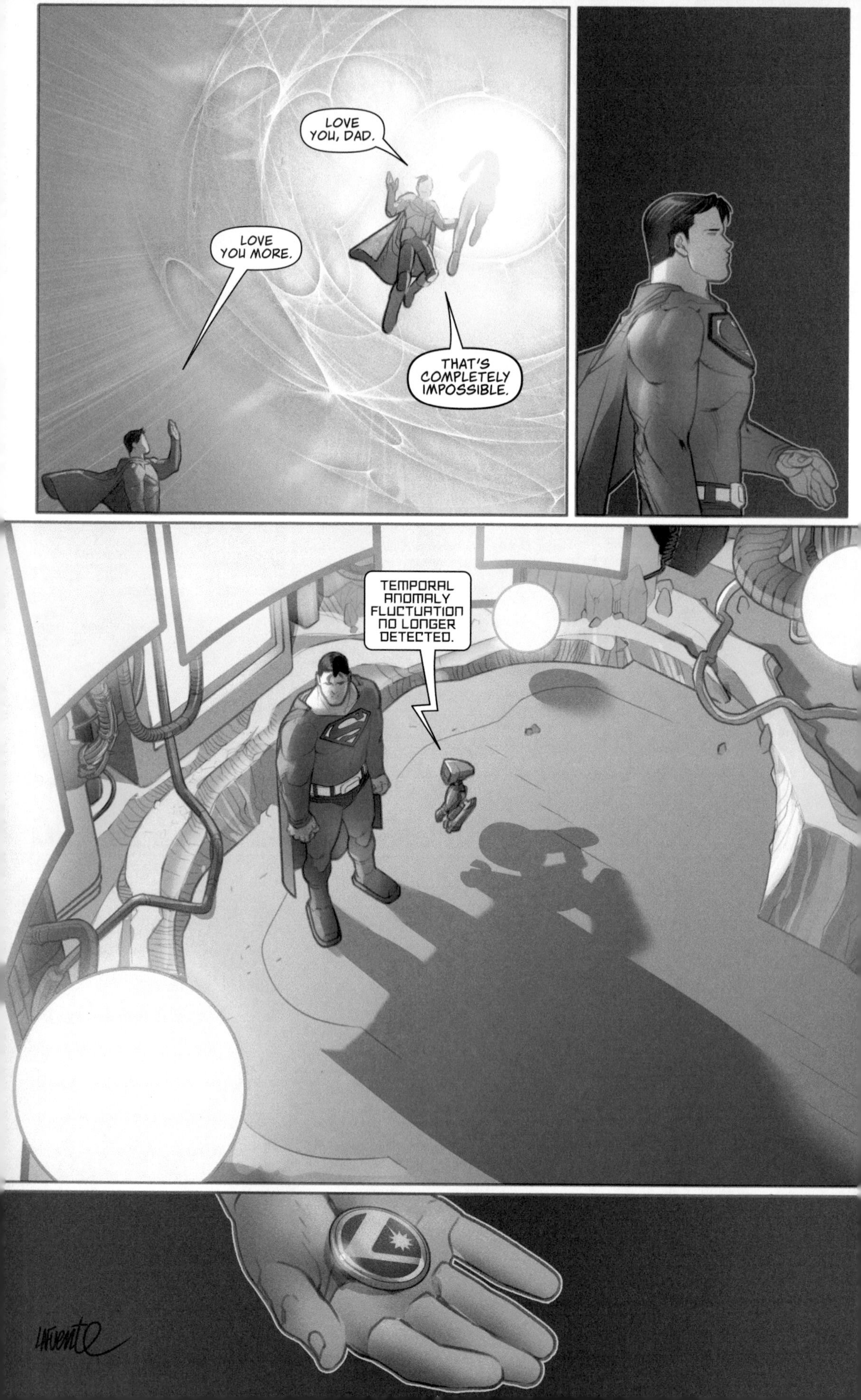
LOVE YOU, DAD.
LOVE YOU MORE.
THAT'S COMPLETELY IMPOSSIBLE.
TEMPORAL ANOMALY FLUCTUATION NO LONGER DETECTED.

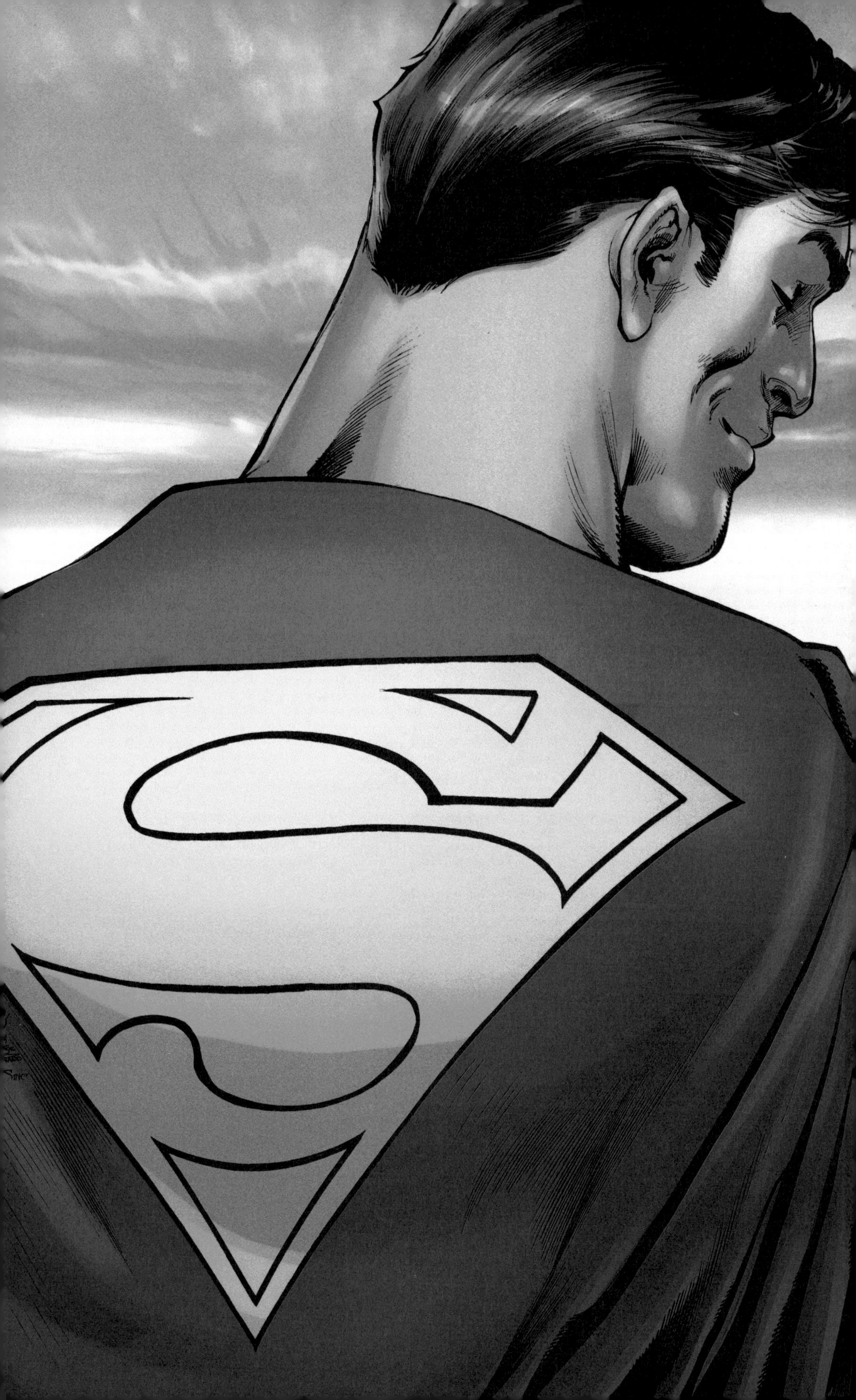

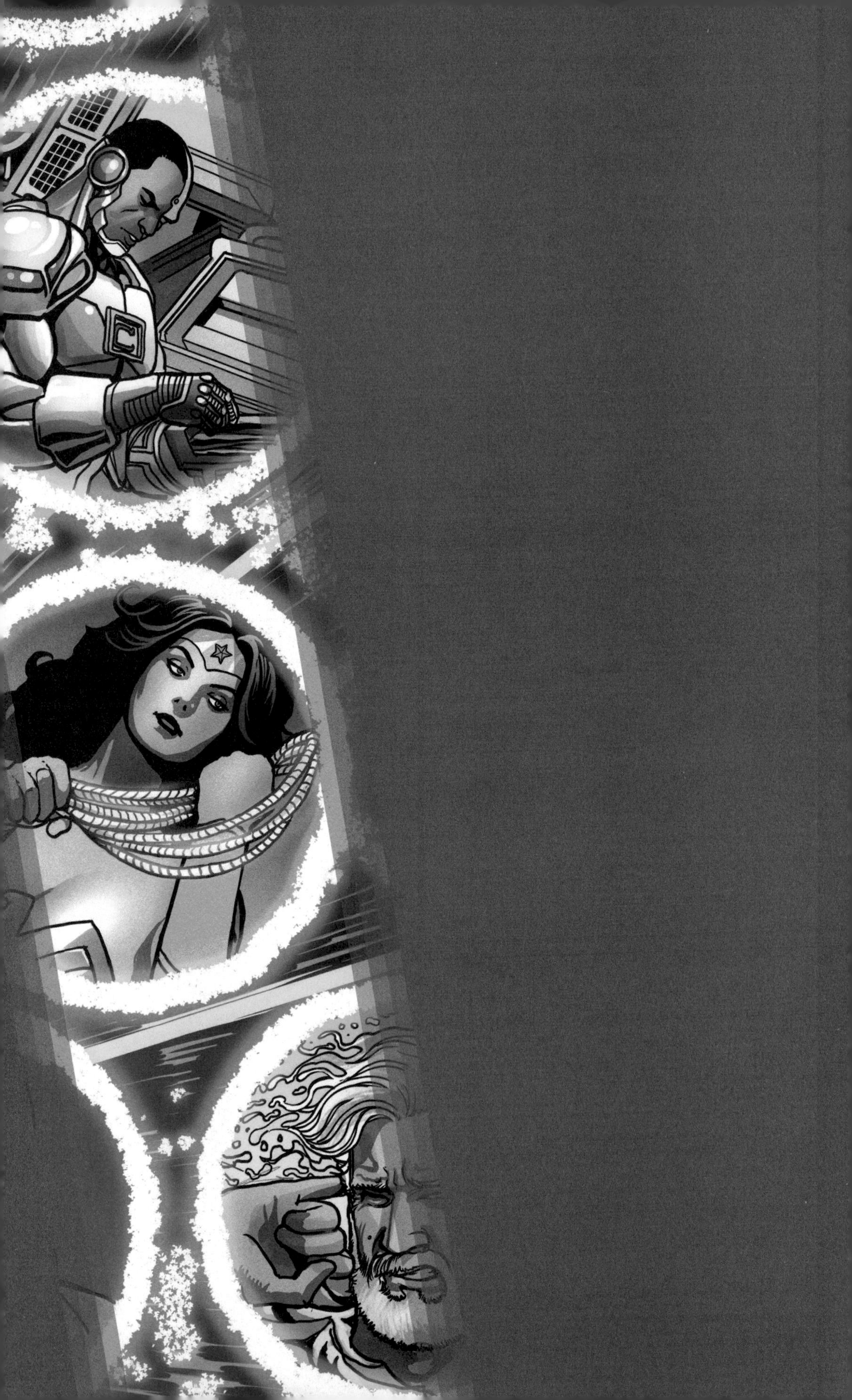

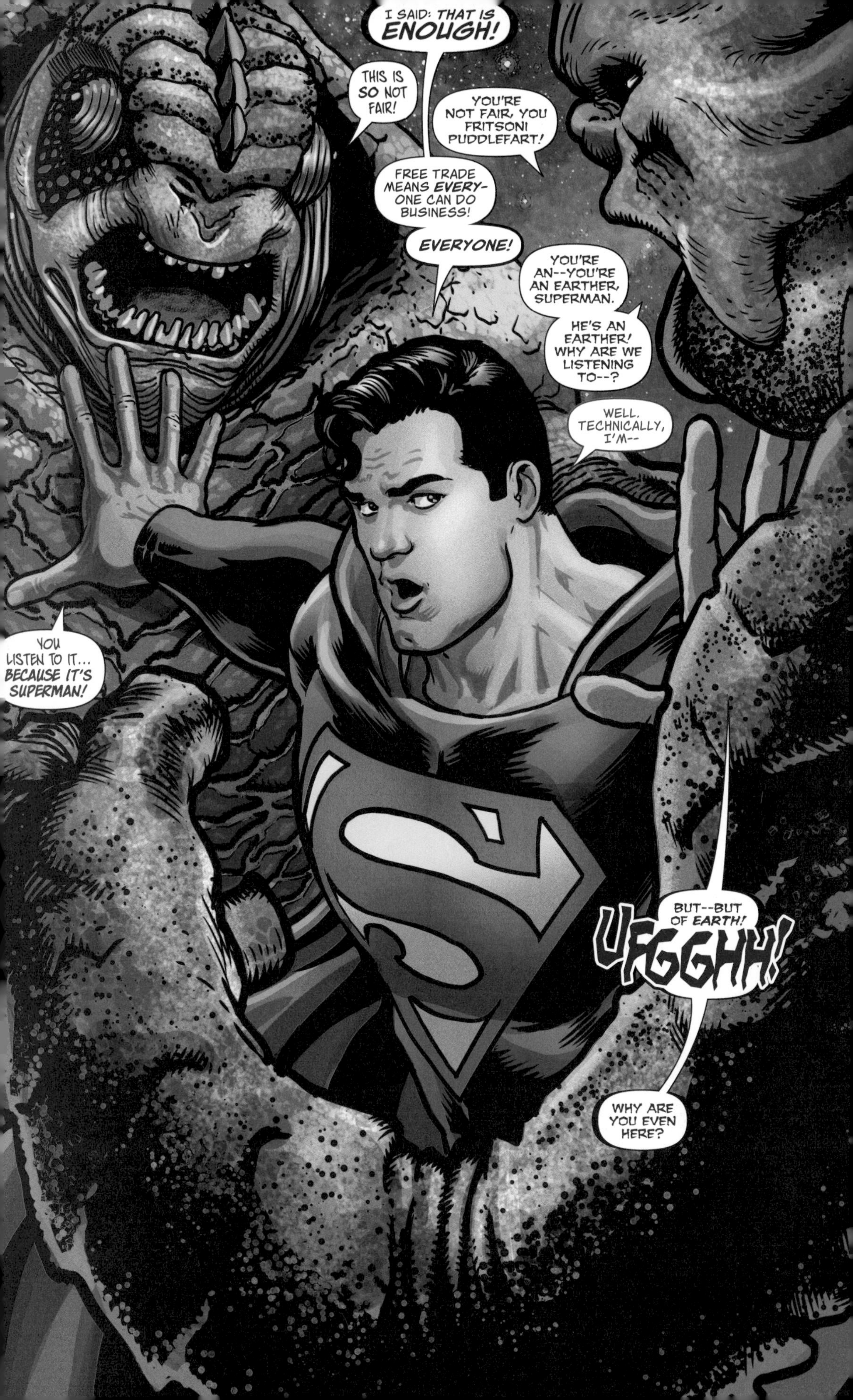
I SAID: THAT IS ENOUGH!
THIS IS SO NOT FAIR!
YOU'RE NOT FAIR, YOU FRITSONI PUDDLEFART!
FREE TRADE MEANS EVERY-ONE CAN DO BUSINESS!
EVERYONE!
YOU'RE AN--YOU'RE AN EARTHER, SUPERMAN.
HE'S AN EARTHER! WHY ARE WE LISTENING TO--?
WELL. TECHNICALLY, I'M--
YOU LISTEN TO IT... BECAUSE IT'S SUPERMAN!
BUT--BUT OF EARTH!
UFGGHH!
WHY ARE YOU EVEN HERE?

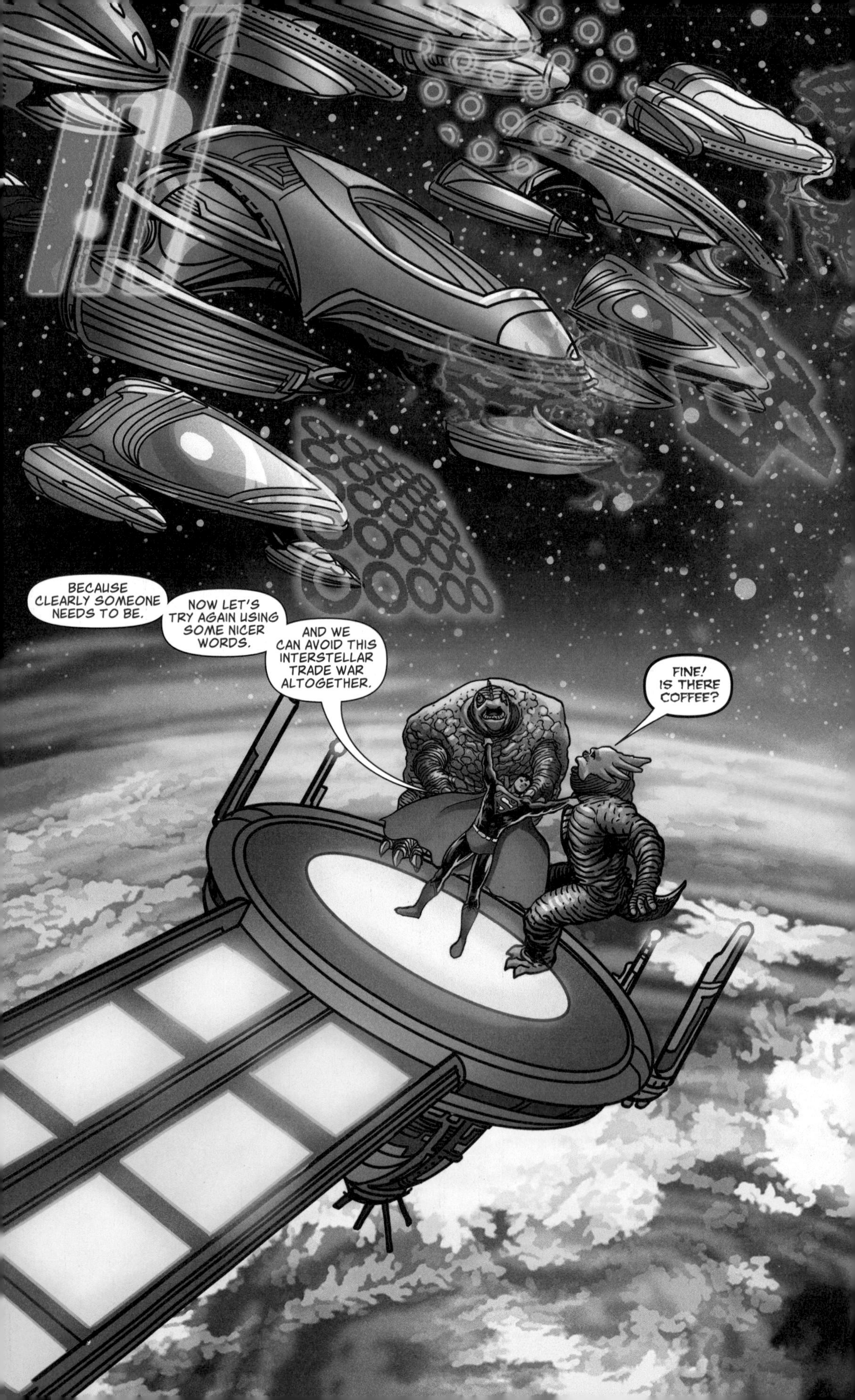
BECAUSE CLEARLY SOMEONE NEEDS TO BE.
NOW LET'S TRY AGAIN USING SOME NICER WORDS.
AND WE CAN AVOID THIS INTERSTELLAR TRADE WAR ALTOGETHER.
FINE! IS THERE COFFEE?

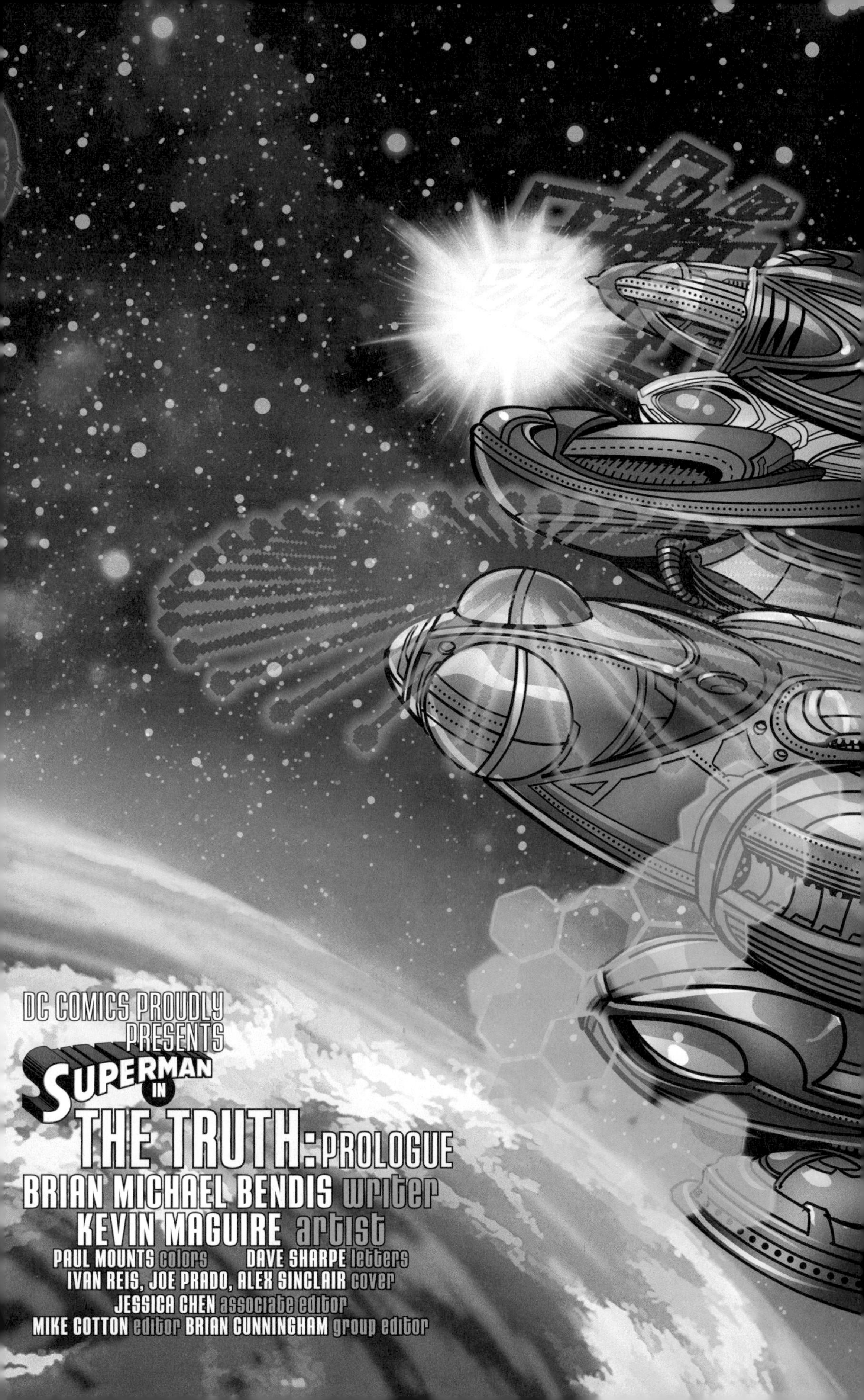
DC COMICS PROUDLY PRESENTS
SUPERMAN IN
THE TRUTH: PROLOGUE
BRIAN MICHAEL BENDIS writer
KEVIN MAGUIRE artist
PAUL MOUNTS colors DAVE SHARPE letters
IVAN REIS, JOE PRADO, ALEX SINCLAIR cover
JESSICA CHEN associate editor
MIKE COTTON editor BRIAN CUNNINGHAM group editor

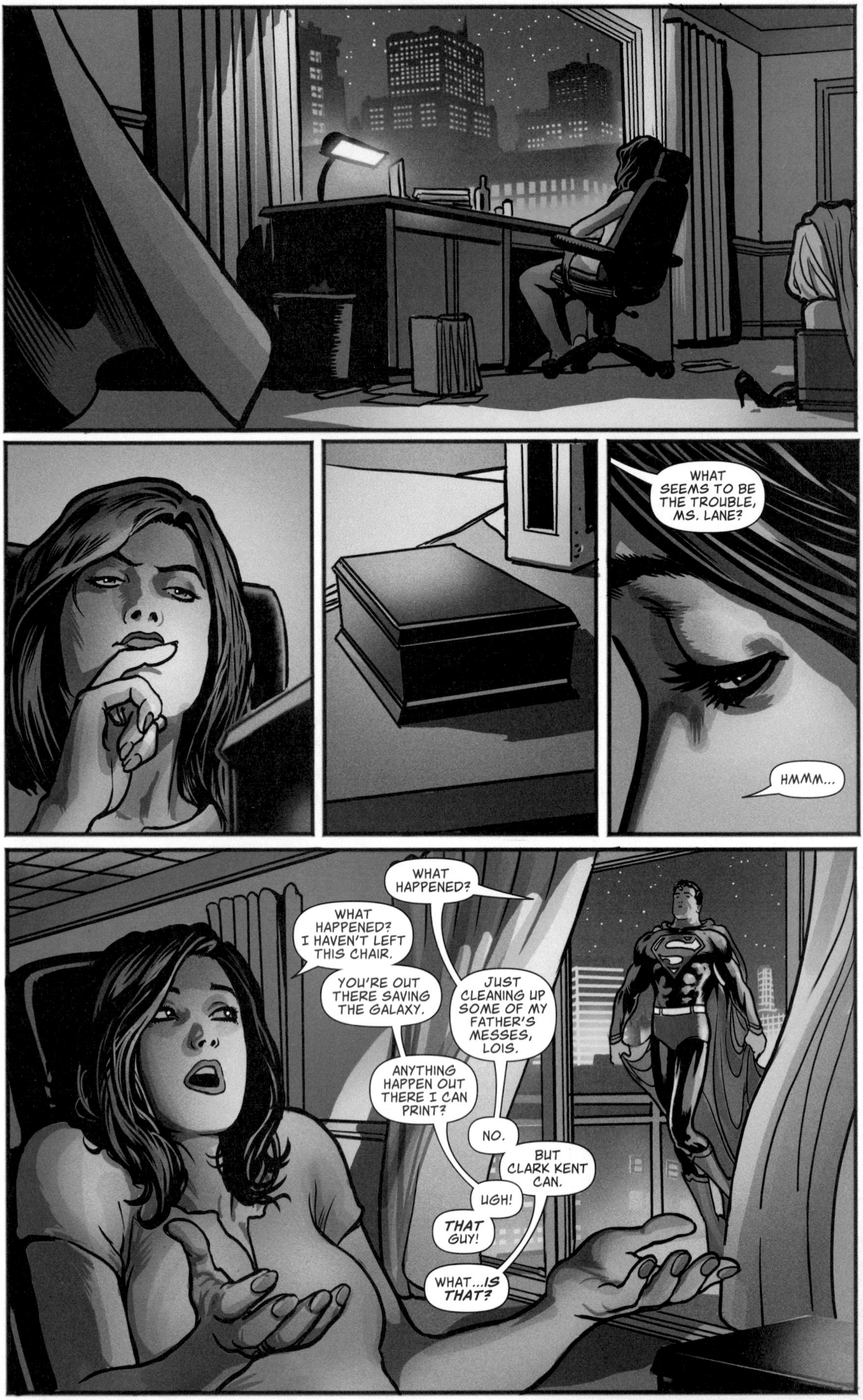
WHAT SEEMS TO BE THE TROUBLE, MS. LANE?
HMMM...
WHAT HAPPENED?
WHAT HAPPENED? I HAVEN'T LEFT THIS CHAIR.
YOU'RE OUT THERE SAVING THE GALAXY.
JUST CLEANING UP SOME OF MY FATHER'S MESSES, LOIS.
ANYTHING HAPPEN OUT THERE I CAN PRINT?
NO.
BUT CLARK KENT CAN.
UGH!
THAT GUY!
WHAT...*IS THAT?*

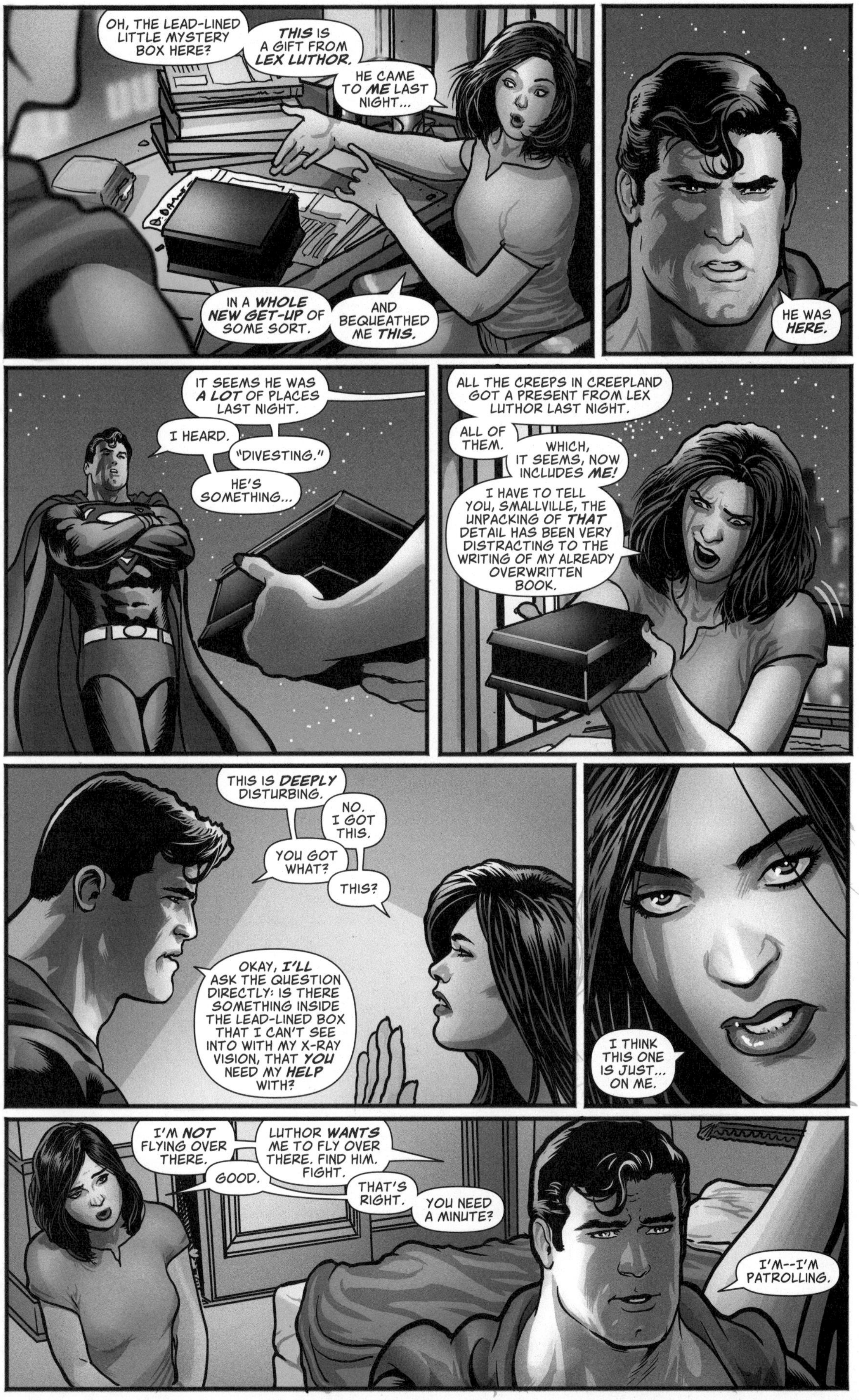

OH, THE LEAD-LINED LITTLE MYSTERY BOX HERE?
THIS IS A GIFT FROM LEX LUTHOR.
HE CAME TO ME LAST NIGHT...
IN A WHOLE NEW GET-UP OF SOME SORT.
AND BEQUEATHED ME THIS.
HE WAS HERE.
IT SEEMS HE WAS A LOT OF PLACES LAST NIGHT.
I HEARD.
"DIVESTING."
HE'S SOMETHING...
ALL THE CREEPS IN CREEPLAND GOT A PRESENT FROM LEX LUTHOR LAST NIGHT.
ALL OF THEM.
WHICH, IT SEEMS, NOW INCLUDES ME!
I HAVE TO TELL YOU, SMALLVILLE, THE UNPACKING OF THAT DETAIL HAS BEEN VERY DISTRACTING TO THE WRITING OF MY ALREADY OVERWRITTEN BOOK.
THIS IS DEEPLY DISTURBING.
NO. I GOT THIS.
YOU GOT WHAT?
THIS?
OKAY, I'LL ASK THE QUESTION DIRECTLY: IS THERE SOMETHING INSIDE THE LEAD-LINED BOX THAT I CAN'T SEE INTO WITH MY X-RAY VISION, THAT YOU NEED MY HELP WITH?
I THINK THIS ONE IS JUST... ON ME.
I'M NOT FLYING OVER THERE.
LUTHOR WANTS ME TO FLY OVER THERE. FIND HIM. FIGHT.
GOOD.
THAT'S RIGHT.
YOU NEED A MINUTE?
I'M--I'M PATROLLING.

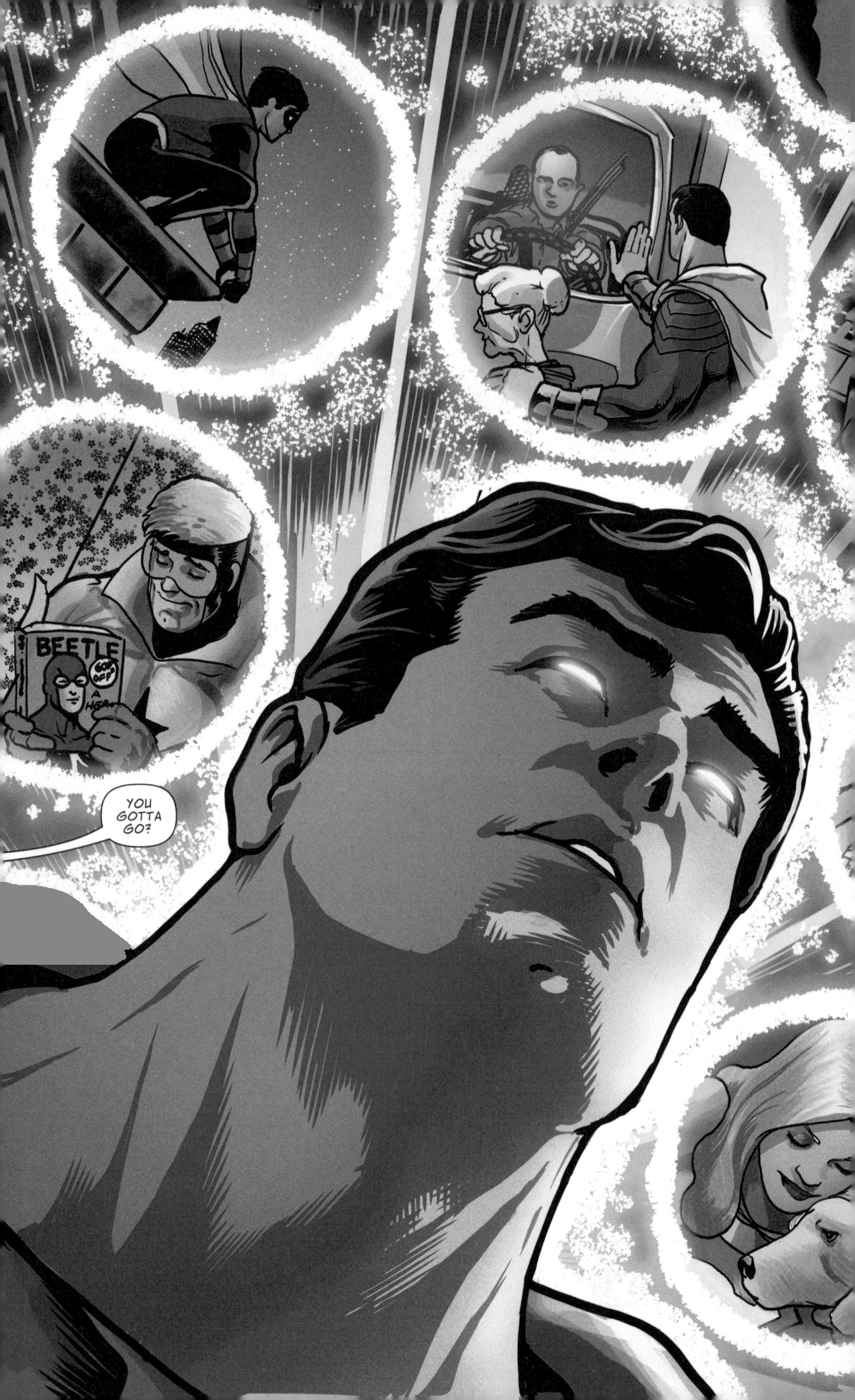
BEETLE
GOS OFF
YOU GOTTA GO?

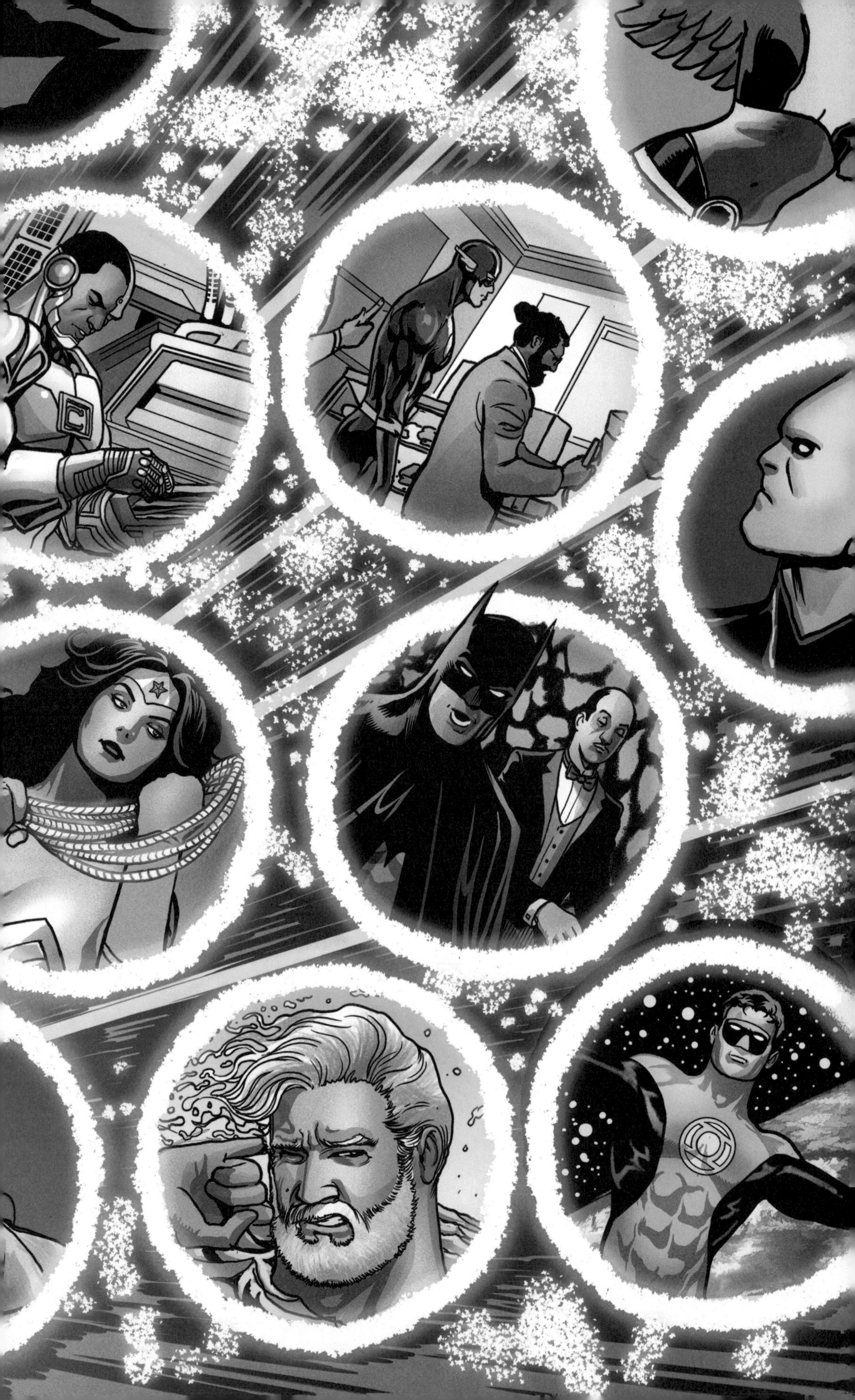

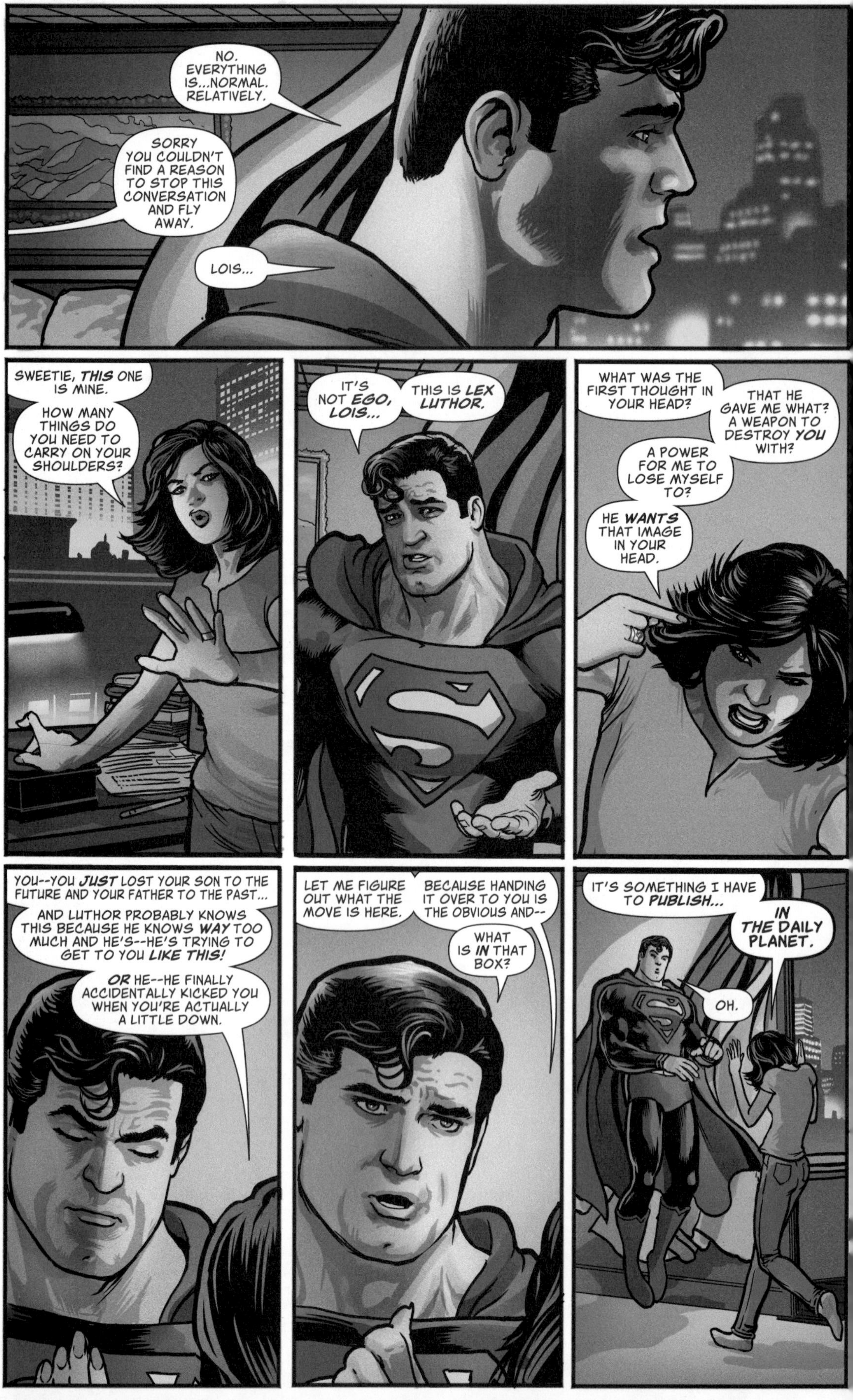
NO. EVERYTHING IS...NORMAL. RELATIVELY.
SORRY YOU COULDN'T FIND A REASON TO STOP THIS CONVERSATION AND FLY AWAY.
LOIS...
SWEETIE, **THIS** ONE IS MINE.
HOW MANY THINGS DO YOU NEED TO CARRY ON YOUR SHOULDERS?
IT'S NOT **EGO, LOIS...**
THIS IS **LEX LUTHOR.**
WHAT WAS THE FIRST THOUGHT IN YOUR HEAD?
THAT HE GAVE ME WHAT? A WEAPON TO DESTROY **YOU** WITH?
A POWER FOR ME TO LOSE MYSELF TO?
HE **WANTS** THAT IMAGE IN YOUR HEAD.
YOU--YOU **JUST** LOST YOUR SON TO THE FUTURE AND YOUR FATHER TO THE PAST...
AND LUTHOR PROBABLY KNOWS THIS BECAUSE HE KNOWS **WAY** TOO MUCH AND HE'S--HE'S TRYING TO GET TO YOU **LIKE THIS!**
OR HE--HE FINALLY ACCIDENTALLY KICKED YOU WHEN YOU'RE ACTUALLY A LITTLE DOWN.
LET ME FIGURE OUT WHAT THE MOVE IS HERE.
BECAUSE HANDING IT OVER TO YOU IS THE OBVIOUS AND--
WHAT IS **IN** THAT BOX?
IT'S SOMETHING I HAVE TO **PUBLISH...**
IN THE DAILY **PLANET.**
OH.

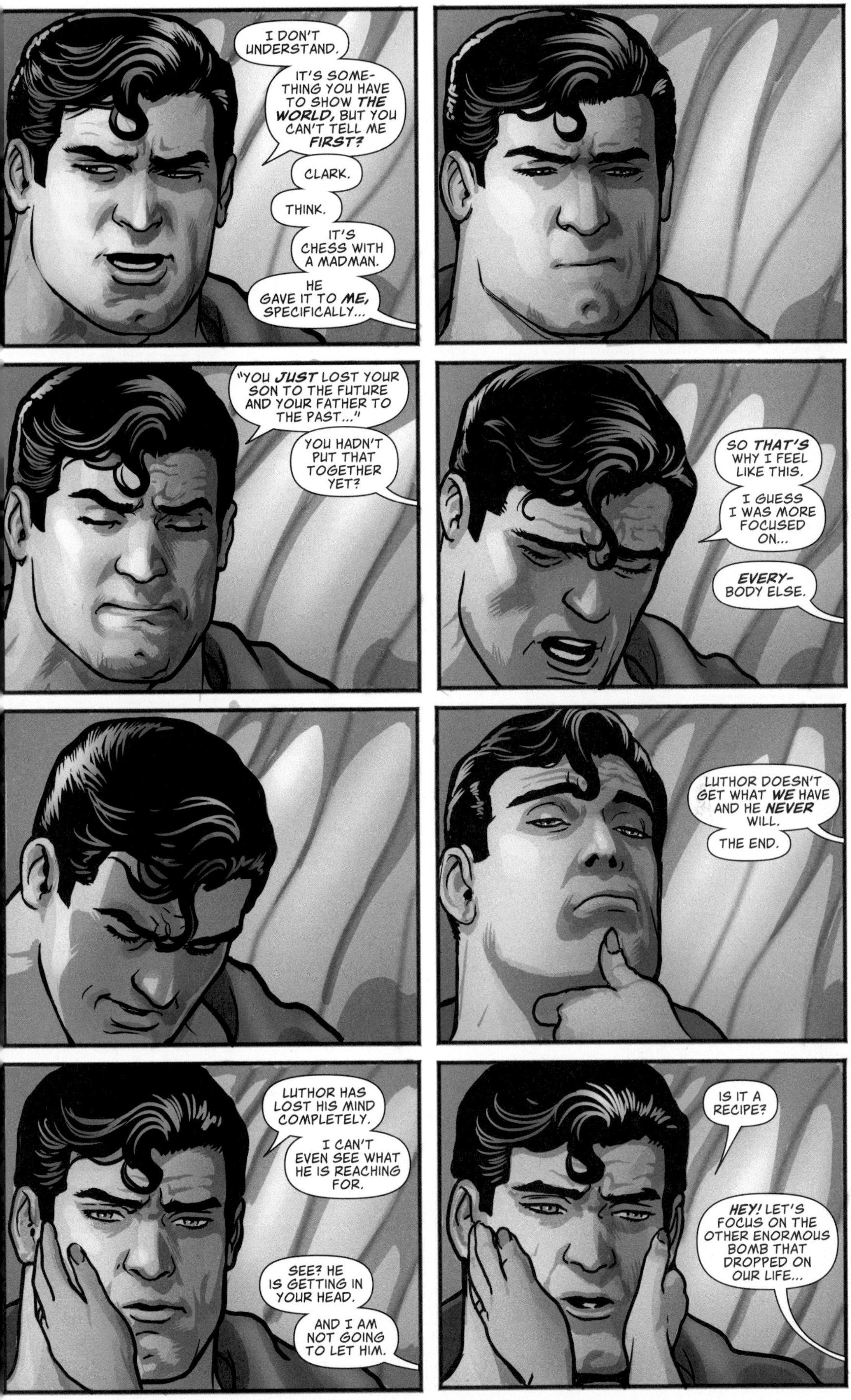
I DON'T UNDERSTAND.
IT'S SOMETHING YOU HAVE TO SHOW THE WORLD, BUT YOU CAN'T TELL ME FIRST?
CLARK.
THINK.
IT'S CHESS WITH A MADMAN.
HE GAVE IT TO ME, SPECIFICALLY...
"YOU JUST LOST YOUR SON TO THE FUTURE AND YOUR FATHER TO THE PAST..."
YOU HADN'T PUT THAT TOGETHER YET?
SO THAT'S WHY I FEEL LIKE THIS.
I GUESS I WAS MORE FOCUSED ON...
EVERYBODY ELSE.
LUTHOR DOESN'T GET WHAT WE HAVE AND HE NEVER WILL.
THE END.
LUTHOR HAS LOST HIS MIND COMPLETELY.
I CAN'T EVEN SEE WHAT HE IS REACHING FOR.
SEE? HE IS GETTING IN YOUR HEAD.
AND I AM NOT GOING TO LET HIM.
IS IT A RECIPE?
HEY! LET'S FOCUS ON THE OTHER ENORMOUS BOMB THAT DROPPED ON OUR LIFE...

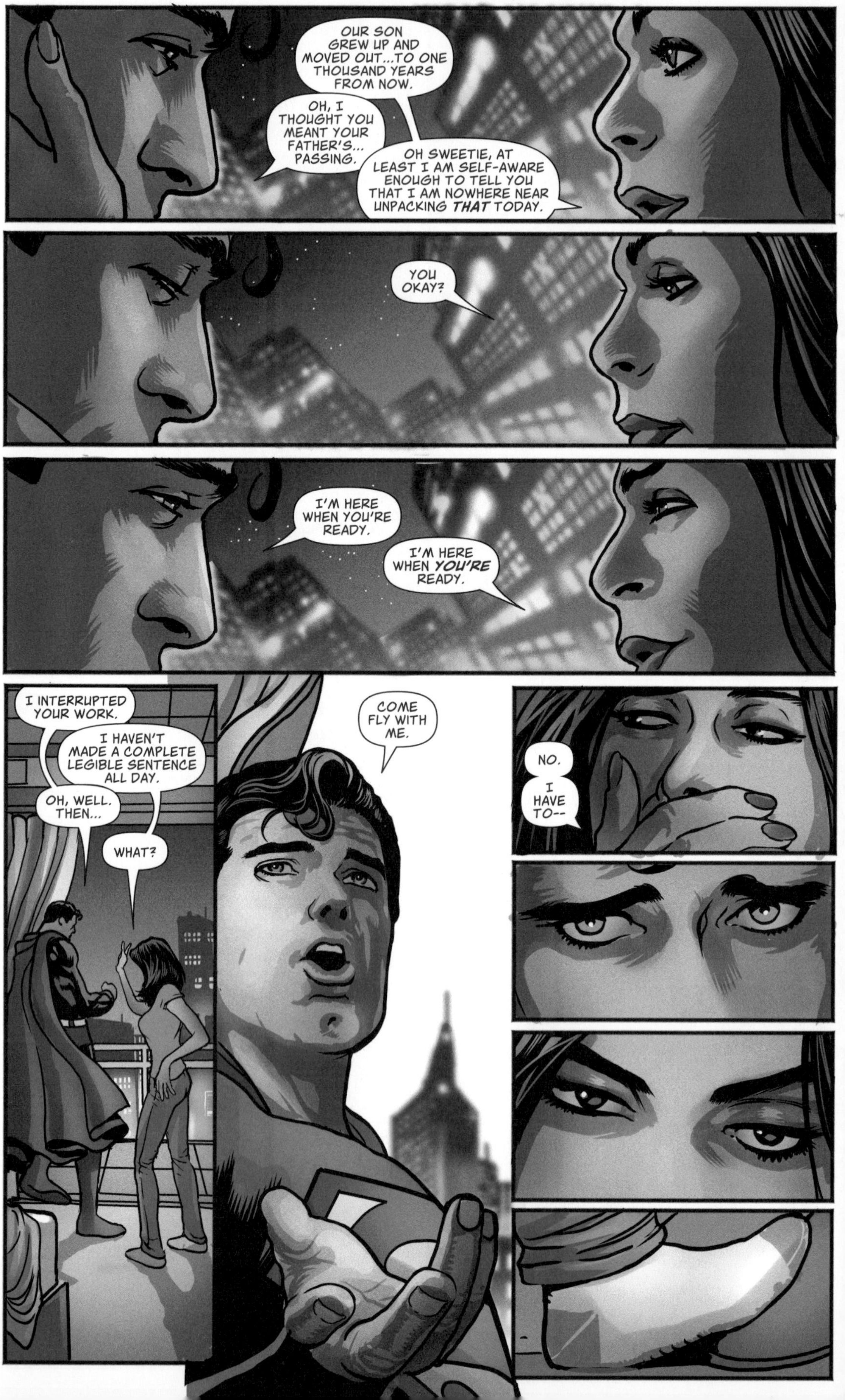
OUR SON GREW UP AND MOVED OUT...TO ONE THOUSAND YEARS FROM NOW.
OH, I THOUGHT YOU MEANT YOUR FATHER'S... PASSING.
OH SWEETIE, AT LEAST I AM SELF-AWARE ENOUGH TO TELL YOU THAT I AM NOWHERE NEAR UNPACKING **THAT** TODAY.
YOU OKAY?
I'M HERE WHEN YOU'RE READY.
I'M HERE WHEN **YOU'RE** READY.
I INTERRUPTED YOUR WORK.
I HAVEN'T MADE A COMPLETE LEGIBLE SENTENCE ALL DAY.
OH, WELL. THEN...
WHAT?
COME FLY WITH ME.
NO.
I HAVE TO--

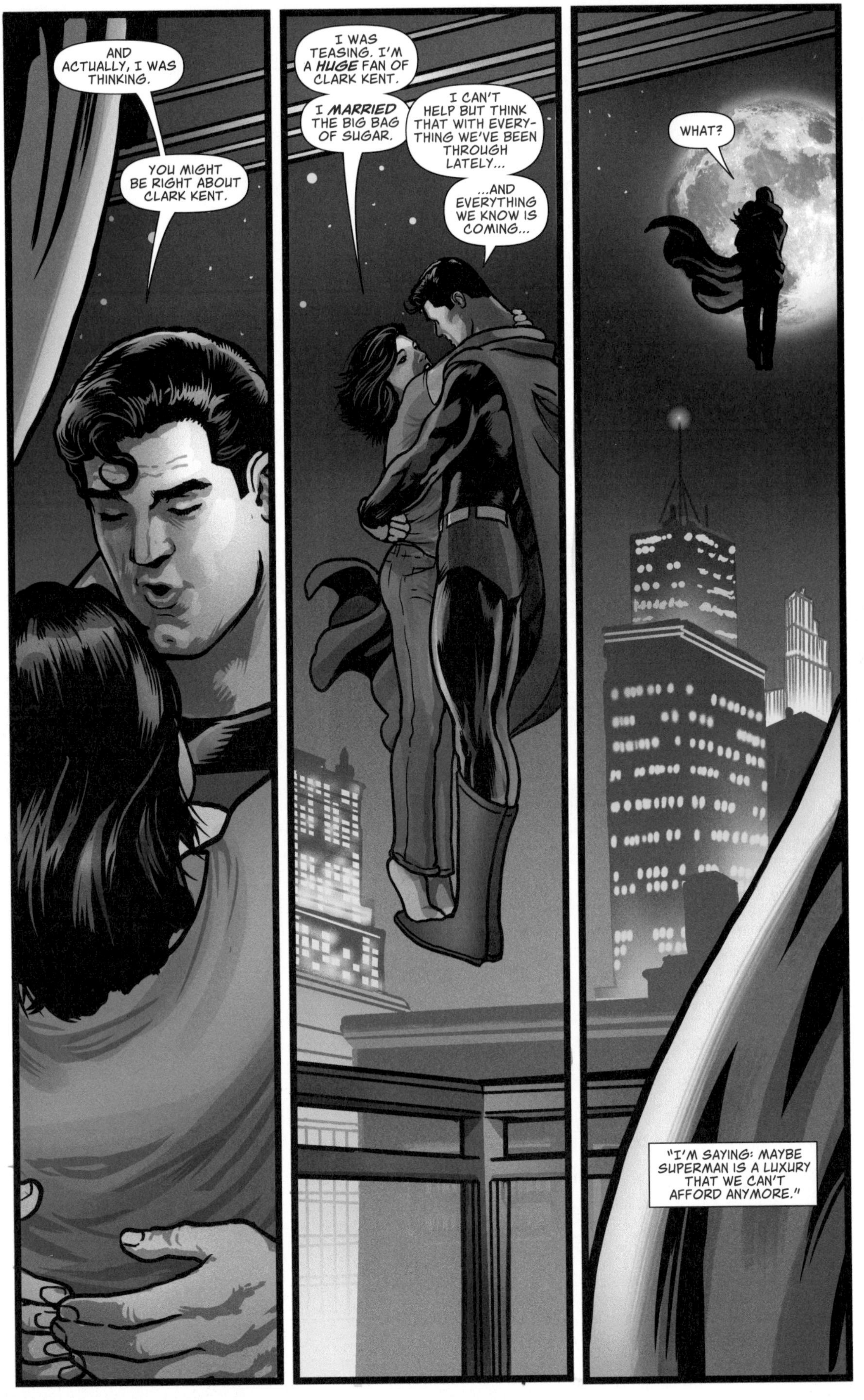
AND ACTUALLY, I WAS THINKING.
YOU MIGHT BE RIGHT ABOUT CLARK KENT.
I WAS TEASING. I'M A HUGE FAN OF CLARK KENT.
I MARRIED THE BIG BAG OF SUGAR.
I CAN'T HELP BUT THINK THAT WITH EVERYTHING WE'VE BEEN THROUGH LATELY...
...AND EVERYTHING WE KNOW IS COMING...
WHAT?
"I'M SAYING: MAYBE SUPERMAN IS A LUXURY THAT WE CAN'T AFFORD ANYMORE."

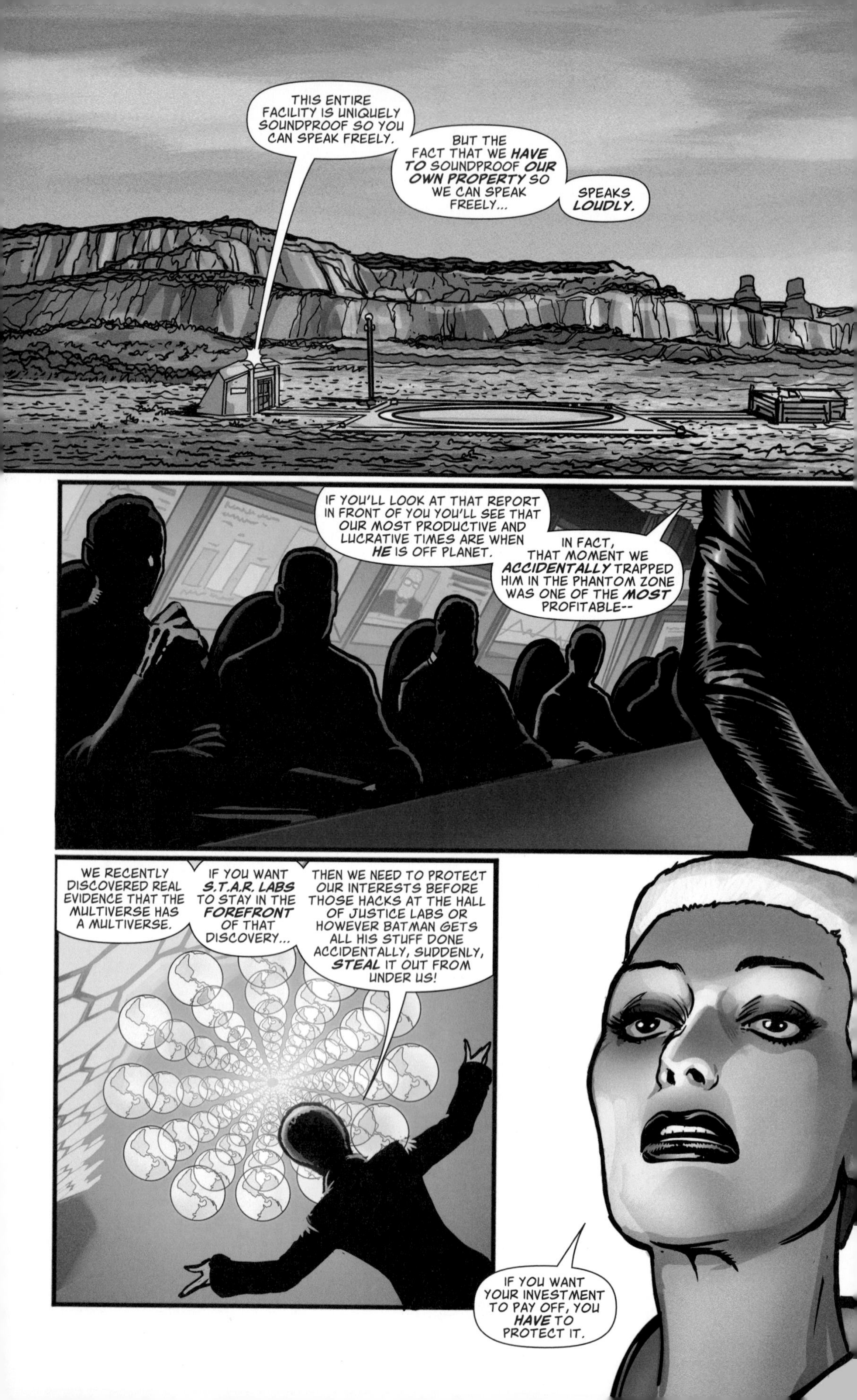
THIS ENTIRE FACILITY IS UNIQUELY SOUNDPROOF SO YOU CAN SPEAK FREELY.
BUT THE FACT THAT WE *HAVE TO* SOUNDPROOF *OUR OWN PROPERTY* SO WE CAN SPEAK FREELY...
SPEAKS *LOUDLY.*
IF YOU'LL LOOK AT THAT REPORT IN FRONT OF YOU YOU'LL SEE THAT OUR MOST PRODUCTIVE AND LUCRATIVE TIMES ARE WHEN *HE* IS OFF PLANET.
IN FACT, THAT MOMENT WE *ACCIDENTALLY* TRAPPED HIM IN THE PHANTOM ZONE WAS ONE OF THE *MOST* PROFITABLE--
WE RECENTLY DISCOVERED REAL EVIDENCE THAT THE MULTIVERSE HAS A MULTIVERSE.
IF YOU WANT *S.T.A.R. LABS* TO STAY IN THE *FOREFRONT* OF THAT DISCOVERY...
THEN WE NEED TO PROTECT OUR INTERESTS BEFORE THOSE HACKS AT THE HALL OF JUSTICE LABS OR HOWEVER BATMAN GETS ALL HIS STUFF DONE ACCIDENTALLY, SUDDENLY, *STEAL* IT OUT FROM UNDER US!
IF YOU WANT YOUR INVESTMENT TO PAY OFF, YOU *HAVE* TO PROTECT IT.

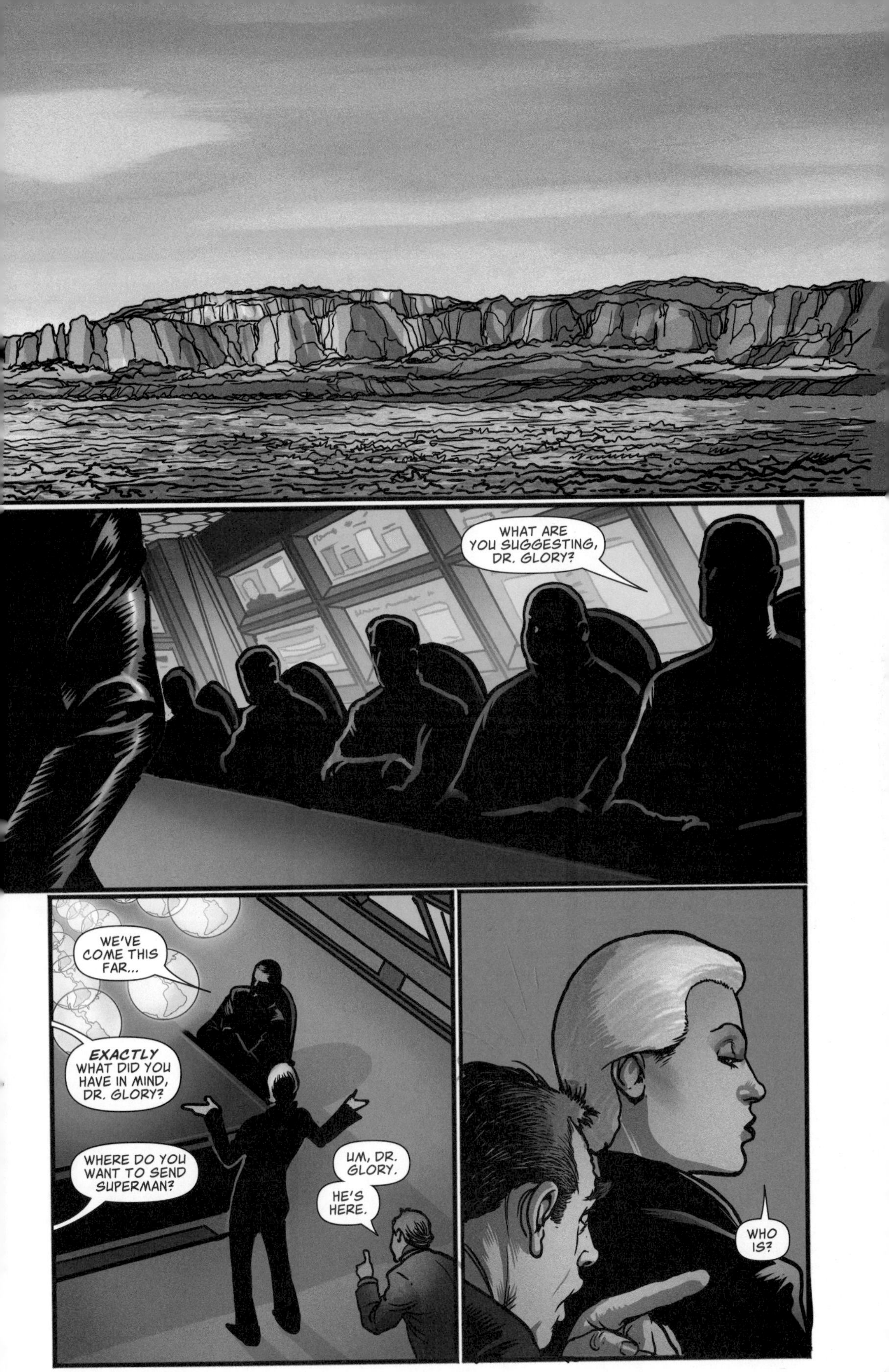
WHAT ARE YOU SUGGESTING, DR. GLORY?
WE'VE COME THIS FAR...
EXACTLY WHAT DID YOU HAVE IN MIND, DR. GLORY?
WHERE DO YOU WANT TO SEND SUPERMAN?
UM, DR. GLORY.
HE'S HERE.
WHO IS?

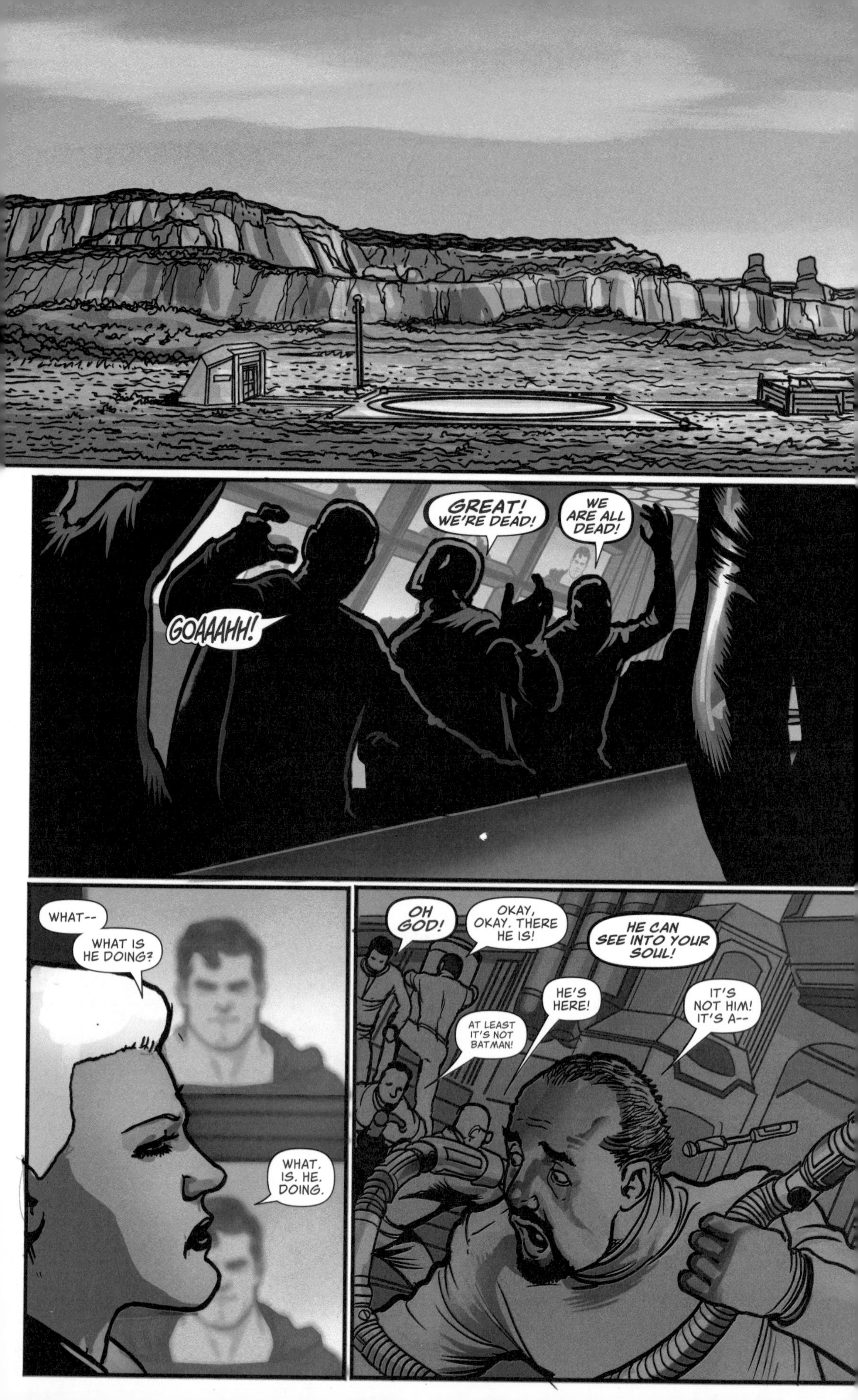
GREAT! WE'RE DEAD!
WE ARE ALL DEAD!
GOAAAHH!
WHAT--
WHAT IS HE DOING?
WHAT. IS. HE. DOING.
OH GOD!
OKAY, OKAY. THERE HE IS!
HE CAN SEE INTO YOUR SOUL!
AT LEAST IT'S NOT BATMAN!
HE'S HERE!
IT'S NOT HIM! IT'S A--

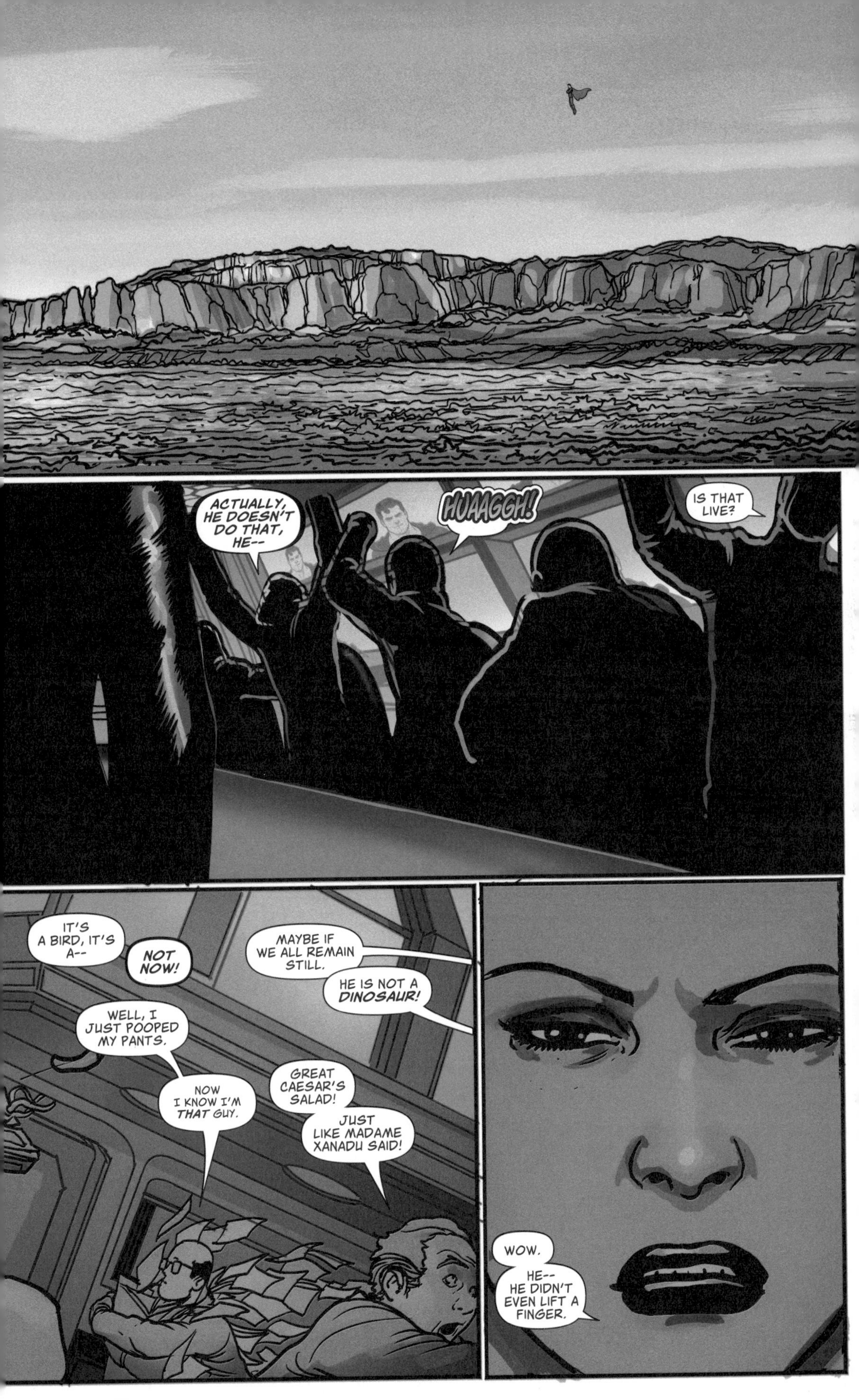

ACTUALLY, HE DOESN'T DO THAT, HE--
HUAAGGH!
IS THAT LIVE?
IT'S A BIRD, IT'S A--
NOT NOW!
MAYBE IF WE ALL REMAIN STILL.
HE IS NOT A DINOSAUR!
WELL, I JUST POOPED MY PANTS.
NOW I KNOW I'M THAT GUY.
GREAT CAESAR'S SALAD!
JUST LIKE MADAME XANADU SAID!
WOW.
HE-- HE DIDN'T EVEN LIFT A FINGER.

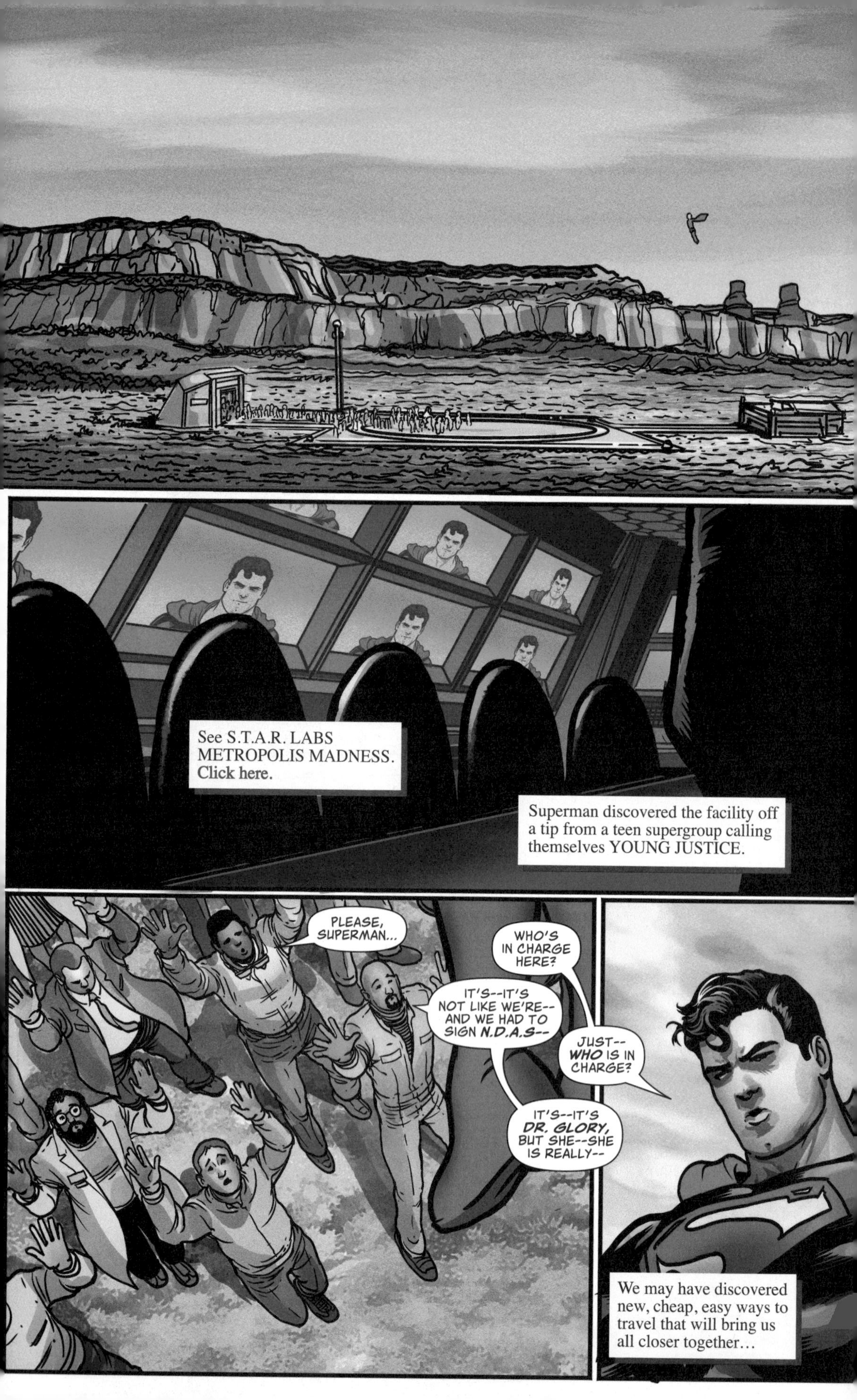
See S.T.A.R. LABS METROPOLIS MADNESS. Click here.
Superman discovered the facility off a tip from a teen supergroup calling themselves YOUNG JUSTICE.
PLEASE, SUPERMAN...
WHO'S IN CHARGE HERE?
IT'S--IT'S NOT LIKE WE'RE-- AND WE HAD TO SIGN N.D.A.S--
JUST-- WHO IS IN CHARGE?
IT'S--IT'S DR. GLORY, BUT SHE--SHE IS REALLY--
We may have discovered new, cheap, easy ways to travel that will bring us all closer together…

S.T.A.R. LABS SUPER SHUTDOWN!
by Clark Kent

Another challenging day for the people behind multi-hyphenate science conglomerate S.T.A.R. Labs. Superman located a secret, unsanctioned S.T.A.R. Labs facility, code-named THE CONSTELLATION, hidden away in the low plains of the Utah deserts.

The Constellation was caught actively engaging in unlicensed and unlawful interdimensional science experiments without supervision or governmental regulation of any kind.

All of these experiments were "off the books" and not for the public. "This was a fully funded black bag science initiative," said one source. "They didn't care what the cost. They just wanted the next new thing to be from S.T.A.R. Labs."

Members of that group reported themselves as victims of "illegal interdimensional experiments." When Superman went to investigate, he discovered dozens more illegal experiments like the ones found recently at the Metropolis S.T.A.R. Labs.

"The teleportation science we're working with is so new, we don't know what the cost of it is. It could be nothing or it could be enormous, said another S.T.A.R. Labs employee speaking with anonymity.

Or these S.T.A.R. Lab monsters, with no one looking over their shoulder, may have torn open the fabric of reality, beyond repair, and we're all in a lot of trouble.

The leader of the illegal Constellation program escaped, some say taking much of S.T.A.R. Labs future with her, leaving more questions than answers.

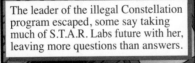

Representatives for S.T.A.R. Labs could not be reached for comment. The S.T.A.R. Labs LASDAC stock plummeted to an all-time low.

SECRETS.

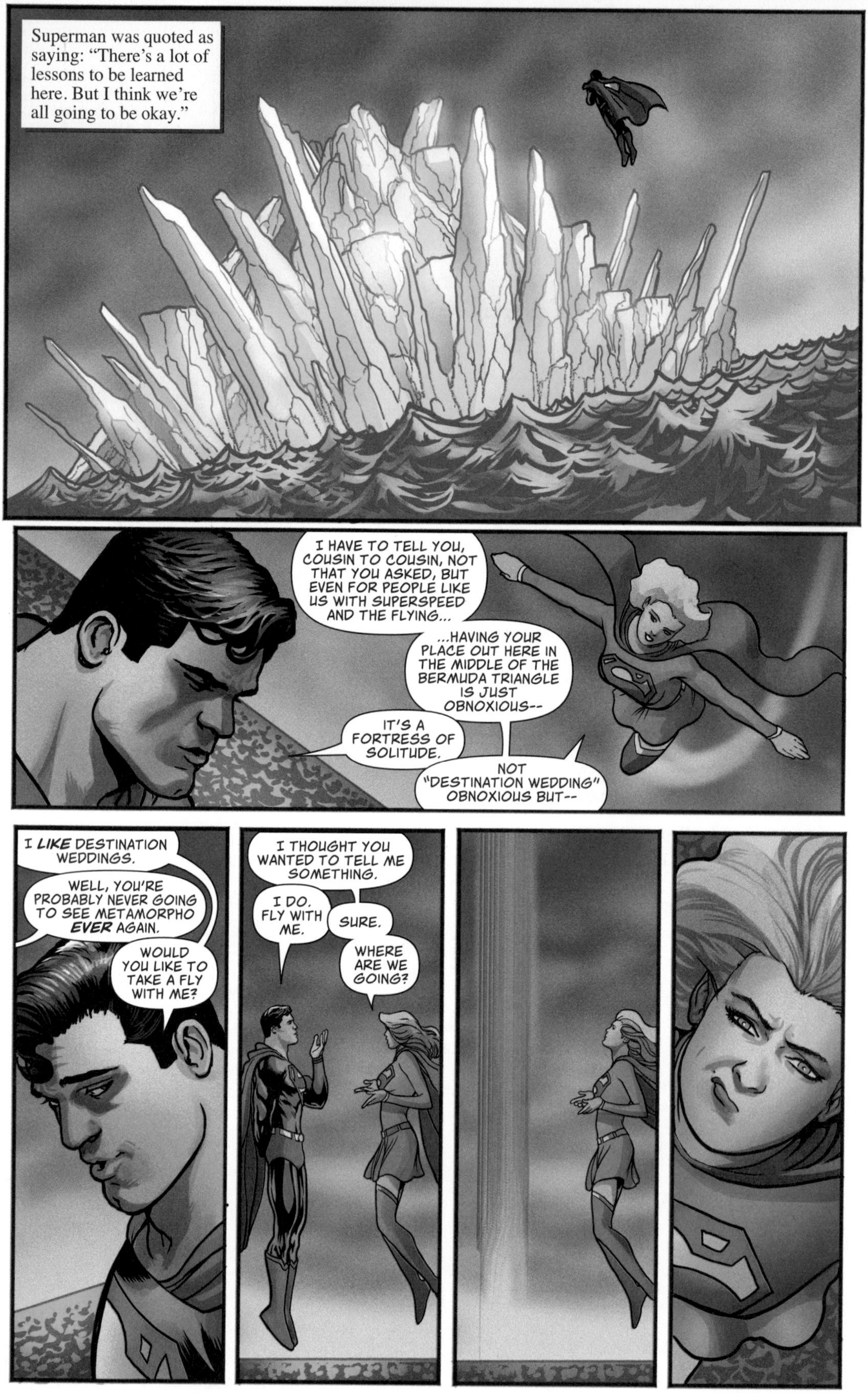

Superman was quoted as saying: "There's a lot of lessons to be learned here. But I think we're all going to be okay."
I HAVE TO TELL YOU, COUSIN TO COUSIN, NOT THAT YOU ASKED, BUT EVEN FOR PEOPLE LIKE US WITH SUPERSPEED AND THE FLYING...
...HAVING YOUR PLACE OUT HERE IN THE MIDDLE OF THE BERMUDA TRIANGLE IS JUST OBNOXIOUS--
IT'S A FORTRESS OF SOLITUDE.
NOT "DESTINATION WEDDING" OBNOXIOUS BUT--
I *LIKE* DESTINATION WEDDINGS.
WELL, YOU'RE PROBABLY NEVER GOING TO SEE METAMORPHO *EVER* AGAIN.
WOULD YOU LIKE TO TAKE A FLY WITH ME?
I THOUGHT YOU WANTED TO TELL ME SOMETHING.
I DO. FLY WITH ME.
SURE.
WHERE ARE WE GOING?

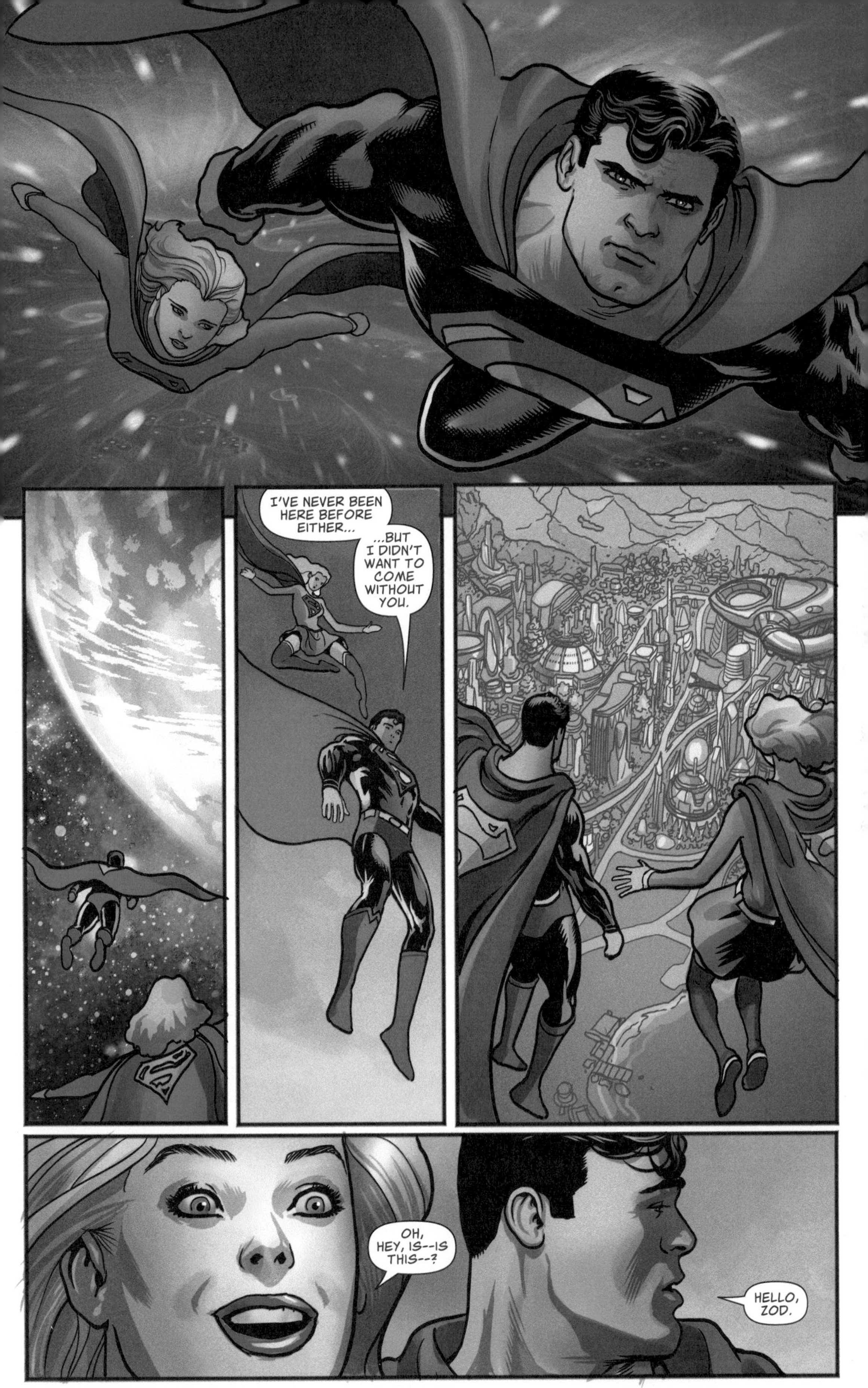
I'VE NEVER BEEN HERE BEFORE EITHER...
...BUT I DIDN'T WANT TO COME WITHOUT YOU.
OH, HEY, IS--IS THIS--?
HELLO, ZOD.

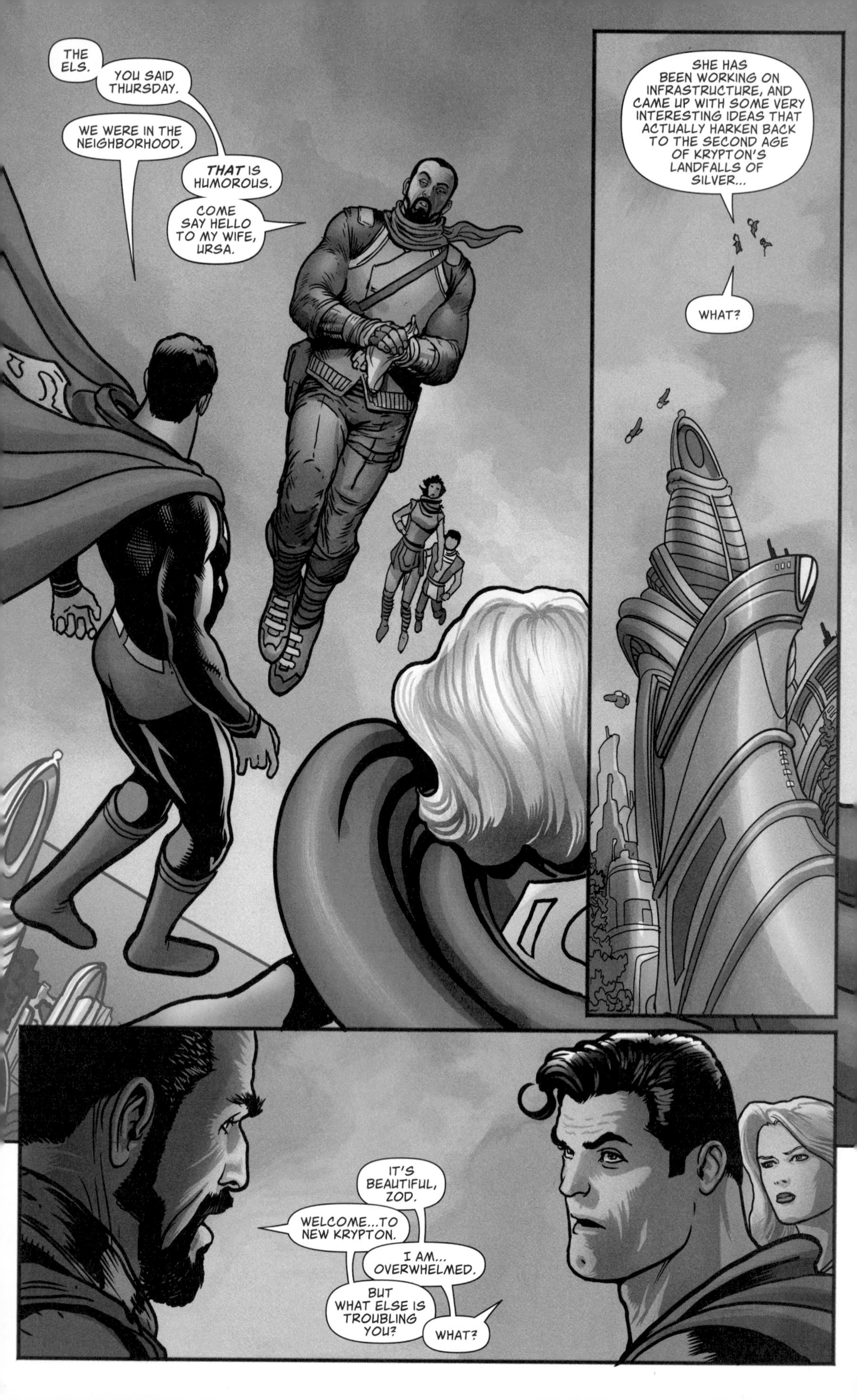
THE ELS.
YOU SAID THURSDAY.
WE WERE IN THE NEIGHBORHOOD.
THAT IS HUMOROUS.
COME SAY HELLO TO MY WIFE, URSA.
SHE HAS BEEN WORKING ON INFRASTRUCTURE, AND CAME UP WITH SOME VERY INTERESTING IDEAS THAT ACTUALLY HARKEN BACK TO THE SECOND AGE OF KRYPTON'S LANDFALLS OF SILVER...
WHAT?
WELCOME...TO NEW KRYPTON.
IT'S BEAUTIFUL, ZOD.
I AM... OVERWHELMED.
BUT WHAT ELSE IS TROUBLING YOU?
WHAT?

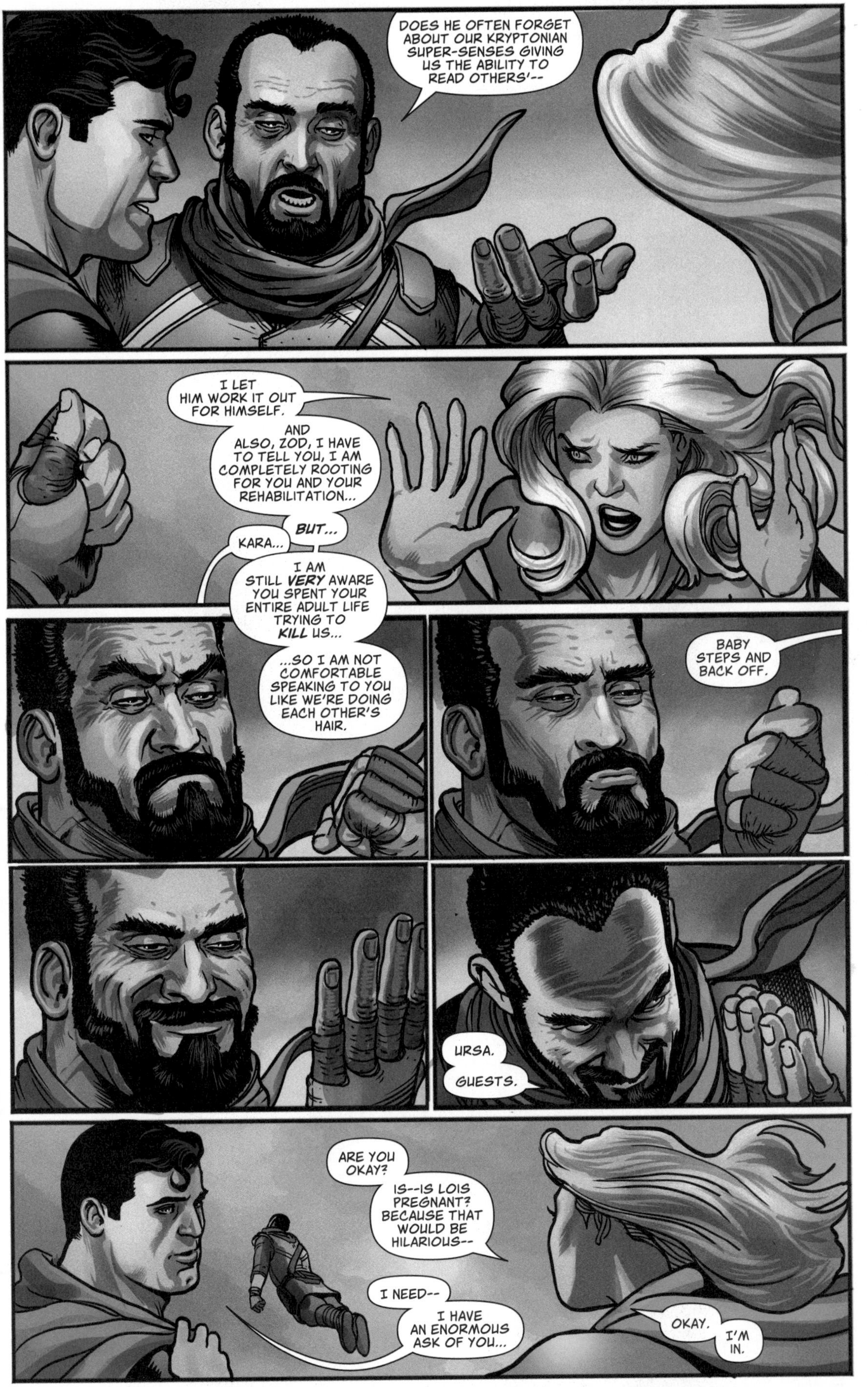
DOES HE OFTEN FORGET ABOUT OUR KRYPTONIAN SUPER-SENSES GIVING US THE ABILITY TO READ OTHERS'--
I LET HIM WORK IT OUT FOR HIMSELF.
AND ALSO, ZOD, I HAVE TO TELL YOU, I AM COMPLETELY ROOTING FOR YOU AND YOUR REHABILITATION...
BUT...
KARA...
I AM STILL VERY AWARE YOU SPENT YOUR ENTIRE ADULT LIFE TRYING TO KILL US...
...SO I AM NOT COMFORTABLE SPEAKING TO YOU LIKE WE'RE DOING EACH OTHER'S HAIR.
BABY STEPS AND BACK OFF.
URSA.
GUESTS.
ARE YOU OKAY?
IS--IS LOIS PREGNANT? BECAUSE THAT WOULD BE HILARIOUS--
I NEED--
I HAVE AN ENORMOUS ASK OF YOU...
OKAY.
I'M IN.

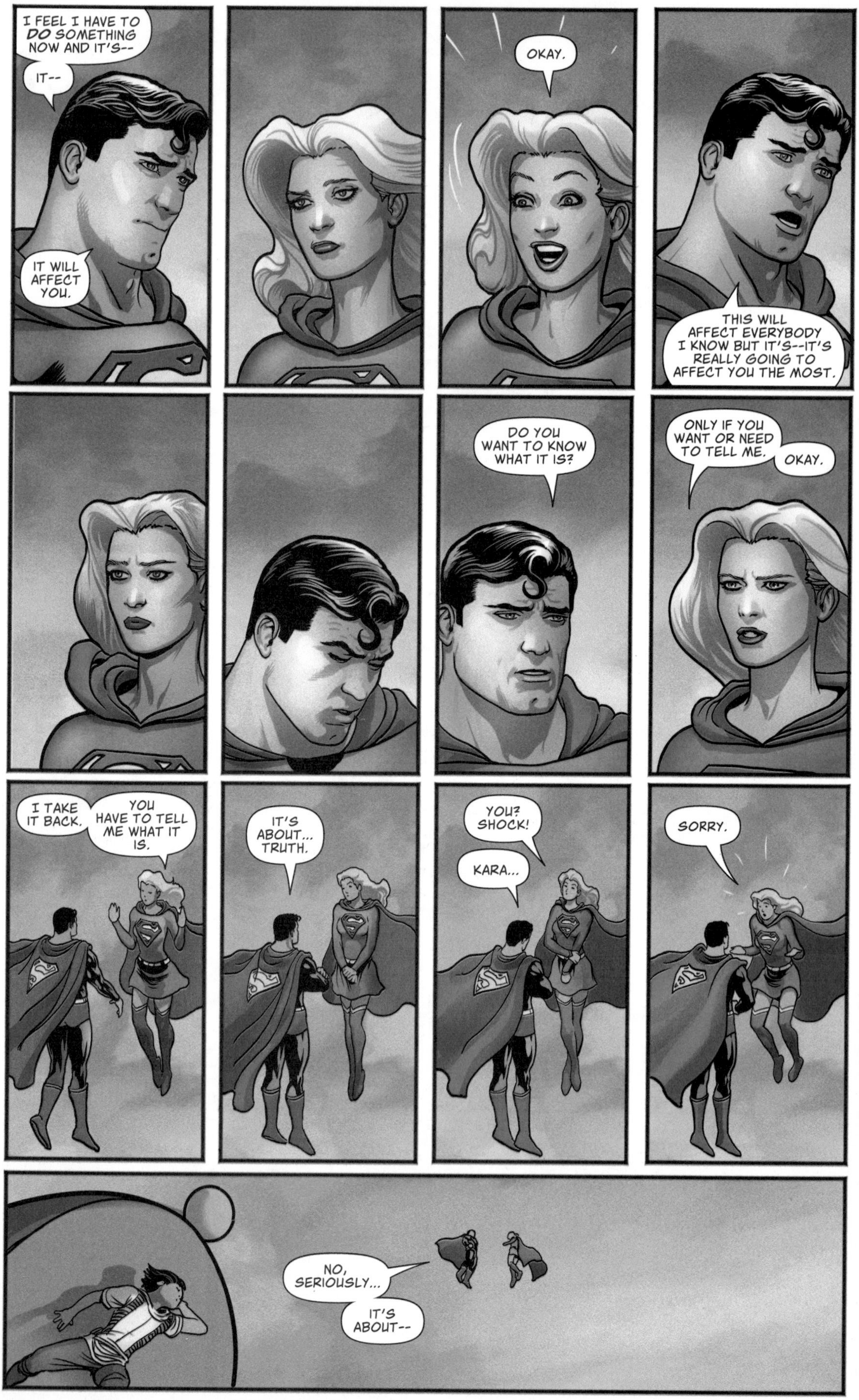

I FEEL I HAVE TO **DO** SOMETHING NOW AND IT'S--
IT--
IT WILL AFFECT YOU.
OKAY.
THIS WILL AFFECT EVERYBODY I KNOW BUT IT'S--IT'S REALLY GOING TO AFFECT YOU THE MOST.
DO YOU WANT TO KNOW WHAT IT IS?
ONLY IF YOU WANT OR NEED TO TELL ME.
OKAY.
I TAKE IT BACK.
YOU HAVE TO TELL ME WHAT IT IS.
IT'S ABOUT... TRUTH.
YOU? SHOCK!
KARA...
SORRY.
NO, SERIOUSLY...
IT'S ABOUT--

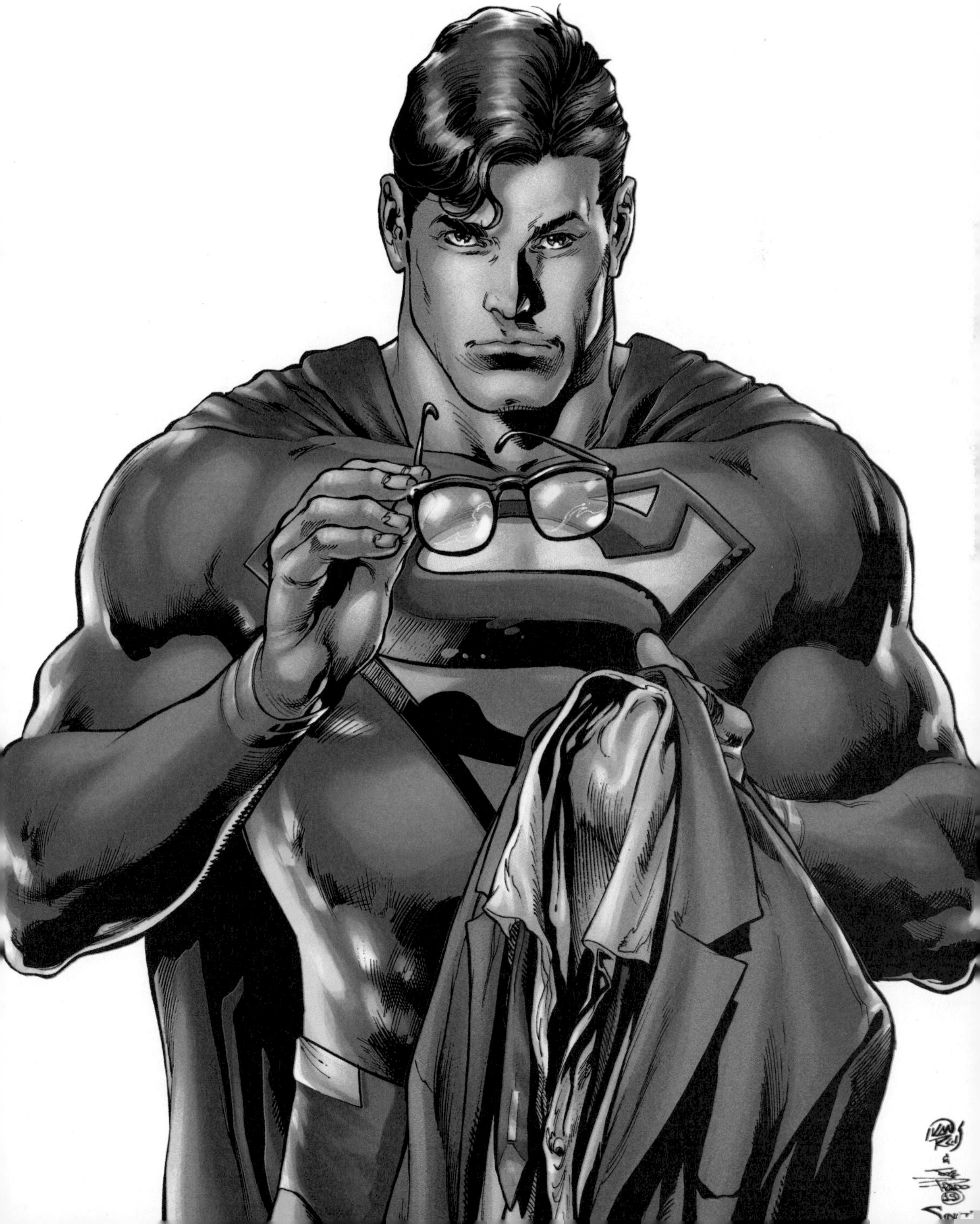

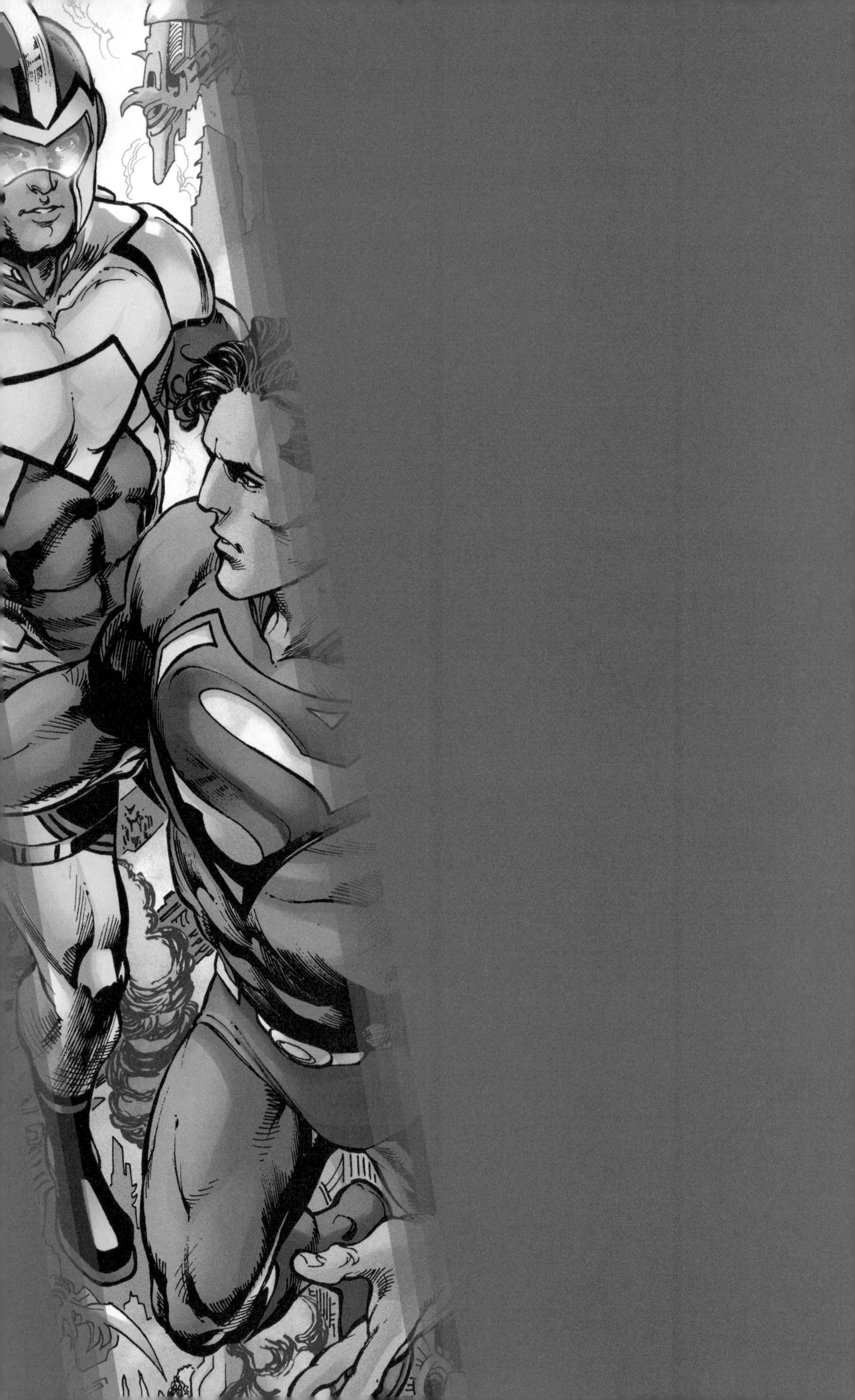

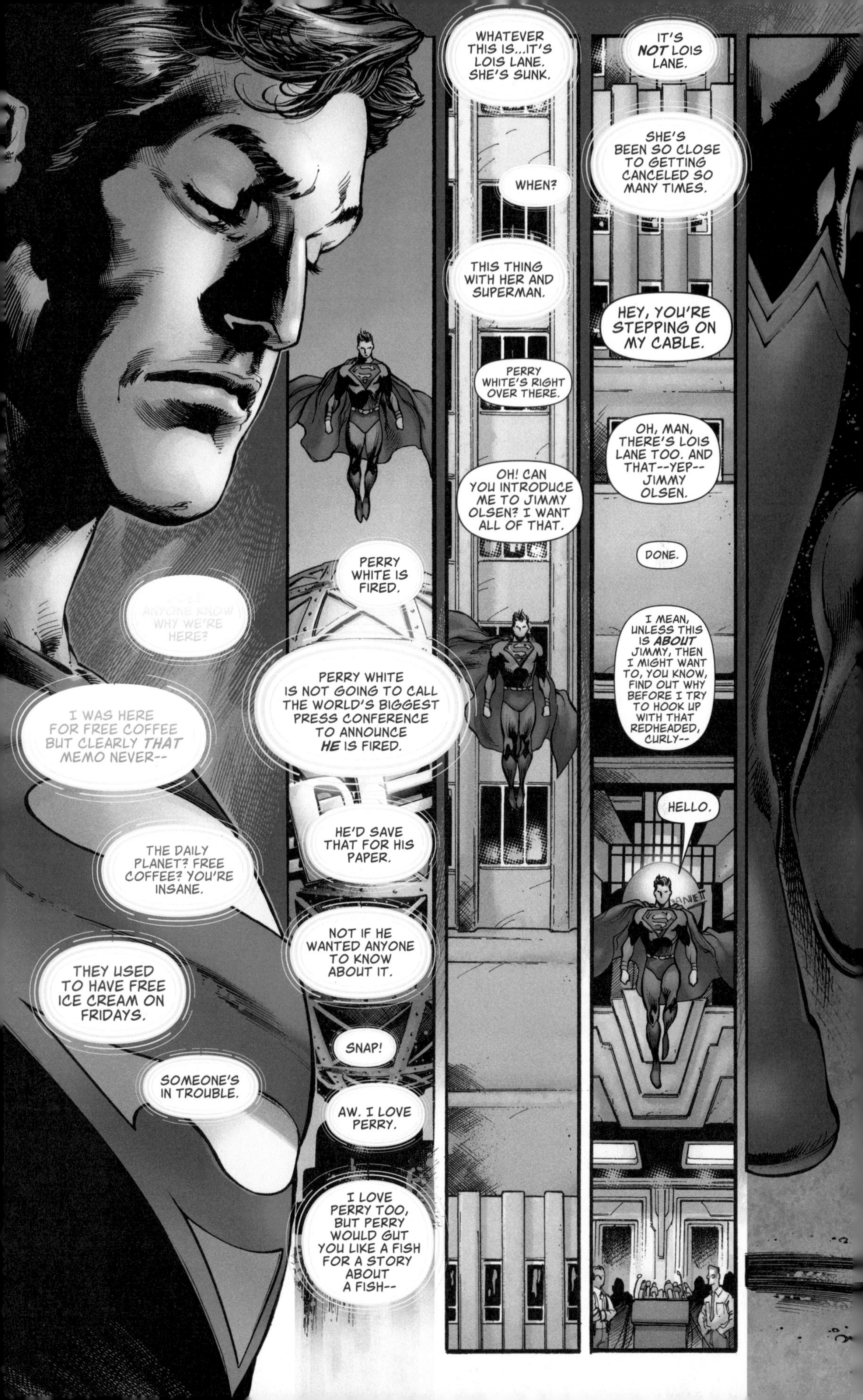
ANYONE KNOW WHY WE'RE HERE?
PERRY WHITE IS FIRED.
I WAS HERE FOR FREE COFFEE BUT CLEARLY *THAT* MEMO NEVER--
PERRY WHITE IS NOT GOING TO CALL THE WORLD'S BIGGEST PRESS CONFERENCE TO ANNOUNCE *HE* IS FIRED.
HE'D SAVE THAT FOR HIS PAPER.
THE DAILY PLANET? FREE COFFEE? YOU'RE INSANE.
NOT IF HE WANTED ANYONE TO KNOW ABOUT IT.
THEY USED TO HAVE FREE ICE CREAM ON FRIDAYS.
SNAP!
SOMEONE'S IN TROUBLE.
AW. I LOVE PERRY.
I LOVE PERRY TOO, BUT PERRY WOULD GUT YOU LIKE A FISH FOR A STORY ABOUT A FISH--
WHATEVER THIS IS...IT'S LOIS LANE. SHE'S SUNK.
WHEN?
THIS THING WITH HER AND SUPERMAN.
PERRY WHITE'S RIGHT OVER THERE.
OH! CAN YOU INTRODUCE ME TO JIMMY OLSEN? I WANT ALL OF THAT.
IT'S *NOT* LOIS LANE.
SHE'S BEEN SO CLOSE TO GETTING CANCELED SO MANY TIMES.
HEY, YOU'RE STEPPING ON MY CABLE.
OH, MAN, THERE'S LOIS LANE TOO. AND THAT--YEP-- JIMMY OLSEN.
DONE.
I MEAN, UNLESS THIS IS *ABOUT* JIMMY, THEN I MIGHT WANT TO, YOU KNOW, FIND OUT WHY BEFORE I TRY TO HOOK UP WITH THAT REDHEADED, CURLY--
HELLO.

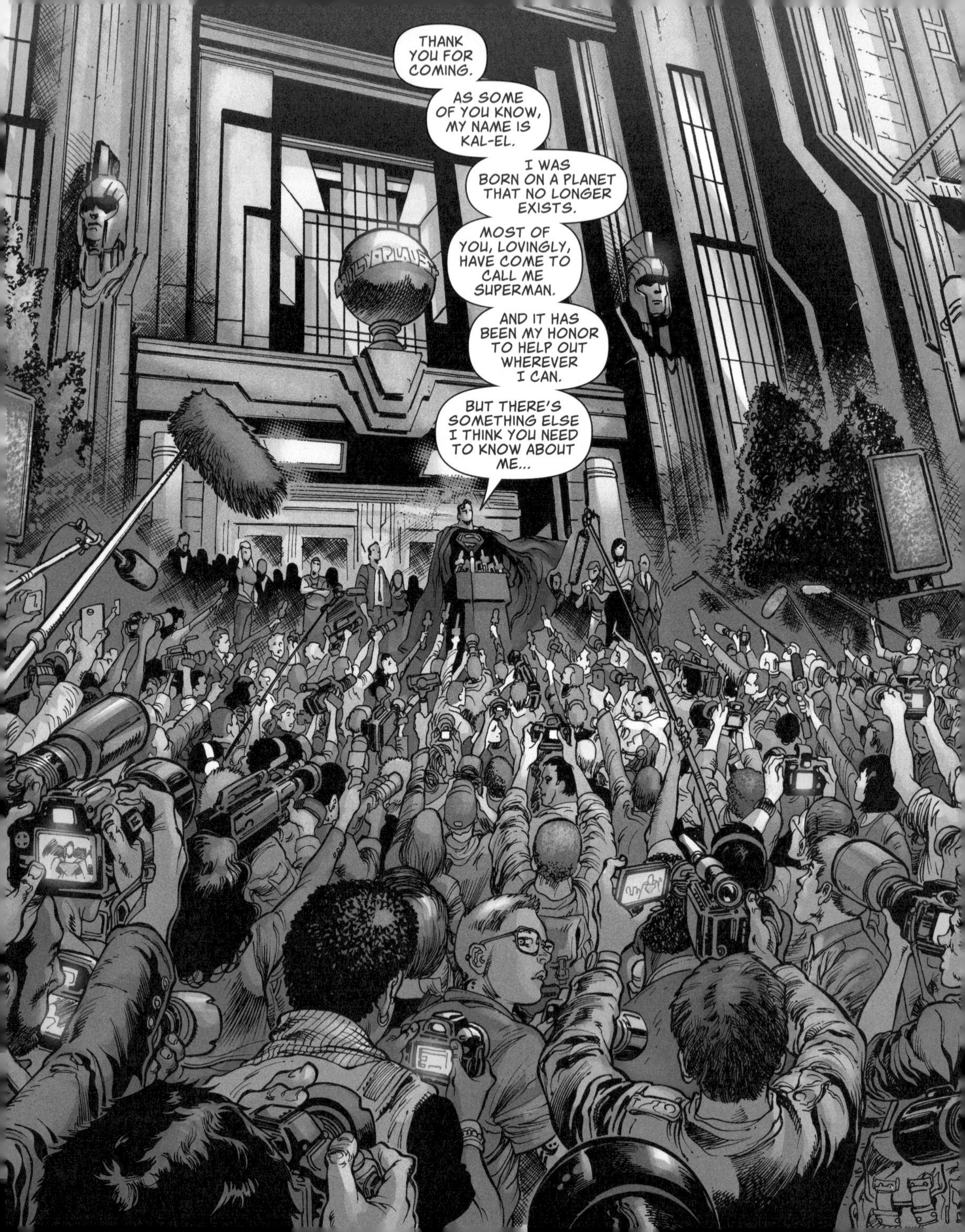
THANK YOU FOR COMING.
AS SOME OF YOU KNOW, MY NAME IS KAL-EL.
I WAS BORN ON A PLANET THAT NO LONGER EXISTS.
MOST OF YOU, LOVINGLY, HAVE COME TO CALL ME SUPERMAN.
AND IT HAS BEEN MY HONOR TO HELP OUT WHEREVER I CAN.
BUT THERE'S SOMETHING ELSE I THINK YOU NEED TO KNOW ABOUT ME...

DC COMICS PROUDLY PRESENTS

SUPERMAN TRUTH

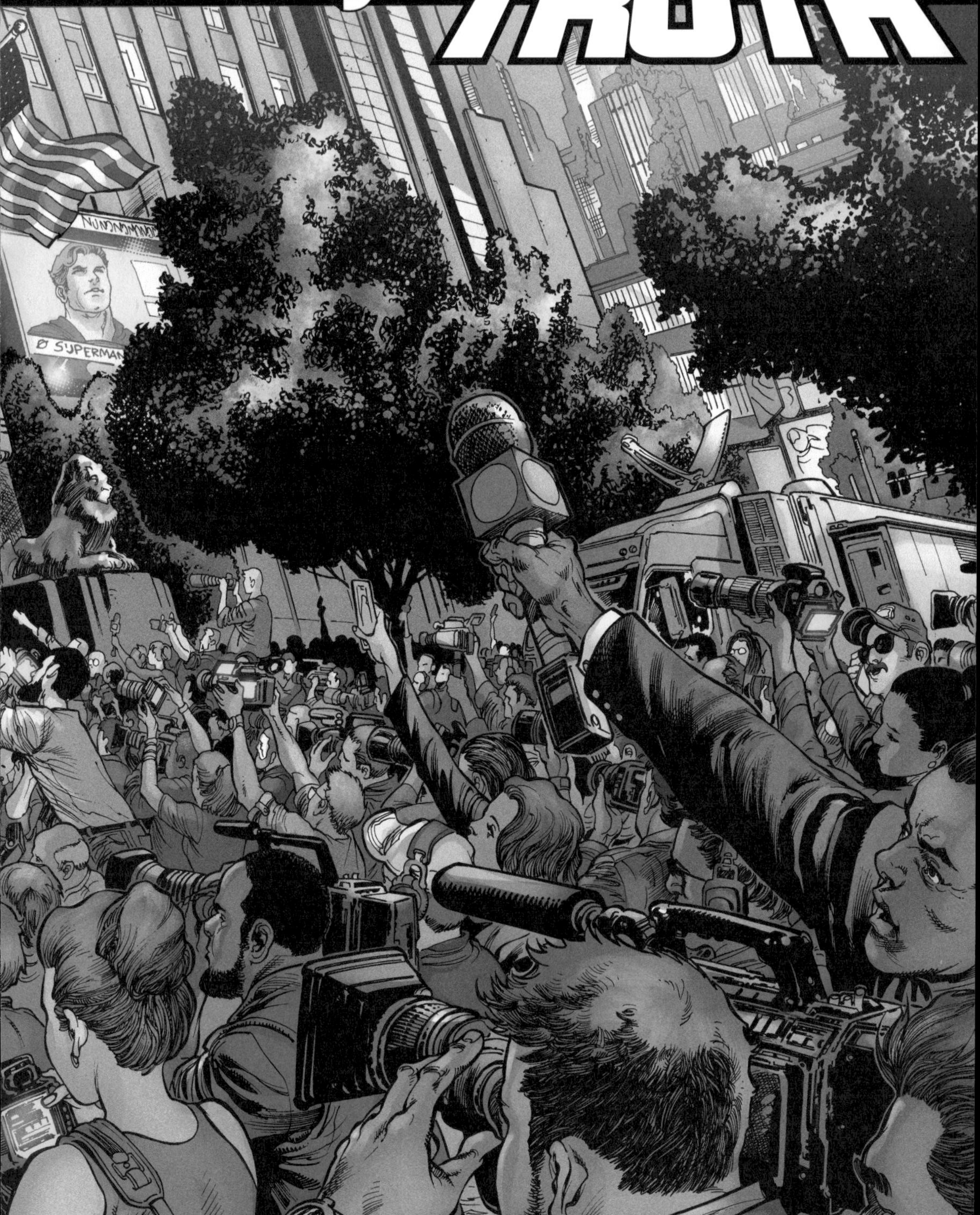
Ø SUPERMAN

BRIAN MICHAEL BENDIS writer IVAN REIS pencils JOE PRADO inks

ALEX SINCLAIR colors DAVE SHARPE letters IVAN REIS, JOE PRADO, ALEX SINCLAIR cover

JESSICA CHEN associate editor MIKE COTTON editor BRIAN CUNNINGHAM group editor

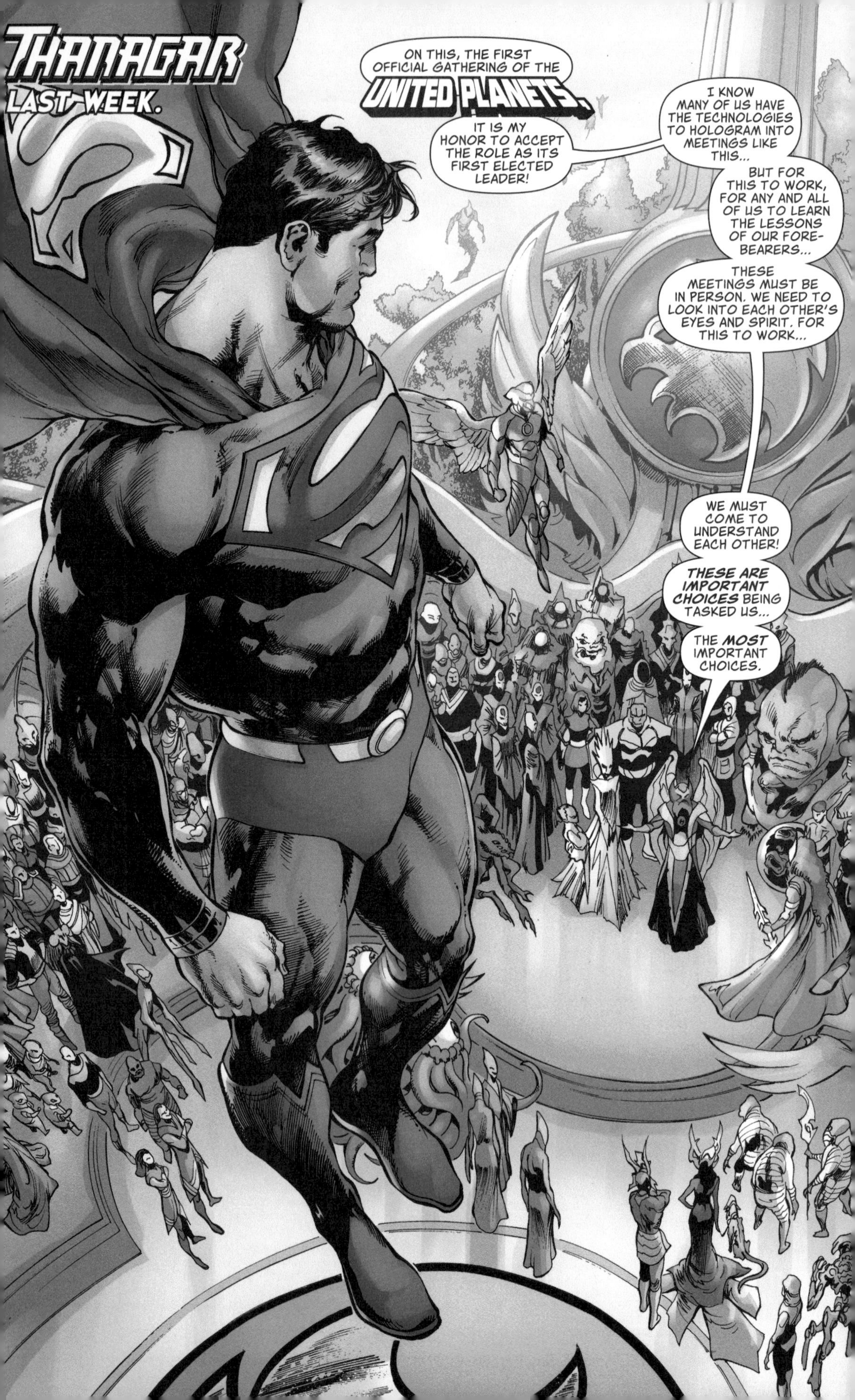
THANAGAR
LAST WEEK.
ON THIS, THE FIRST OFFICIAL GATHERING OF THE UNITED PLANETS,
IT IS MY HONOR TO ACCEPT THE ROLE AS ITS FIRST ELECTED LEADER!
I KNOW MANY OF US HAVE THE TECHNOLOGIES TO HOLOGRAM INTO MEETINGS LIKE THIS...
BUT FOR THIS TO WORK, FOR ANY AND ALL OF US TO LEARN THE LESSONS OF OUR FORE-BEARERS...
THESE MEETINGS MUST BE IN PERSON. WE NEED TO LOOK INTO EACH OTHER'S EYES AND SPIRIT. FOR THIS TO WORK...
WE MUST COME TO UNDERSTAND EACH OTHER!
THESE ARE IMPORTANT CHOICES BEING TASKED US...
THE MOST IMPORTANT CHOICES.

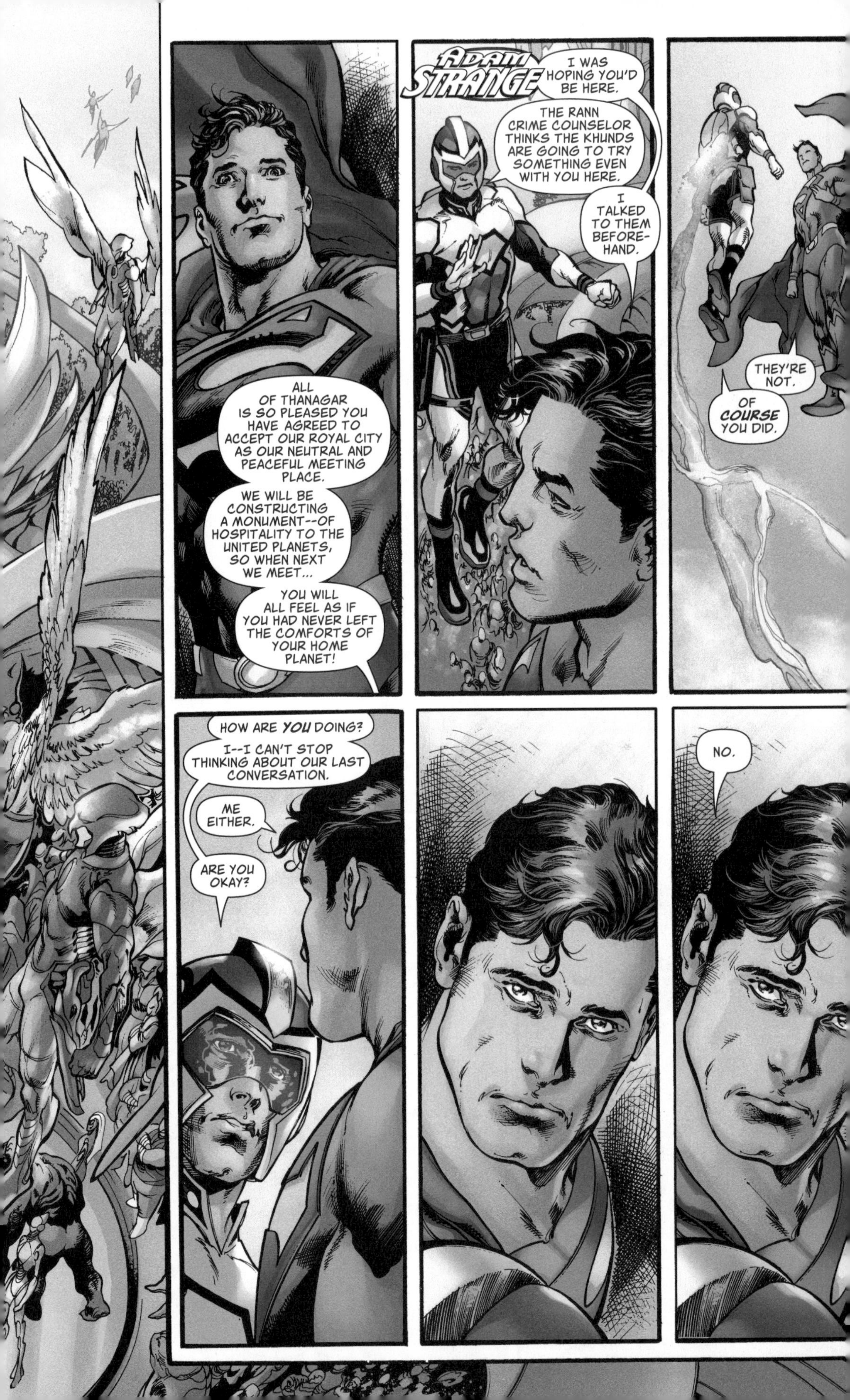
ALL OF THANAGAR IS SO PLEASED YOU HAVE AGREED TO ACCEPT OUR ROYAL CITY AS OUR NEUTRAL AND PEACEFUL MEETING PLACE.
WE WILL BE CONSTRUCTING A MONUMENT--OF HOSPITALITY TO THE UNITED PLANETS, SO WHEN NEXT WE MEET...
YOU WILL ALL FEEL AS IF YOU HAD NEVER LEFT THE COMFORTS OF YOUR HOME PLANET!
ADAM STRANGE
I WAS HOPING YOU'D BE HERE.
THE RANN CRIME COUNSELOR THINKS THE KHUNDS ARE GOING TO TRY SOMETHING EVEN WITH YOU HERE.
I TALKED TO THEM BEFORE-HAND.
THEY'RE NOT.
OF COURSE YOU DID.
HOW ARE YOU DOING?
I--I CAN'T STOP THINKING ABOUT OUR LAST CONVERSATION.
ME EITHER.
ARE YOU OKAY?
NO.

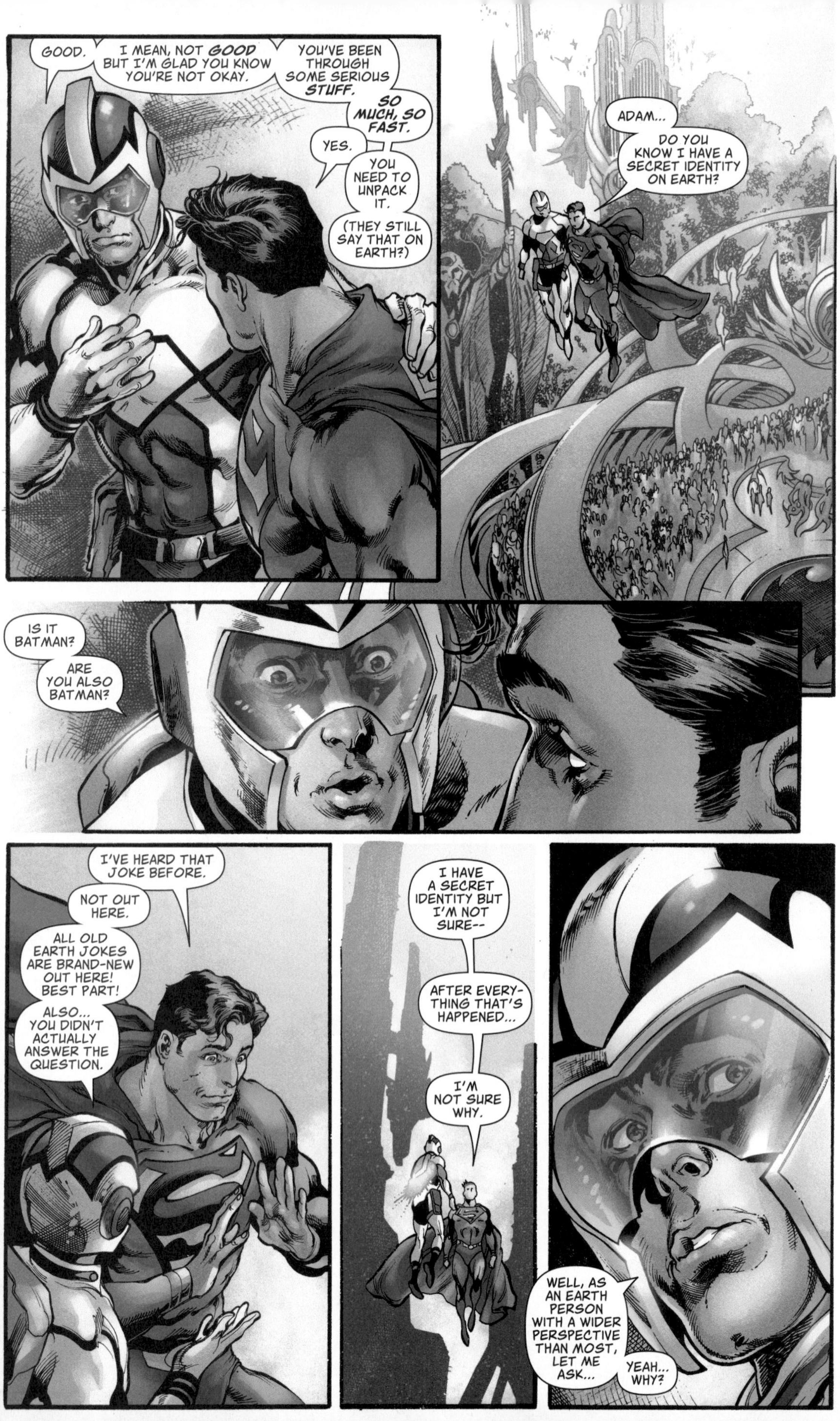

GOOD.
I MEAN, NOT GOOD BUT I'M GLAD YOU KNOW YOU'RE NOT OKAY.
YOU'VE BEEN THROUGH SOME SERIOUS STUFF.
SO MUCH, SO FAST.
YES.
YOU NEED TO UNPACK IT.
(THEY STILL SAY THAT ON EARTH?)
ADAM...
DO YOU KNOW I HAVE A SECRET IDENTITY ON EARTH?
IS IT BATMAN?
ARE YOU ALSO BATMAN?
I'VE HEARD THAT JOKE BEFORE.
NOT OUT HERE.
ALL OLD EARTH JOKES ARE BRAND-NEW OUT HERE! BEST PART!
ALSO... YOU DIDN'T ACTUALLY ANSWER THE QUESTION.
I HAVE A SECRET IDENTITY BUT I'M NOT SURE--
AFTER EVERY-THING THAT'S HAPPENED...
I'M NOT SURE WHY.
WELL, AS AN EARTH PERSON WITH A WIDER PERSPECTIVE THAN MOST, LET ME ASK...
YEAH... WHY?

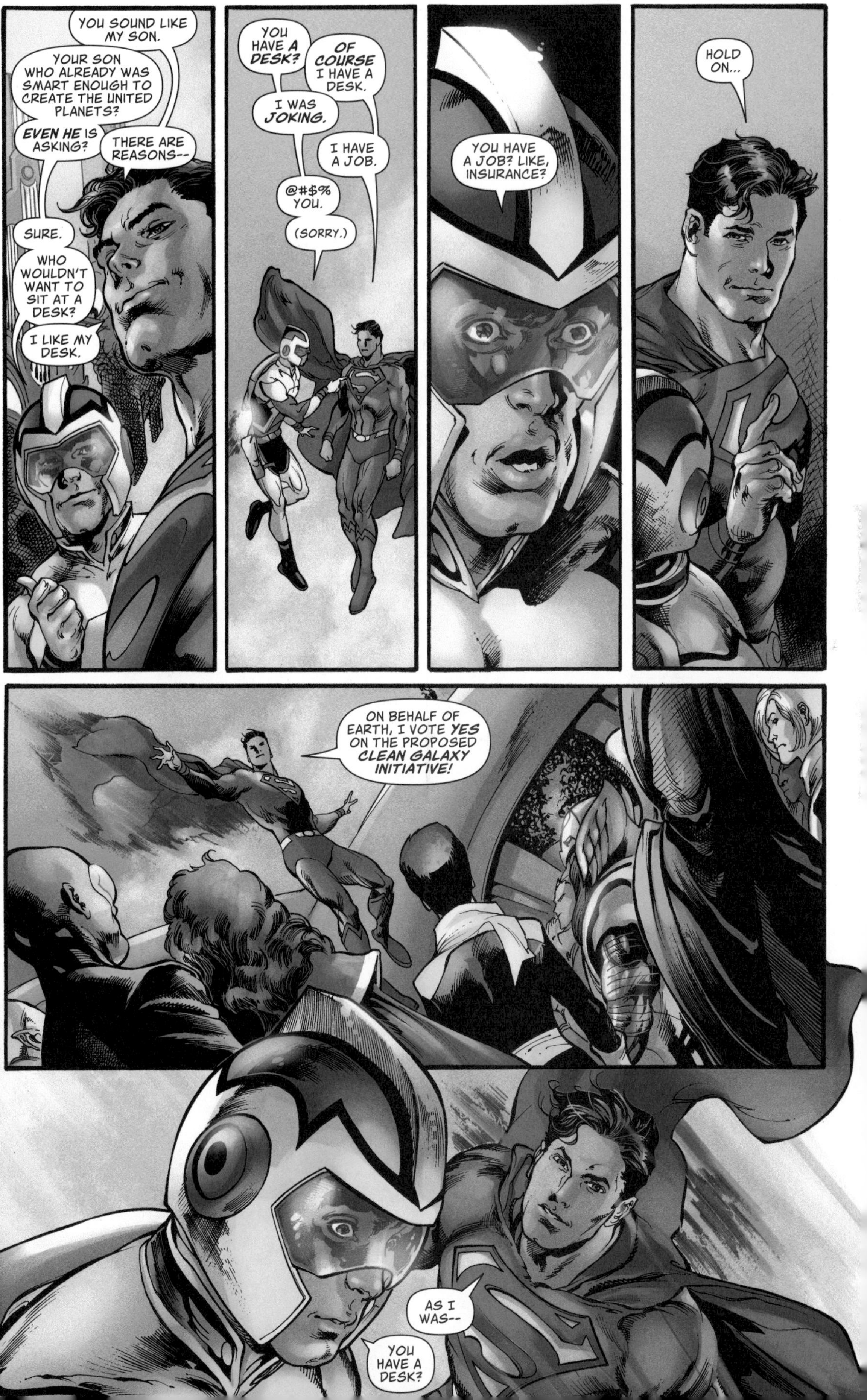
YOU SOUND LIKE MY SON.
YOUR SON WHO ALREADY WAS SMART ENOUGH TO CREATE THE UNITED PLANETS?
EVEN HE IS ASKING?
THERE ARE REASONS--
SURE.
WHO WOULDN'T WANT TO SIT AT A DESK?
I LIKE MY DESK.
YOU HAVE A DESK?
OF COURSE I HAVE A DESK.
I WAS JOKING.
I HAVE A JOB.
@#$% YOU.
(SORRY.)
YOU HAVE A JOB? LIKE, INSURANCE?
HOLD ON...
ON BEHALF OF EARTH, I VOTE YES ON THE PROPOSED CLEAN GALAXY INITIATIVE!
AS I WAS--
YOU HAVE A DESK?

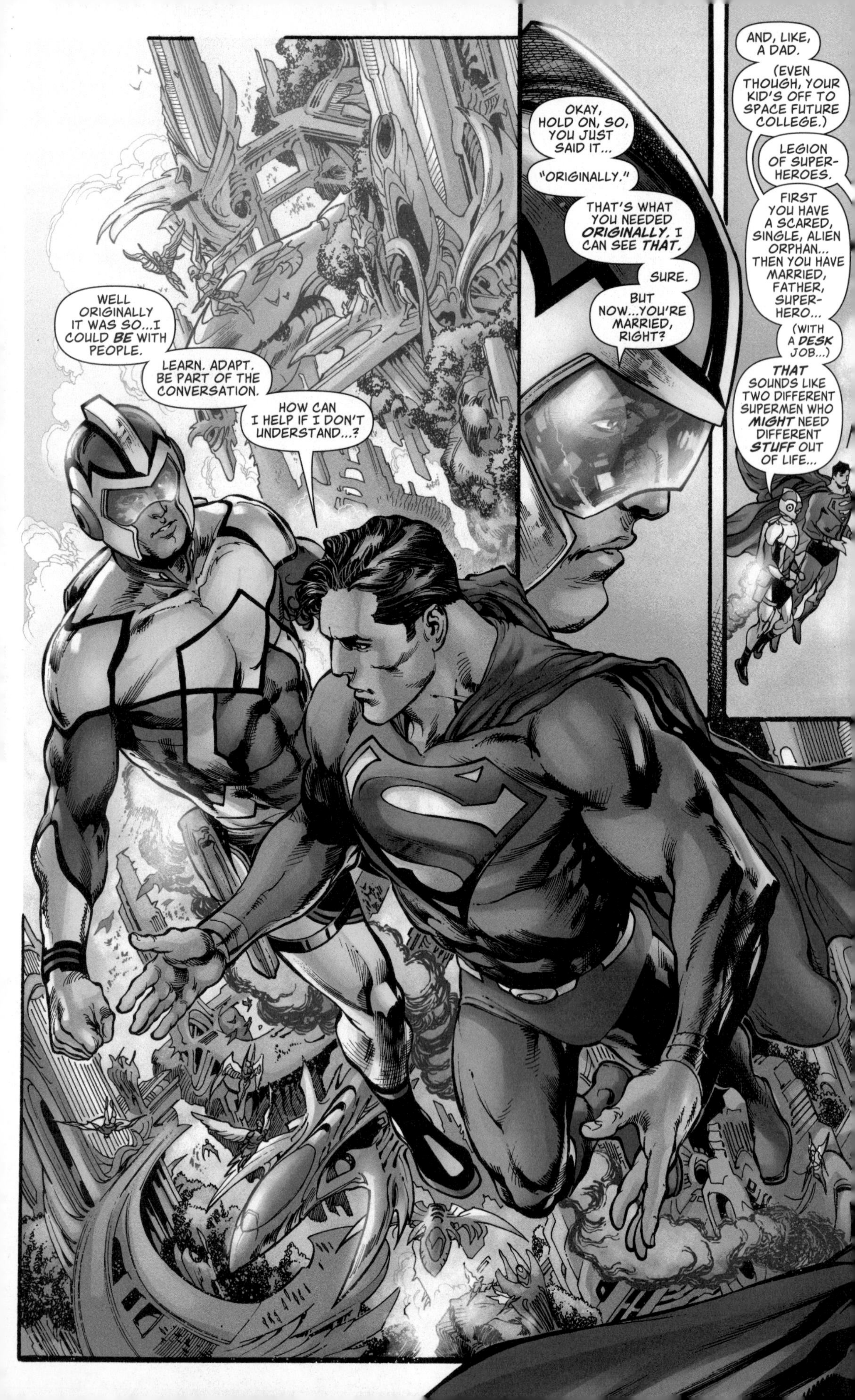
WELL ORIGINALLY IT WAS SO...I COULD BE WITH PEOPLE.
LEARN. ADAPT. BE PART OF THE CONVERSATION.
HOW CAN I HELP IF I DON'T UNDERSTAND...?
OKAY, HOLD ON, SO, YOU JUST SAID IT...
"ORIGINALLY."
THAT'S WHAT YOU NEEDED ORIGINALLY. I CAN SEE THAT.
SURE.
BUT NOW...YOU'RE MARRIED, RIGHT?
AND, LIKE, A DAD.
(EVEN THOUGH, YOUR KID'S OFF TO SPACE FUTURE COLLEGE.)
LEGION OF SUPER-HEROES.
FIRST YOU HAVE A SCARED, SINGLE, ALIEN ORPHAN... THEN YOU HAVE MARRIED, FATHER, SUPER-HERO...
(WITH A DESK JOB...)
THAT SOUNDS LIKE TWO DIFFERENT SUPERMEN WHO MIGHT NEED DIFFERENT STUFF OUT OF LIFE...

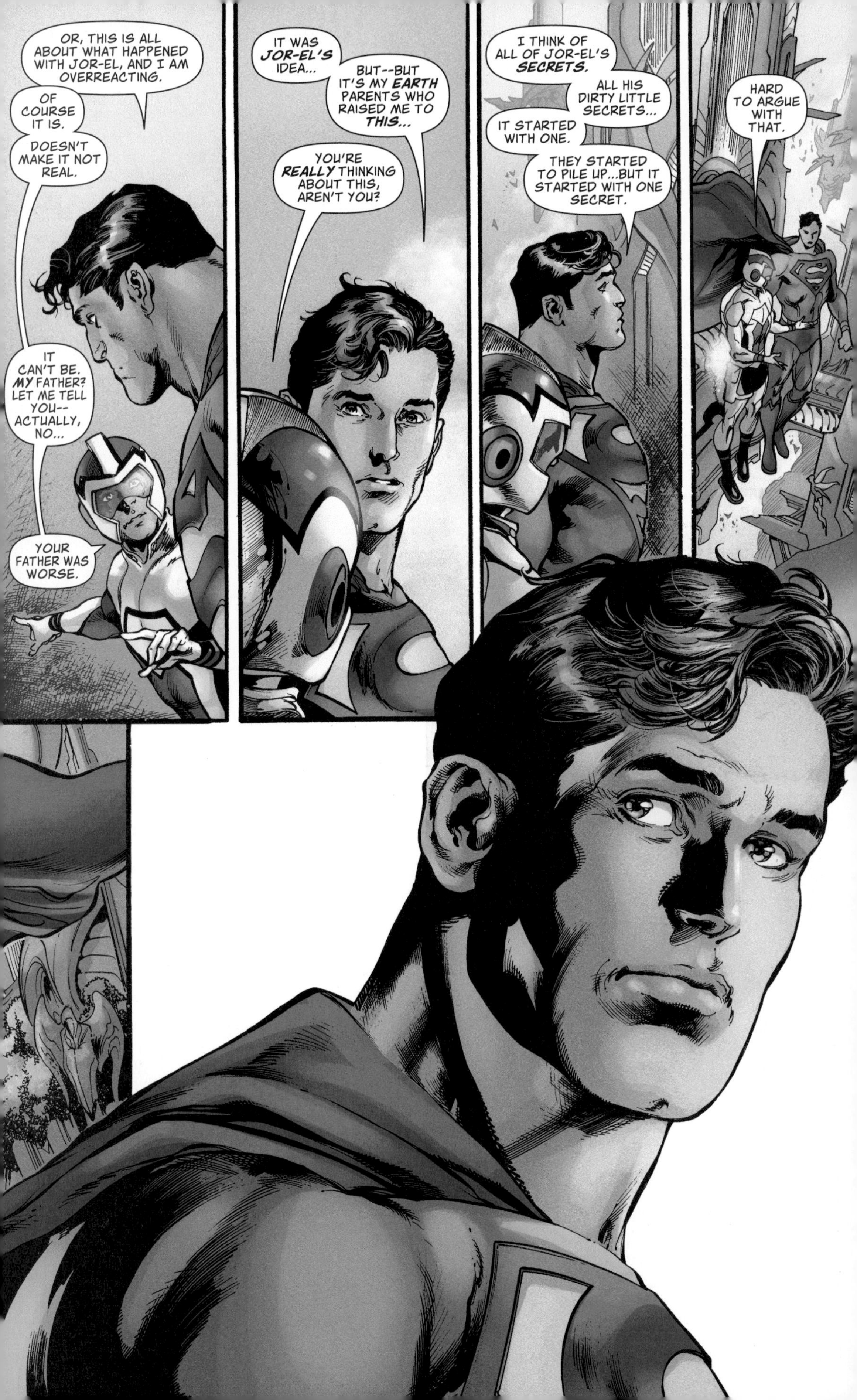
OR, THIS IS ALL ABOUT WHAT HAPPENED WITH JOR-EL, AND I AM OVERREACTING.
OF COURSE IT IS.
DOESN'T MAKE IT NOT REAL.
IT CAN'T BE. MY FATHER? LET ME TELL YOU-- ACTUALLY, NO...
YOUR FATHER WAS WORSE.
IT WAS JOR-EL'S IDEA...
BUT--BUT IT'S MY EARTH PARENTS WHO RAISED ME TO THIS...
YOU'RE REALLY THINKING ABOUT THIS, AREN'T YOU?
I THINK OF ALL OF JOR-EL'S SECRETS.
ALL HIS DIRTY LITTLE SECRETS...
IT STARTED WITH ONE.
THEY STARTED TO PILE UP...BUT IT STARTED WITH ONE SECRET.
HARD TO ARGUE WITH THAT.

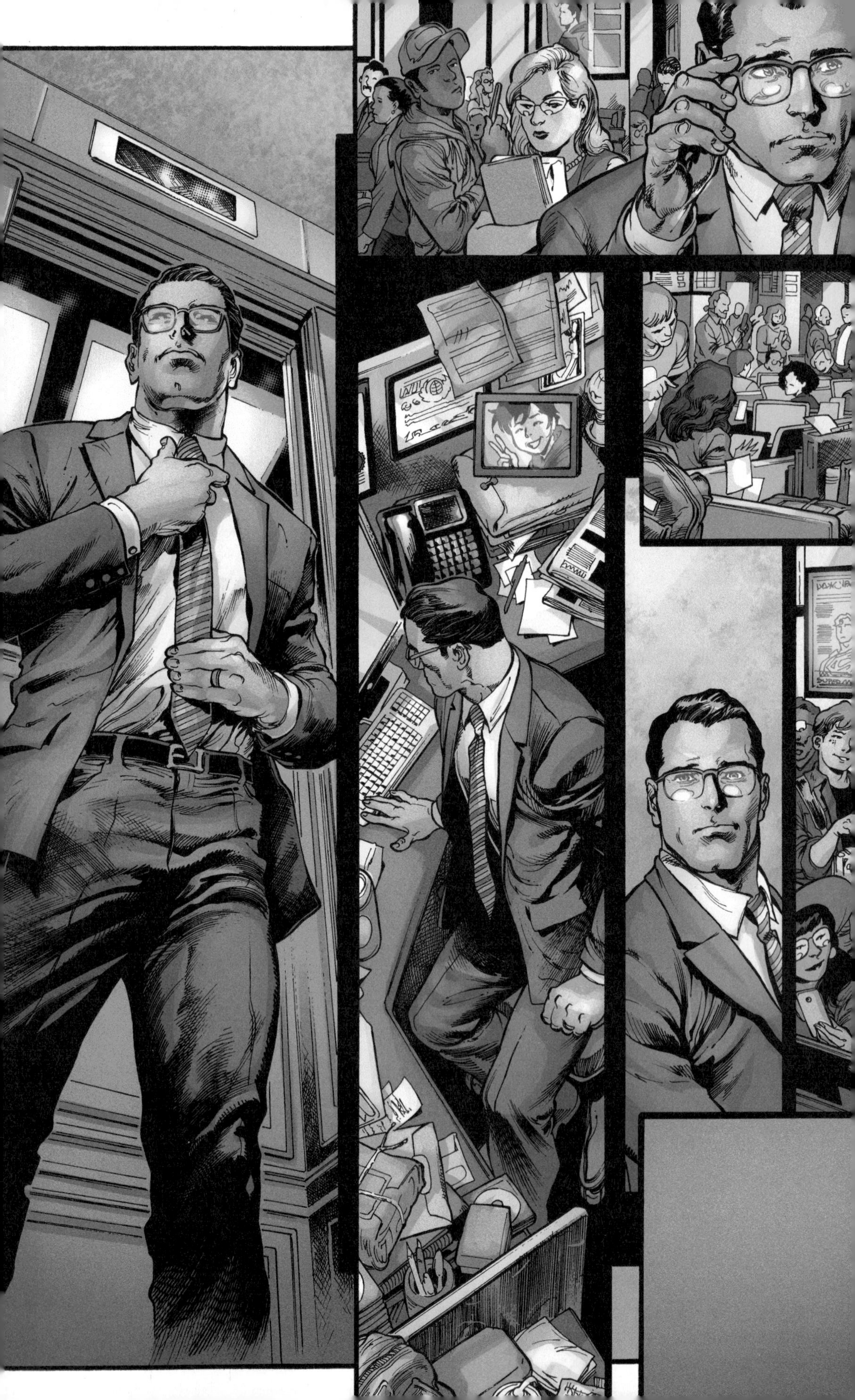

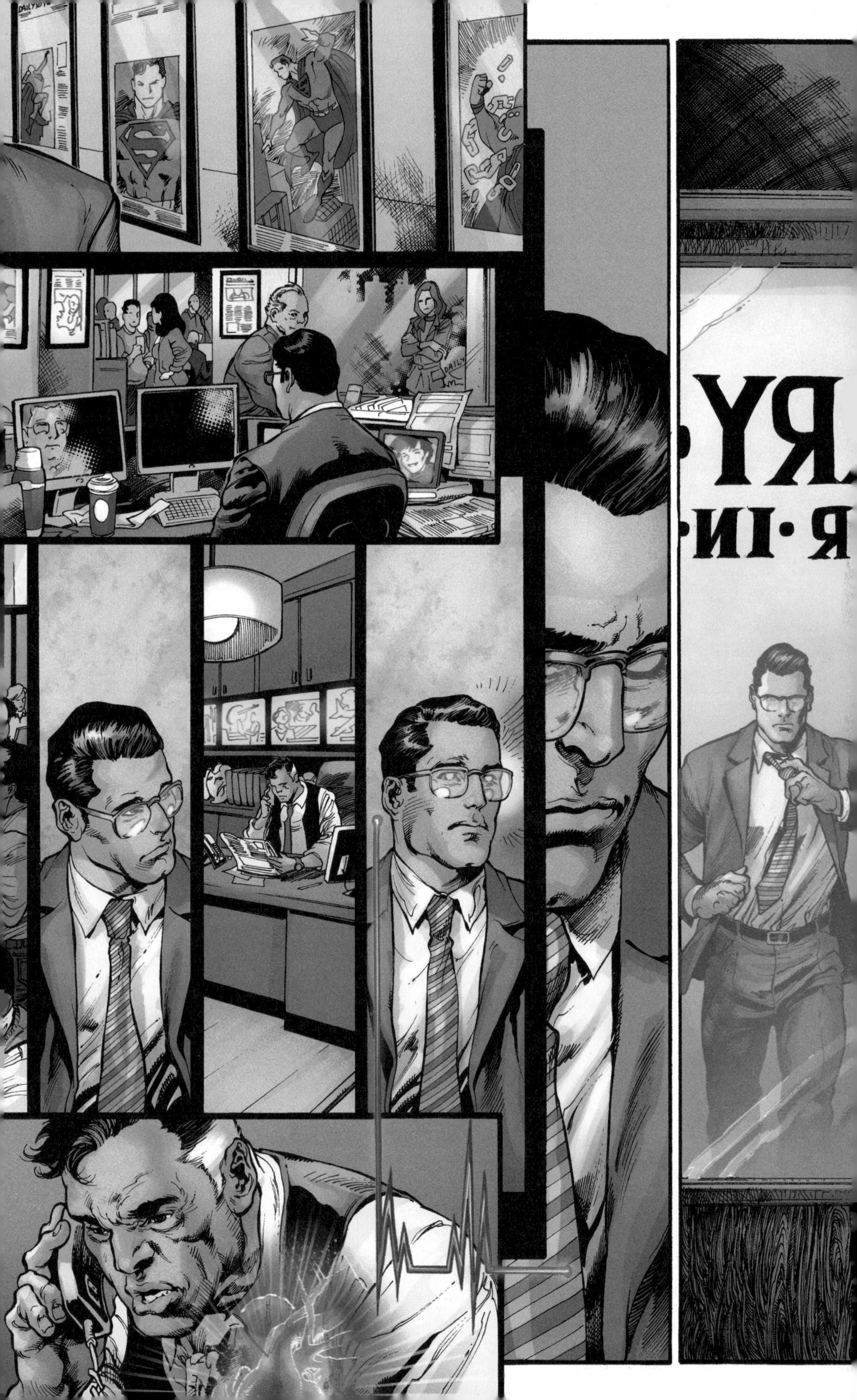

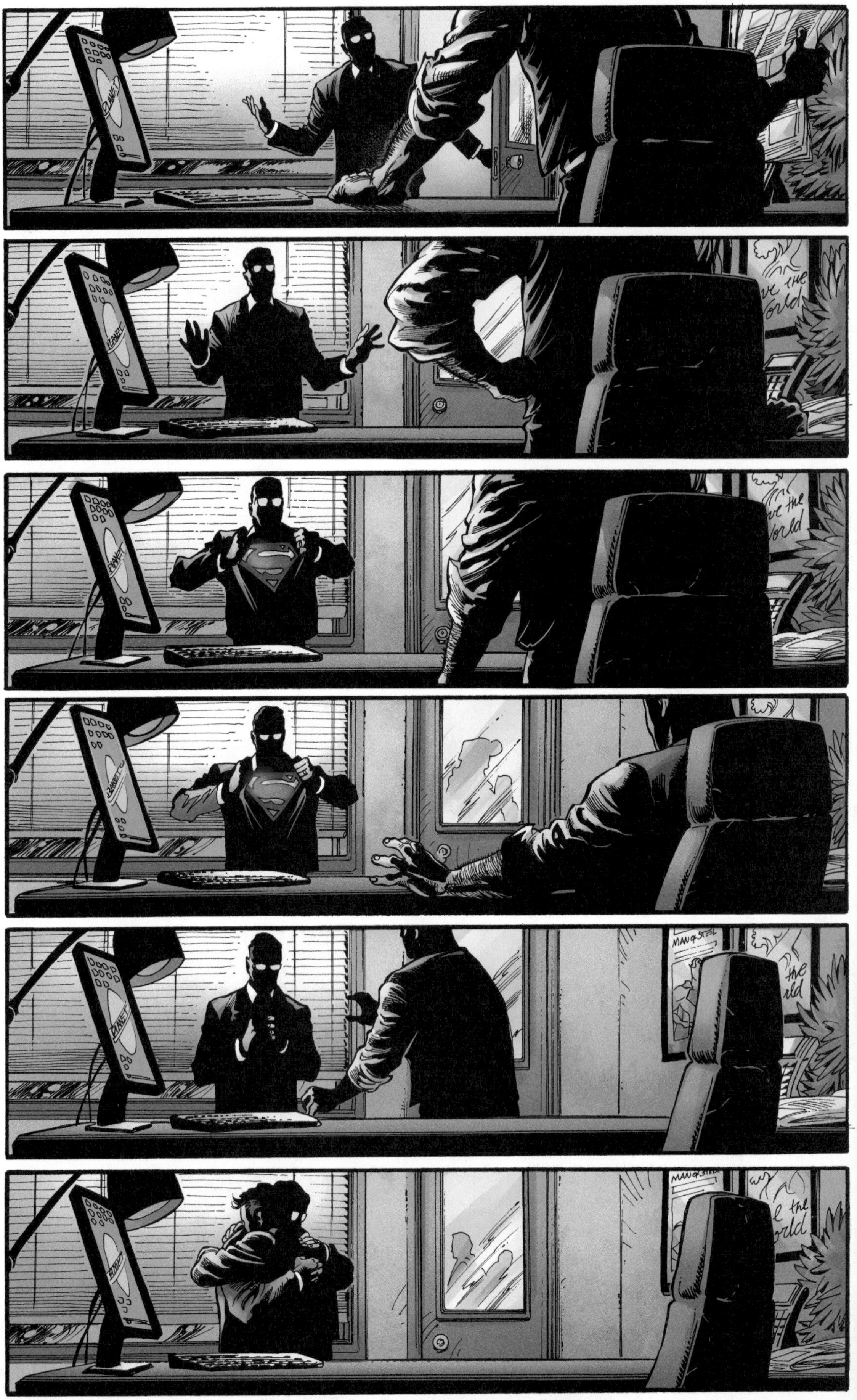
MAN of STEEL

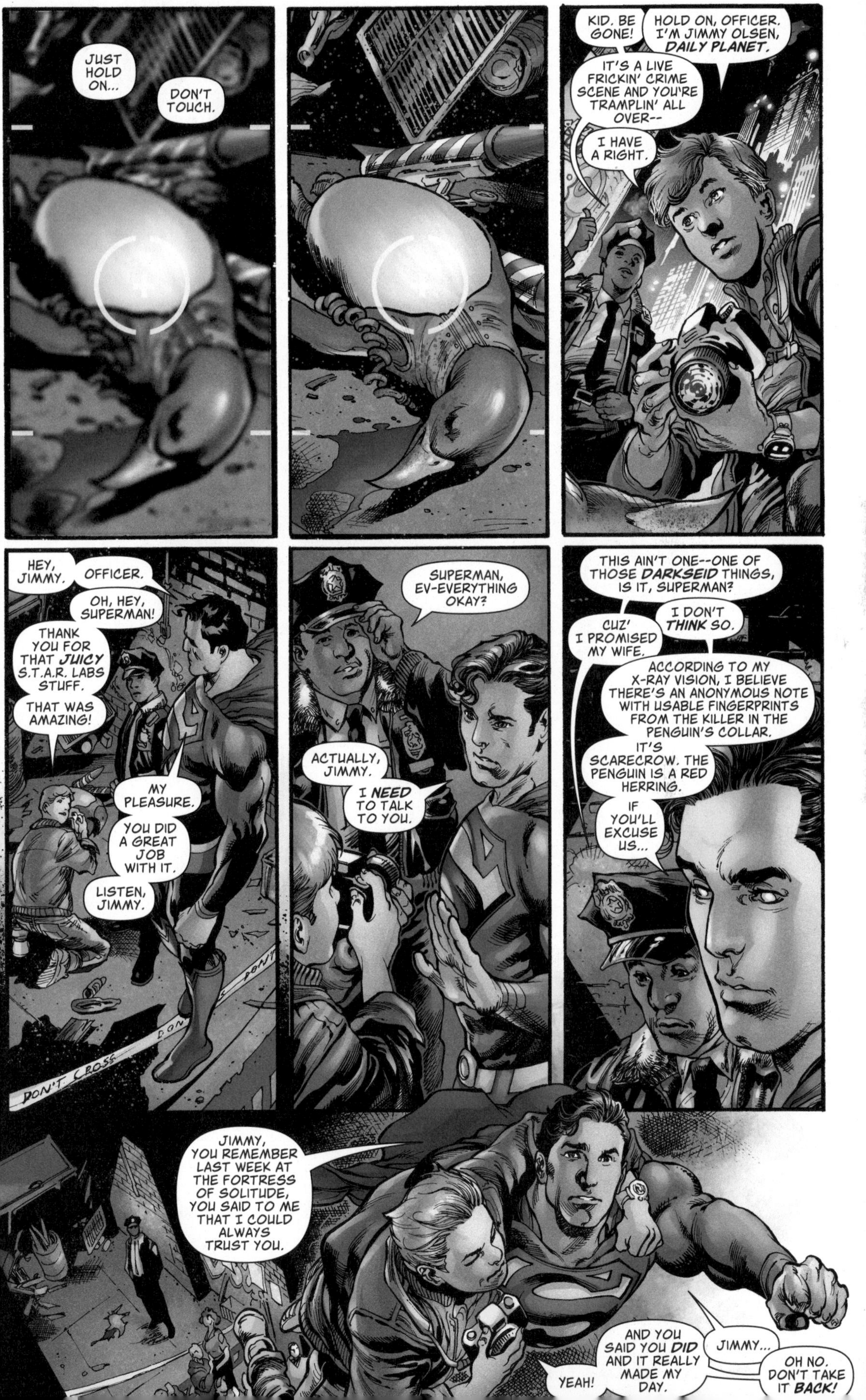
JUST HOLD ON...
DON'T TOUCH.
KID. BE GONE!
HOLD ON, OFFICER. I'M JIMMY OLSEN, DAILY PLANET.
IT'S A LIVE FRICKIN' CRIME SCENE AND YOU'RE TRAMPLIN' ALL OVER--
I HAVE A RIGHT.
HEY, JIMMY.
OFFICER.
OH, HEY, SUPERMAN!
THANK YOU FOR THAT JUICY S.T.A.R. LABS STUFF.
THAT WAS AMAZING!
MY PLEASURE.
YOU DID A GREAT JOB WITH IT.
LISTEN, JIMMY.
DON'T CROSS
SUPERMAN, EV-EVERYTHING OKAY?
ACTUALLY, JIMMY.
I NEED TO TALK TO YOU.
THIS AIN'T ONE--ONE OF THOSE DARKSEID THINGS, IS IT, SUPERMAN?
I DON'T THINK SO.
CUZ' I PROMISED MY WIFE.
ACCORDING TO MY X-RAY VISION, I BELIEVE THERE'S AN ANONYMOUS NOTE WITH USABLE FINGERPRINTS FROM THE KILLER IN THE PENGUIN'S COLLAR.
IT'S SCARECROW. THE PENGUIN IS A RED HERRING.
IF YOU'LL EXCUSE US...
JIMMY, YOU REMEMBER LAST WEEK AT THE FORTRESS OF SOLITUDE, YOU SAID TO ME THAT I COULD ALWAYS TRUST YOU.
YEAH!
AND YOU SAID YOU DID AND IT REALLY MADE MY DAY.
JIMMY...
OH NO. DON'T TAKE IT BACK!

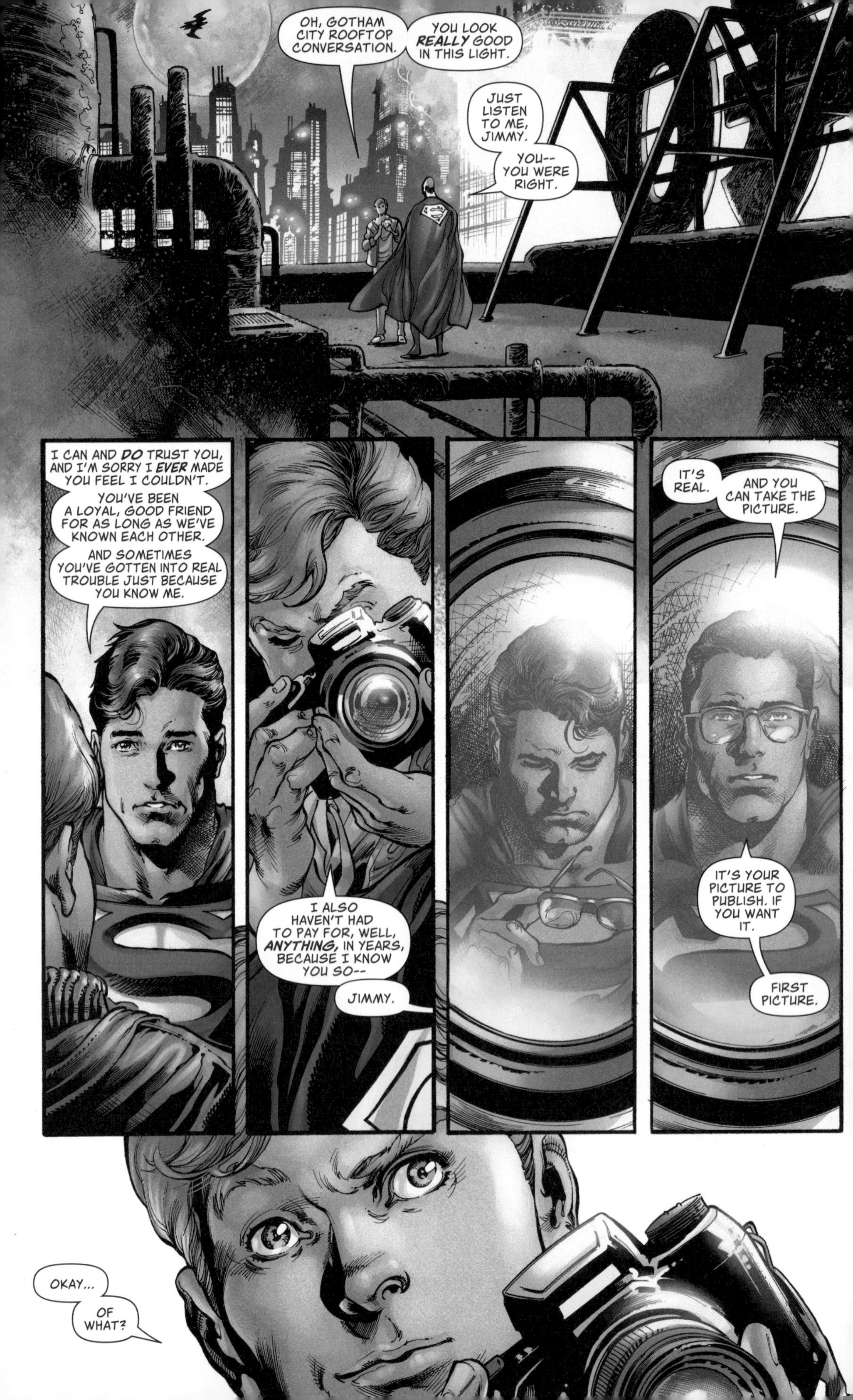
OH, GOTHAM CITY ROOFTOP CONVERSATION.
YOU LOOK REALLY GOOD IN THIS LIGHT.
JUST LISTEN TO ME, JIMMY.
YOU-- YOU WERE RIGHT.
I CAN AND DO TRUST YOU, AND I'M SORRY I EVER MADE YOU FEEL I COULDN'T.
YOU'VE BEEN A LOYAL, GOOD FRIEND FOR AS LONG AS WE'VE KNOWN EACH OTHER.
AND SOMETIMES YOU'VE GOTTEN INTO REAL TROUBLE JUST BECAUSE YOU KNOW ME.
I ALSO HAVEN'T HAD TO PAY FOR, WELL, ANYTHING, IN YEARS, BECAUSE I KNOW YOU SO--
JIMMY.
IT'S REAL.
AND YOU CAN TAKE THE PICTURE.
IT'S YOUR PICTURE TO PUBLISH. IF YOU WANT IT.
FIRST PICTURE.
OKAY...
OF WHAT?

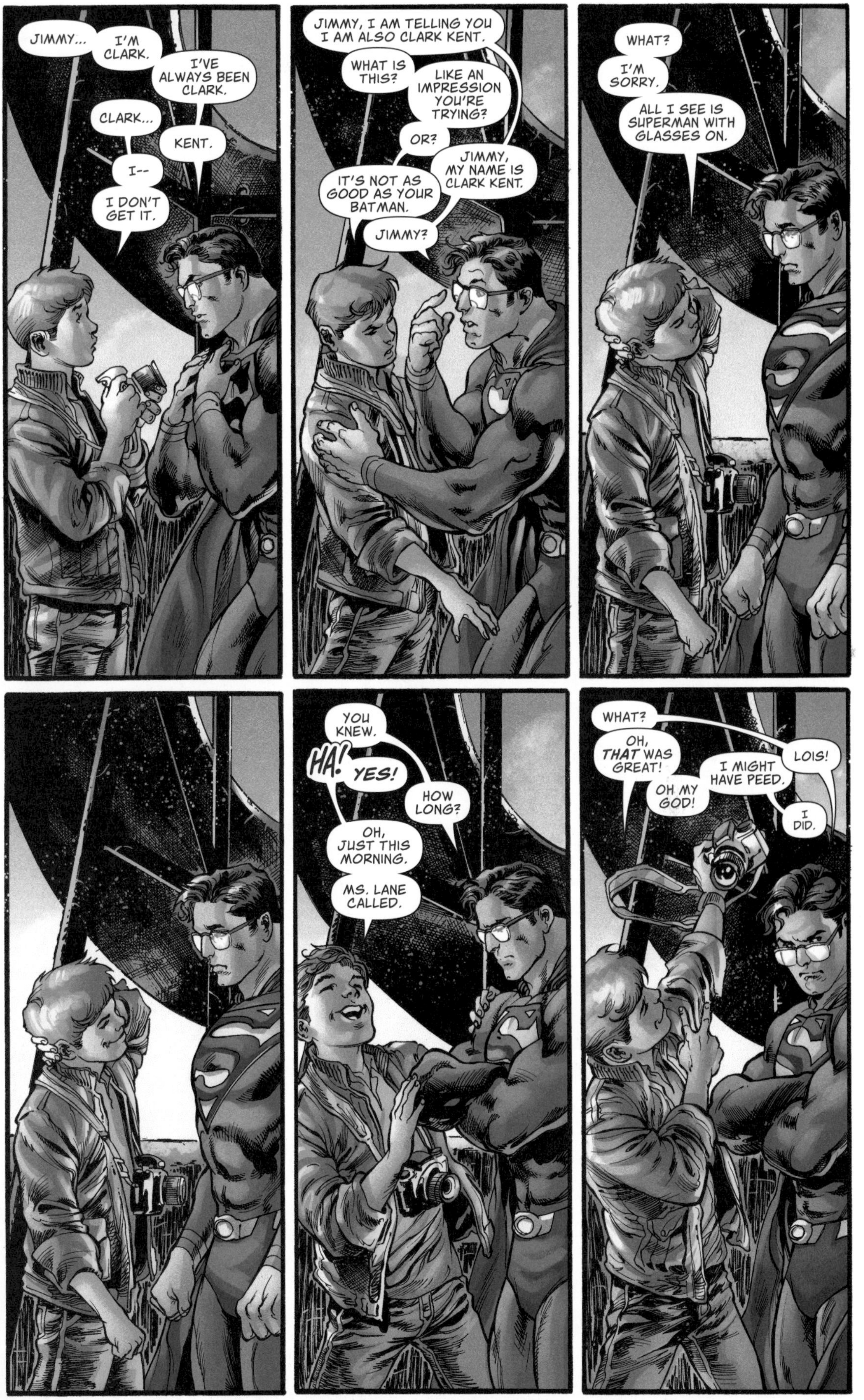
JIMMY...
I'M CLARK.
I'VE ALWAYS BEEN CLARK.
CLARK...
KENT.
I--
I DON'T GET IT.
JIMMY, I AM TELLING YOU I AM ALSO CLARK KENT.
WHAT IS THIS?
LIKE AN IMPRESSION YOU'RE TRYING?
OR?
IT'S NOT AS GOOD AS YOUR BATMAN.
JIMMY, MY NAME IS CLARK KENT.
JIMMY?
WHAT?
I'M SORRY.
ALL I SEE IS SUPERMAN WITH GLASSES ON.
YOU KNEW.
HA!
YES!
HOW LONG?
OH, JUST THIS MORNING.
MS. LANE CALLED.
WHAT?
OH, THAT WAS GREAT!
OH MY GOD!
I MIGHT HAVE PEED.
LOIS!
I DID.

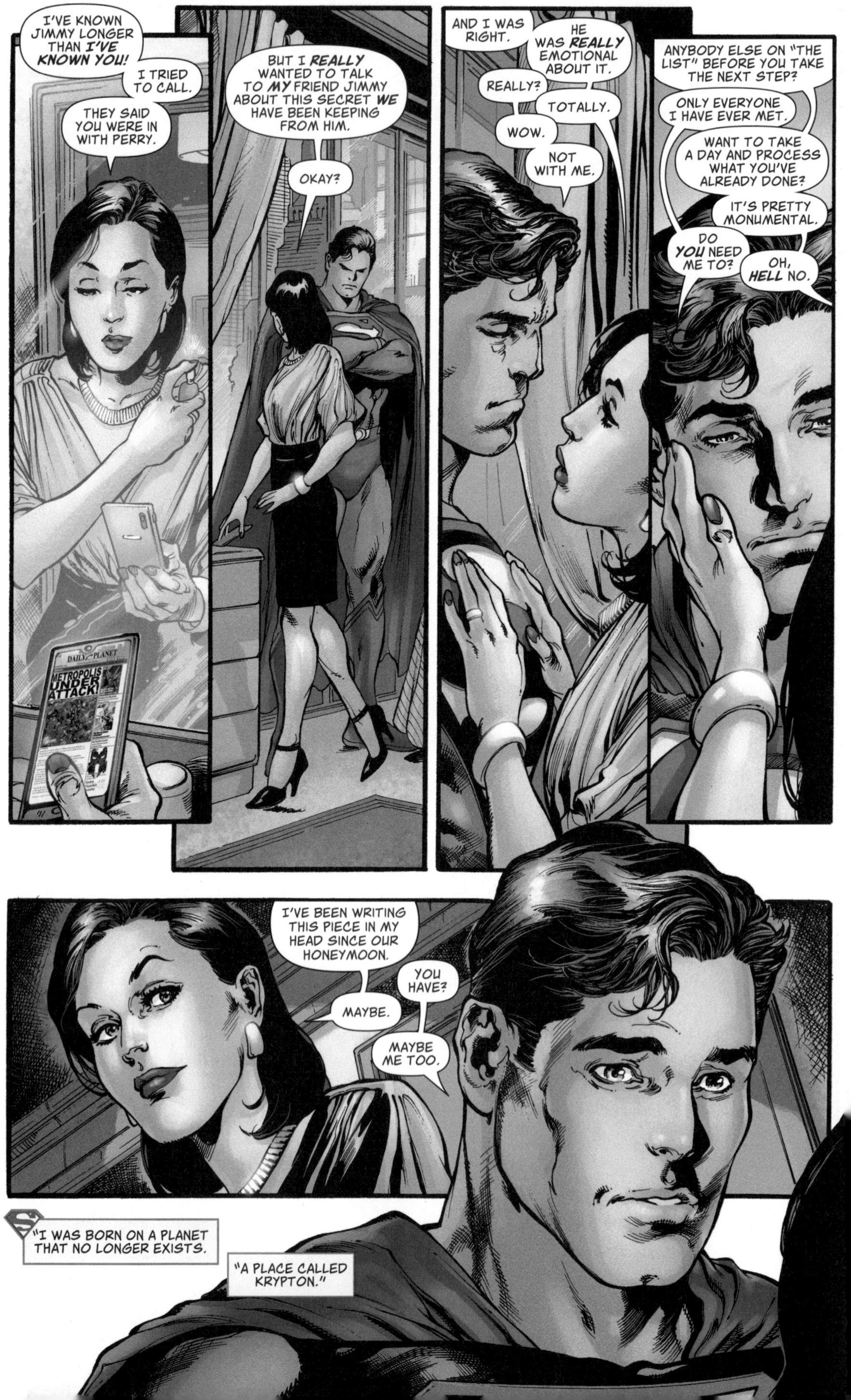

I'VE KNOWN JIMMY LONGER THAN I'VE KNOWN YOU!
I TRIED TO CALL.
THEY SAID YOU WERE IN WITH PERRY.
DAILY PLANET
METROPOLIS UNDER ATTACK!
BUT I REALLY WANTED TO TALK TO MY FRIEND JIMMY ABOUT THIS SECRET WE HAVE BEEN KEEPING FROM HIM.
OKAY?
AND I WAS RIGHT.
HE WAS REALLY EMOTIONAL ABOUT IT.
REALLY?
TOTALLY.
WOW.
NOT WITH ME.
ANYBODY ELSE ON "THE LIST" BEFORE YOU TAKE THE NEXT STEP?
ONLY EVERYONE I HAVE EVER MET.
WANT TO TAKE A DAY AND PROCESS WHAT YOU'VE ALREADY DONE?
IT'S PRETTY MONUMENTAL.
DO YOU NEED ME TO?
OH, HELL NO.
I'VE BEEN WRITING THIS PIECE IN MY HEAD SINCE OUR HONEYMOON.
YOU HAVE?
MAYBE.
MAYBE ME TOO.
"I WAS BORN ON A PLANET THAT NO LONGER EXISTS.
"A PLACE CALLED KRYPTON."

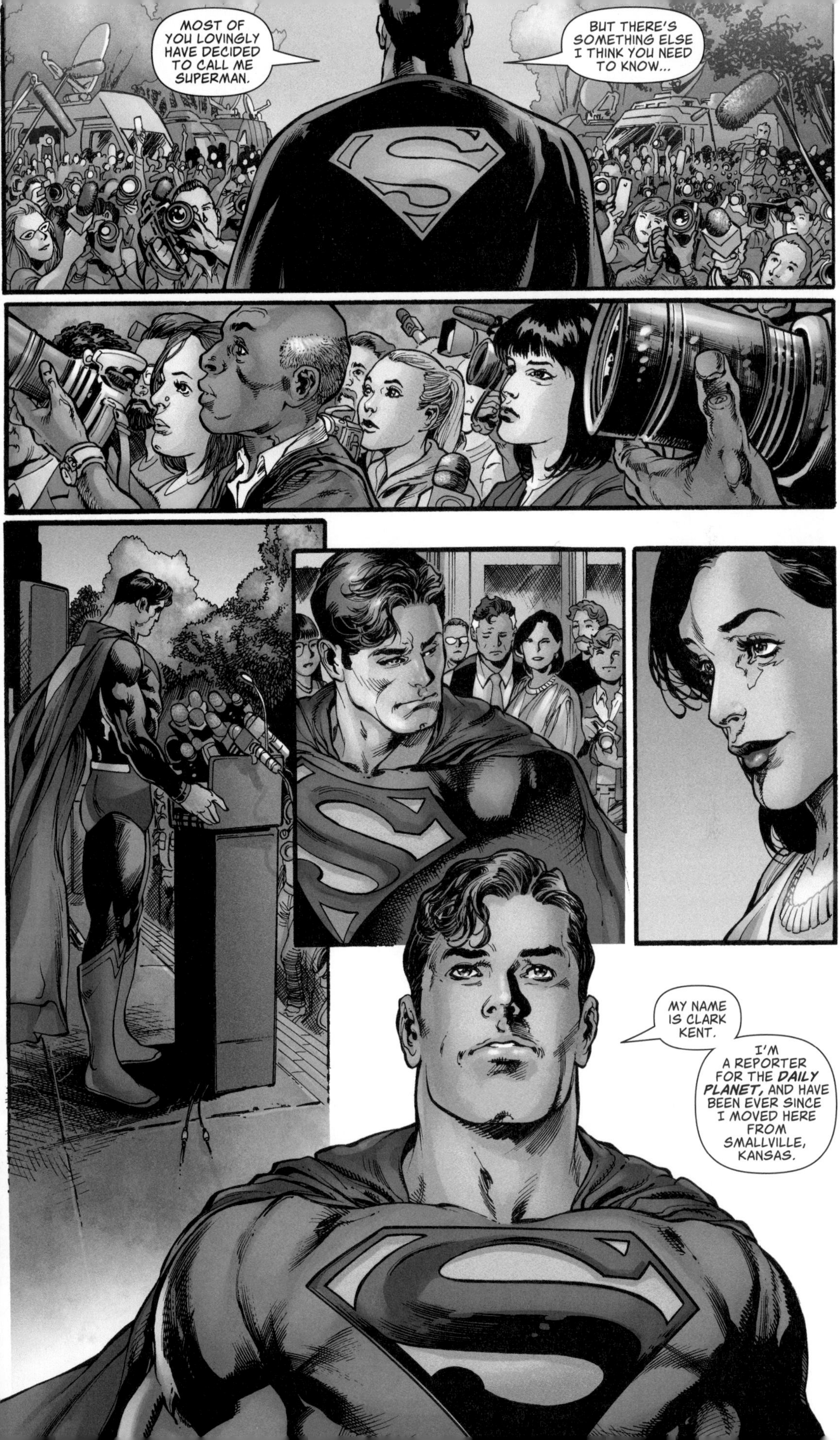
MOST OF YOU LOVINGLY HAVE DECIDED TO CALL ME SUPERMAN.
BUT THERE'S SOMETHING ELSE I THINK YOU NEED TO KNOW...
MY NAME IS CLARK KENT.
I'M A REPORTER FOR THE *DAILY PLANET,* AND HAVE BEEN EVER SINCE I MOVED HERE FROM SMALLVILLE, KANSAS.

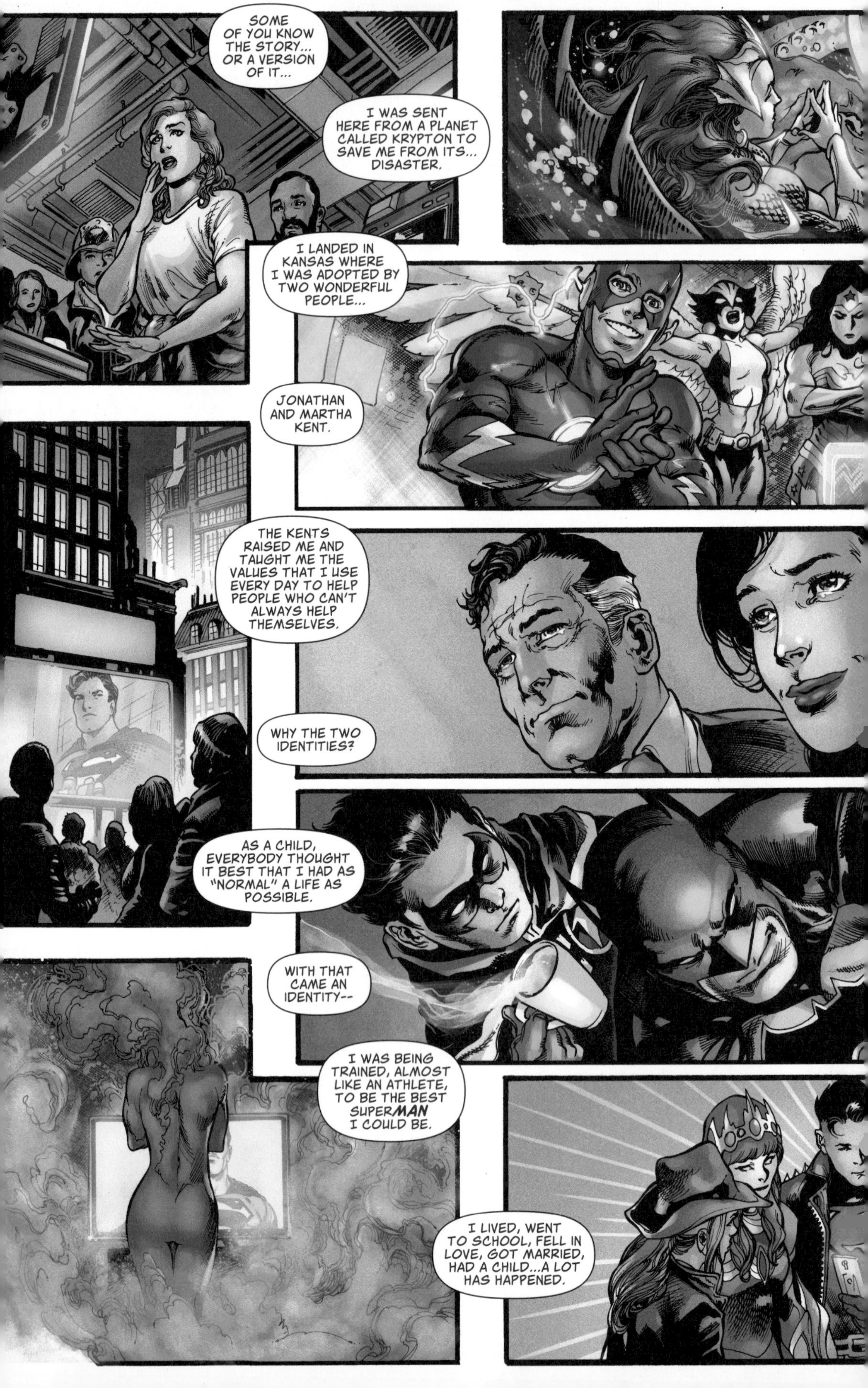
SOME OF YOU KNOW THE STORY... OR A VERSION OF IT...
I WAS SENT HERE FROM A PLANET CALLED KRYPTON TO SAVE ME FROM ITS... DISASTER.
I LANDED IN KANSAS WHERE I WAS ADOPTED BY TWO WONDERFUL PEOPLE...
JONATHAN AND MARTHA KENT.
THE KENTS RAISED ME AND TAUGHT ME THE VALUES THAT I USE EVERY DAY TO HELP PEOPLE WHO CAN'T ALWAYS HELP THEMSELVES.
WHY THE TWO IDENTITIES?
AS A CHILD, EVERYBODY THOUGHT IT BEST THAT I HAD AS "NORMAL" A LIFE AS POSSIBLE.
WITH THAT CAME AN IDENTITY--
I WAS BEING TRAINED, ALMOST LIKE AN ATHLETE, TO BE THE BEST SUPER*MAN* I COULD BE.
I LIVED, WENT TO SCHOOL, FELL IN LOVE, GOT MARRIED, HAD A CHILD...A LOT HAS HAPPENED.

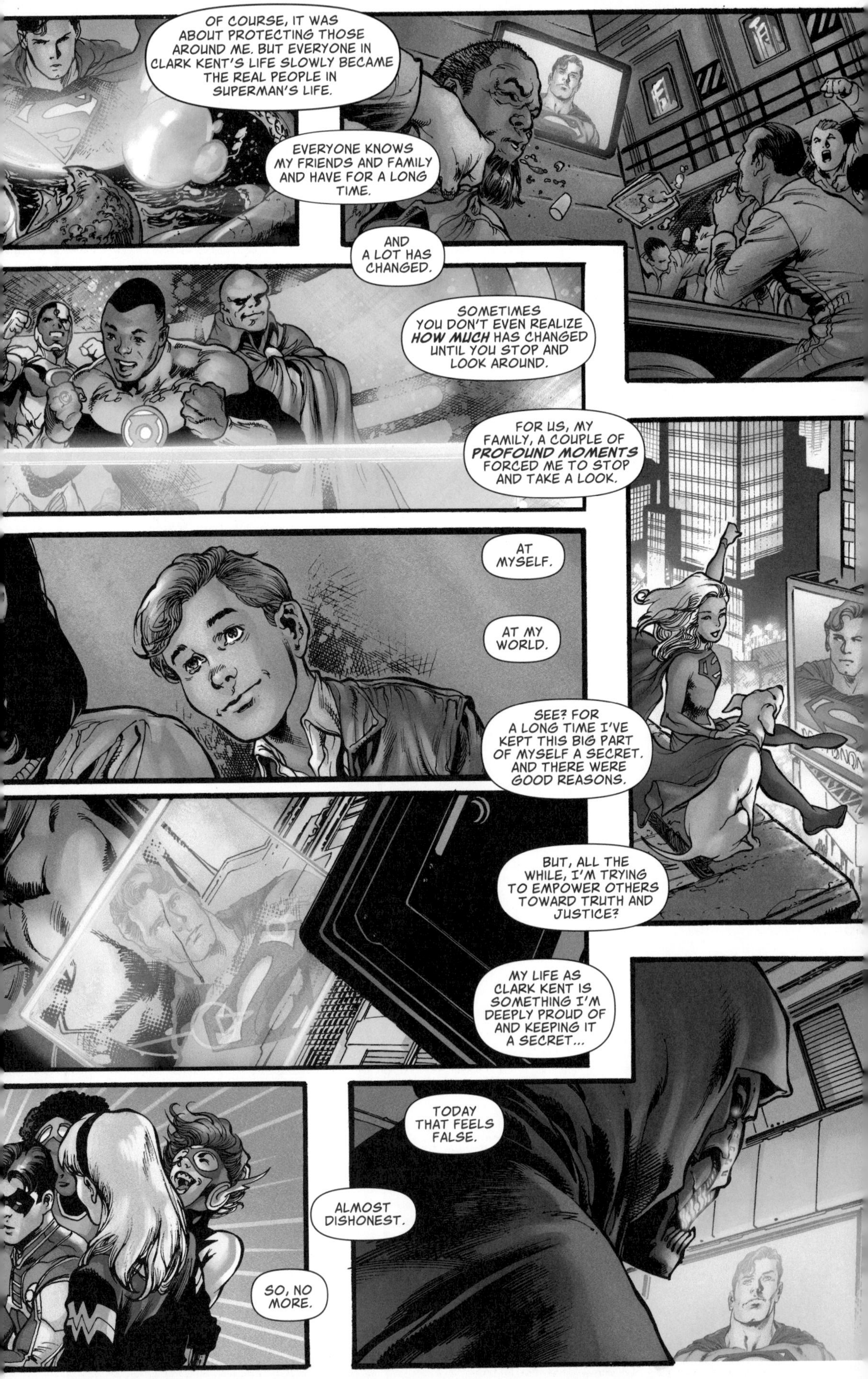
OF COURSE, IT WAS ABOUT PROTECTING THOSE AROUND ME. BUT EVERYONE IN CLARK KENT'S LIFE SLOWLY BECAME THE REAL PEOPLE IN SUPERMAN'S LIFE.
EVERYONE KNOWS MY FRIENDS AND FAMILY AND HAVE FOR A LONG TIME.
AND A LOT HAS CHANGED.
SOMETIMES YOU DON'T EVEN REALIZE HOW MUCH HAS CHANGED UNTIL YOU STOP AND LOOK AROUND.
FOR US, MY FAMILY, A COUPLE OF PROFOUND MOMENTS FORCED ME TO STOP AND TAKE A LOOK.
AT MYSELF.
AT MY WORLD.
SEE? FOR A LONG TIME I'VE KEPT THIS BIG PART OF MYSELF A SECRET. AND THERE WERE GOOD REASONS.
BUT, ALL THE WHILE, I'M TRYING TO EMPOWER OTHERS TOWARD TRUTH AND JUSTICE?
MY LIFE AS CLARK KENT IS SOMETHING I'M DEEPLY PROUD OF AND KEEPING IT A SECRET...
TODAY THAT FEELS FALSE.
ALMOST DISHONEST.
SO, NO MORE.

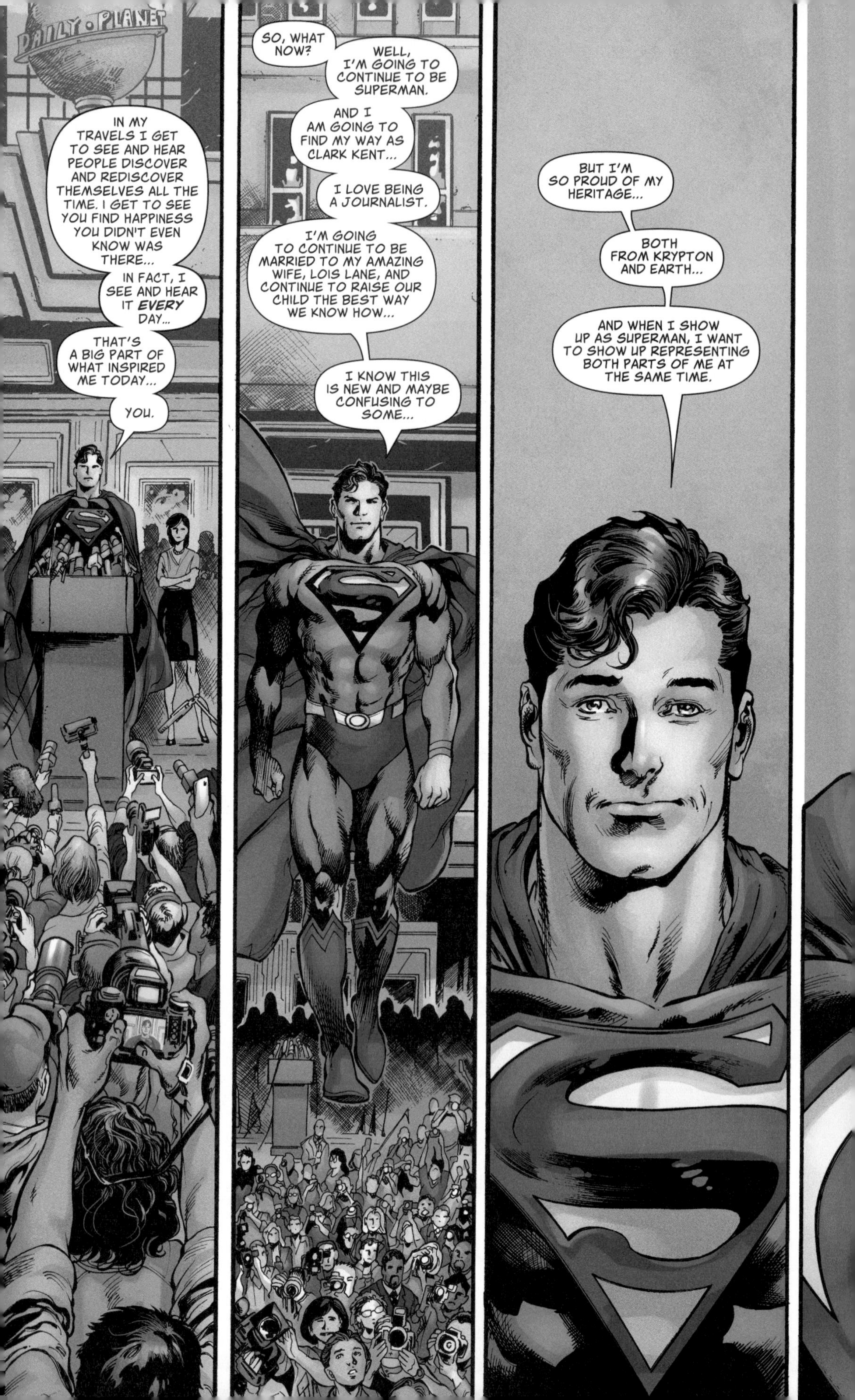
DAILY PLANET
IN MY TRAVELS I GET TO SEE AND HEAR PEOPLE DISCOVER AND REDISCOVER THEMSELVES ALL THE TIME. I GET TO SEE YOU FIND HAPPINESS YOU DIDN'T EVEN KNOW WAS THERE...
IN FACT, I SEE AND HEAR IT **EVERY** DAY...
THAT'S A BIG PART OF WHAT INSPIRED ME TODAY...
YOU.
SO, WHAT NOW?
WELL, I'M GOING TO CONTINUE TO BE SUPERMAN.
AND I AM GOING TO FIND MY WAY AS CLARK KENT...
I LOVE BEING A JOURNALIST.
I'M GOING TO CONTINUE TO BE MARRIED TO MY AMAZING WIFE, LOIS LANE, AND CONTINUE TO RAISE OUR CHILD THE BEST WAY WE KNOW HOW...
I KNOW THIS IS NEW AND MAYBE CONFUSING TO SOME...
BUT I'M SO PROUD OF MY HERITAGE...
BOTH FROM KRYPTON AND EARTH...
AND WHEN I SHOW UP AS SUPERMAN, I WANT TO SHOW UP REPRESENTING BOTH PARTS OF ME AT THE SAME TIME.

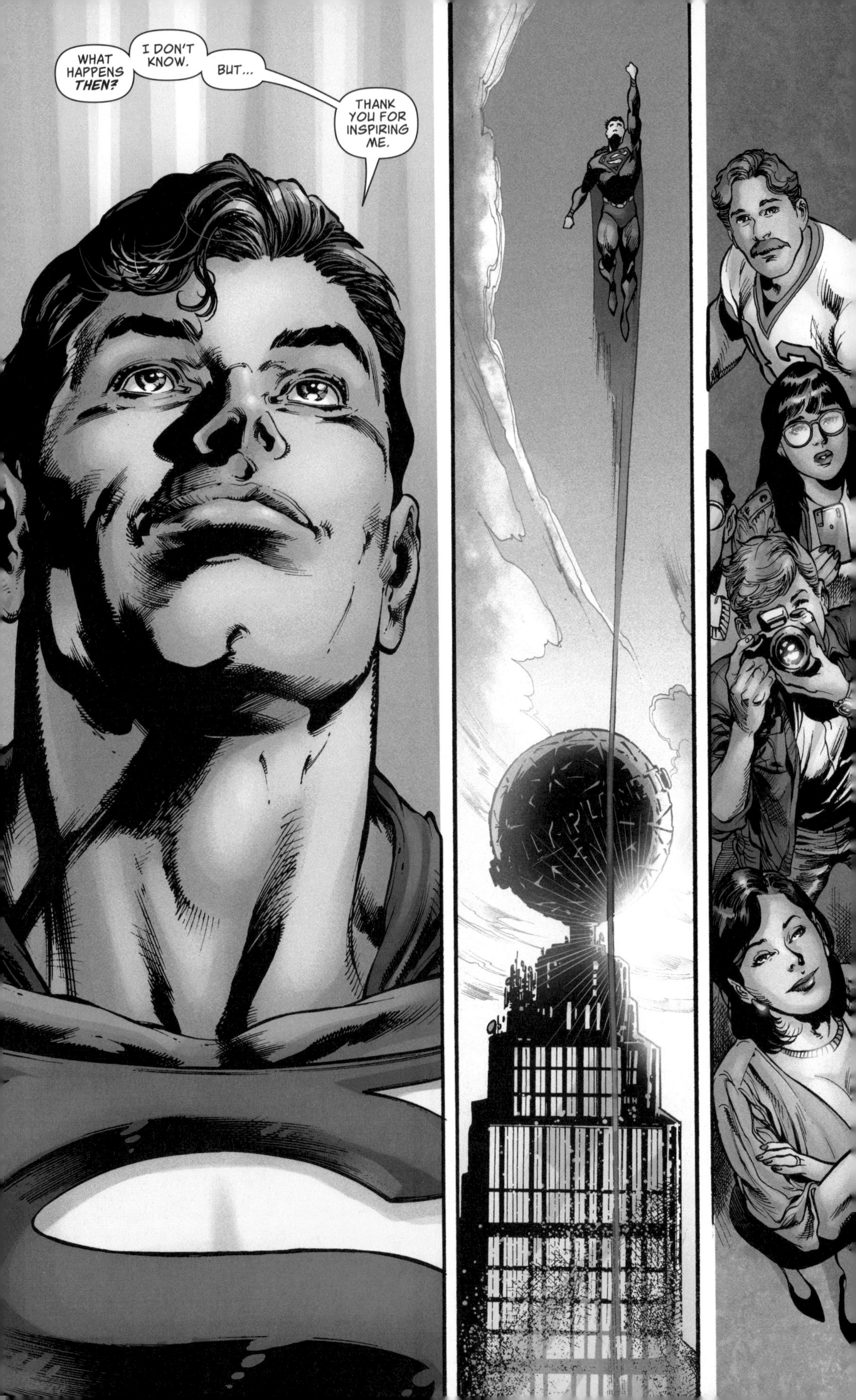
WHAT HAPPENS *THEN?*
I DON'T KNOW.
BUT...
THANK YOU FOR INSPIRING ME.

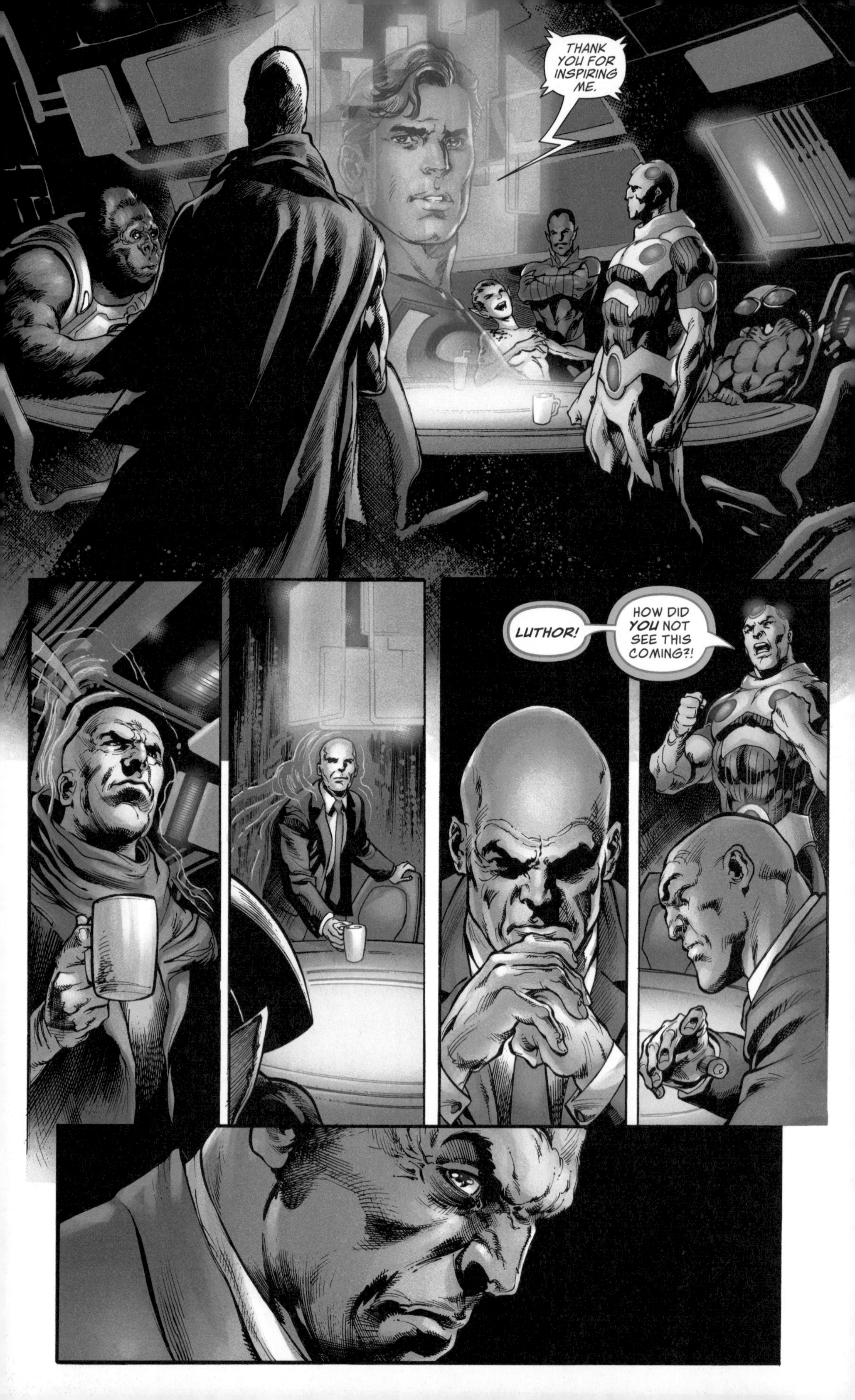
THANK YOU FOR INSPIRING ME.
LUTHOR!
HOW DID YOU NOT SEE THIS COMING?!

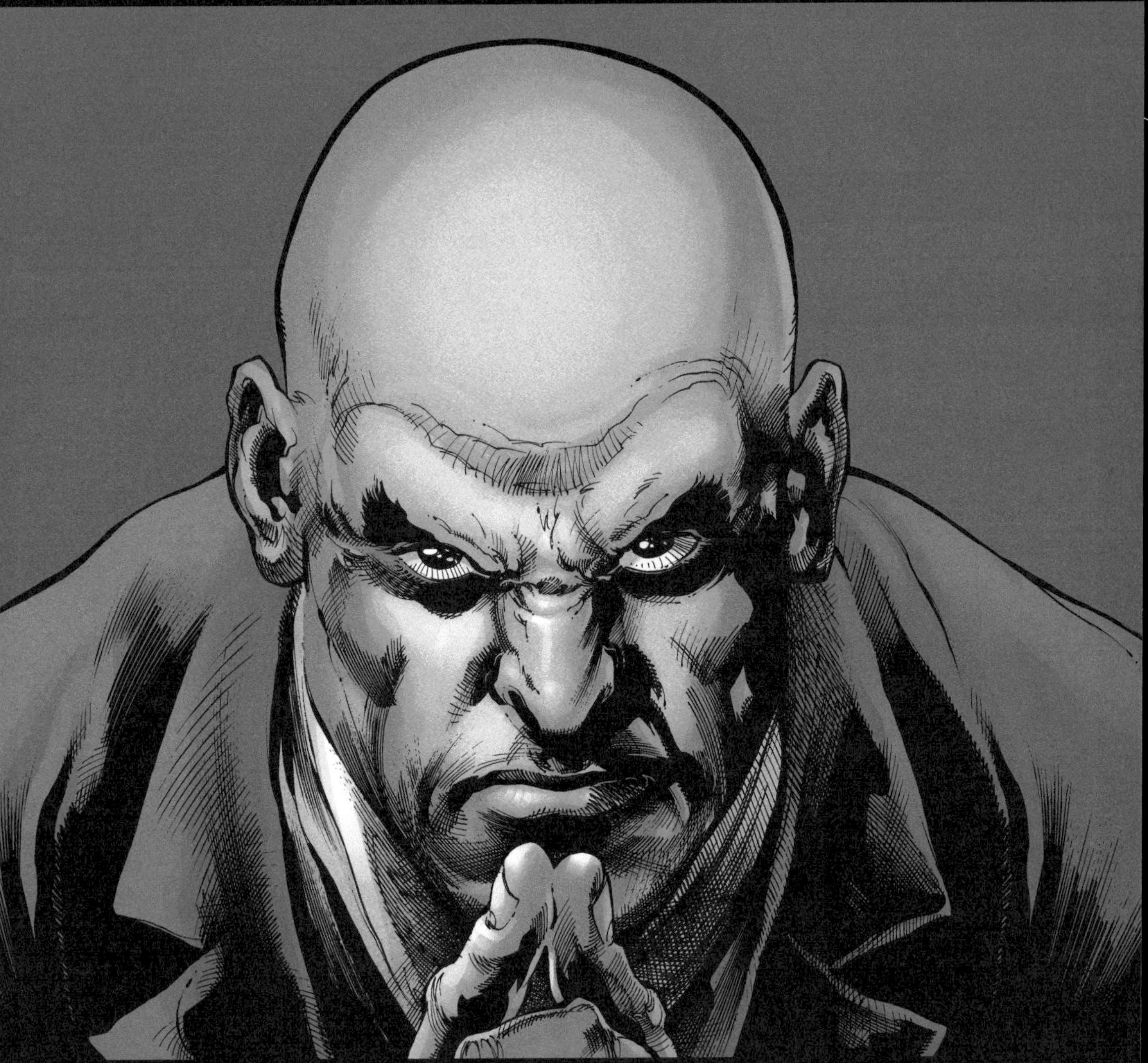

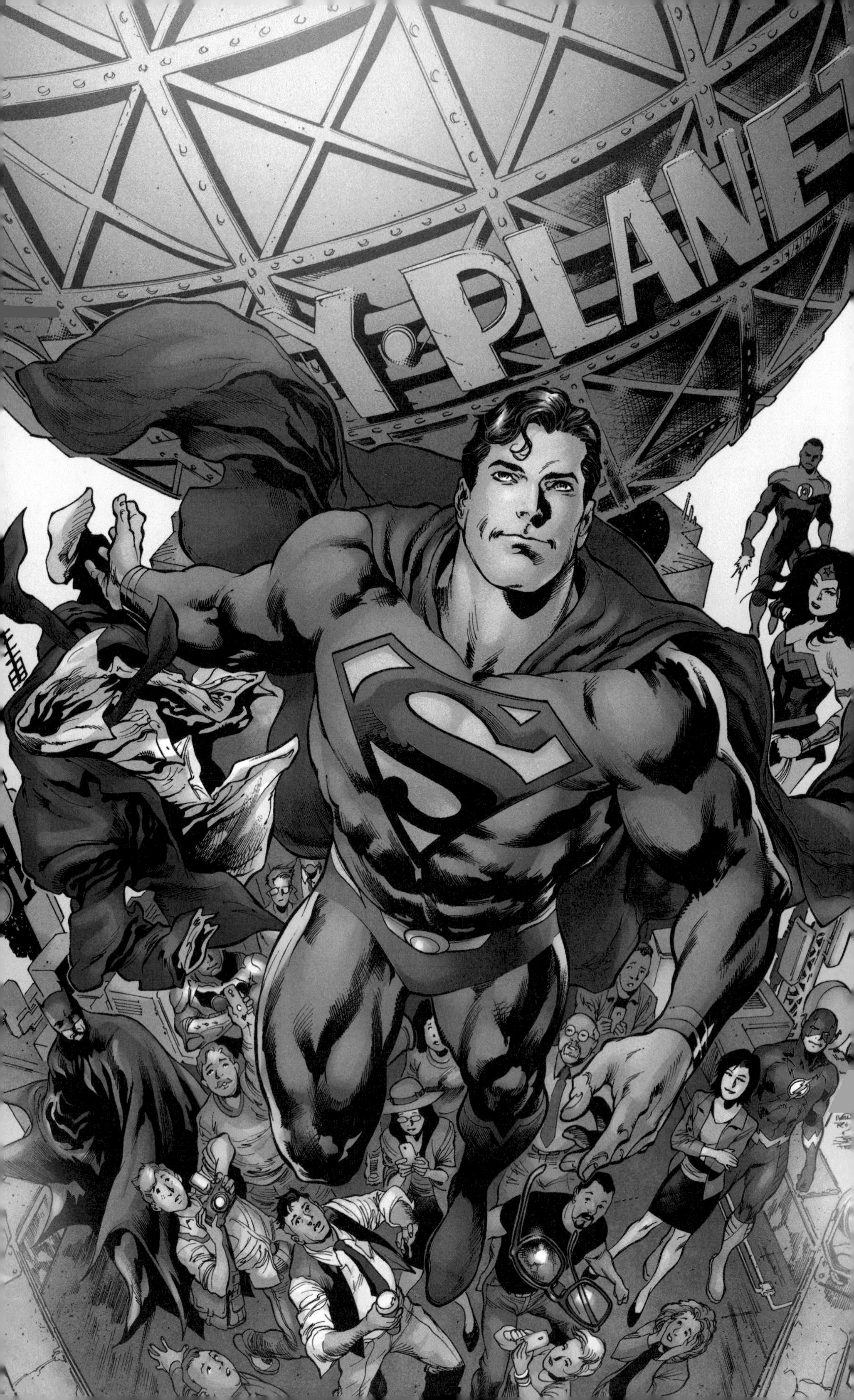
PLANE

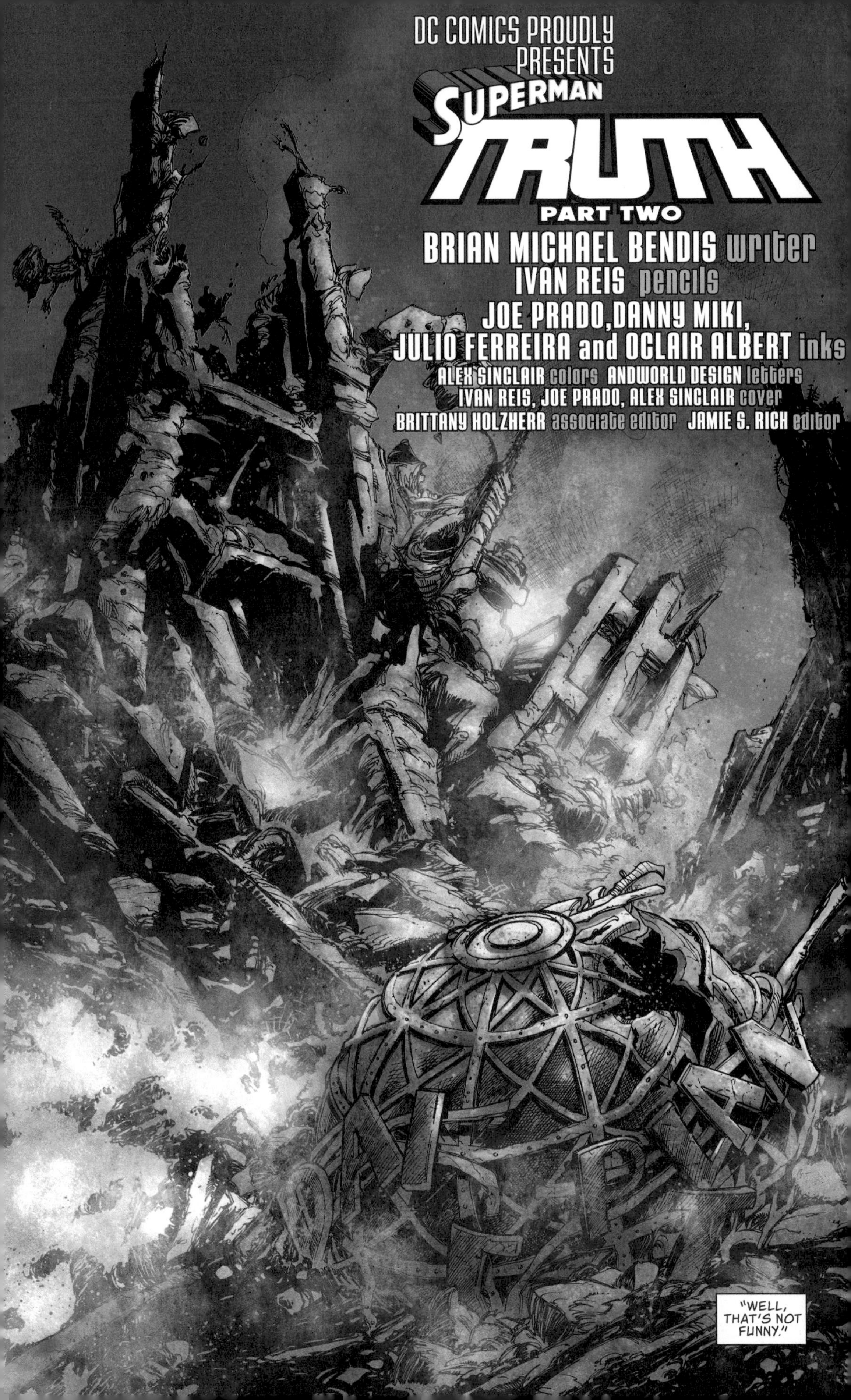
DC COMICS PROUDLY PRESENTS
SUPERMAN
TRUTH
PART TWO
BRIAN MICHAEL BENDIS writer
IVAN REIS pencils
JOE PRADO, DANNY MIKI, JULIO FERREIRA and OCLAIR ALBERT inks
ALEX SINCLAIR colors ANDWORLD DESIGN letters
IVAN REIS, JOE PRADO, ALEX SINCLAIR cover
BRITTANY HOLZHERR associate editor JAMIE S. RICH editor
"WELL, THAT'S NOT FUNNY."

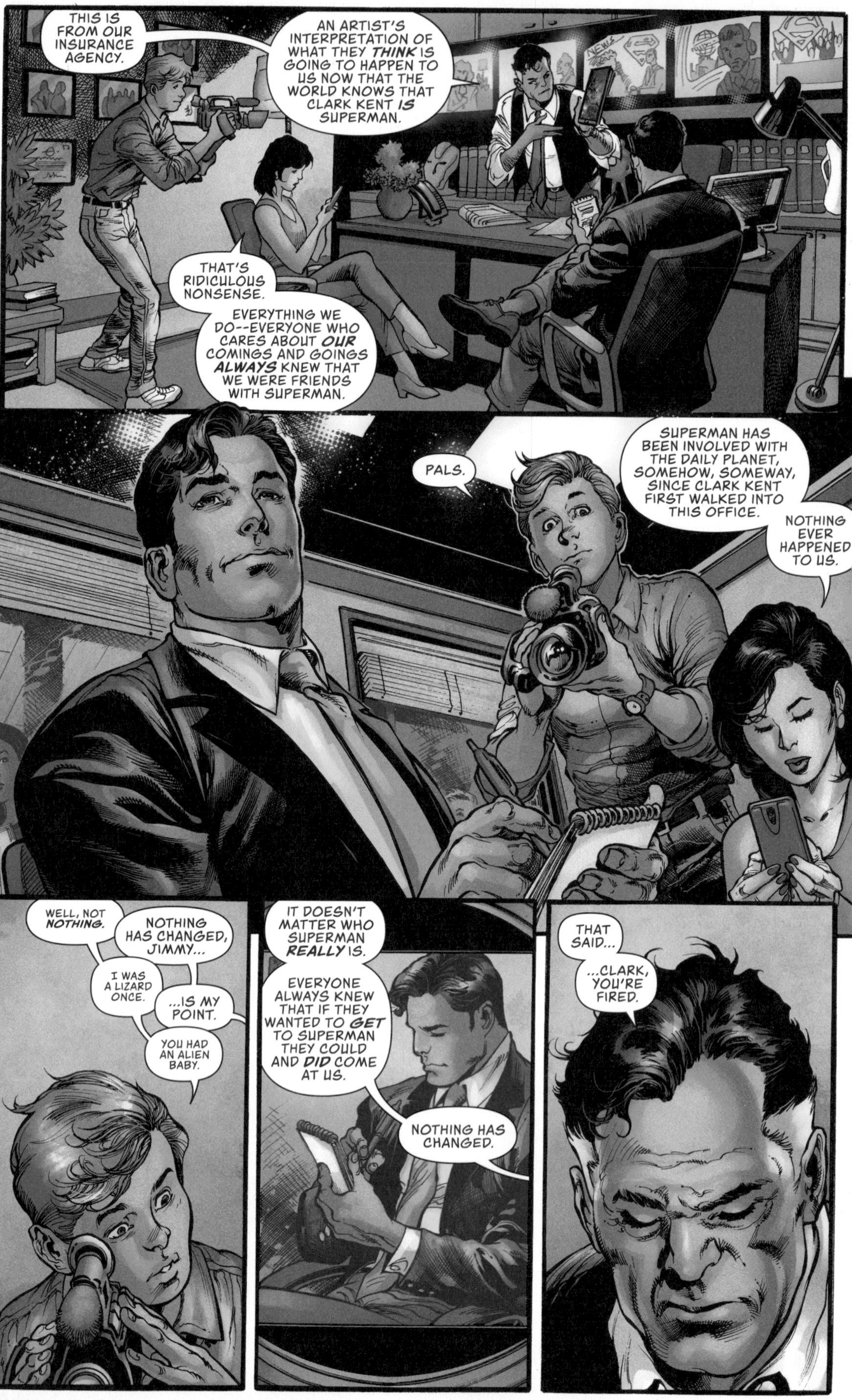
THIS IS FROM OUR INSURANCE AGENCY.
AN ARTIST'S INTERPRETATION OF WHAT THEY *THINK* IS GOING TO HAPPEN TO US NOW THAT THE WORLD KNOWS THAT CLARK KENT *IS* SUPERMAN.
THAT'S RIDICULOUS NONSENSE.
EVERYTHING WE DO--EVERYONE WHO CARES ABOUT *OUR* COMINGS AND GOINGS *ALWAYS* KNEW THAT WE WERE FRIENDS WITH SUPERMAN.
PALS.
SUPERMAN HAS BEEN INVOLVED WITH THE DAILY PLANET, SOMEHOW, SOMEWAY, SINCE CLARK KENT FIRST WALKED INTO THIS OFFICE.
NOTHING EVER HAPPENED TO US.
WELL, NOT *NOTHING*.
NOTHING HAS CHANGED, JIMMY...
I WAS A LIZARD ONCE.
...IS MY POINT.
YOU HAD AN ALIEN BABY.
IT DOESN'T MATTER WHO SUPERMAN *REALLY* IS.
EVERYONE ALWAYS KNEW THAT IF THEY WANTED TO *GET* TO SUPERMAN THEY COULD AND *DID* COME AT US.
NOTHING HAS CHANGED.
THAT SAID...
...CLARK, YOU'RE FIRED.

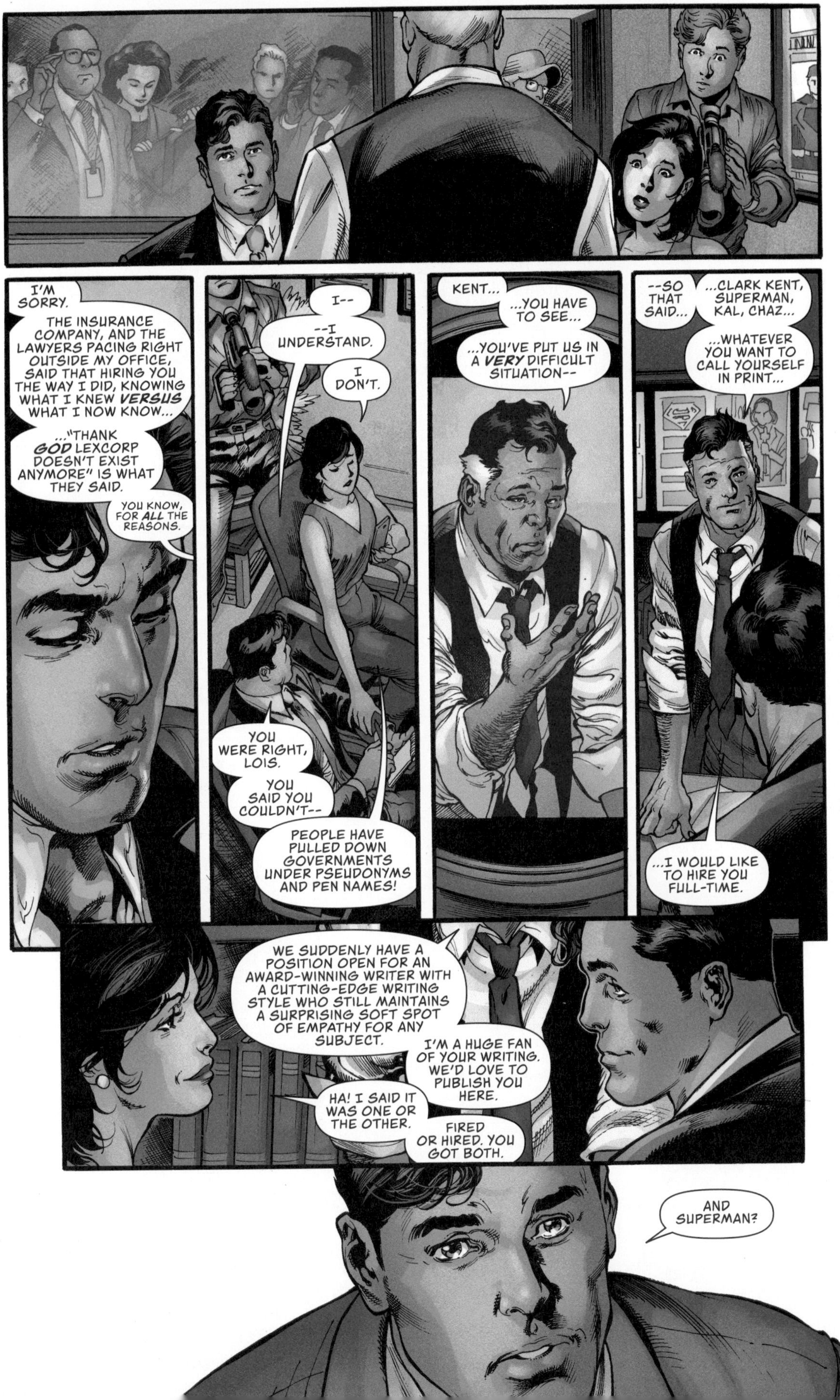
I'M SORRY.
THE INSURANCE COMPANY, AND THE LAWYERS PACING RIGHT OUTSIDE MY OFFICE, SAID THAT HIRING YOU THE WAY I DID, KNOWING WHAT I KNEW VERSUS WHAT I NOW KNOW...
..."THANK GOD LEXCORP DOESN'T EXIST ANYMORE" IS WHAT THEY SAID.
YOU KNOW, FOR ALL THE REASONS.
I--
--I UNDERSTAND.
I DON'T.
YOU WERE RIGHT, LOIS.
YOU SAID YOU COULDN'T--
PEOPLE HAVE PULLED DOWN GOVERNMENTS UNDER PSEUDONYMS AND PEN NAMES!
KENT...
...YOU HAVE TO SEE...
...YOU'VE PUT US IN A VERY DIFFICULT SITUATION--
--SO THAT SAID...
...CLARK KENT, SUPERMAN, KAL, CHAZ...
...WHATEVER YOU WANT TO CALL YOURSELF IN PRINT...
...I WOULD LIKE TO HIRE YOU FULL-TIME.
WE SUDDENLY HAVE A POSITION OPEN FOR AN AWARD-WINNING WRITER WITH A CUTTING-EDGE WRITING STYLE WHO STILL MAINTAINS A SURPRISING SOFT SPOT OF EMPATHY FOR ANY SUBJECT.
I'M A HUGE FAN OF YOUR WRITING. WE'D LOVE TO PUBLISH YOU HERE.
HA! I SAID IT WAS ONE OR THE OTHER.
FIRED OR HIRED. YOU GOT BOTH.
AND SUPERMAN?

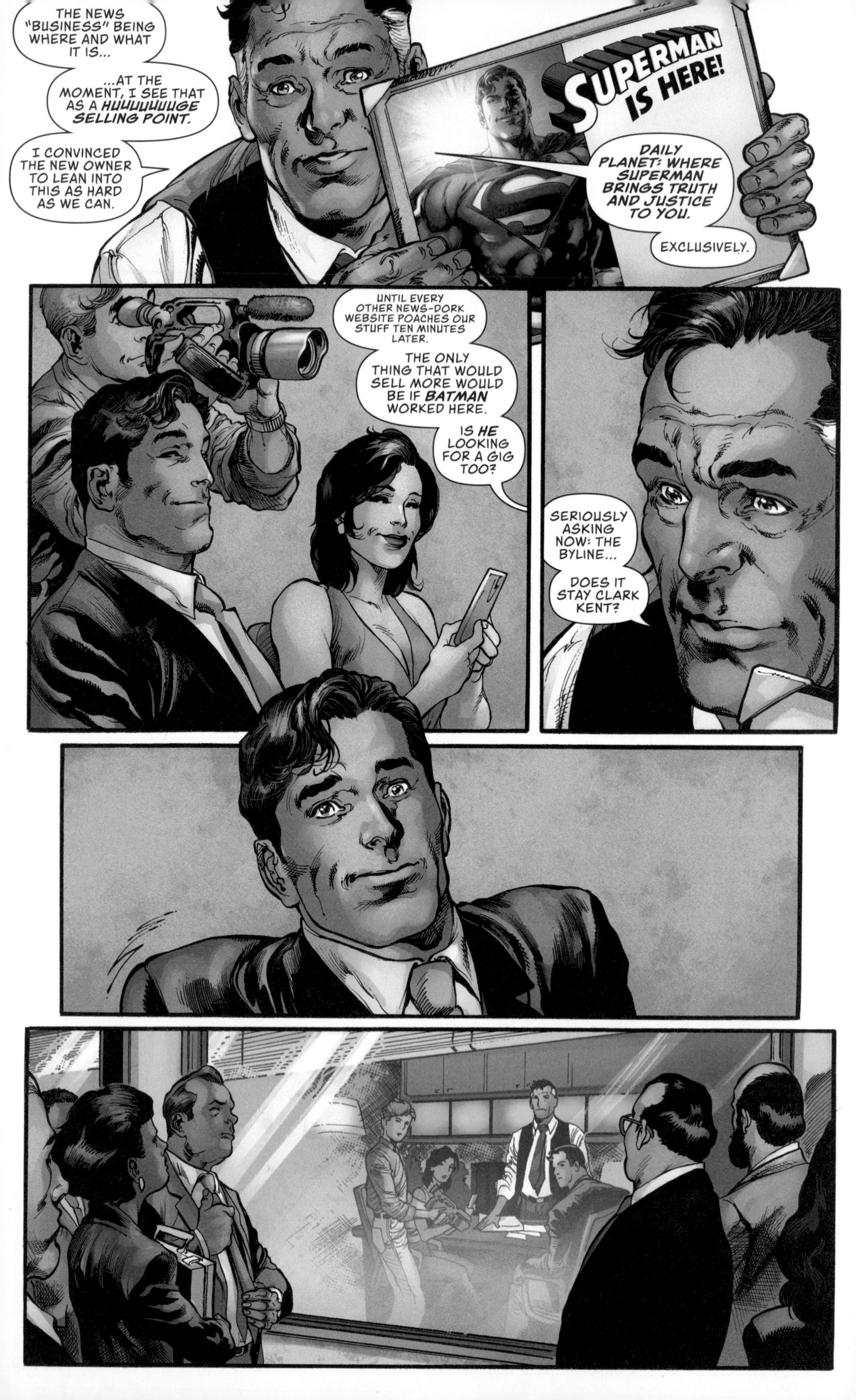
THE NEWS "BUSINESS" BEING WHERE AND WHAT IT IS...
...AT THE MOMENT, I SEE THAT AS A HUUUUUUUGE SELLING POINT.
I CONVINCED THE NEW OWNER TO LEAN INTO THIS AS HARD AS WE CAN.
SUPERMAN IS HERE!
DAILY PLANET: WHERE SUPERMAN BRINGS TRUTH AND JUSTICE TO YOU.
EXCLUSIVELY.
UNTIL EVERY OTHER NEWS-DORK WEBSITE POACHES OUR STUFF TEN MINUTES LATER.
THE ONLY THING THAT WOULD SELL MORE WOULD BE IF BATMAN WORKED HERE.
IS HE LOOKING FOR A GIG TOO?
SERIOUSLY ASKING NOW: THE BYLINE...
DOES IT STAY CLARK KENT?

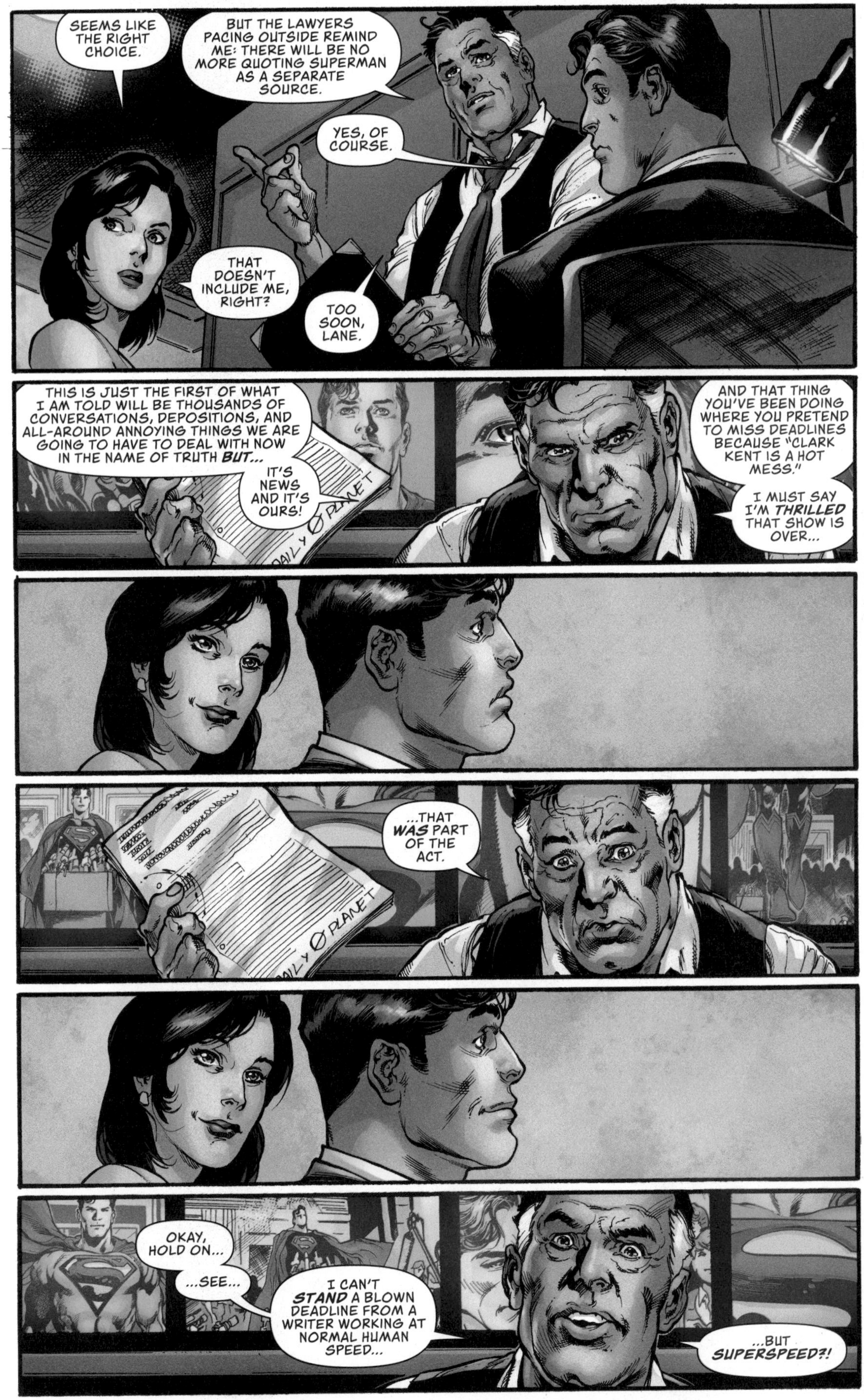
SEEMS LIKE THE RIGHT CHOICE.
BUT THE LAWYERS PACING OUTSIDE REMIND ME: THERE WILL BE NO MORE QUOTING SUPERMAN AS A SEPARATE SOURCE.
YES, OF COURSE.
THAT DOESN'T INCLUDE ME, RIGHT?
TOO SOON, LANE.
THIS IS JUST THE FIRST OF WHAT I AM TOLD WILL BE THOUSANDS OF CONVERSATIONS, DEPOSITIONS, AND ALL-AROUND ANNOYING THINGS WE ARE GOING TO HAVE TO DEAL WITH NOW IN THE NAME OF TRUTH **BUT...**
IT'S NEWS AND IT'S OURS!
DAILY PLANET
AND THAT THING YOU'VE BEEN DOING WHERE YOU PRETEND TO MISS DEADLINES BECAUSE "CLARK KENT IS A HOT MESS."
I MUST SAY I'M ***THRILLED*** THAT SHOW IS OVER...
...THAT ***WAS*** PART OF THE ACT.
DAILY PLANET
OKAY, HOLD ON...
...SEE...
I CAN'T ***STAND*** A BLOWN DEADLINE FROM A WRITER WORKING AT NORMAL HUMAN SPEED...
...BUT ***SUPERSPEED?!***

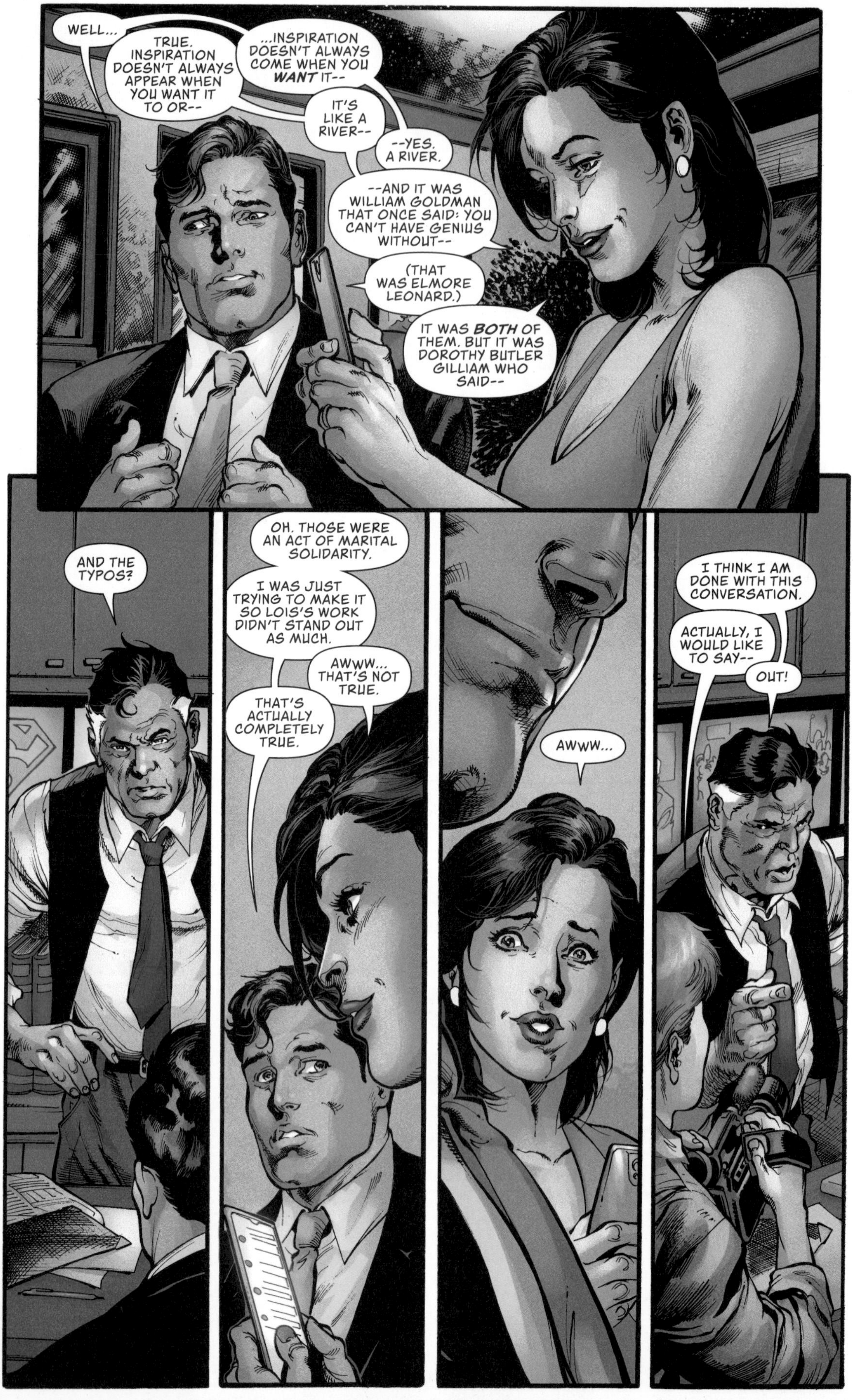
WELL...
TRUE. INSPIRATION DOESN'T ALWAYS APPEAR WHEN YOU WANT IT TO OR--
...INSPIRATION DOESN'T ALWAYS COME WHEN YOU *WANT* IT--
IT'S LIKE A RIVER--
--YES. A RIVER.
--AND IT WAS WILLIAM GOLDMAN THAT ONCE SAID: YOU CAN'T HAVE GENIUS WITHOUT--
(THAT WAS ELMORE LEONARD.)
IT WAS **BOTH** OF THEM. BUT IT WAS DOROTHY BUTLER GILLIAM WHO SAID--
AND THE TYPOS?
OH. THOSE WERE AN ACT OF MARITAL SOLIDARITY.
I WAS JUST TRYING TO MAKE IT SO LOIS'S WORK DIDN'T STAND OUT AS MUCH.
AWWW... THAT'S NOT TRUE.
THAT'S ACTUALLY COMPLETELY TRUE.
AWWW...
I THINK I AM DONE WITH THIS CONVERSATION.
ACTUALLY, I WOULD LIKE TO SAY--
OUT!

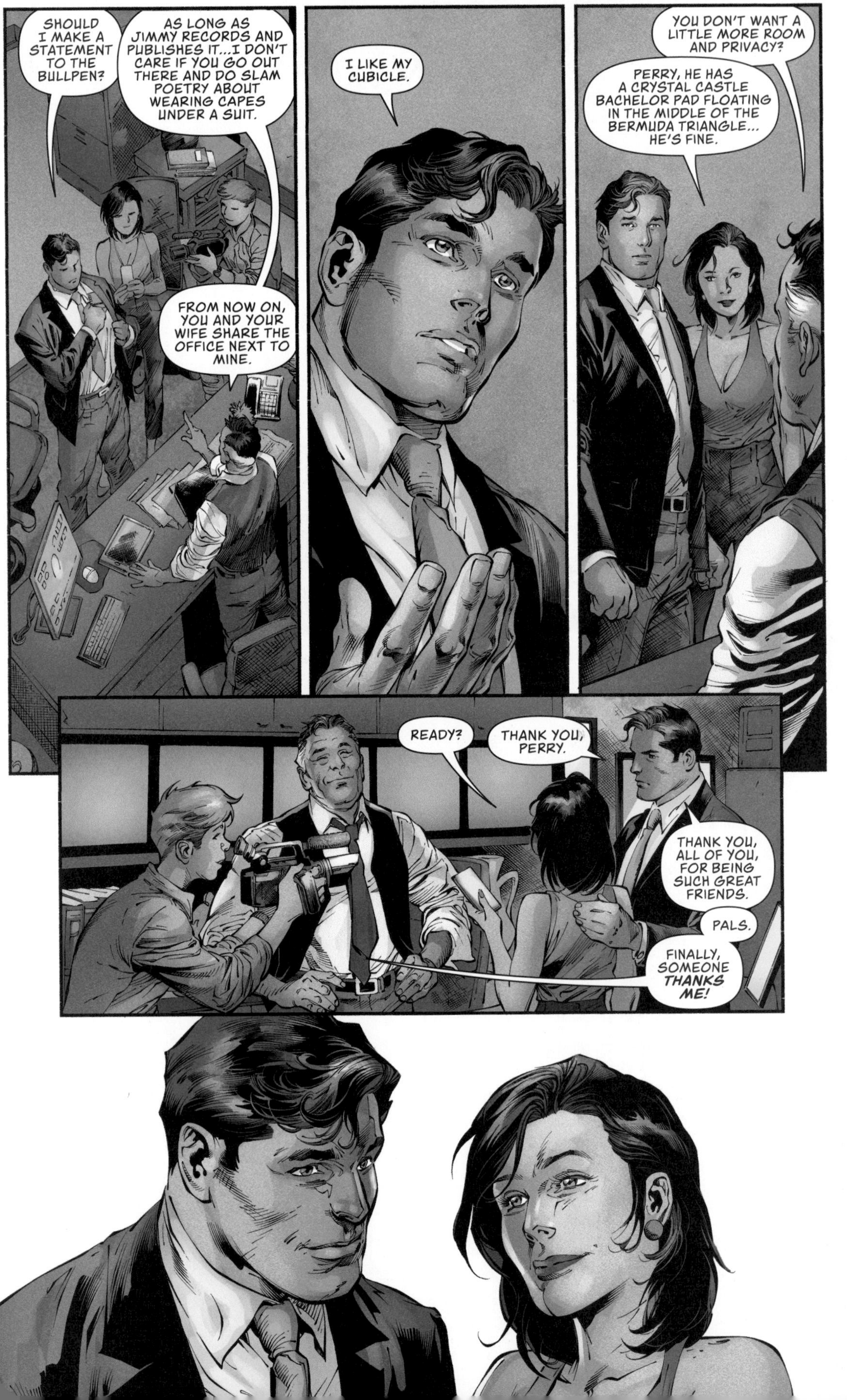
SHOULD I MAKE A STATEMENT TO THE BULLPEN?
AS LONG AS JIMMY RECORDS AND PUBLISHES IT...I DON'T CARE IF YOU GO OUT THERE AND DO SLAM POETRY ABOUT WEARING CAPES UNDER A SUIT.
FROM NOW ON, YOU AND YOUR WIFE SHARE THE OFFICE NEXT TO MINE.
I LIKE MY CUBICLE.
YOU DON'T WANT A LITTLE MORE ROOM AND PRIVACY?
PERRY, HE HAS A CRYSTAL CASTLE BACHELOR PAD FLOATING IN THE MIDDLE OF THE BERMUDA TRIANGLE... HE'S FINE.
READY?
THANK YOU, PERRY.
THANK YOU, ALL OF YOU, FOR BEING SUCH GREAT FRIENDS.
PALS.
FINALLY, SOMEONE THANKS ME!

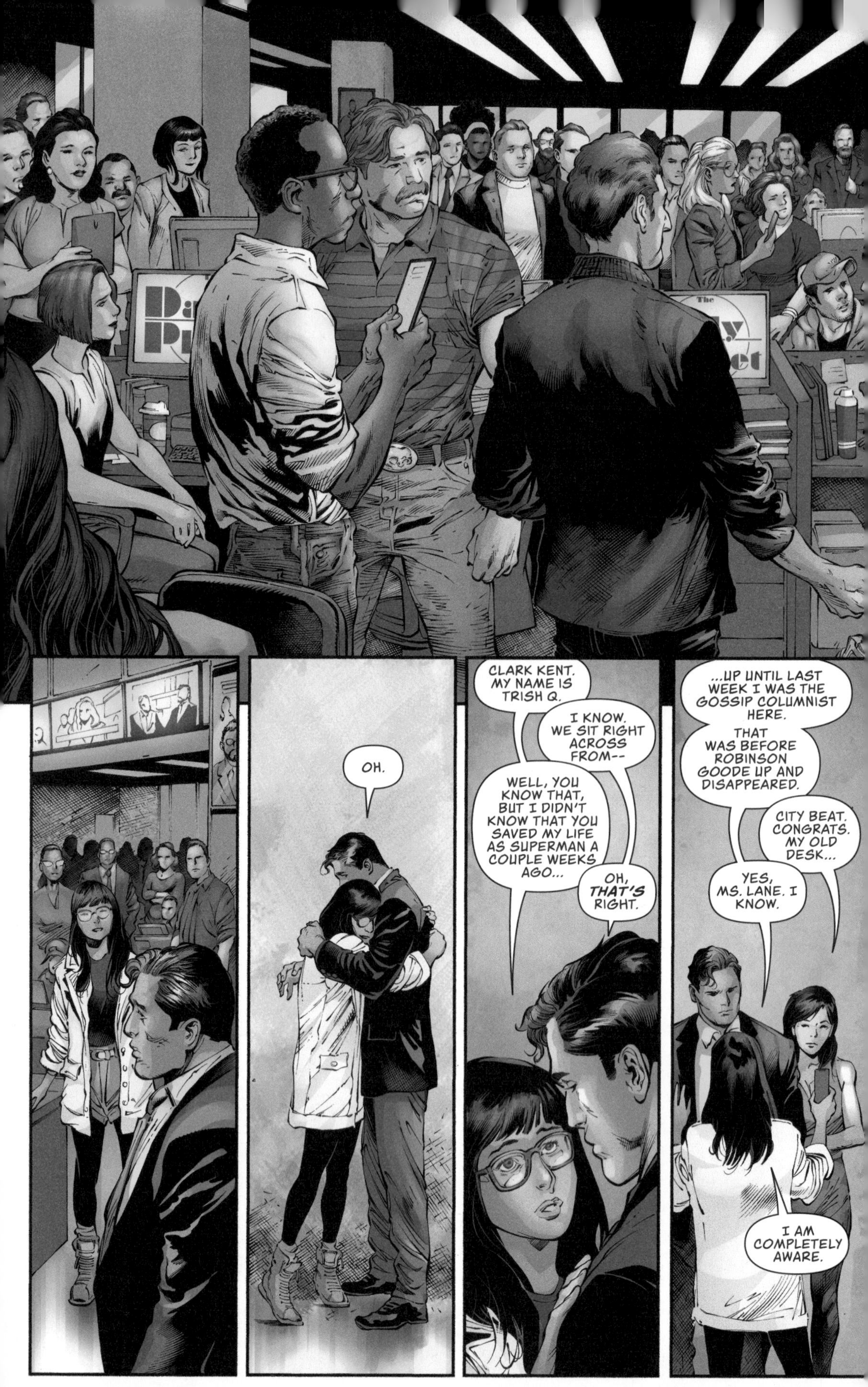
OH.
CLARK KENT. MY NAME IS TRISH Q.
I KNOW. WE SIT RIGHT ACROSS FROM--
WELL, YOU KNOW THAT, BUT I DIDN'T KNOW THAT YOU SAVED MY LIFE AS SUPERMAN A COUPLE WEEKS AGO...
OH, *THAT'S* RIGHT.
...UP UNTIL LAST WEEK I WAS THE GOSSIP COLUMNIST HERE.
THAT WAS BEFORE ROBINSON GOODE UP AND DISAPPEARED.
CITY BEAT. CONGRATS. MY OLD DESK...
YES, MS. LANE. I KNOW.
I AM COMPLETELY AWARE.

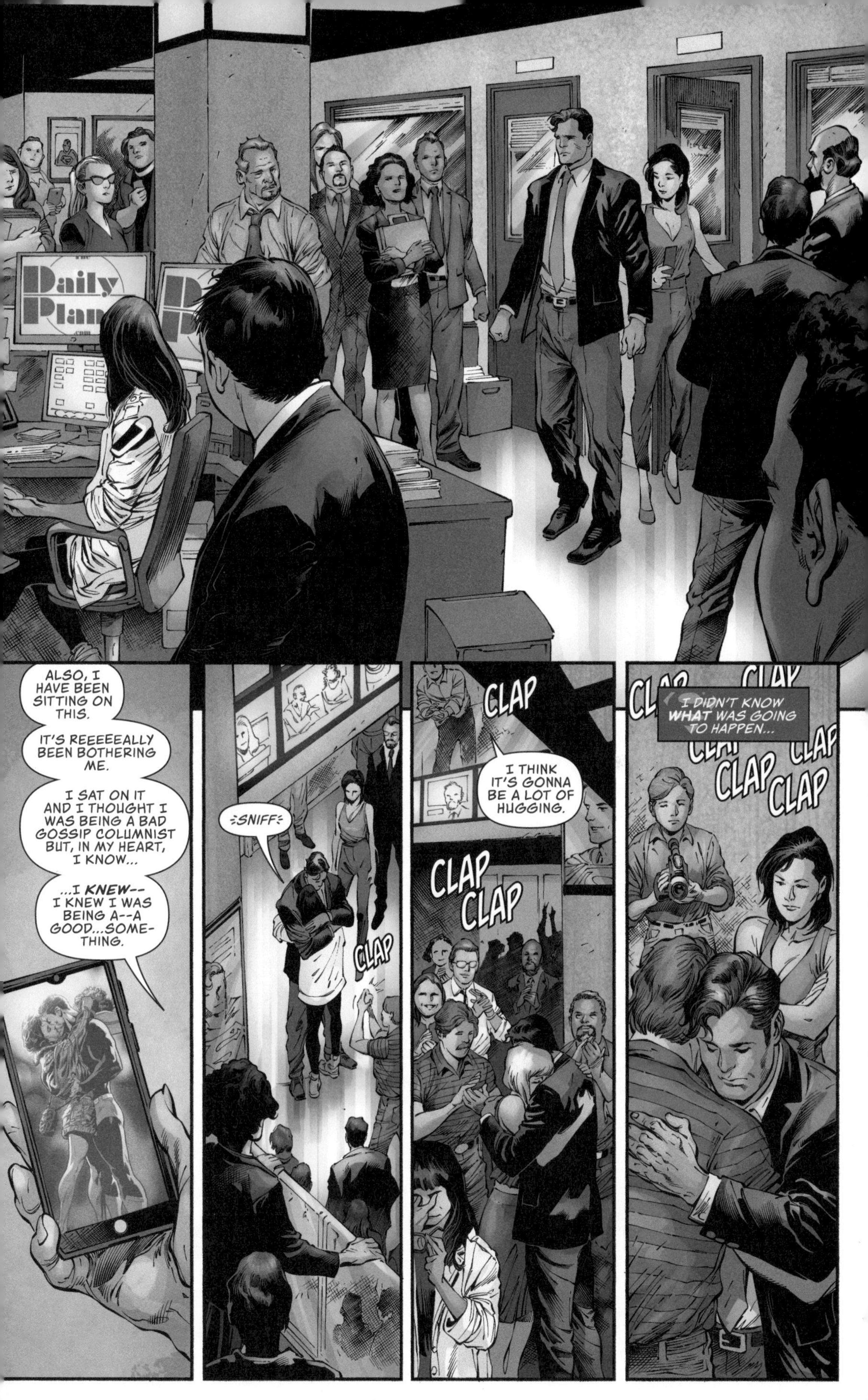
Daily
ALSO, I HAVE BEEN SITTING ON THIS.
IT'S REEEEEALLY BEEN BOTHERING ME.
I SAT ON IT AND I THOUGHT I WAS BEING A BAD GOSSIP COLUMNIST BUT, IN MY HEART, I KNOW...
...I **KNEW**-- I KNEW I WAS BEING A--A GOOD...SOMETHING.
SNIFF
CLAP
CLAP
I THINK IT'S GONNA BE A LOT OF HUGGING.
CLAP CLAP
I DIDN'T KNOW **WHAT** WAS GOING TO HAPPEN...
CLAP CLAP CLAP CLAP CLAP

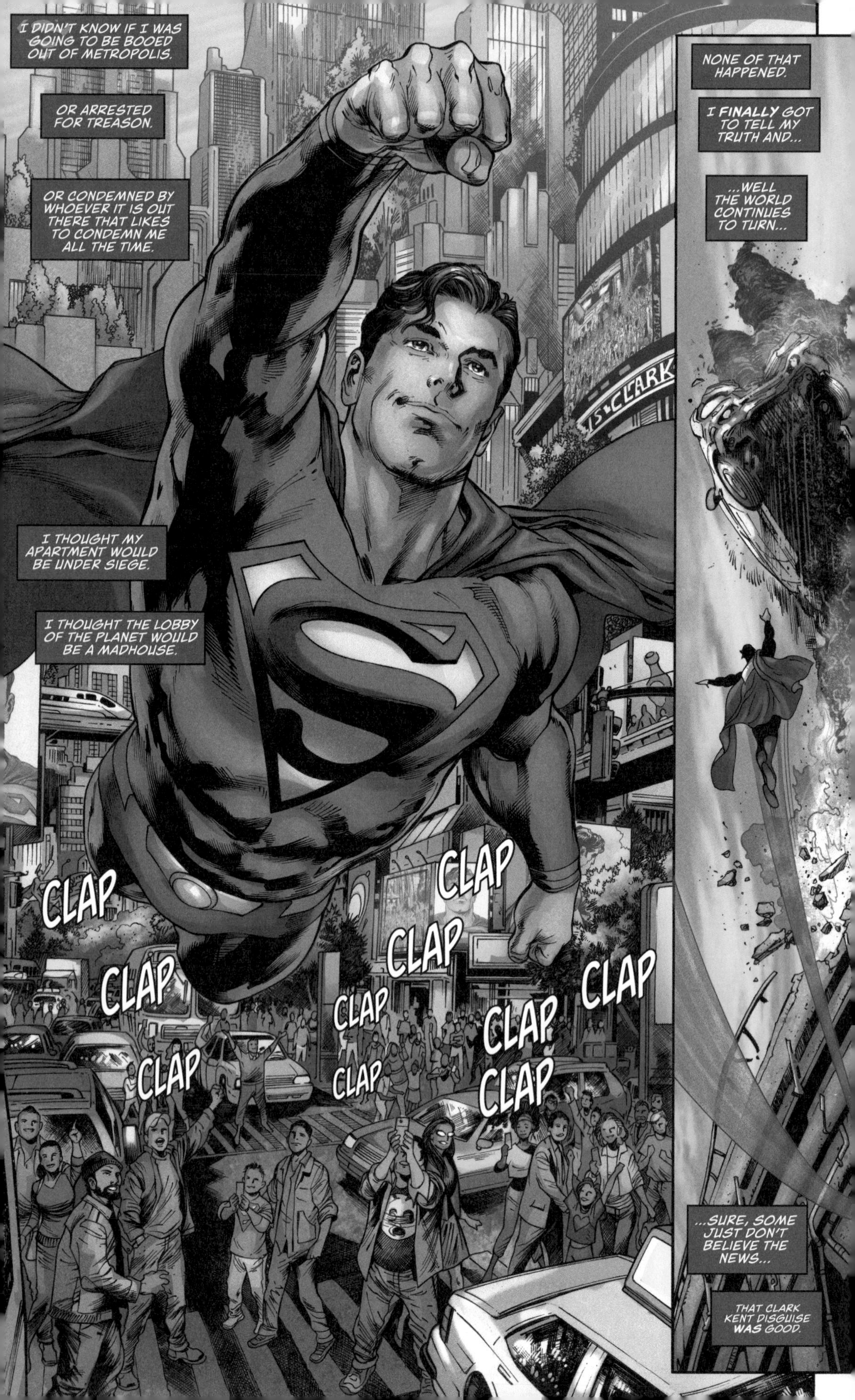
I DIDN'T KNOW IF I WAS GOING TO BE BOOED OUT OF METROPOLIS.
OR ARRESTED FOR TREASON.
OR CONDEMNED BY WHOEVER IT IS OUT THERE THAT LIKES TO CONDEMN ME ALL THE TIME.
I THOUGHT MY APARTMENT WOULD BE UNDER SIEGE.
I THOUGHT THE LOBBY OF THE PLANET WOULD BE A MADHOUSE.
CLAP
CLAP
CLAP
CLAP
CLAP
CLAP
CLAP
CLAP
CLAP
CLAP
NONE OF THAT HAPPENED.
I **FINALLY** GOT TO TELL MY TRUTH AND...
...WELL THE WORLD CONTINUES TO TURN...
...SURE, SOME JUST DON'T BELIEVE THE NEWS...
THAT CLARK KENT DISGUISE **WAS** GOOD.

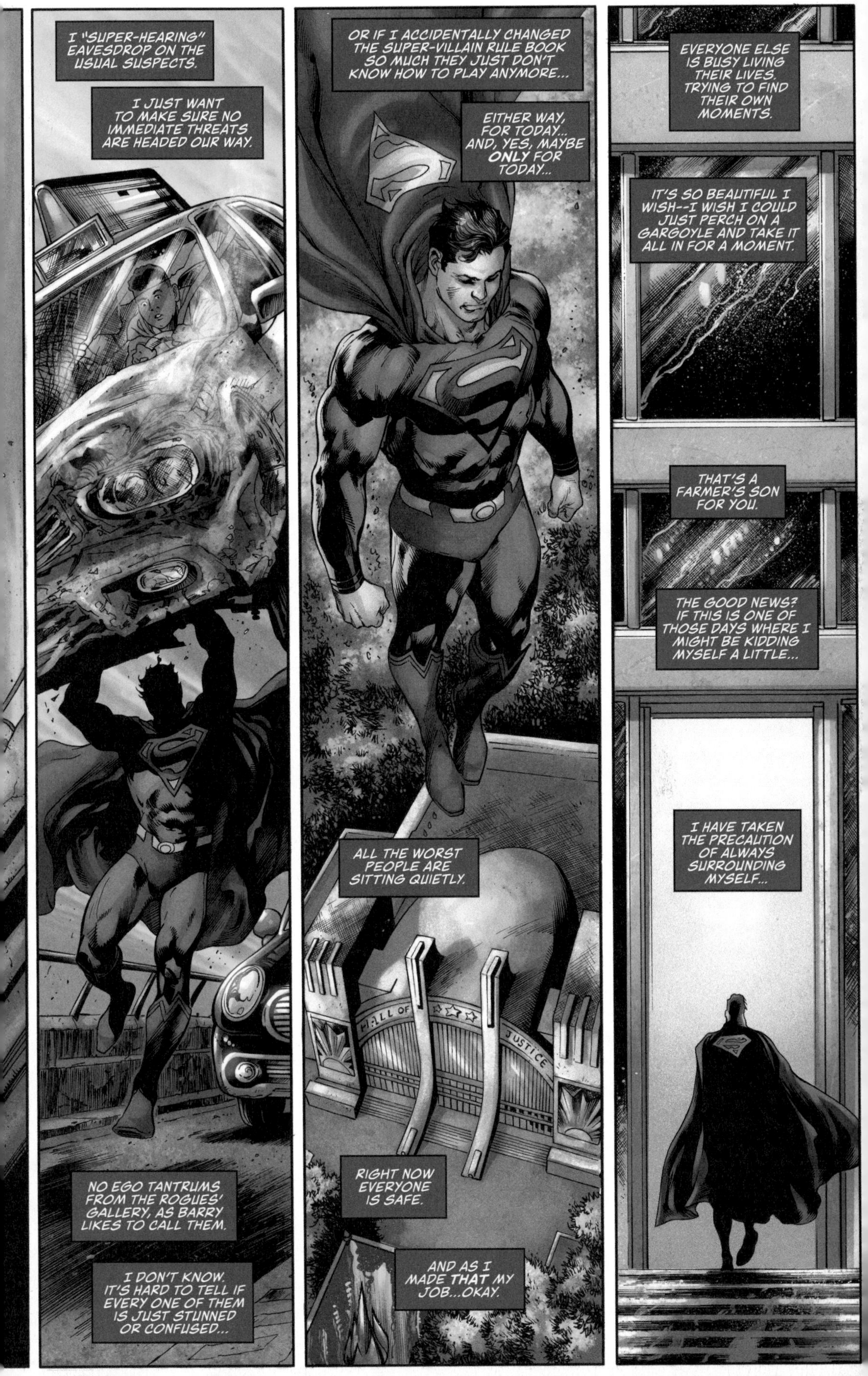
I "SUPER-HEARING" EAVESDROP ON THE USUAL SUSPECTS.
I JUST WANT TO MAKE SURE NO IMMEDIATE THREATS ARE HEADED OUR WAY.
NO EGO TANTRUMS FROM THE ROGUES' GALLERY, AS BARRY LIKES TO CALL THEM.
I DON'T KNOW. IT'S HARD TO TELL IF EVERY ONE OF THEM IS JUST STUNNED OR CONFUSED...
OR IF I ACCIDENTALLY CHANGED THE SUPER-VILLAIN RULE BOOK SO MUCH THEY JUST DON'T KNOW HOW TO PLAY ANYMORE...
EITHER WAY, FOR TODAY... AND, YES, MAYBE ONLY FOR TODAY...
ALL THE WORST PEOPLE ARE SITTING QUIETLY.
HALL OF JUSTICE
RIGHT NOW EVERYONE IS SAFE.
AND AS I MADE THAT MY JOB...OKAY.
EVERYONE ELSE IS BUSY LIVING THEIR LIVES. TRYING TO FIND THEIR OWN MOMENTS.
IT'S SO BEAUTIFUL I WISH--I WISH I COULD JUST PERCH ON A GARGOYLE AND TAKE IT ALL IN FOR A MOMENT.
THAT'S A FARMER'S SON FOR YOU.
THE GOOD NEWS? IF THIS IS ONE OF THOSE DAYS WHERE I MIGHT BE KIDDING MYSELF A LITTLE...
I HAVE TAKEN THE PRECAUTION OF ALWAYS SURROUNDING MYSELF...

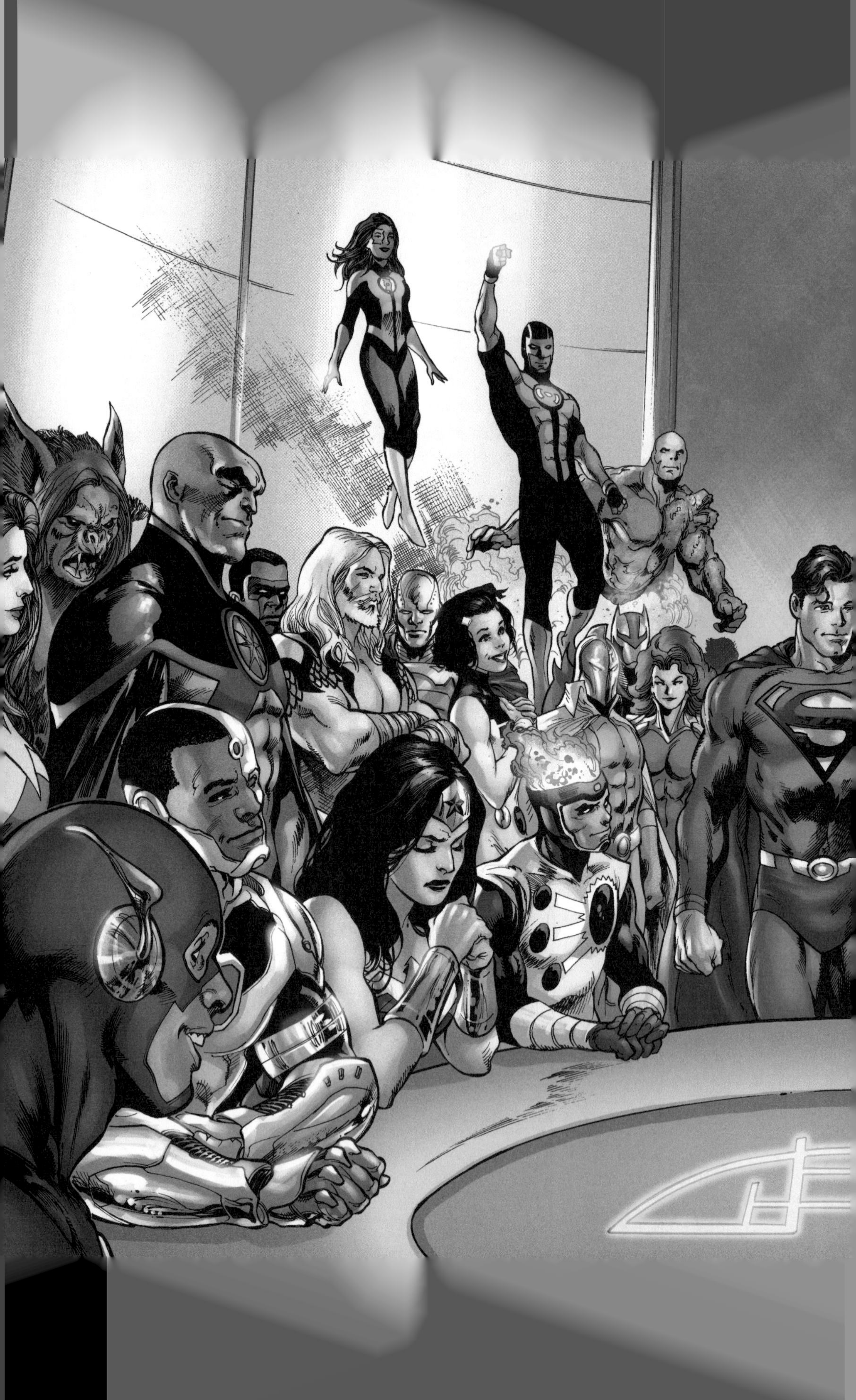

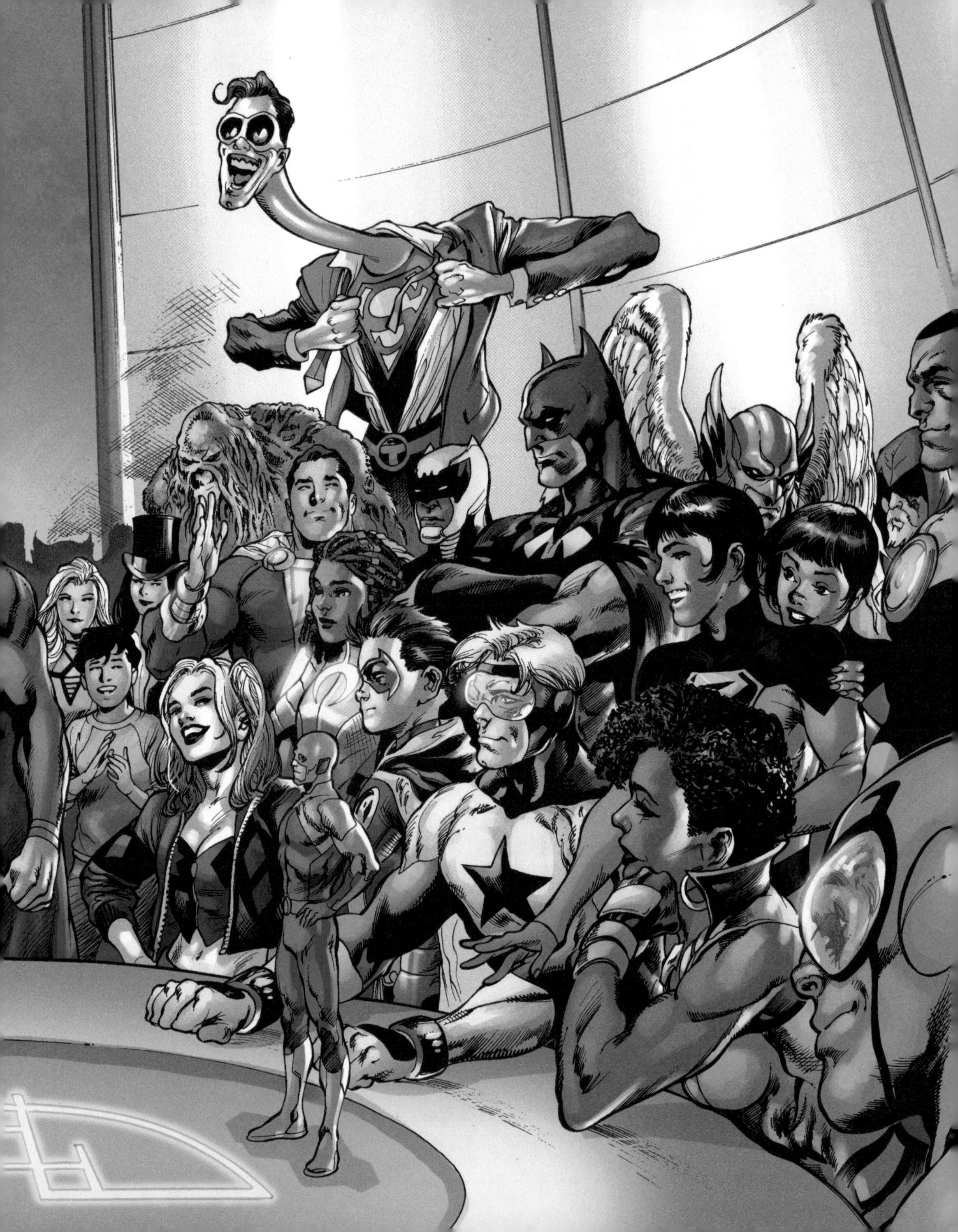

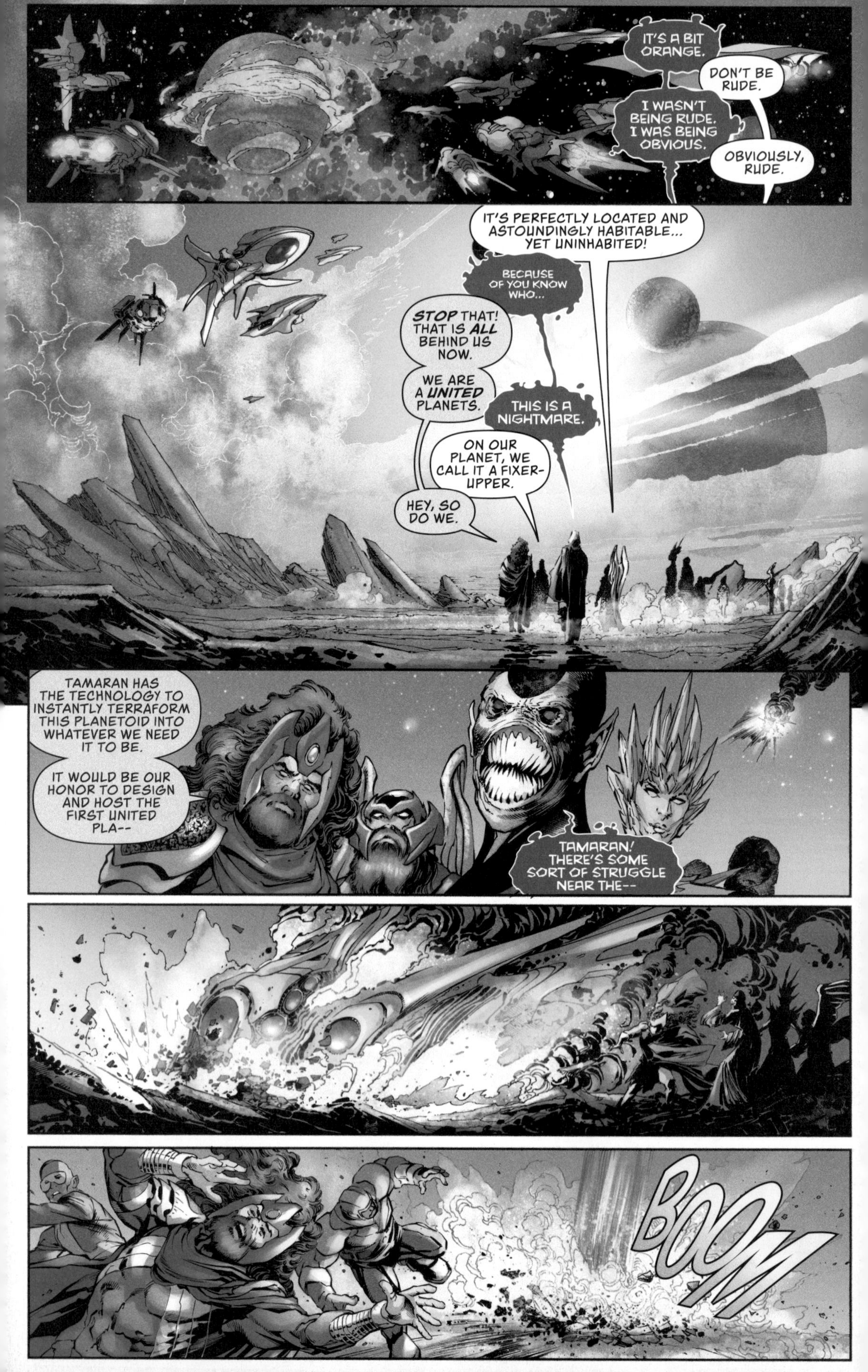
IT'S A BIT ORANGE.
DON'T BE RUDE.
I WASN'T BEING RUDE. I WAS BEING OBVIOUS.
OBVIOUSLY, RUDE.
IT'S PERFECTLY LOCATED AND ASTOUNDINGLY HABITABLE... YET UNINHABITED!
BECAUSE OF YOU KNOW WHO...
STOP THAT! THAT IS ALL BEHIND US NOW.
WE ARE A UNITED PLANETS.
THIS IS A NIGHTMARE.
ON OUR PLANET, WE CALL IT A FIXER-UPPER.
HEY, SO DO WE.
TAMARAN HAS THE TECHNOLOGY TO INSTANTLY TERRAFORM THIS PLANETOID INTO WHATEVER WE NEED IT TO BE.
IT WOULD BE OUR HONOR TO DESIGN AND HOST THE FIRST UNITED PLA--
TAMARAN! THERE'S SOME SORT OF STRUGGLE NEAR THE--
BOOM

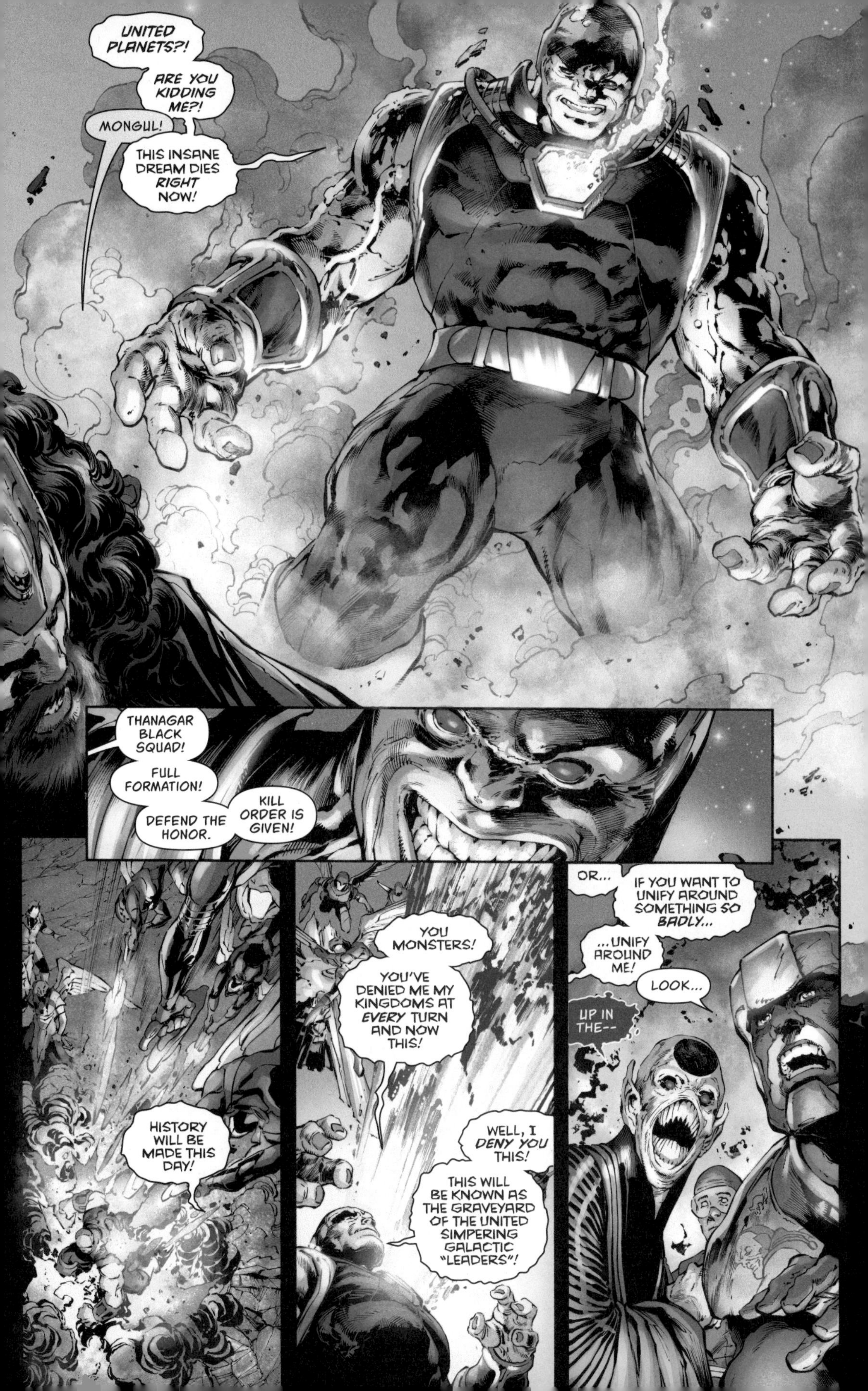
UNITED PLANETS?!
ARE YOU KIDDING ME?!
MONGUL!
THIS INSANE DREAM DIES RIGHT NOW!
THANAGAR BLACK SQUAD!
FULL FORMATION!
DEFEND THE HONOR.
KILL ORDER IS GIVEN!
HISTORY WILL BE MADE THIS DAY!
YOU MONSTERS!
YOU'VE DENIED ME MY KINGDOMS AT EVERY TURN AND NOW THIS!
WELL, I DENY YOU THIS!
THIS WILL BE KNOWN AS THE GRAVEYARD OF THE UNITED SIMPERING GALACTIC "LEADERS"!
OR...
IF YOU WANT TO UNIFY AROUND SOMETHING SO BADLY...
...UNIFY AROUND ME!
LOOK...
UP IN THE--

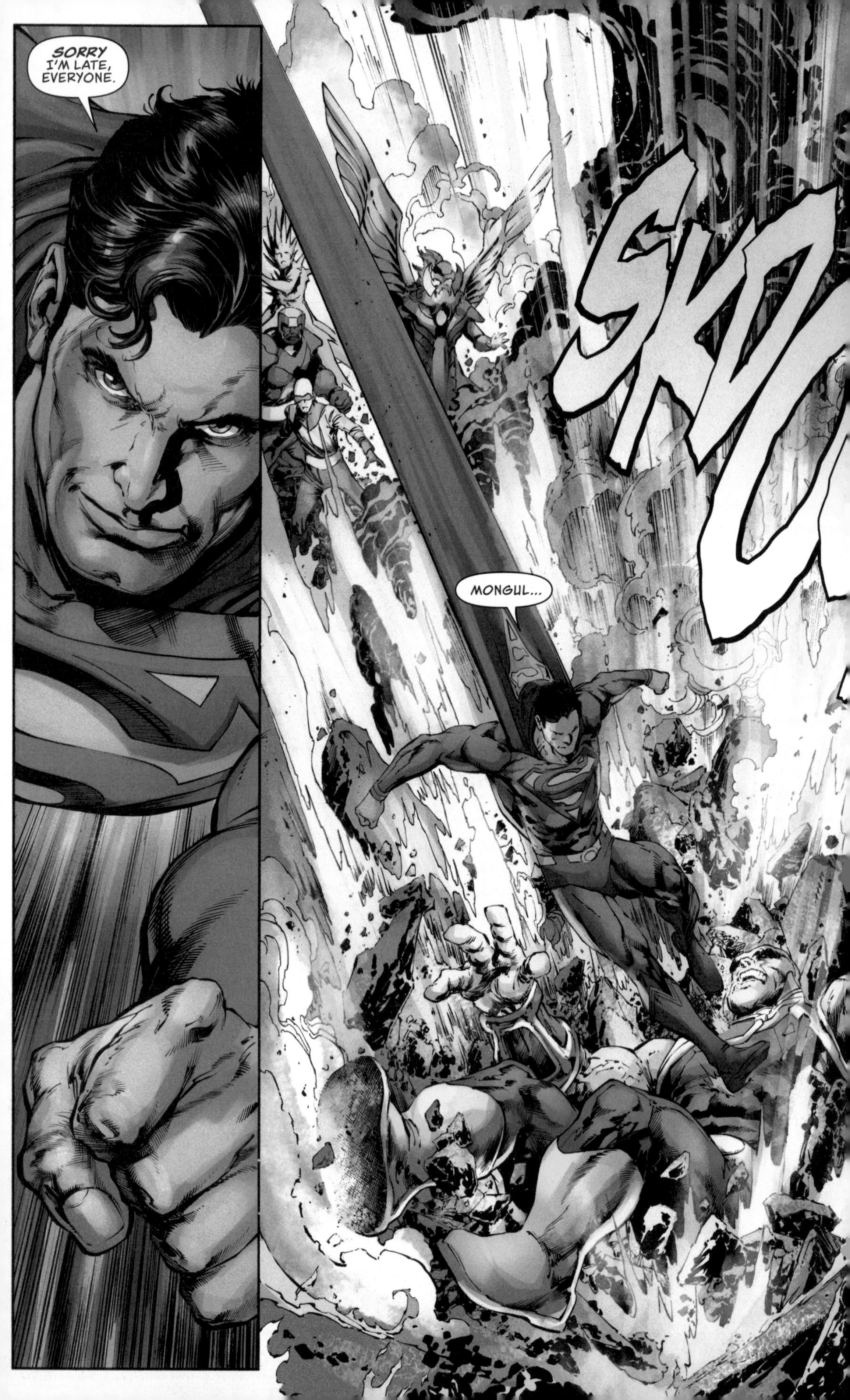
SORRY I'M LATE, EVERYONE.
MONGUL...
SKO

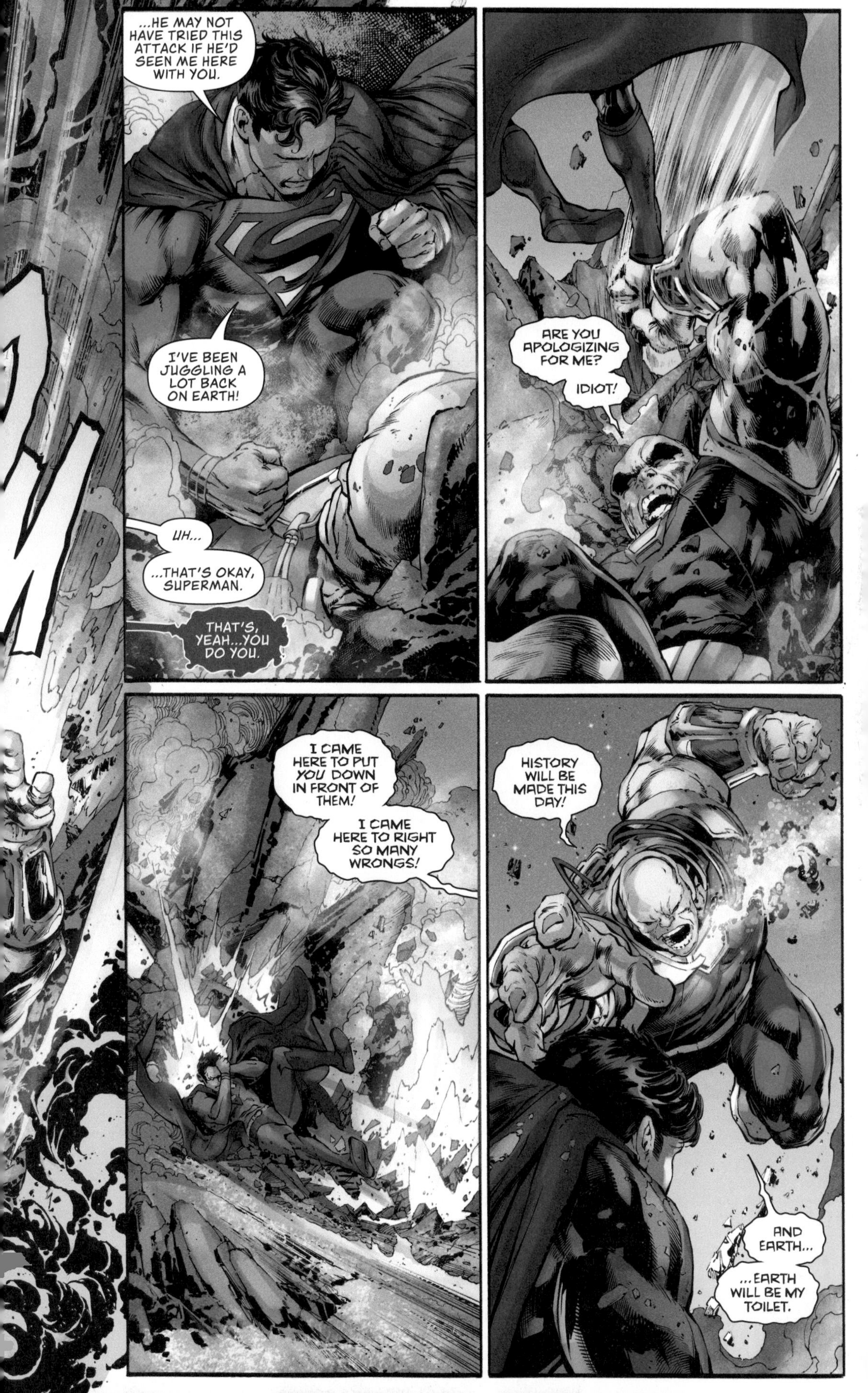
...HE MAY NOT HAVE TRIED THIS ATTACK IF HE'D SEEN ME HERE WITH YOU.
I'VE BEEN JUGGLING A LOT BACK ON EARTH!
UH...
...THAT'S OKAY, SUPERMAN.
THAT'S, YEAH...YOU DO YOU.
ARE YOU APOLOGIZING FOR ME?
IDIOT!
I CAME HERE TO PUT YOU DOWN IN FRONT OF THEM!
I CAME HERE TO RIGHT SO MANY WRONGS!
HISTORY WILL BE MADE THIS DAY!
AND EARTH...
...EARTH WILL BE MY TOILET.

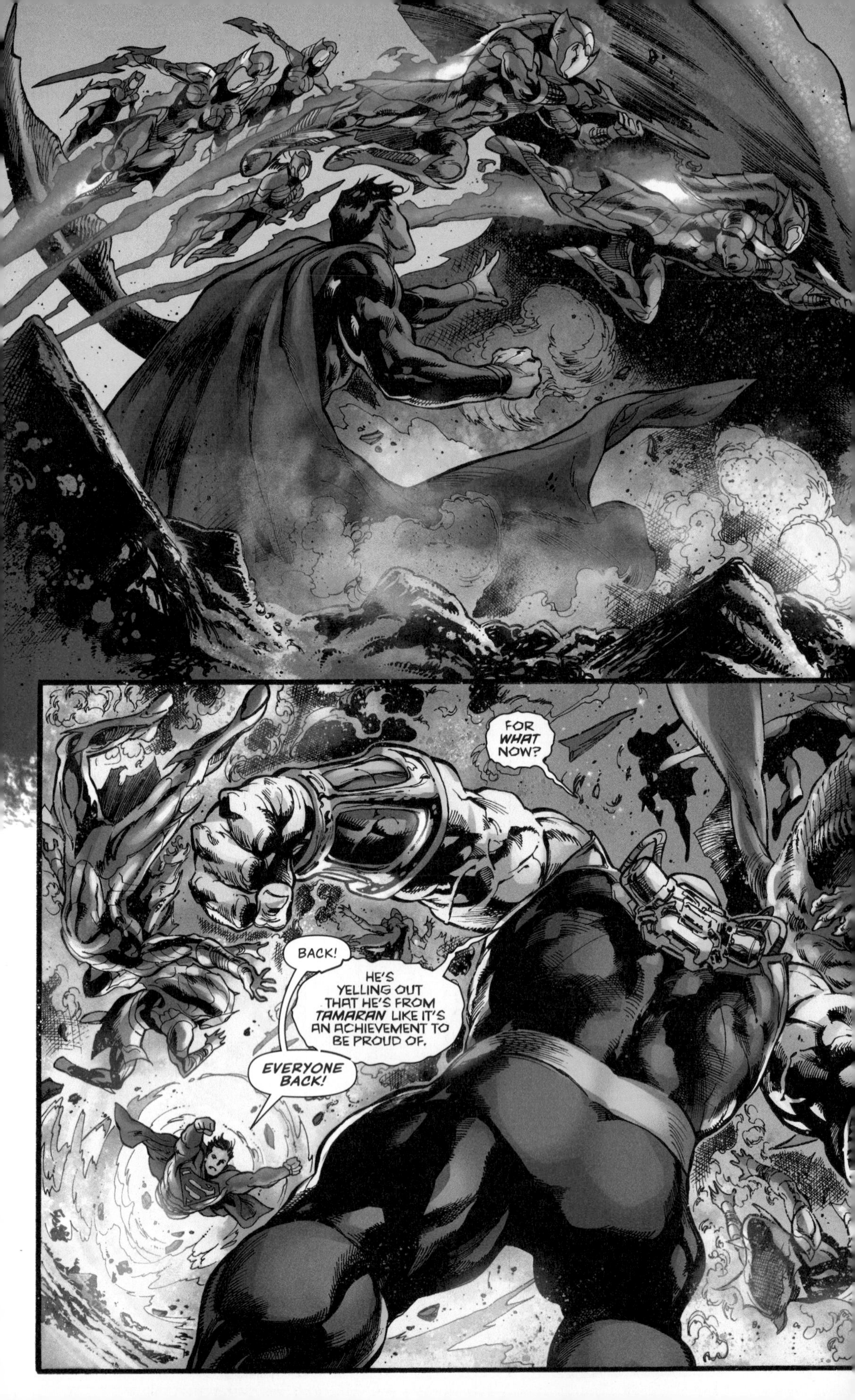

FOR WHAT NOW?
BACK!
HE'S YELLING OUT THAT HE'S FROM TAMARAN LIKE IT'S AN ACHIEVEMENT TO BE PROUD OF.
EVERYONE BACK!

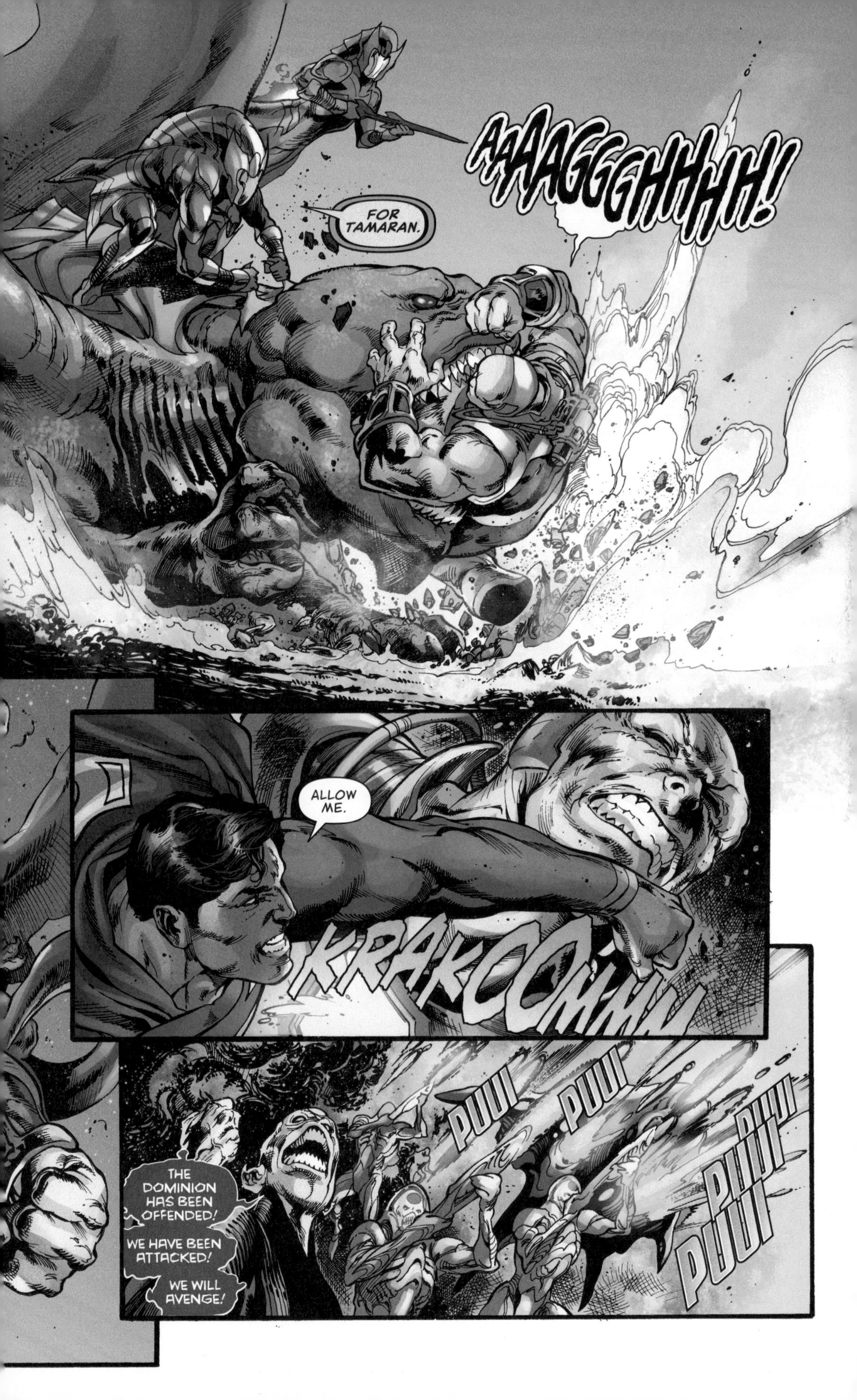

FOR TAMARAN.
AAAAAGGGHHHHH!
ALLOW ME.
KRAKOOMMM
THE DOMINION HAS BEEN OFFENDED!
WE HAVE BEEN ATTACKED!
WE WILL AVENGE!
PUUI
PUUI
PUUI
PUUI

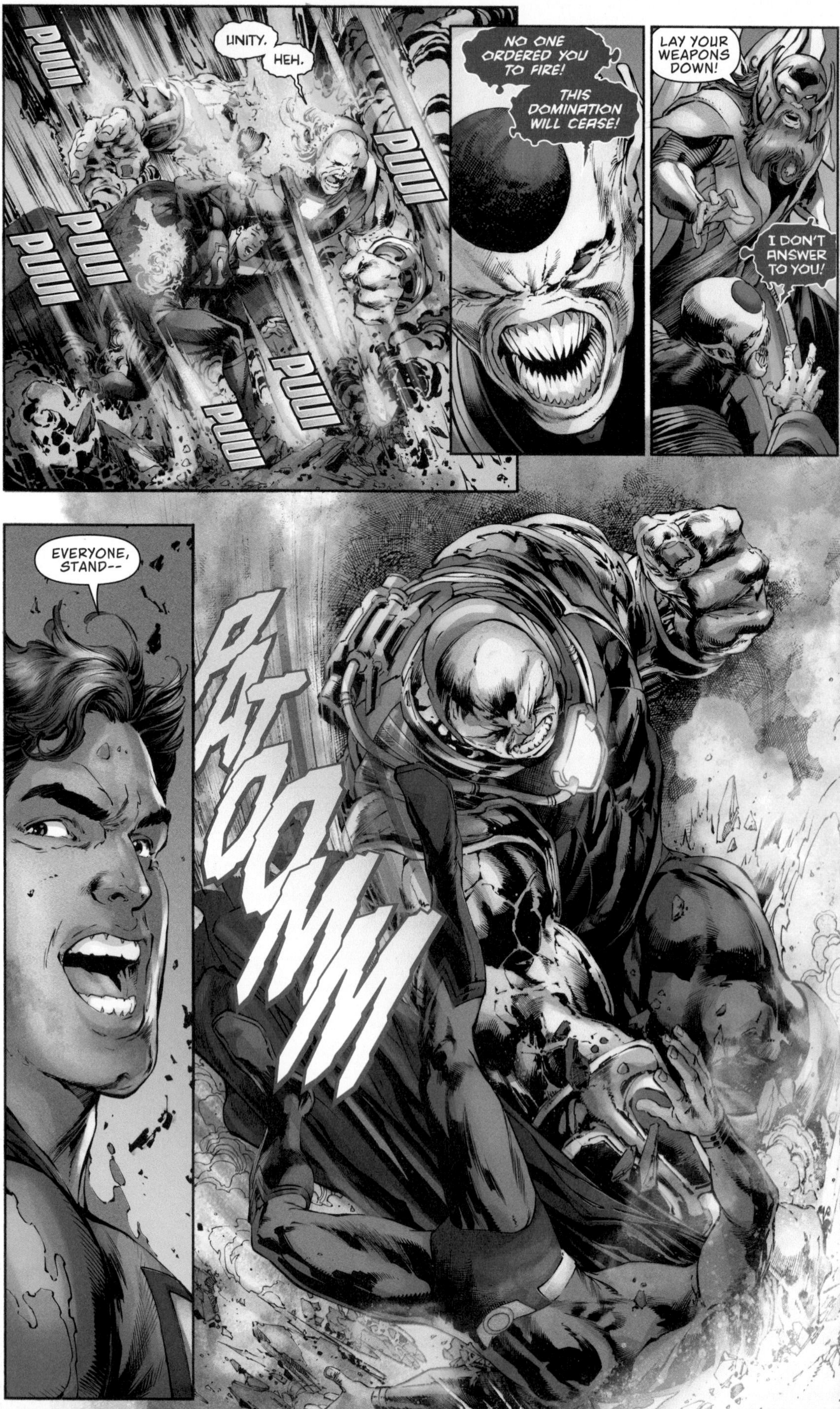

PUUI
UNITY.
HEH.
PUUI
PUUI
PUUI
PUUI
PUUI
NO ONE ORDERED YOU TO FIRE!
THIS DOMINATION WILL CEASE!
LAY YOUR WEAPONS DOWN!
I DON'T ANSWER TO YOU!
EVERYONE, STAND--
BATOOMM

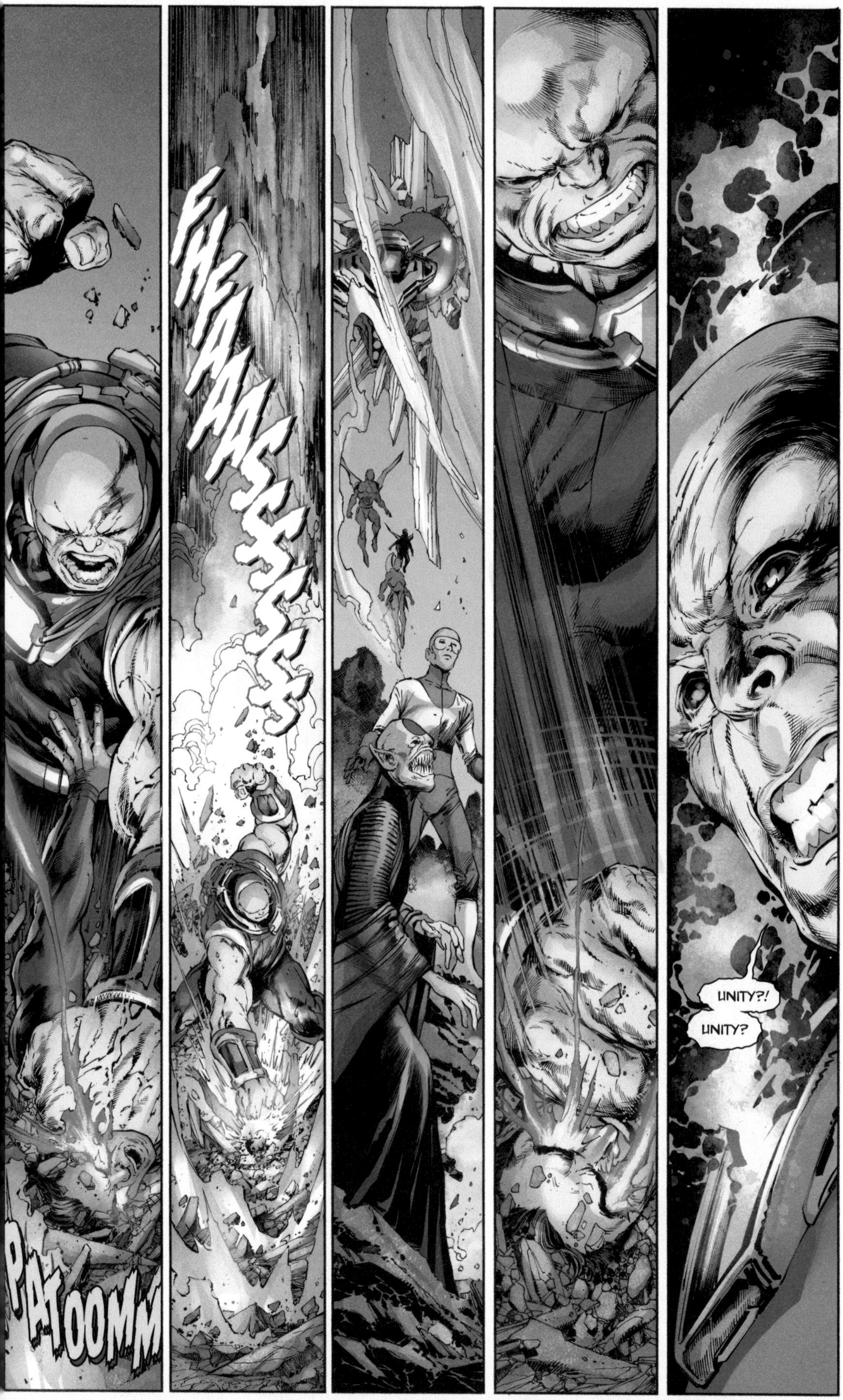
PATOOMM
FWAAAASHSSSS
UNITY?!
UNITY?

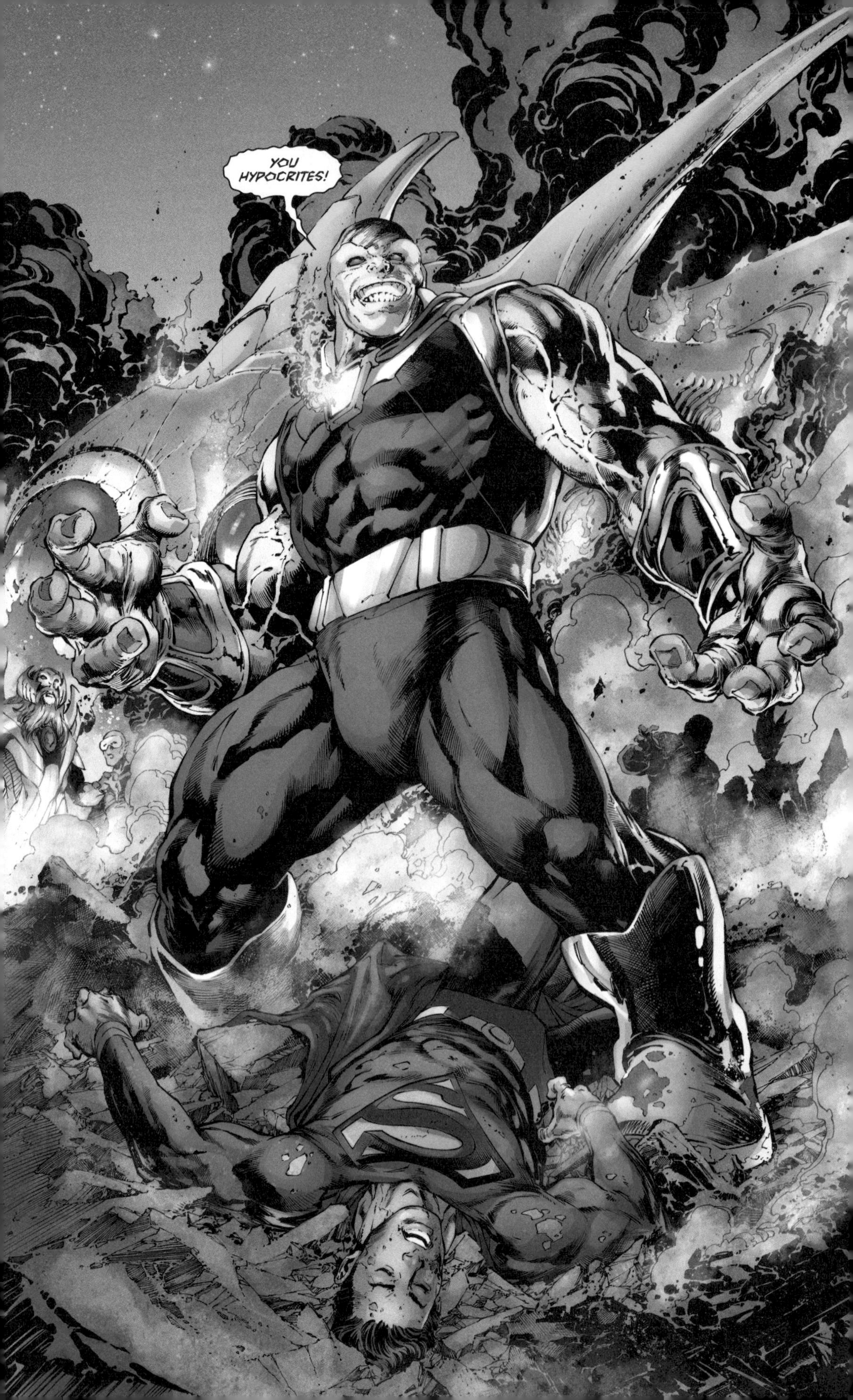
YOU HYPOCRITES!

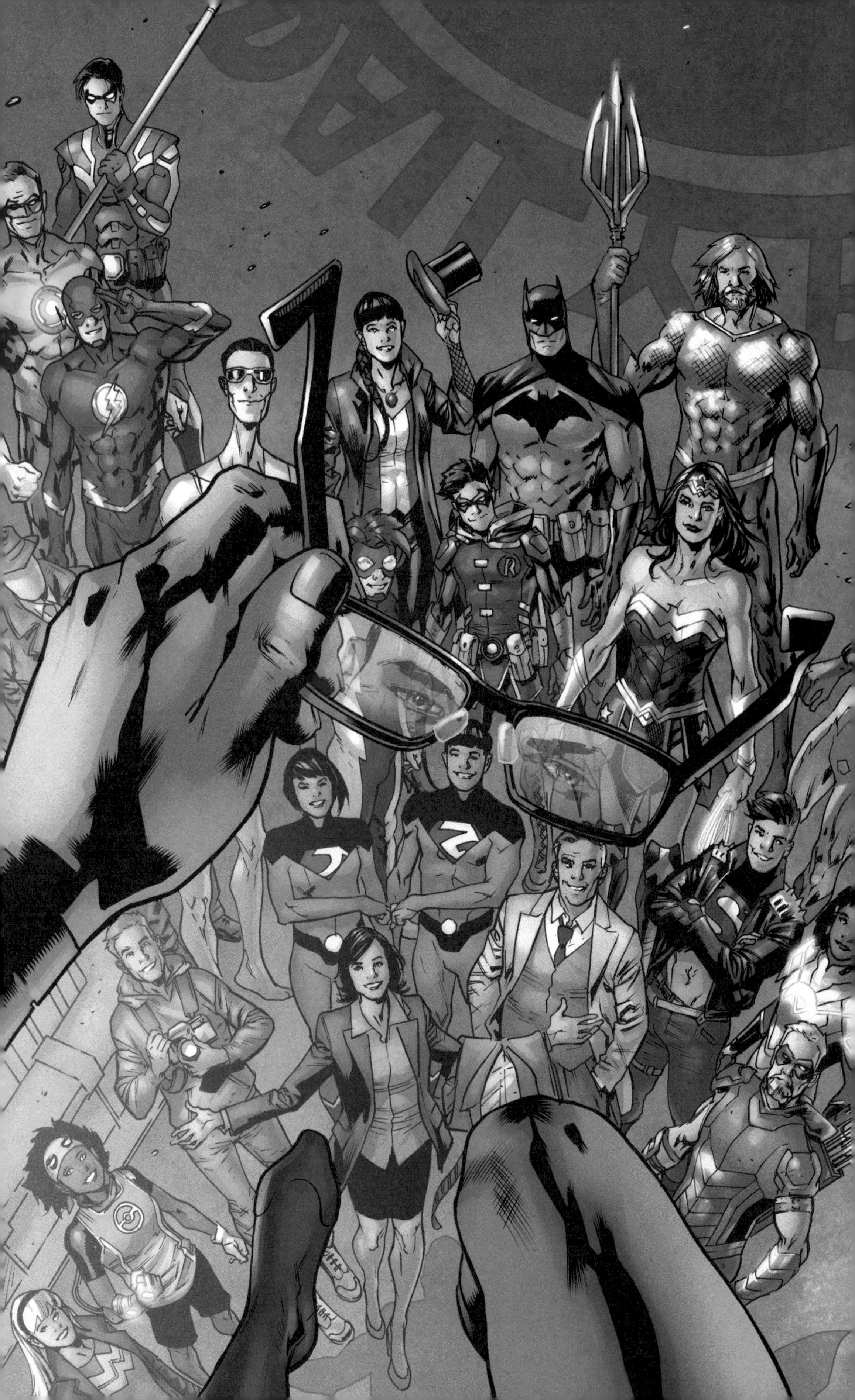

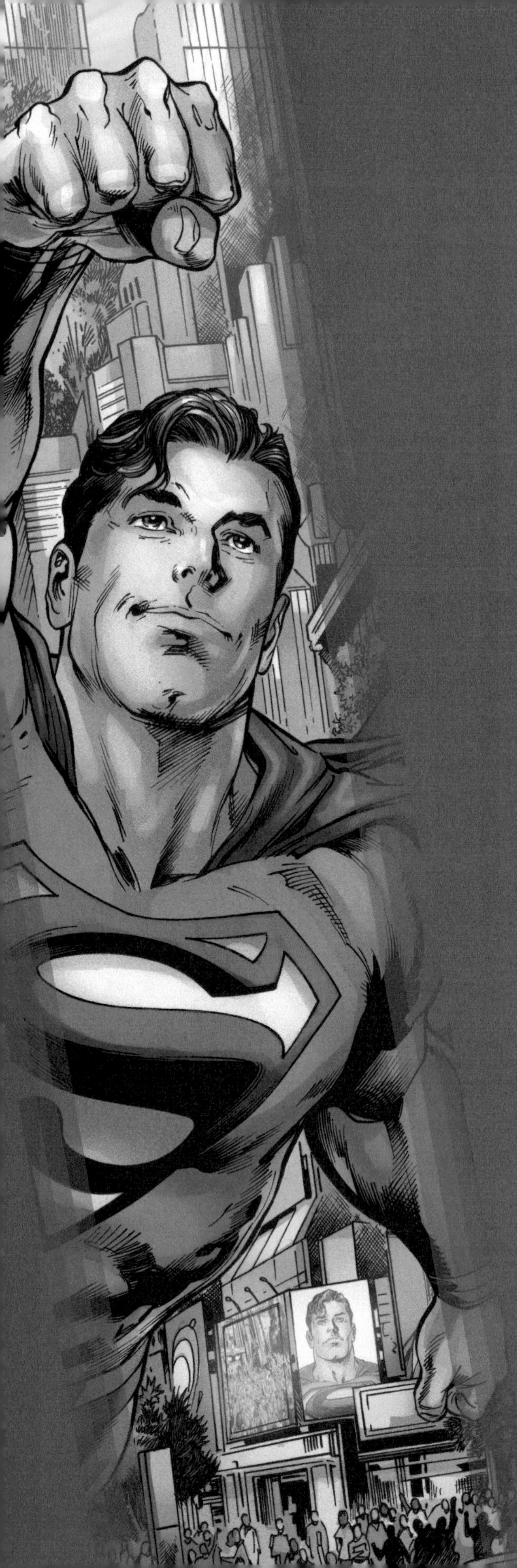

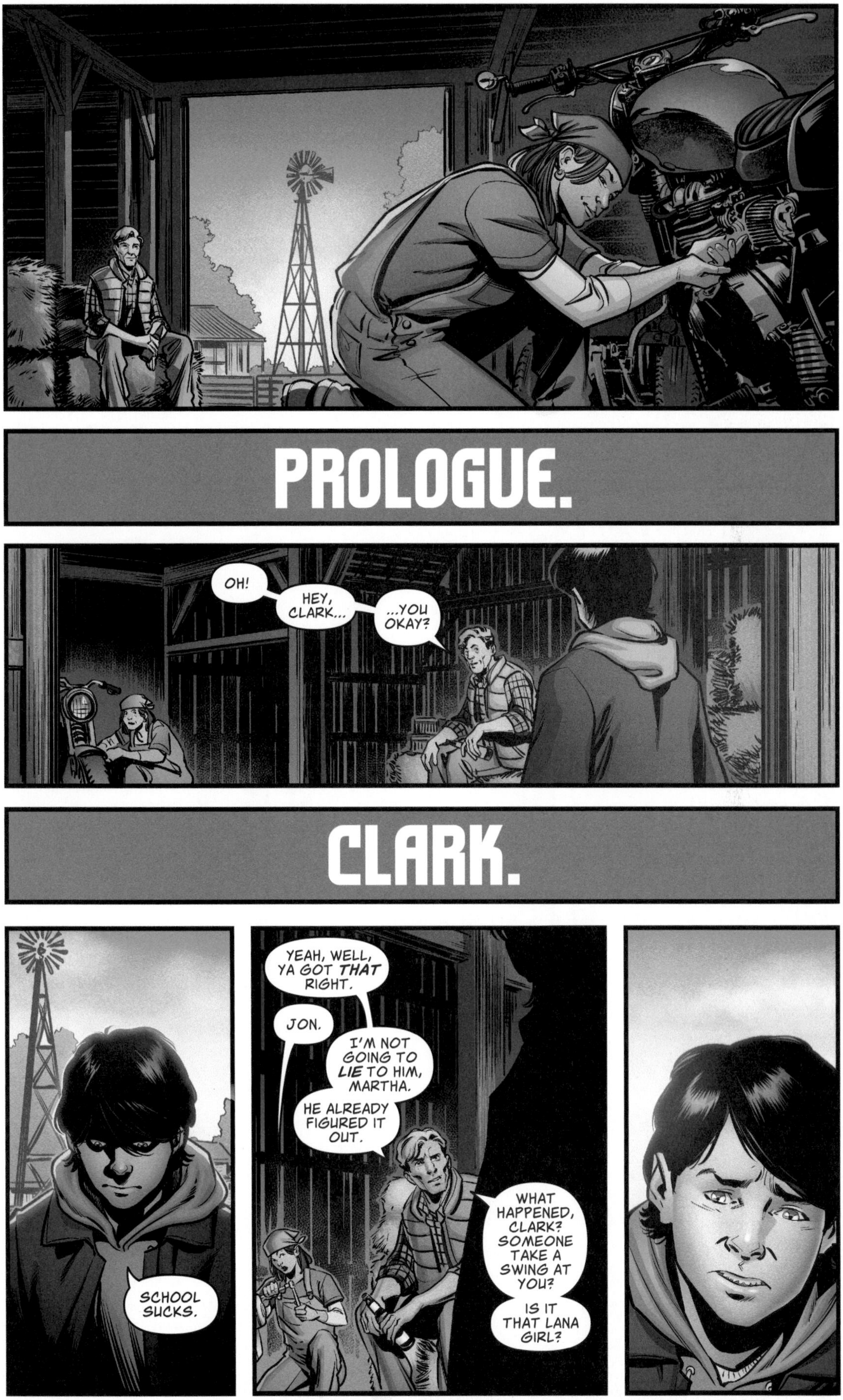
PROLOGUE.
OH!
HEY, CLARK...
...YOU OKAY?
CLARK.
SCHOOL SUCKS.
YEAH, WELL, YA GOT THAT RIGHT.
JON.
I'M NOT GOING TO LIE TO HIM, MARTHA.
HE ALREADY FIGURED IT OUT.
WHAT HAPPENED, CLARK? SOMEONE TAKE A SWING AT YOU?
IS IT THAT LANA GIRL?

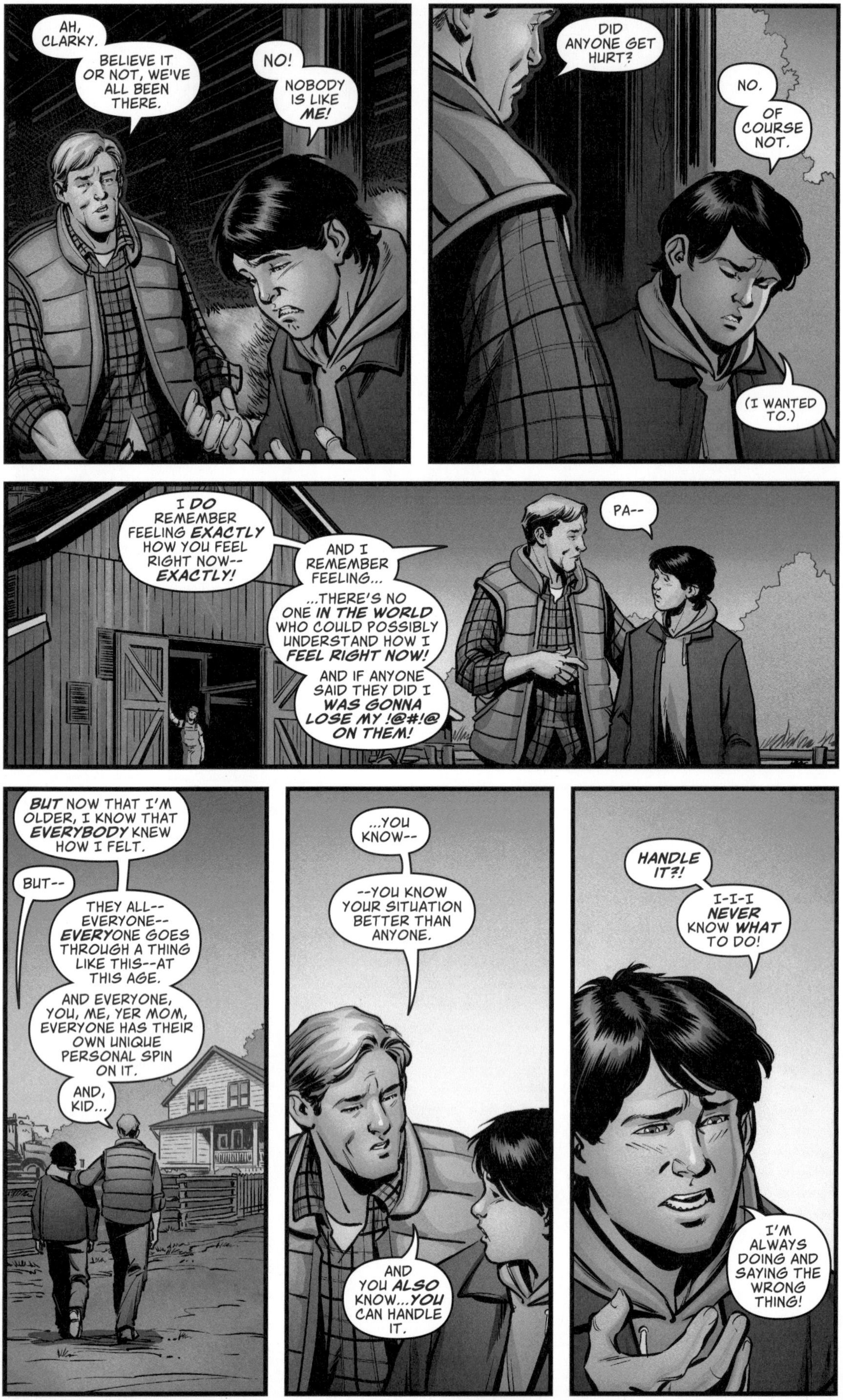

AH, CLARKY.
BELIEVE IT OR NOT, WE'VE ALL BEEN THERE.
NO!
NOBODY IS LIKE ME!
DID ANYONE GET HURT?
NO.
OF COURSE NOT.
(I WANTED TO.)
I DO REMEMBER FEELING EXACTLY HOW YOU FEEL RIGHT NOW-- EXACTLY!
AND I REMEMBER FEELING...
...THERE'S NO ONE IN THE WORLD WHO COULD POSSIBLY UNDERSTAND HOW I FEEL RIGHT NOW!
AND IF ANYONE SAID THEY DID I WAS GONNA LOSE MY !@#!@ ON THEM!
PA--
BUT NOW THAT I'M OLDER, I KNOW THAT EVERYBODY KNEW HOW I FELT.
BUT--
THEY ALL-- EVERYONE-- EVERYONE GOES THROUGH A THING LIKE THIS--AT THIS AGE.
AND EVERYONE, YOU, ME, YER MOM, EVERYONE HAS THEIR OWN UNIQUE PERSONAL SPIN ON IT.
AND, KID...
...YOU KNOW--
--YOU KNOW YOUR SITUATION BETTER THAN ANYONE.
AND YOU ALSO KNOW...YOU CAN HANDLE IT.
HANDLE IT?!
I-I-I NEVER KNOW WHAT TO DO!
I'M ALWAYS DOING AND SAYING THE WRONG THING!

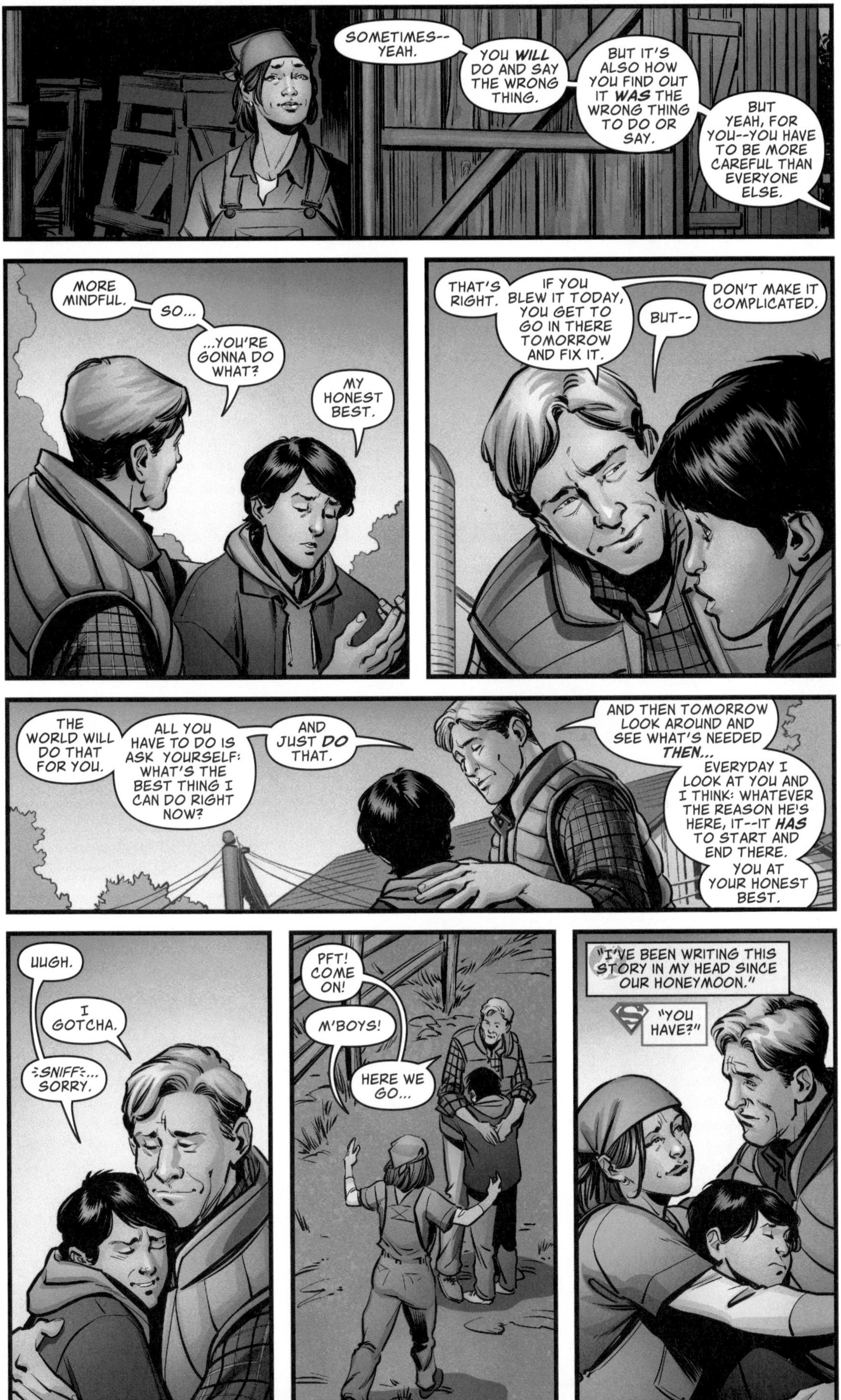
SOMETIMES--YEAH.
YOU WILL DO AND SAY THE WRONG THING.
BUT IT'S ALSO HOW YOU FIND OUT IT WAS THE WRONG THING TO DO OR SAY.
BUT YEAH, FOR YOU--YOU HAVE TO BE MORE CAREFUL THAN EVERYONE ELSE.
MORE MINDFUL.
SO...
...YOU'RE GONNA DO WHAT?
MY HONEST BEST.
THAT'S RIGHT.
IF YOU BLEW IT TODAY, YOU GET TO GO IN THERE TOMORROW AND FIX IT.
BUT--
DON'T MAKE IT COMPLICATED.
THE WORLD WILL DO THAT FOR YOU.
ALL YOU HAVE TO DO IS ASK YOURSELF: WHAT'S THE BEST THING I CAN DO RIGHT NOW?
AND JUST DO THAT.
AND THEN TOMORROW LOOK AROUND AND SEE WHAT'S NEEDED THEN...
EVERYDAY I LOOK AT YOU AND I THINK: WHATEVER THE REASON HE'S HERE, IT--IT HAS TO START AND END THERE.
YOU AT YOUR HONEST BEST.
UUGH.
I GOTCHA.
SNIFF... SORRY.
PFT! COME ON!
M'BOYS!
HERE WE GO...
"I'VE BEEN WRITING THIS STORY IN MY HEAD SINCE OUR HONEYMOON."
"YOU HAVE?"

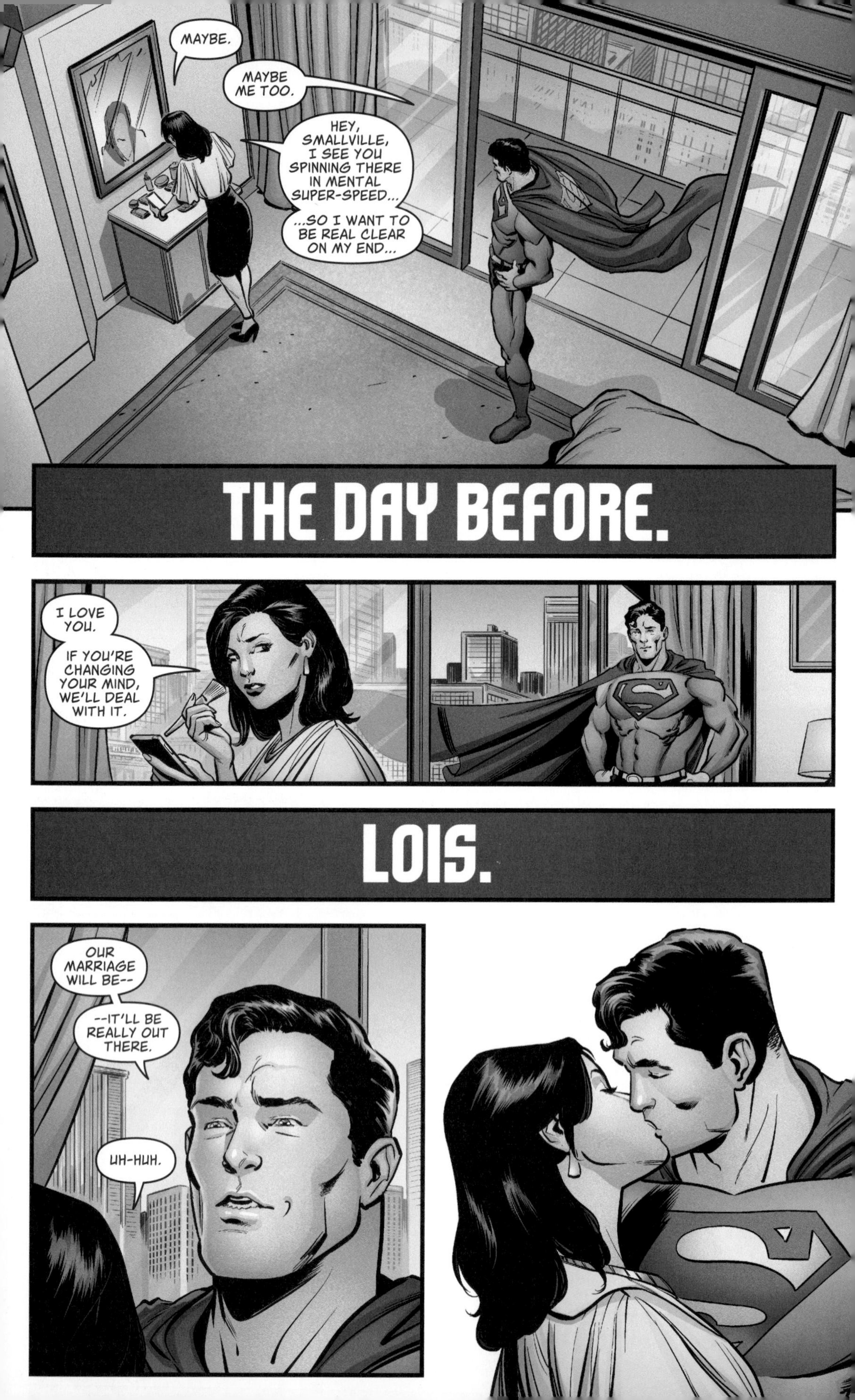
MAYBE.
MAYBE ME TOO.
HEY, SMALLVILLE, I SEE YOU SPINNING THERE IN MENTAL SUPER-SPEED...
...SO I WANT TO BE REAL CLEAR ON MY END...
THE DAY BEFORE.
I LOVE YOU.
IF YOU'RE CHANGING YOUR MIND, WE'LL DEAL WITH IT.
LOIS.
OUR MARRIAGE WILL BE--
--IT'LL BE REALLY OUT THERE.
UH-HUH.

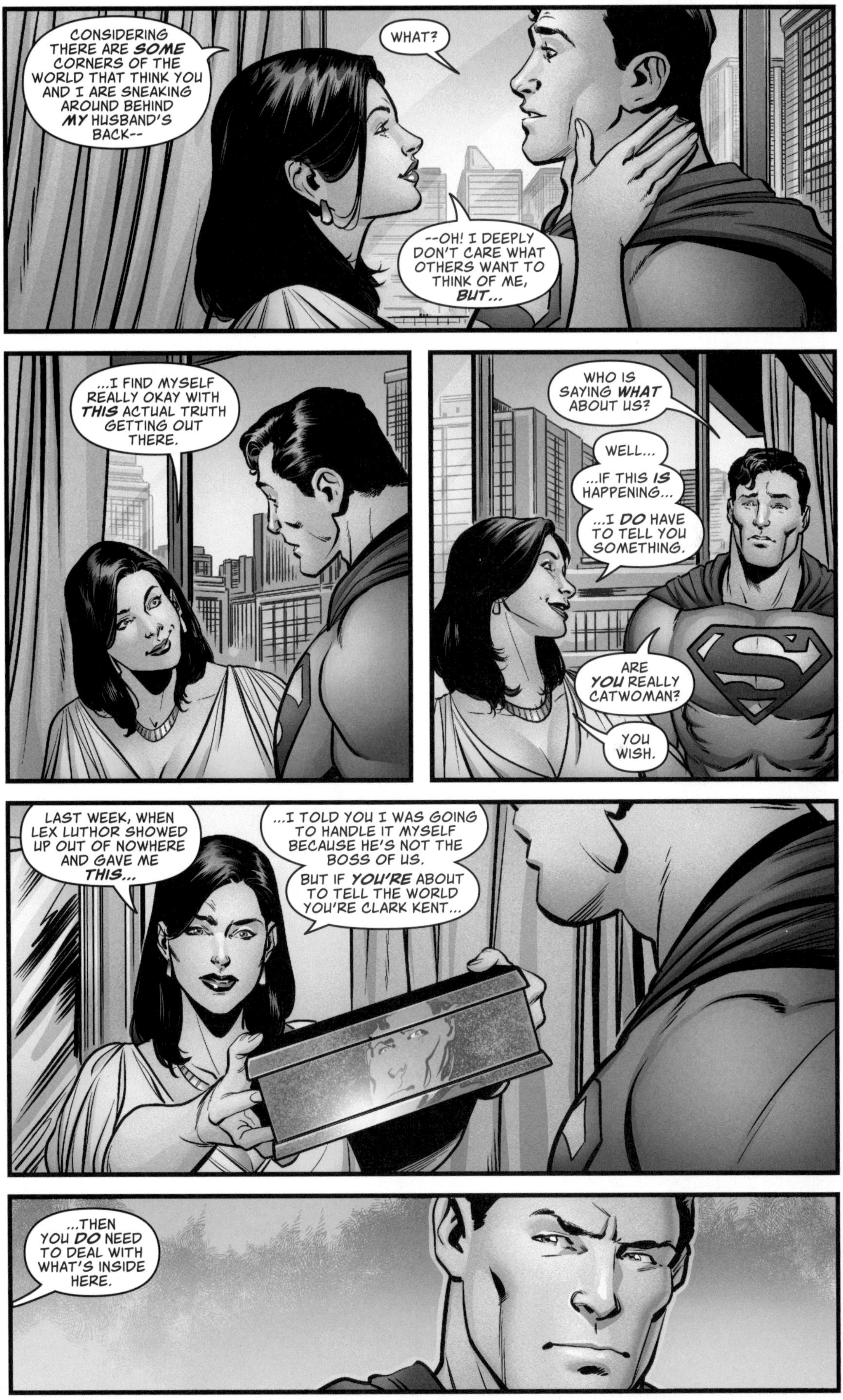
CONSIDERING THERE ARE SOME CORNERS OF THE WORLD THAT THINK YOU AND I ARE SNEAKING AROUND BEHIND MY HUSBAND'S BACK--
WHAT?
--OH! I DEEPLY DON'T CARE WHAT OTHERS WANT TO THINK OF ME, BUT...
...I FIND MYSELF REALLY OKAY WITH THIS ACTUAL TRUTH GETTING OUT THERE.
WHO IS SAYING WHAT ABOUT US?
WELL...
...IF THIS IS HAPPENING...
...I DO HAVE TO TELL YOU SOMETHING.
ARE YOU REALLY CATWOMAN?
YOU WISH.
LAST WEEK, WHEN LEX LUTHOR SHOWED UP OUT OF NOWHERE AND GAVE ME THIS...
...I TOLD YOU I WAS GOING TO HANDLE IT MYSELF BECAUSE HE'S NOT THE BOSS OF US.
BUT IF YOU'RE ABOUT TO TELL THE WORLD YOU'RE CLARK KENT...
...THEN YOU DO NEED TO DEAL WITH WHAT'S INSIDE HERE.

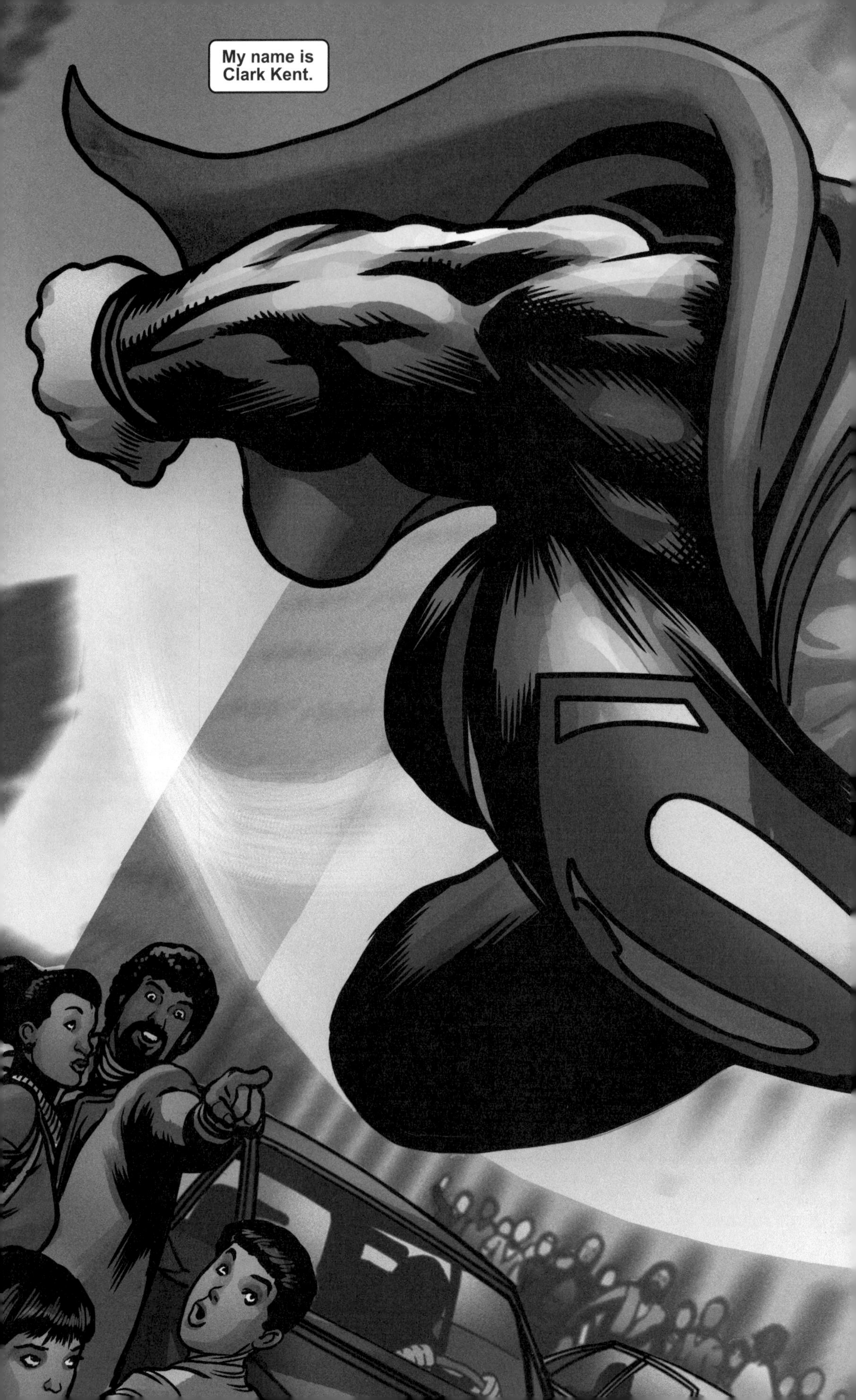
My name is
Clark Kent.

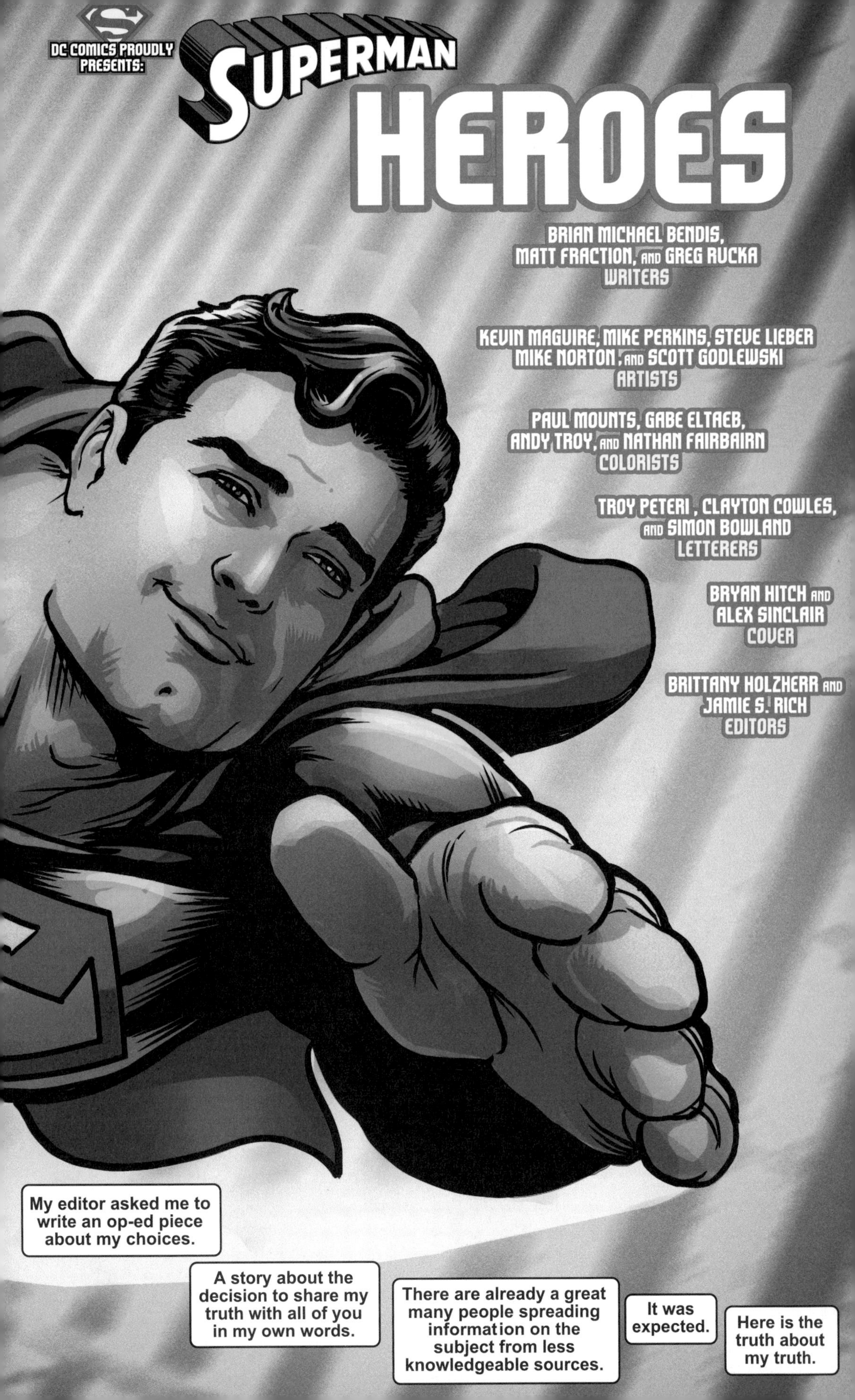
DC COMICS PROUDLY PRESENTS:
SUPERMAN
HEROES
BRIAN MICHAEL BENDIS, MATT FRACTION, AND GREG RUCKA WRITERS
KEVIN MAGUIRE, MIKE PERKINS, STEVE LIEBER MIKE NORTON, AND SCOTT GODLEWSKI ARTISTS
PAUL MOUNTS, GABE ELTAEB, ANDY TROY, AND NATHAN FAIRBAIRN COLORISTS
TROY PETERI, CLAYTON COWLES, AND SIMON BOWLAND LETTERERS
BRYAN HITCH AND ALEX SINCLAIR COVER
BRITTANY HOLZHERR AND JAMIE S. RICH EDITORS
My editor asked me to write an op-ed piece about my choices.
A story about the decision to share my truth with all of you in my own words.
There are already a great many people spreading information on the subject from less knowledgeable sources.
It was expected.
Here is the truth about my truth.

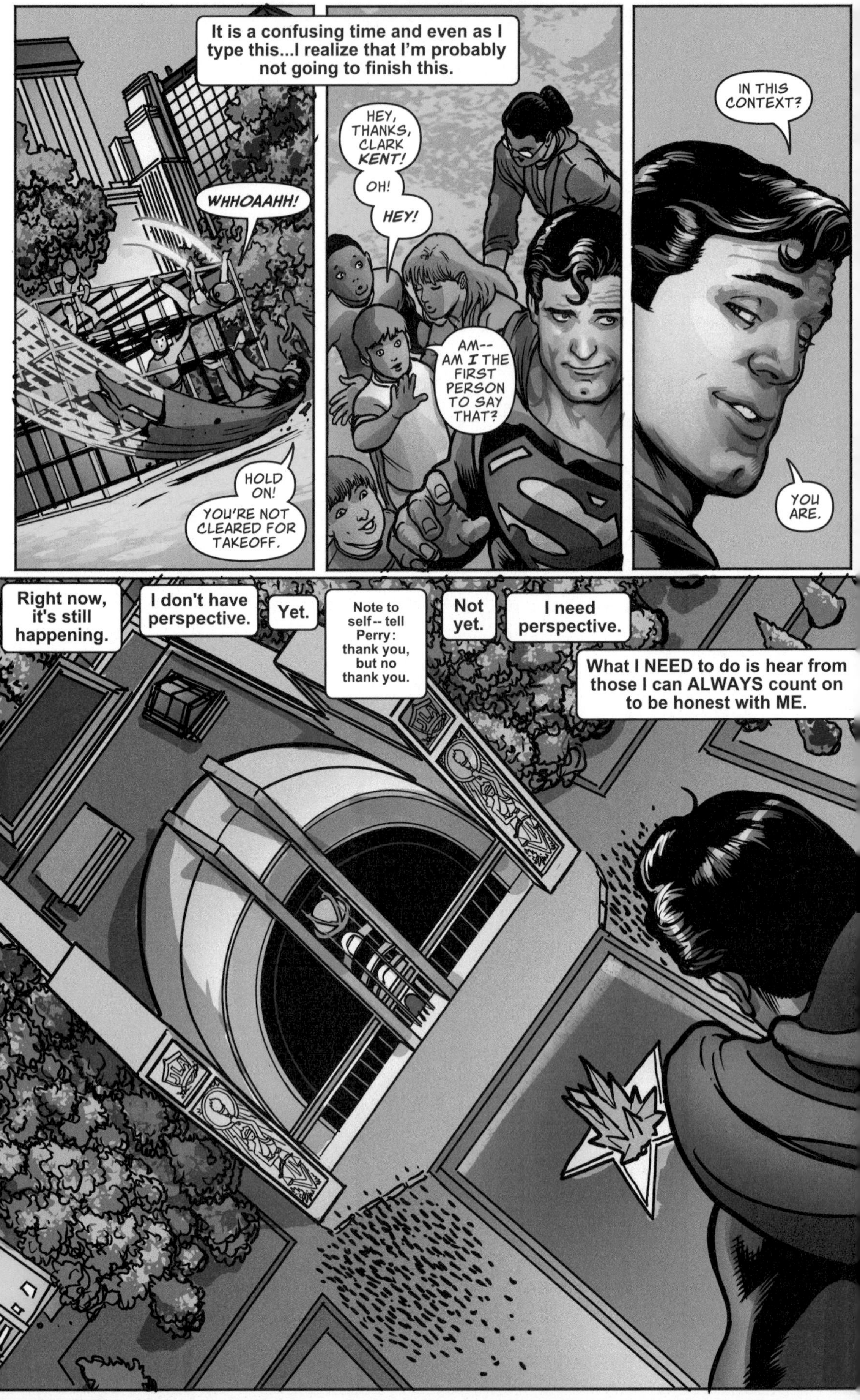

It is a confusing time and even as I type this...I realize that I'm probably not going to finish this.
WHHOAAHH!
HOLD ON!
YOU'RE NOT CLEARED FOR TAKEOFF.
HEY, THANKS, CLARK KENT!
OH!
HEY!
AM-- AM I THE FIRST PERSON TO SAY THAT?
IN THIS CONTEXT?
YOU ARE.
Right now, it's still happening.
I don't have perspective.
Yet.
Note to self-- tell Perry: thank you, but no thank you.
Not yet.
I need perspective.
What I NEED to do is hear from those I can ALWAYS count on to be honest with ME.

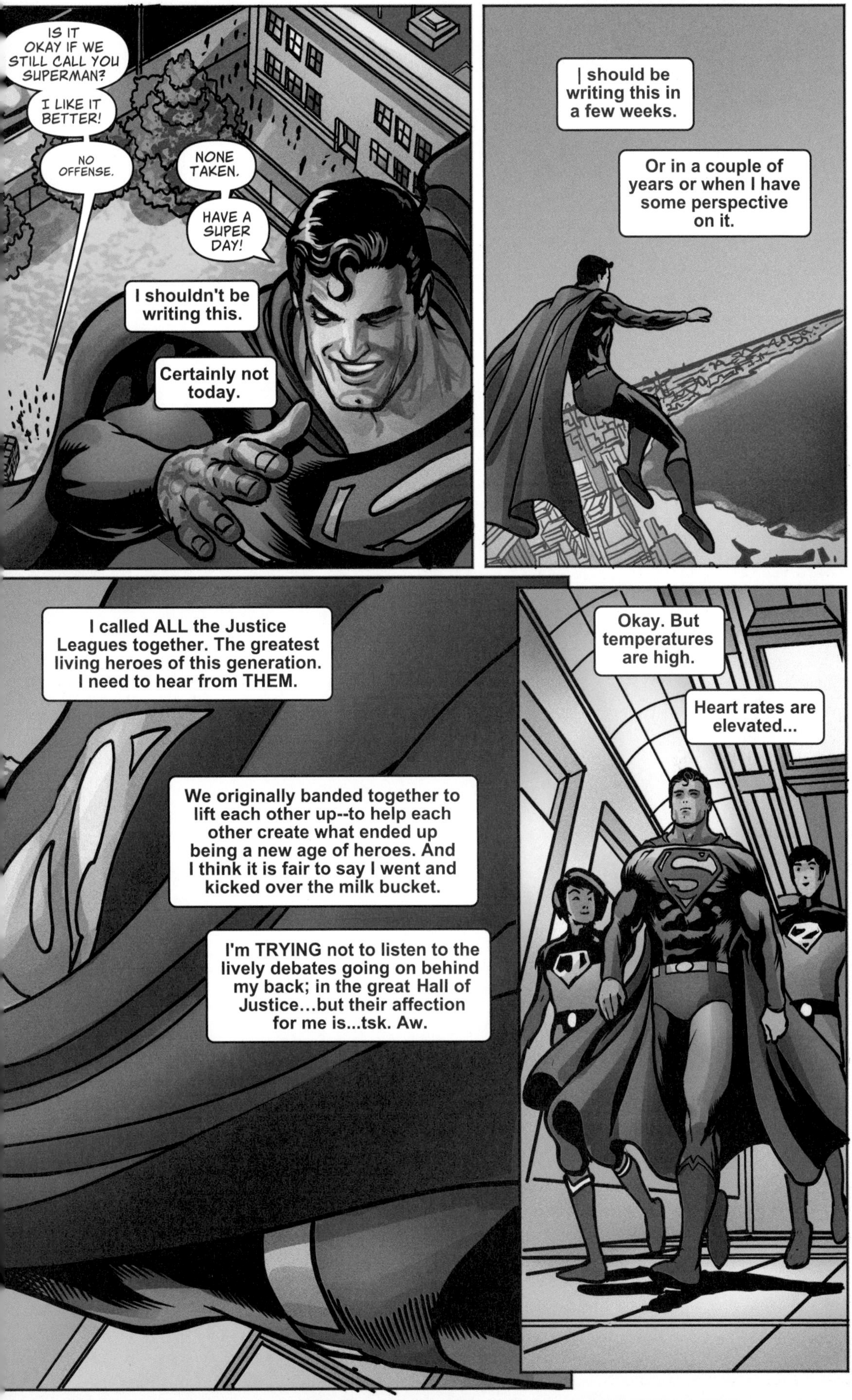
IS IT OKAY IF WE STILL CALL YOU SUPERMAN?
I LIKE IT BETTER!
NO OFFENSE.
NONE TAKEN.
HAVE A SUPER DAY!
I shouldn't be writing this.
Certainly not today.
I should be writing this in a few weeks.
Or in a couple of years or when I have some perspective on it.
I called ALL the Justice Leagues together. The greatest living heroes of this generation. I need to hear from THEM.
We originally banded together to lift each other up--to help each other create what ended up being a new age of heroes. And I think it is fair to say I went and kicked over the milk bucket.
I'm TRYING not to listen to the lively debates going on behind my back; in the great Hall of Justice…but their affection for me is...tsk. Aw.
Okay. But temperatures are high.
Heart rates are elevated...

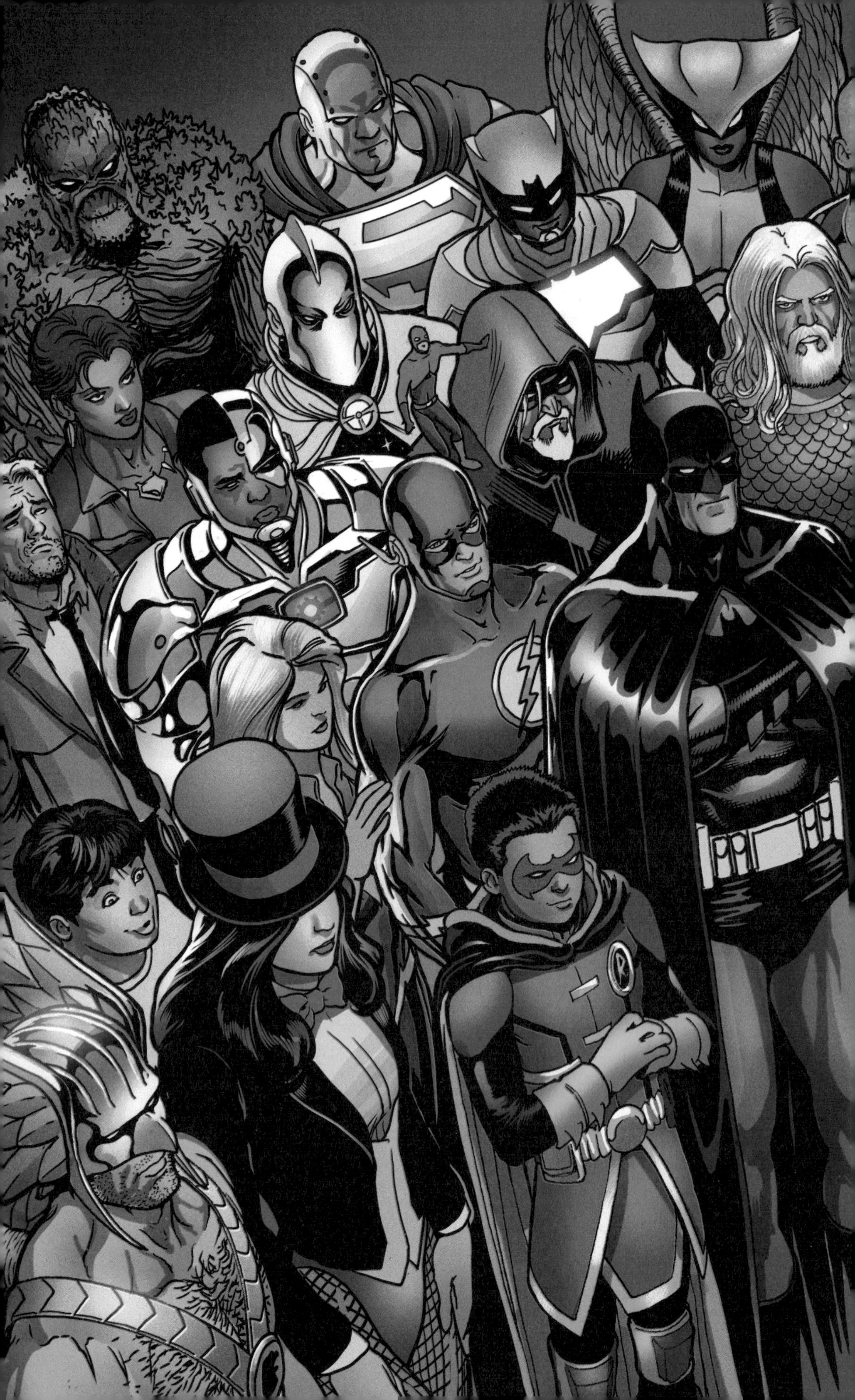

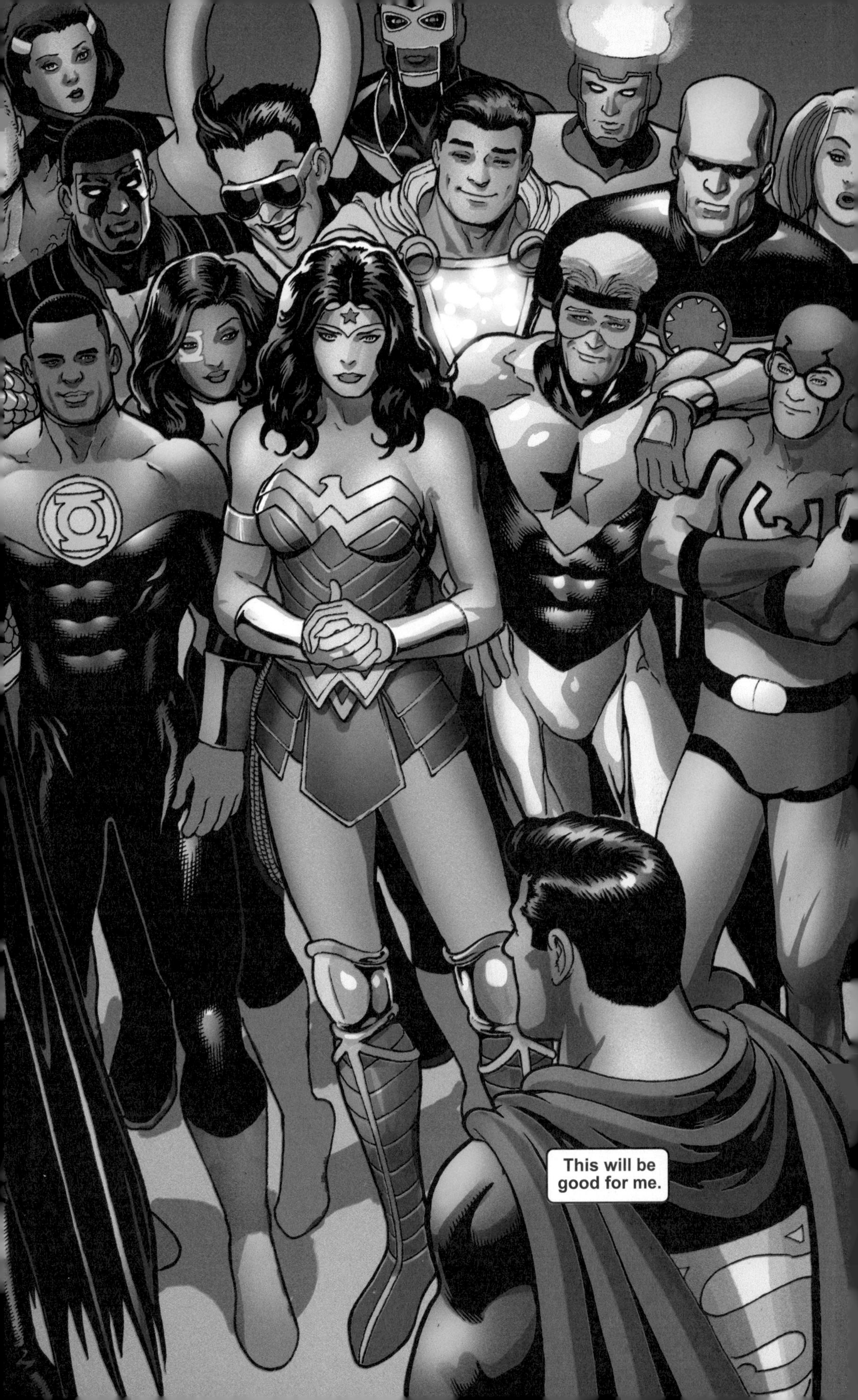
This will be good for me.

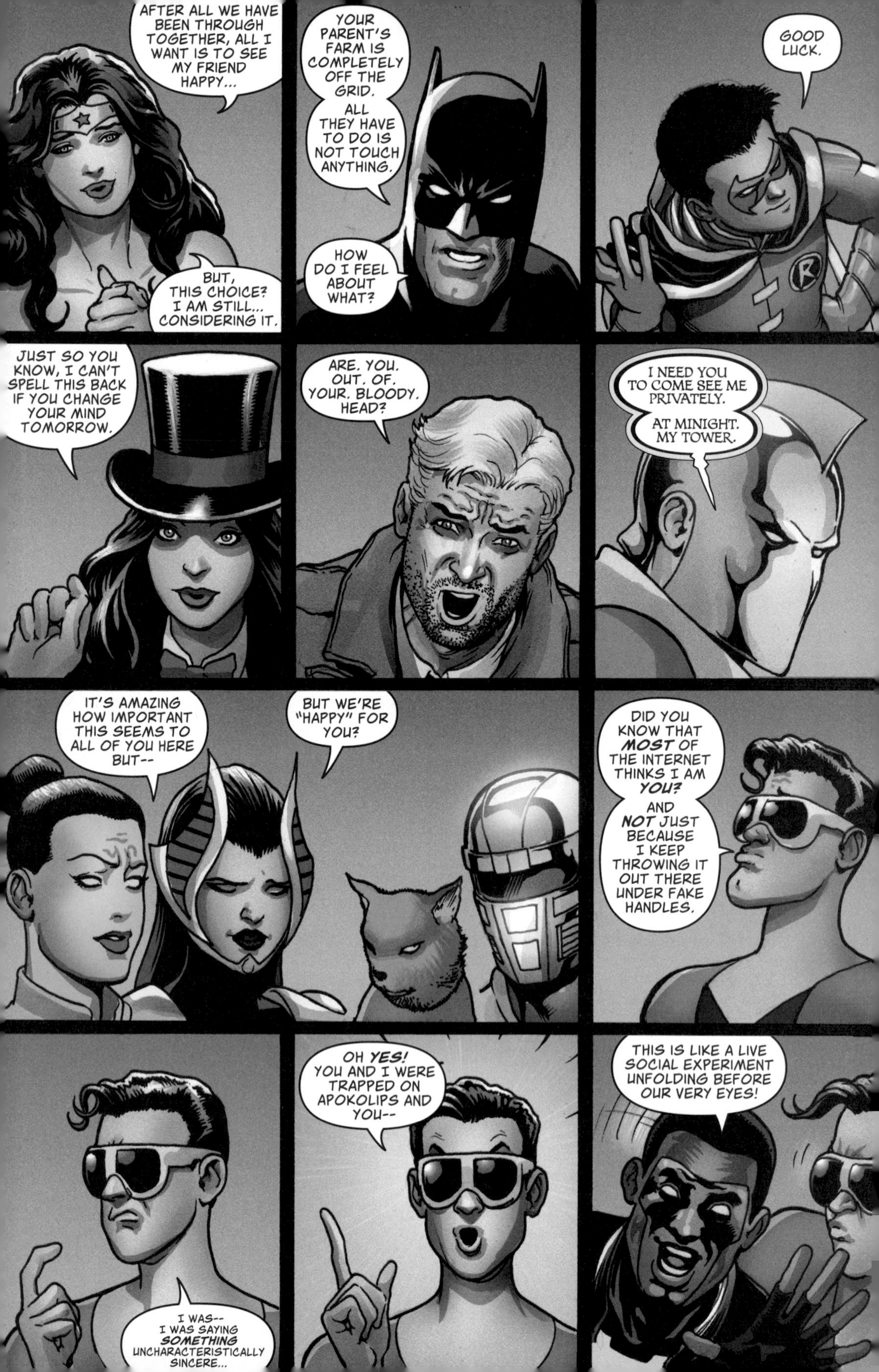
AFTER ALL WE HAVE BEEN THROUGH TOGETHER, ALL I WANT IS TO SEE MY FRIEND HAPPY...
BUT, THIS CHOICE? I AM STILL... CONSIDERING IT.
YOUR PARENT'S FARM IS COMPLETELY OFF THE GRID.
ALL THEY HAVE TO DO IS NOT TOUCH ANYTHING.
HOW DO I FEEL ABOUT WHAT?
GOOD LUCK.
JUST SO YOU KNOW, I CAN'T SPELL THIS BACK IF YOU CHANGE YOUR MIND TOMORROW.
ARE. YOU. OUT. OF. YOUR. BLOODY. HEAD?
I NEED YOU TO COME SEE ME PRIVATELY.
AT MINIGHT. MY TOWER.
IT'S AMAZING HOW IMPORTANT THIS SEEMS TO ALL OF YOU HERE BUT--
BUT WE'RE "HAPPY" FOR YOU?
DID YOU KNOW THAT MOST OF THE INTERNET THINKS I AM YOU?
AND NOT JUST BECAUSE I KEEP THROWING IT OUT THERE UNDER FAKE HANDLES.
I WAS-- I WAS SAYING SOMETHING UNCHARACTERISTICALLY SINCERE...
OH YES! YOU AND I WERE TRAPPED ON APOKOLIPS AND YOU--
THIS IS LIKE A LIVE SOCIAL EXPERIMENT UNFOLDING BEFORE OUR VERY EYES!

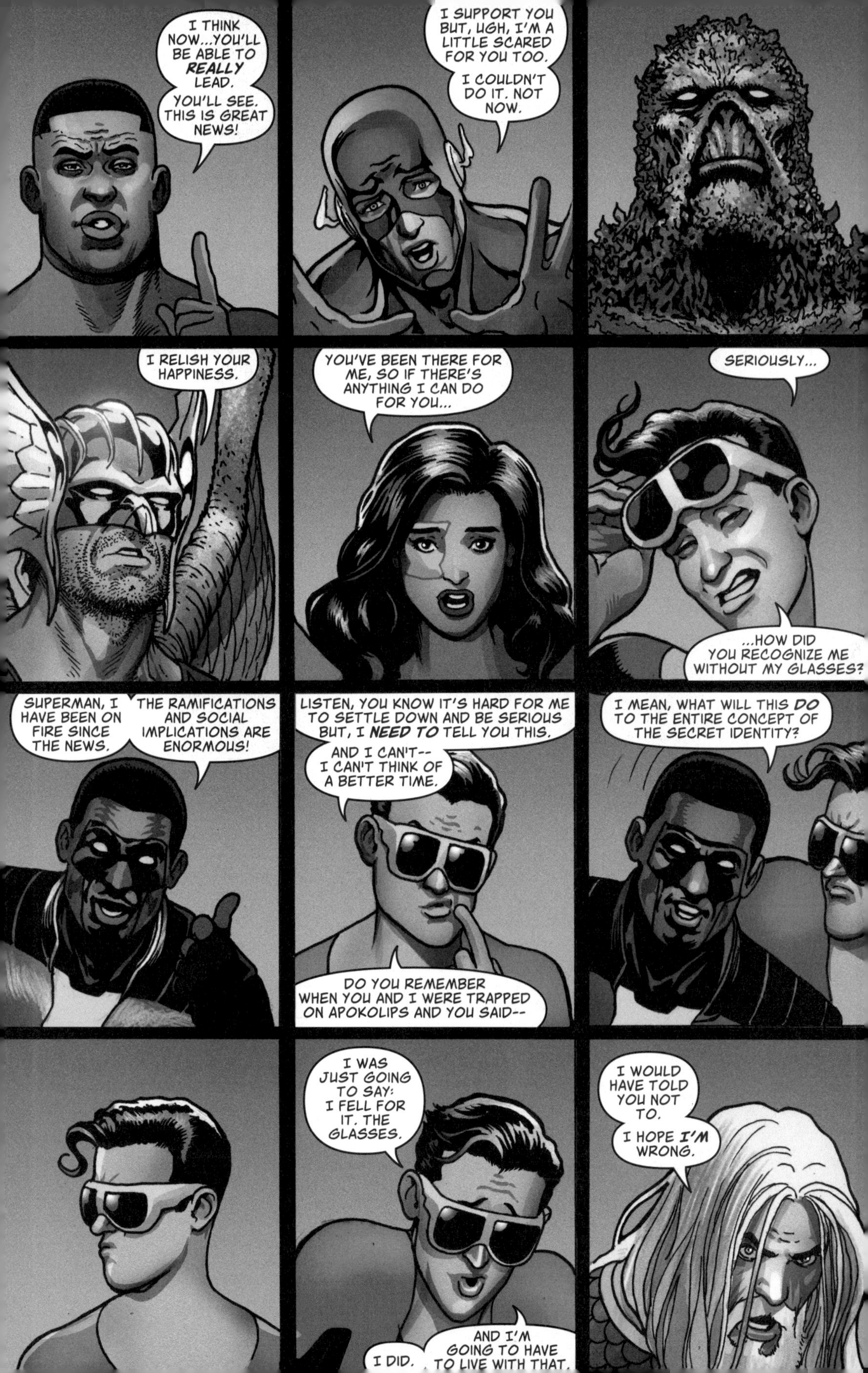
I THINK NOW...YOU'LL BE ABLE TO **REALLY** LEAD.
YOU'LL SEE. THIS IS GREAT NEWS!
I SUPPORT YOU BUT, UGH, I'M A LITTLE SCARED FOR YOU TOO.
I COULDN'T DO IT. NOT NOW.
I RELISH YOUR HAPPINESS.
YOU'VE BEEN THERE FOR ME, SO IF THERE'S ANYTHING I CAN DO FOR YOU...
SERIOUSLY...
...HOW DID YOU RECOGNIZE ME WITHOUT MY GLASSES?
SUPERMAN, I HAVE BEEN ON FIRE SINCE THE NEWS.
THE RAMIFICATIONS AND SOCIAL IMPLICATIONS ARE ENORMOUS!
LISTEN, YOU KNOW IT'S HARD FOR ME TO SETTLE DOWN AND BE SERIOUS BUT, I **NEED TO** TELL YOU THIS.
AND I CAN'T-- I CAN'T THINK OF A BETTER TIME.
DO YOU REMEMBER WHEN YOU AND I WERE TRAPPED ON APOKOLIPS AND YOU SAID--
I MEAN, WHAT WILL THIS **DO** TO THE ENTIRE CONCEPT OF THE SECRET IDENTITY?
I WAS JUST GOING TO SAY: I FELL FOR IT. THE GLASSES.
I DID.
AND I'M GOING TO HAVE TO LIVE WITH THAT.
I WOULD HAVE TOLD YOU NOT TO.
I HOPE **I'M** WRONG.

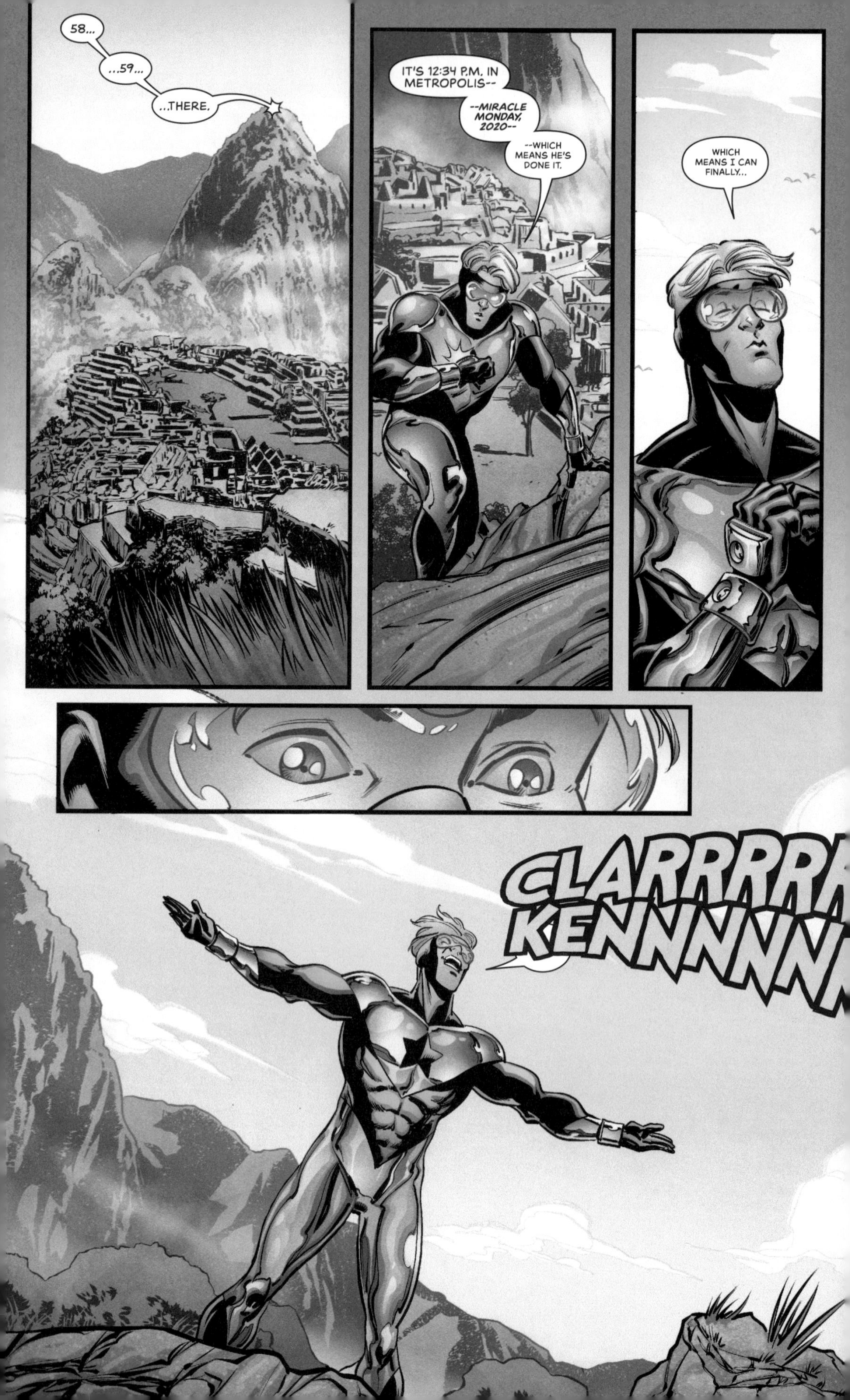
58...
...59...
...THERE.
IT'S 12:34 P.M. IN METROPOLIS--
--MIRACLE MONDAY, 2020--
--WHICH MEANS HE'S DONE IT.
WHICH MEANS I CAN FINALLY...
CLARRRRR
KENNNNNN

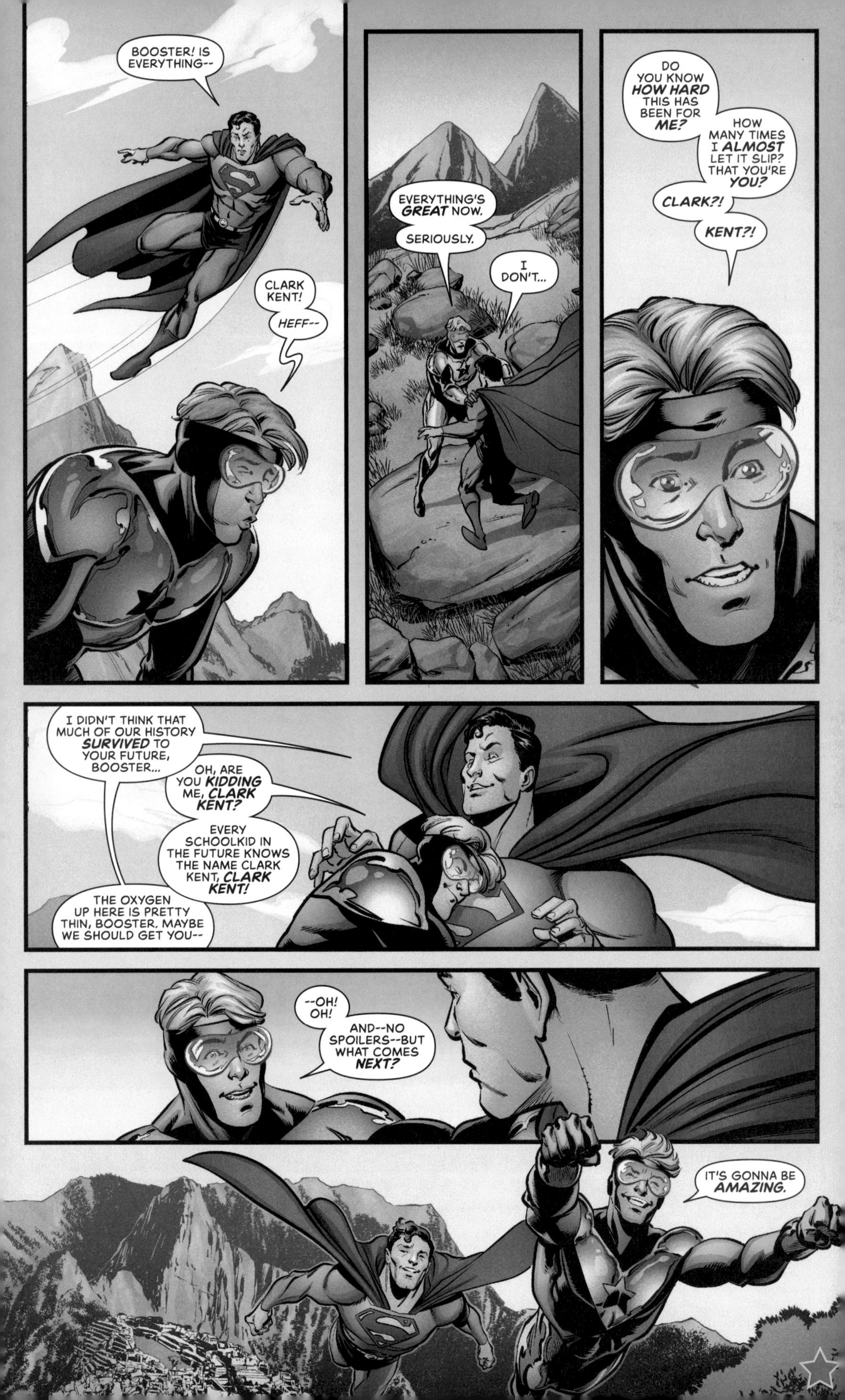
BOOSTER! IS EVERYTHING--
CLARK KENT!
HEFF--
EVERYTHING'S GREAT NOW.
SERIOUSLY.
I DON'T...
DO YOU KNOW HOW HARD THIS HAS BEEN FOR ME?
HOW MANY TIMES I ALMOST LET IT SLIP? THAT YOU'RE YOU?
CLARK?!
KENT?!
I DIDN'T THINK THAT MUCH OF OUR HISTORY SURVIVED TO YOUR FUTURE, BOOSTER...
OH, ARE YOU KIDDING ME, CLARK KENT?
EVERY SCHOOLKID IN THE FUTURE KNOWS THE NAME CLARK KENT, CLARK KENT!
THE OXYGEN UP HERE IS PRETTY THIN, BOOSTER. MAYBE WE SHOULD GET YOU--
--OH! OH!
AND--NO SPOILERS--BUT WHAT COMES NEXT?
IT'S GONNA BE AMAZING.

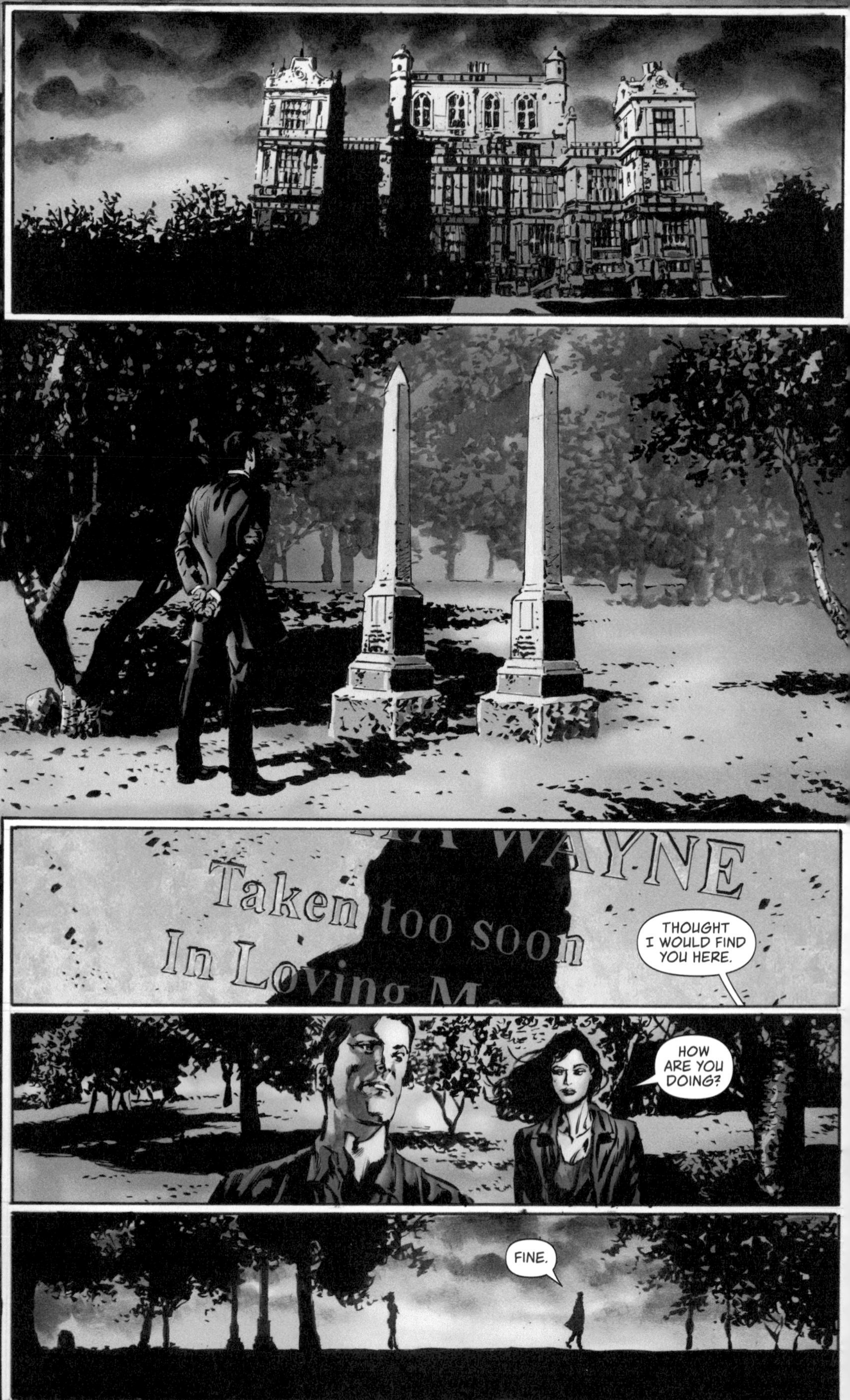
WAYNE
Taken too soon
In Loving
THOUGHT I WOULD FIND YOU HERE.
HOW ARE YOU DOING?
FINE.

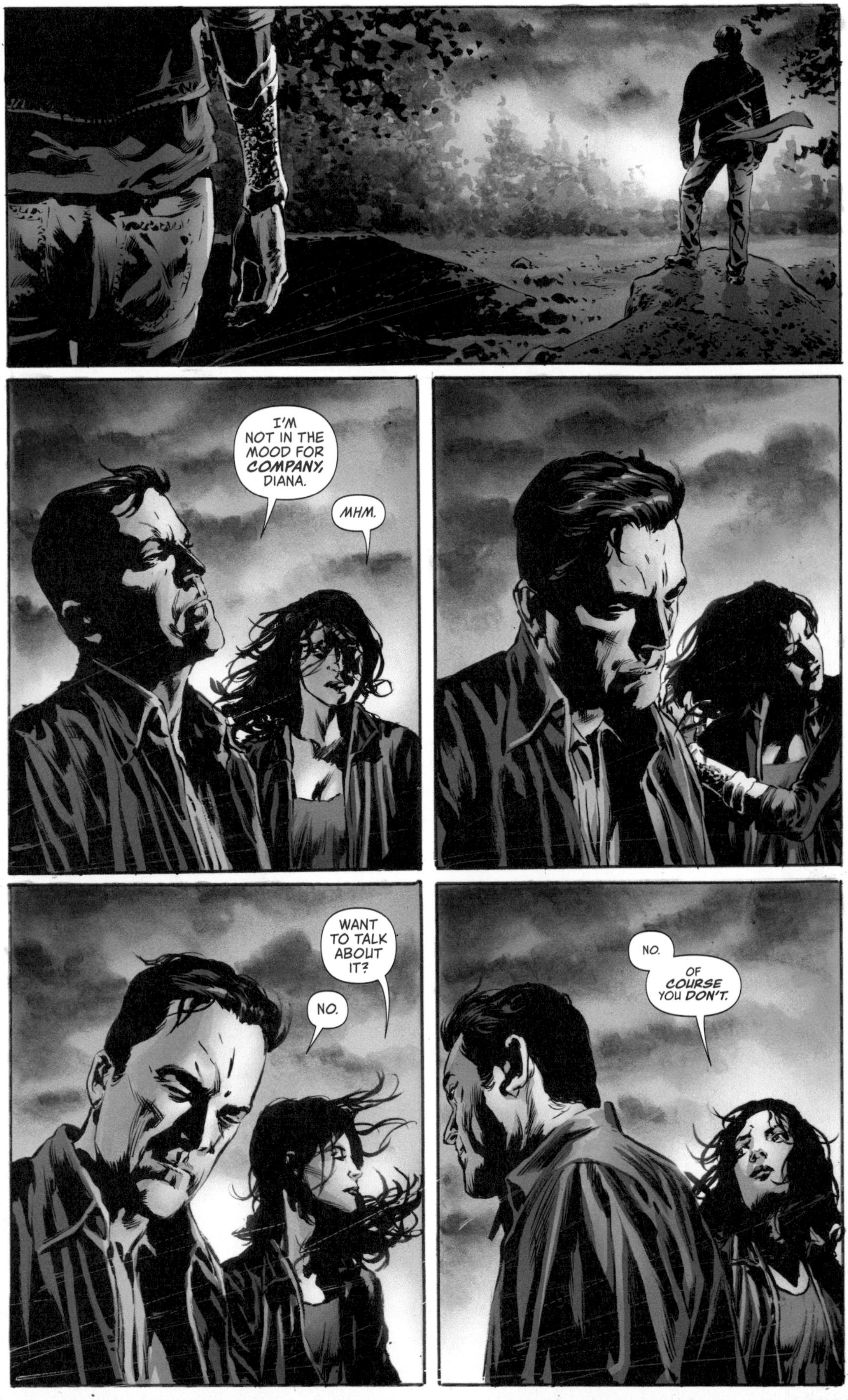
I'M NOT IN THE MOOD FOR COMPANY, DIANA.
MHM.
WANT TO TALK ABOUT IT?
NO.
NO.
OF COURSE YOU DON'T.

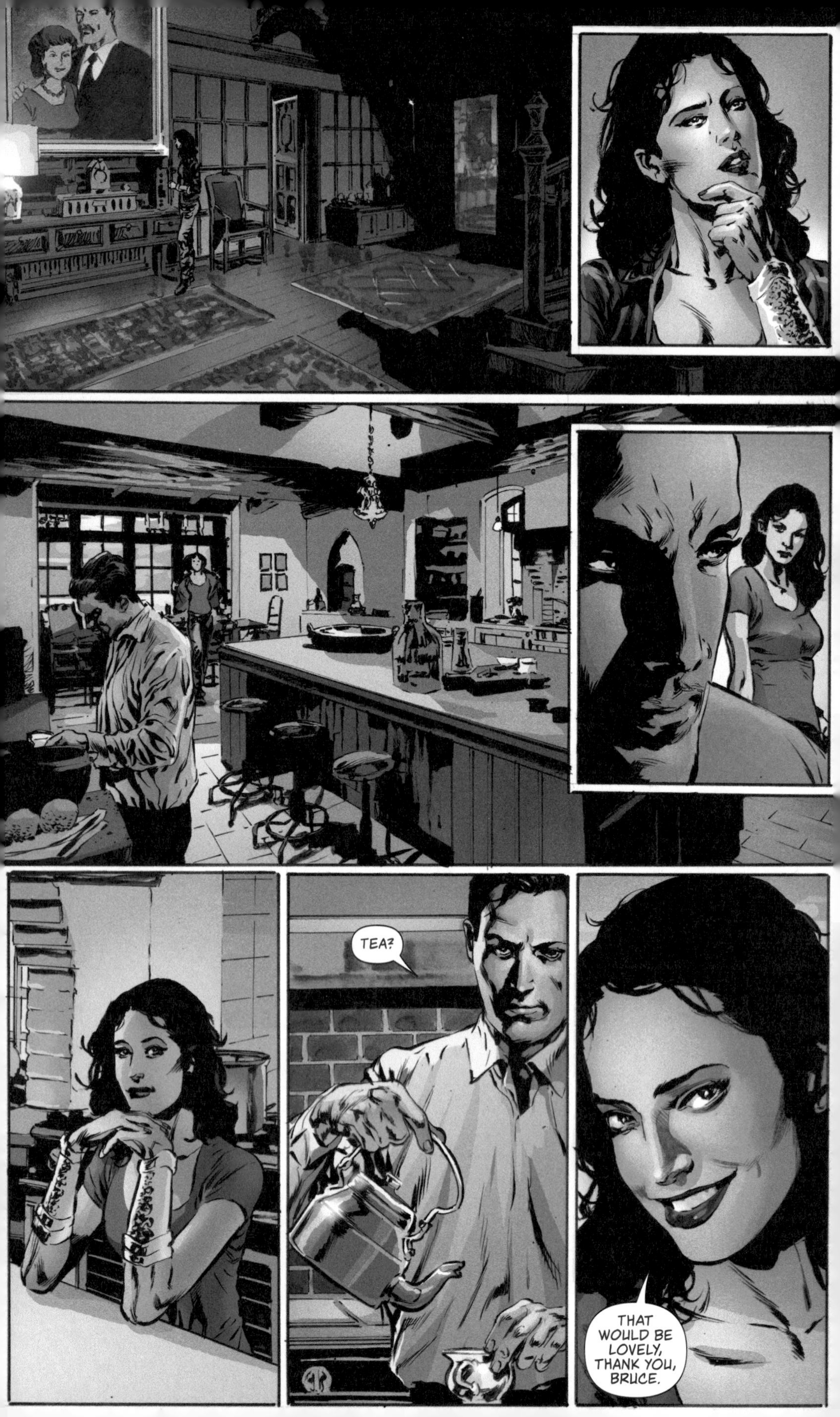
TEA?
THAT WOULD BE LOVELY, THANK YOU, BRUCE.

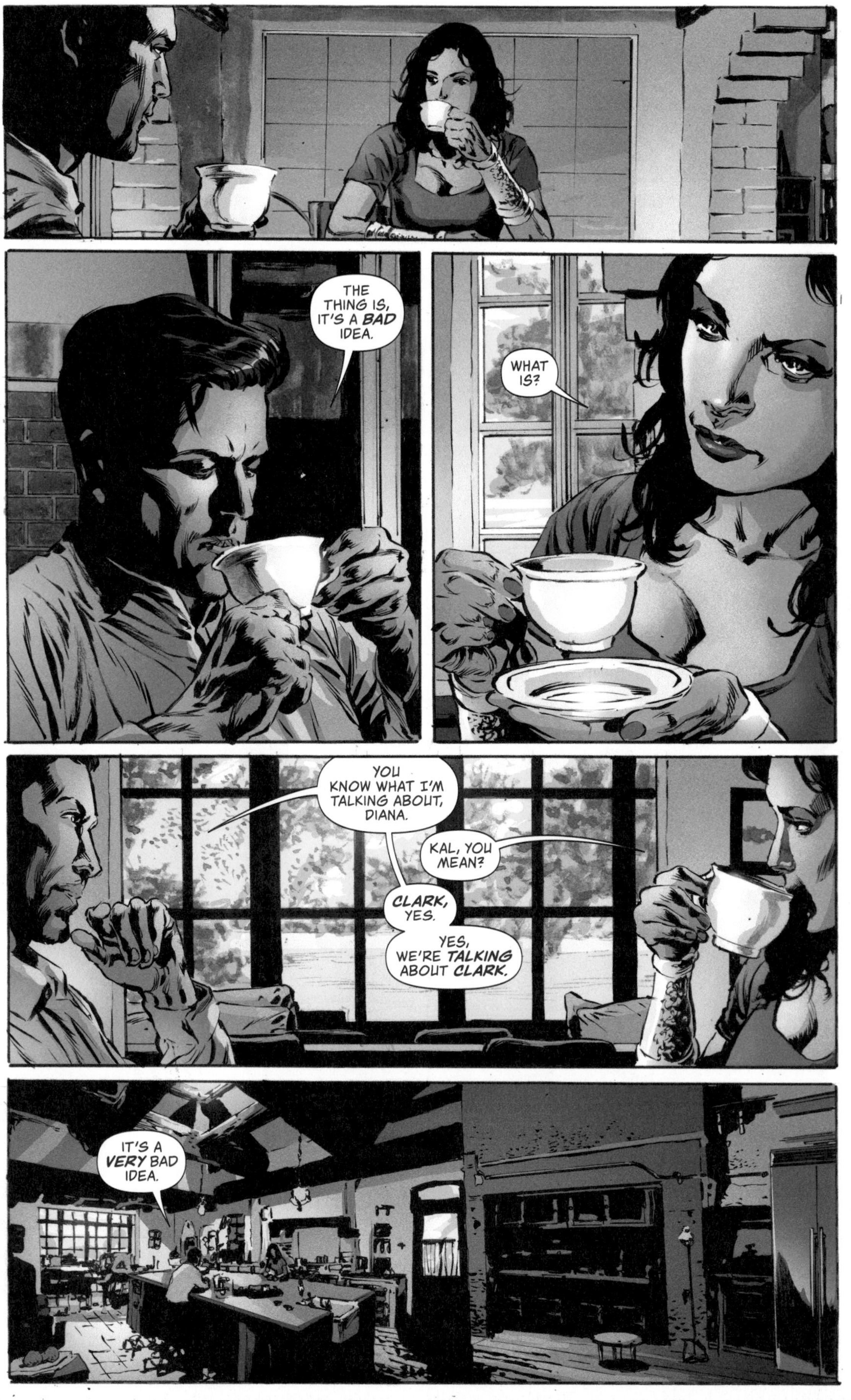
THE THING IS, IT'S A BAD IDEA.
WHAT IS?
YOU KNOW WHAT I'M TALKING ABOUT, DIANA.
KAL, YOU MEAN?
CLARK, YES.
YES, WE'RE TALKING ABOUT CLARK.
IT'S A VERY BAD IDEA.

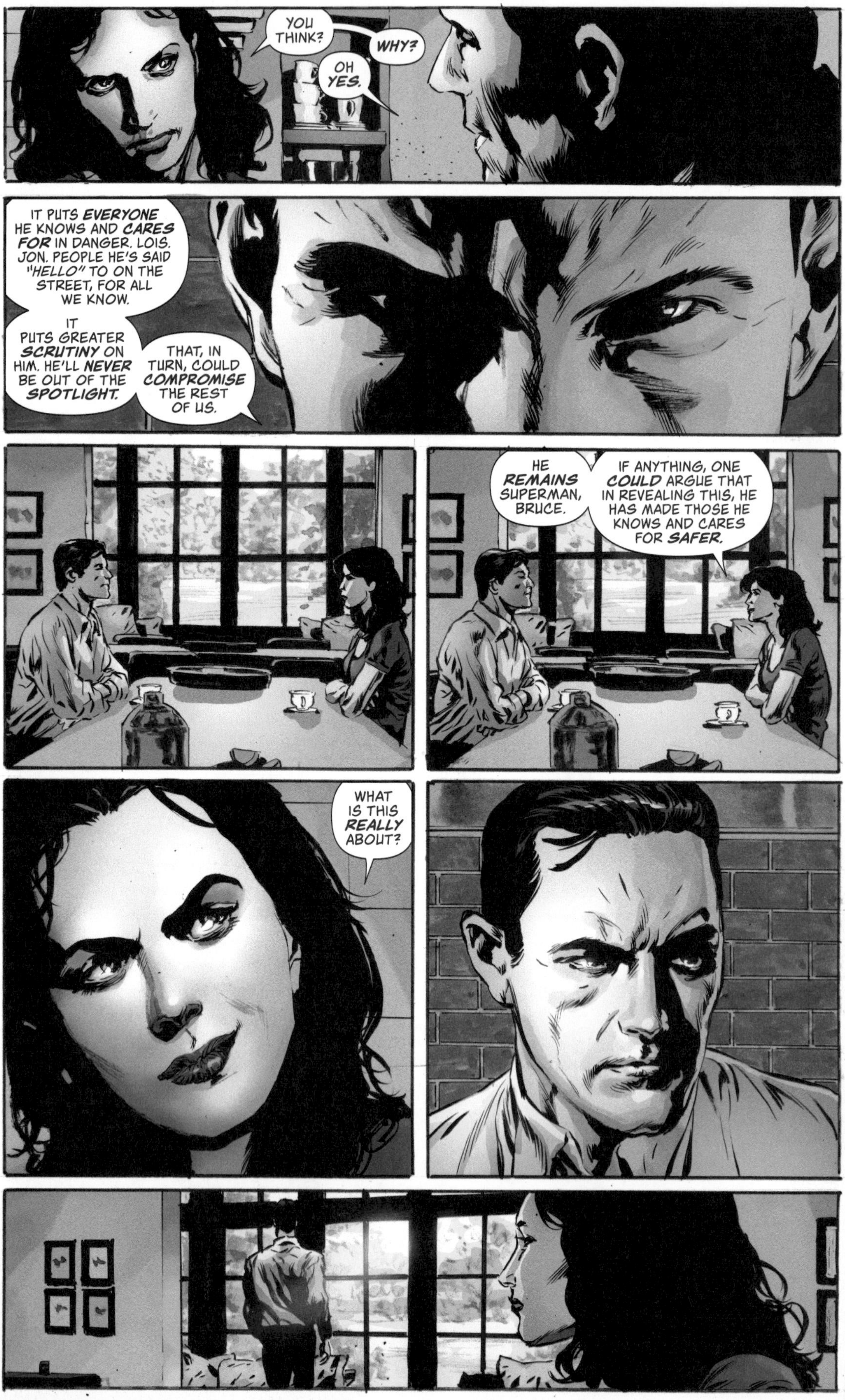
YOU THINK?
WHY?
OH YES.
IT PUTS EVERYONE HE KNOWS AND CARES FOR IN DANGER. LOIS. JON. PEOPLE HE'S SAID "HELLO" TO ON THE STREET, FOR ALL WE KNOW.
IT PUTS GREATER SCRUTINY ON HIM. HE'LL NEVER BE OUT OF THE SPOTLIGHT.
THAT, IN TURN, COULD COMPROMISE THE REST OF US.
HE REMAINS SUPERMAN, BRUCE.
IF ANYTHING, ONE COULD ARGUE THAT IN REVEALING THIS, HE HAS MADE THOSE HE KNOWS AND CARES FOR SAFER.
WHAT IS THIS REALLY ABOUT?

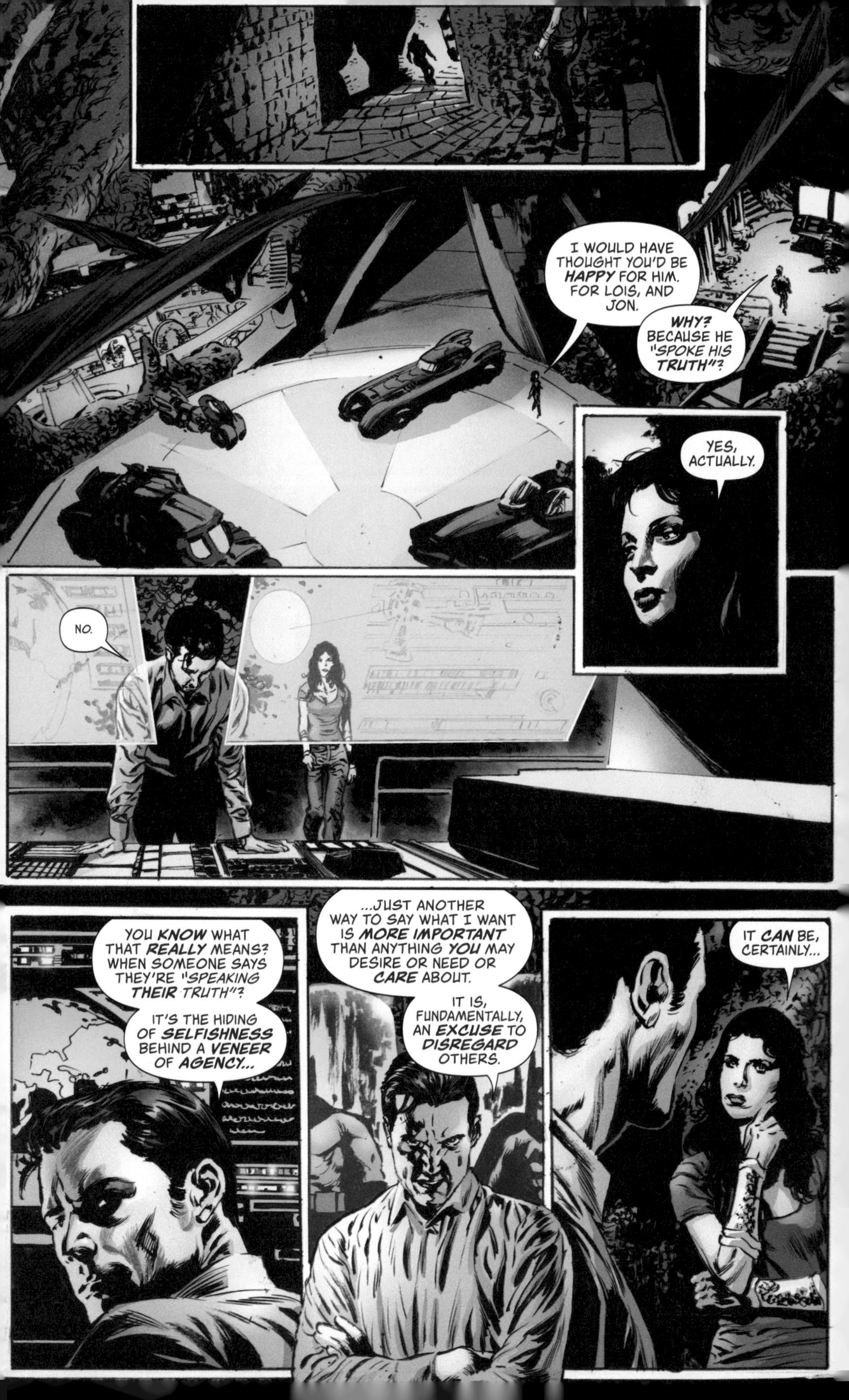
I WOULD HAVE THOUGHT YOU'D BE HAPPY FOR HIM. FOR LOIS, AND JON.
WHY? BECAUSE HE "SPOKE HIS TRUTH"?
YES, ACTUALLY.
NO.
YOU KNOW WHAT THAT REALLY MEANS? WHEN SOMEONE SAYS THEY'RE "SPEAKING THEIR TRUTH"?
IT'S THE HIDING OF SELFISHNESS BEHIND A VENEER OF AGENCY...
...JUST ANOTHER WAY TO SAY WHAT I WANT IS MORE IMPORTANT THAN ANYTHING YOU MAY DESIRE OR NEED OR CARE ABOUT.
IT IS, FUNDAMENTALLY, AN EXCUSE TO DISREGARD OTHERS.
IT CAN BE, CERTAINLY...

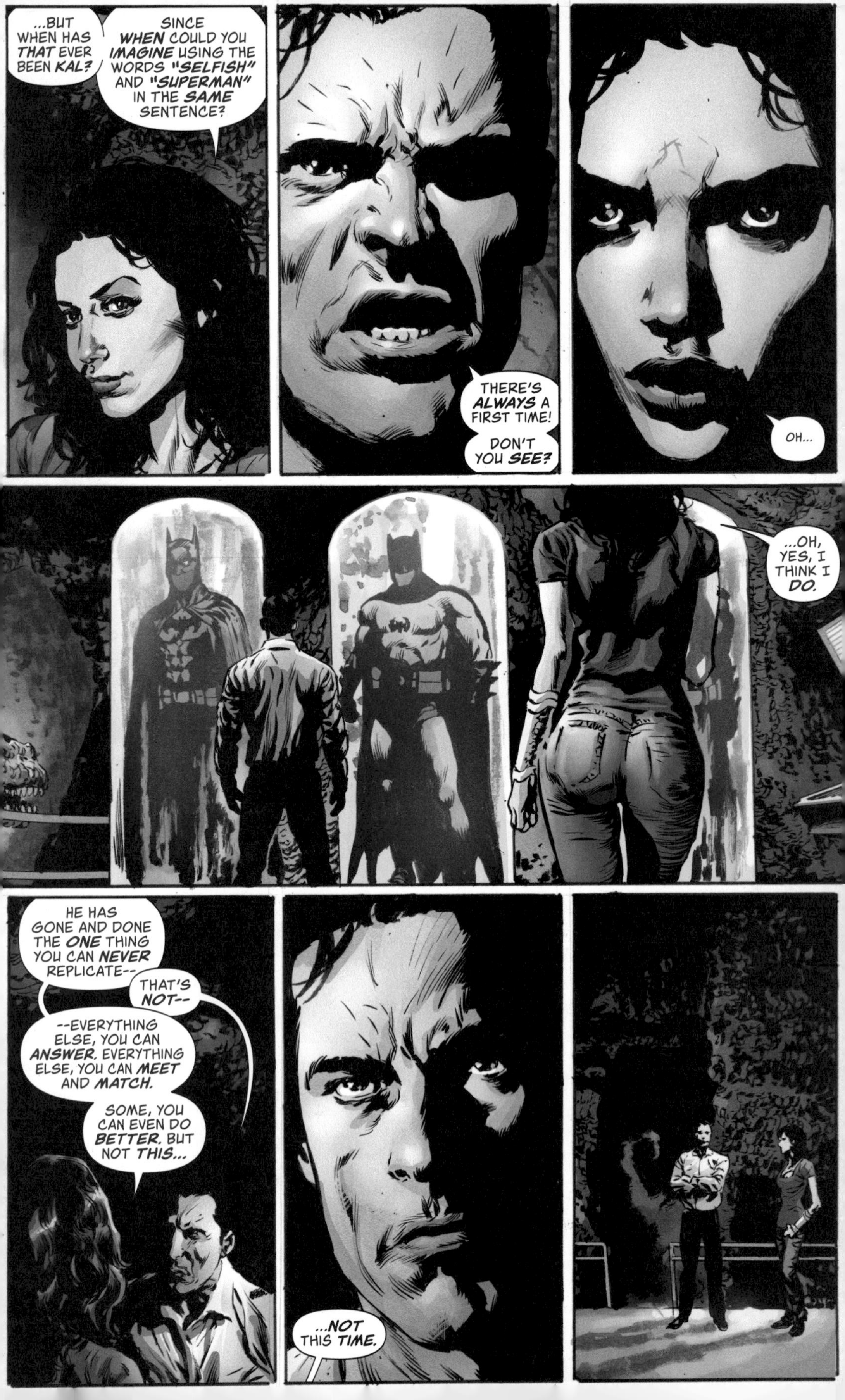
...BUT WHEN HAS THAT EVER BEEN KAL?
SINCE WHEN COULD YOU IMAGINE USING THE WORDS "SELFISH" AND "SUPERMAN" IN THE SAME SENTENCE?
THERE'S ALWAYS A FIRST TIME!
DON'T YOU SEE?
OH...
...OH, YES, I THINK I DO.
HE HAS GONE AND DONE THE ONE THING YOU CAN NEVER REPLICATE--
THAT'S NOT--
--EVERYTHING ELSE, YOU CAN ANSWER. EVERYTHING ELSE, YOU CAN MEET AND MATCH.
SOME, YOU CAN EVEN DO BETTER. BUT NOT THIS...
...NOT THIS TIME.

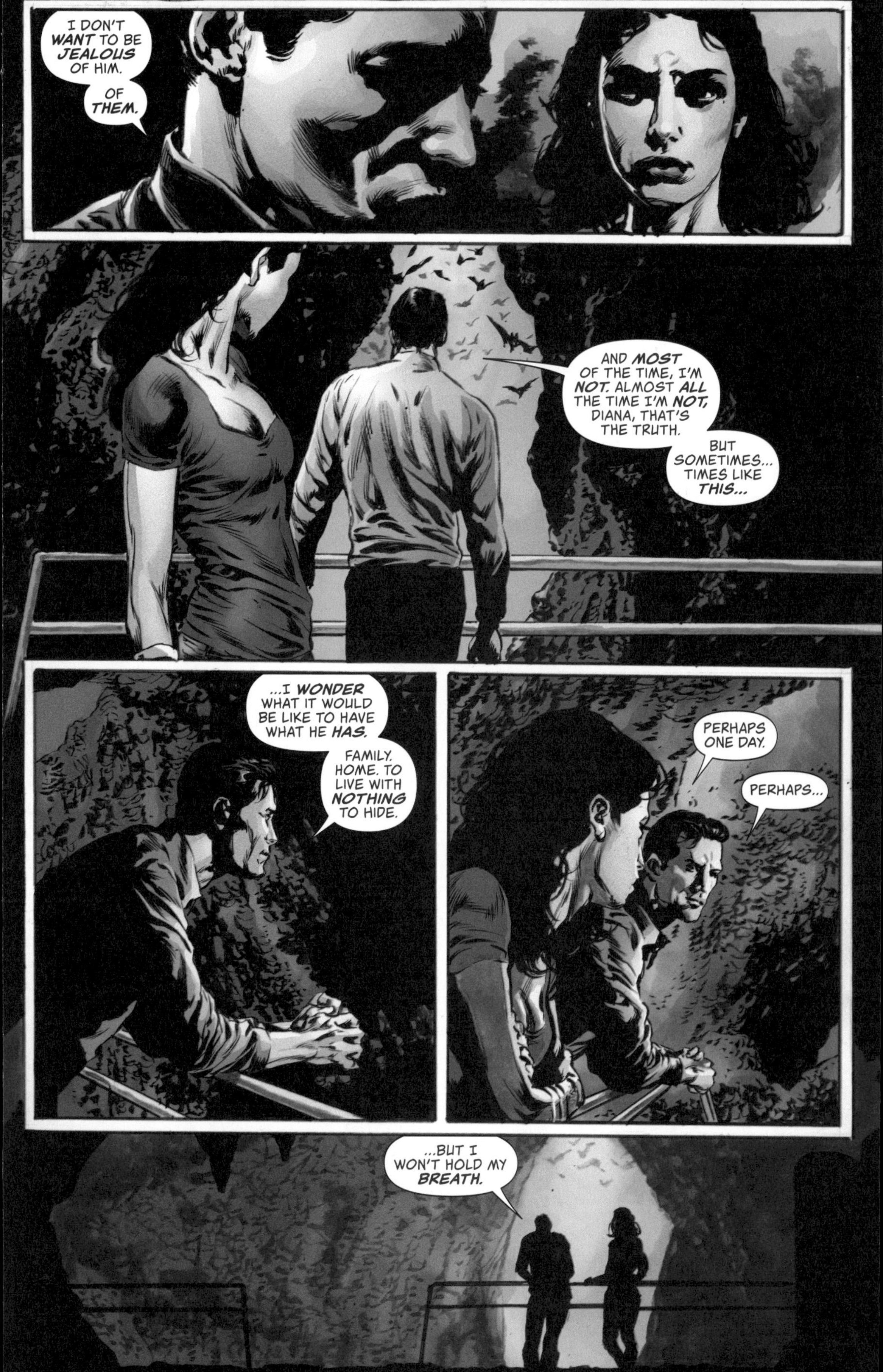
I DON'T WANT TO BE JEALOUS OF HIM.
OF THEM.
AND MOST OF THE TIME, I'M NOT. ALMOST ALL THE TIME I'M NOT, DIANA, THAT'S THE TRUTH.
BUT SOMETIMES... TIMES LIKE THIS...
...I WONDER WHAT IT WOULD BE LIKE TO HAVE WHAT HE HAS.
FAMILY. HOME. TO LIVE WITH NOTHING TO HIDE.
PERHAPS ONE DAY.
PERHAPS...
...BUT I WON'T HOLD MY BREATH.

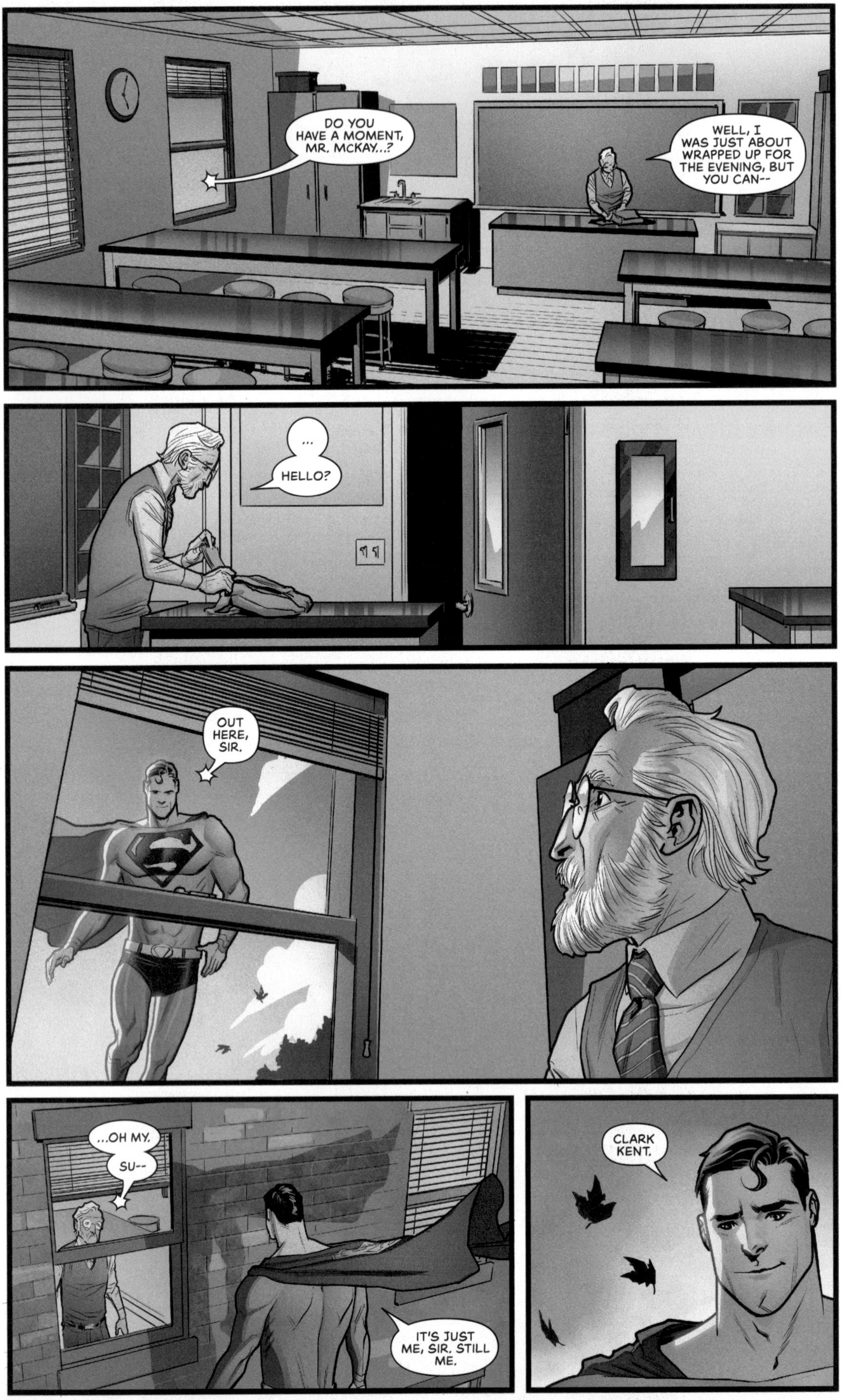
DO YOU HAVE A MOMENT, MR. MCKAY...?
WELL, I WAS JUST ABOUT WRAPPED UP FOR THE EVENING, BUT YOU CAN--
...
HELLO?
OUT HERE, SIR.
...OH MY.
SU--
IT'S JUST ME, SIR. STILL ME.
CLARK KENT.

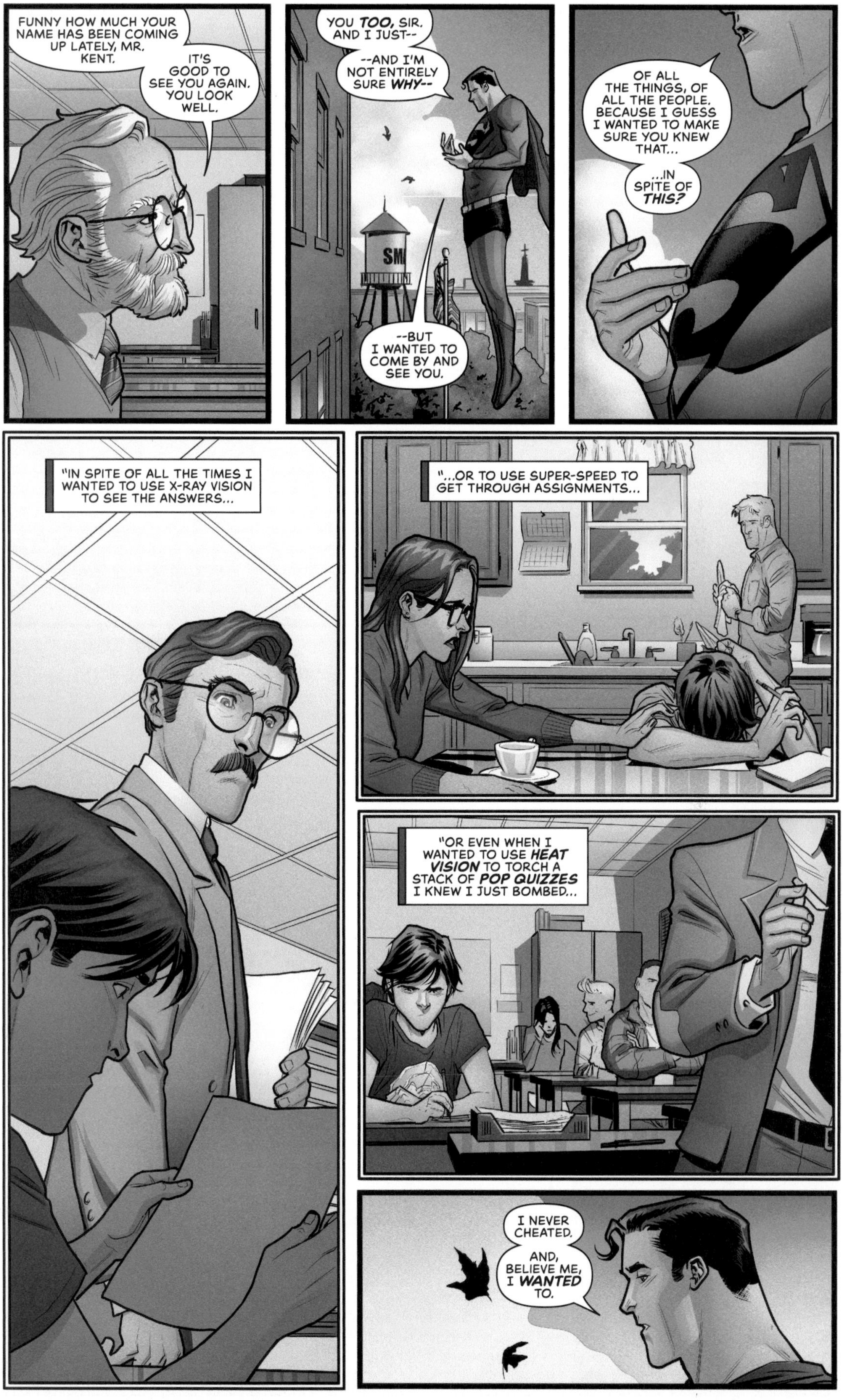
FUNNY HOW MUCH YOUR NAME HAS BEEN COMING UP LATELY, MR. KENT.
IT'S GOOD TO SEE YOU AGAIN. YOU LOOK WELL.
YOU TOO, SIR. AND I JUST--
--AND I'M NOT ENTIRELY SURE WHY--
SM
--BUT I WANTED TO COME BY AND SEE YOU.
OF ALL THE THINGS, OF ALL THE PEOPLE. BECAUSE I GUESS I WANTED TO MAKE SURE YOU KNEW THAT...
...IN SPITE OF THIS?
"IN SPITE OF ALL THE TIMES I WANTED TO USE X-RAY VISION TO SEE THE ANSWERS...
"...OR TO USE SUPER-SPEED TO GET THROUGH ASSIGNMENTS...
"OR EVEN WHEN I WANTED TO USE HEAT VISION TO TORCH A STACK OF POP QUIZZES I KNEW I JUST BOMBED...
I NEVER CHEATED.
AND, BELIEVE ME, I WANTED TO.

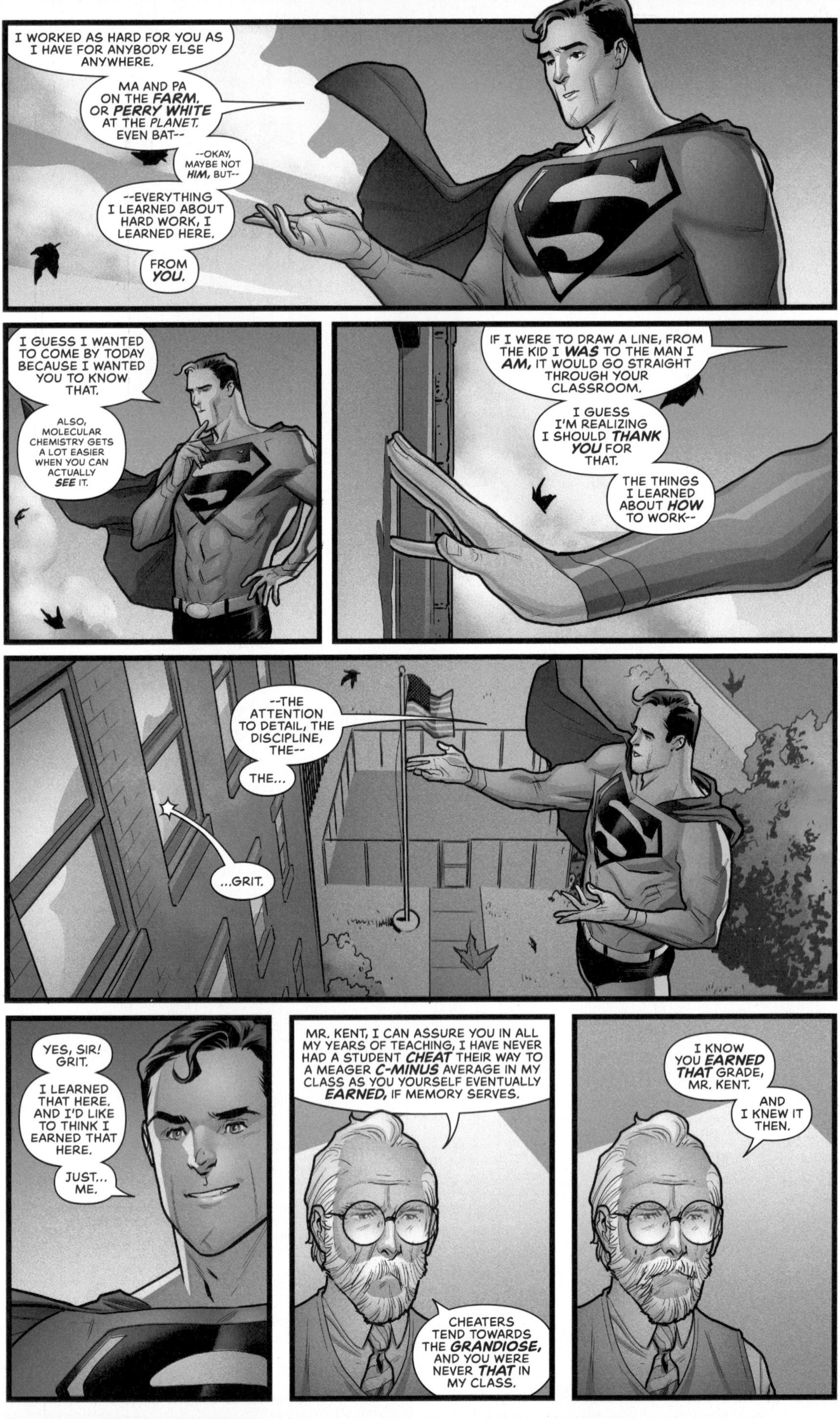
I WORKED AS HARD FOR YOU AS I HAVE FOR ANYBODY ELSE ANYWHERE.
MA AND PA ON THE FARM. OR PERRY WHITE AT THE PLANET. EVEN BAT--
--OKAY, MAYBE NOT HIM, BUT--
--EVERYTHING I LEARNED ABOUT HARD WORK, I LEARNED HERE.
FROM YOU.
I GUESS I WANTED TO COME BY TODAY BECAUSE I WANTED YOU TO KNOW THAT.
ALSO, MOLECULAR CHEMISTRY GETS A LOT EASIER WHEN YOU CAN ACTUALLY SEE IT.
IF I WERE TO DRAW A LINE, FROM THE KID I WAS TO THE MAN I AM, IT WOULD GO STRAIGHT THROUGH YOUR CLASSROOM.
I GUESS I'M REALIZING I SHOULD THANK YOU FOR THAT.
THE THINGS I LEARNED ABOUT HOW TO WORK--
--THE ATTENTION TO DETAIL, THE DISCIPLINE, THE--
THE...
...GRIT.
YES, SIR! GRIT.
I LEARNED THAT HERE. AND I'D LIKE TO THINK I EARNED THAT HERE.
JUST... ME.
MR. KENT, I CAN ASSURE YOU IN ALL MY YEARS OF TEACHING, I HAVE NEVER HAD A STUDENT CHEAT THEIR WAY TO A MEAGER C-MINUS AVERAGE IN MY CLASS AS YOU YOURSELF EVENTUALLY EARNED, IF MEMORY SERVES.
CHEATERS TEND TOWARDS THE GRANDIOSE, AND YOU WERE NEVER THAT IN MY CLASS.
I KNOW YOU EARNED THAT GRADE, MR. KENT.
AND I KNEW IT THEN.

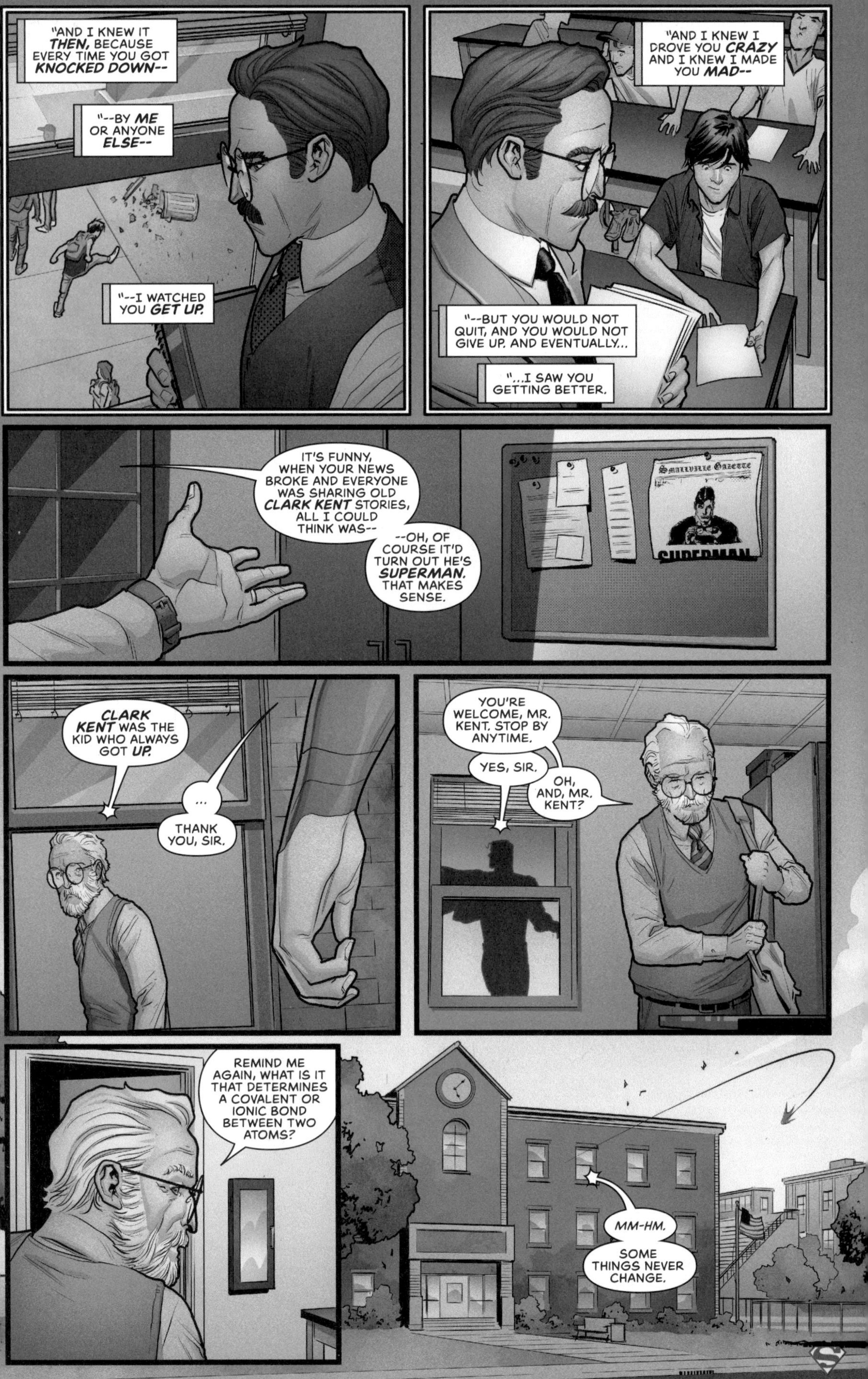
"AND I KNEW IT THEN, BECAUSE EVERY TIME YOU GOT KNOCKED DOWN--
"--BY ME OR ANYONE ELSE--
"--I WATCHED YOU GET UP.
"AND I KNEW I DROVE YOU CRAZY AND I KNEW I MADE YOU MAD--
"--BUT YOU WOULD NOT QUIT, AND YOU WOULD NOT GIVE UP. AND EVENTUALLY...
"...I SAW YOU GETTING BETTER.
IT'S FUNNY, WHEN YOUR NEWS BROKE AND EVERYONE WAS SHARING OLD CLARK KENT STORIES, ALL I COULD THINK WAS--
--OH, OF COURSE IT'D TURN OUT HE'S SUPERMAN. THAT MAKES SENSE.
Smallville Gazette
CLARK KENT WAS THE KID WHO ALWAYS GOT UP.
...
THANK YOU, SIR.
YOU'RE WELCOME, MR. KENT. STOP BY ANYTIME.
YES, SIR.
OH, AND, MR. KENT?
REMIND ME AGAIN, WHAT IS IT THAT DETERMINES A COVALENT OR IONIC BOND BETWEEN TWO ATOMS?
MM-HM.
SOME THINGS NEVER CHANGE.

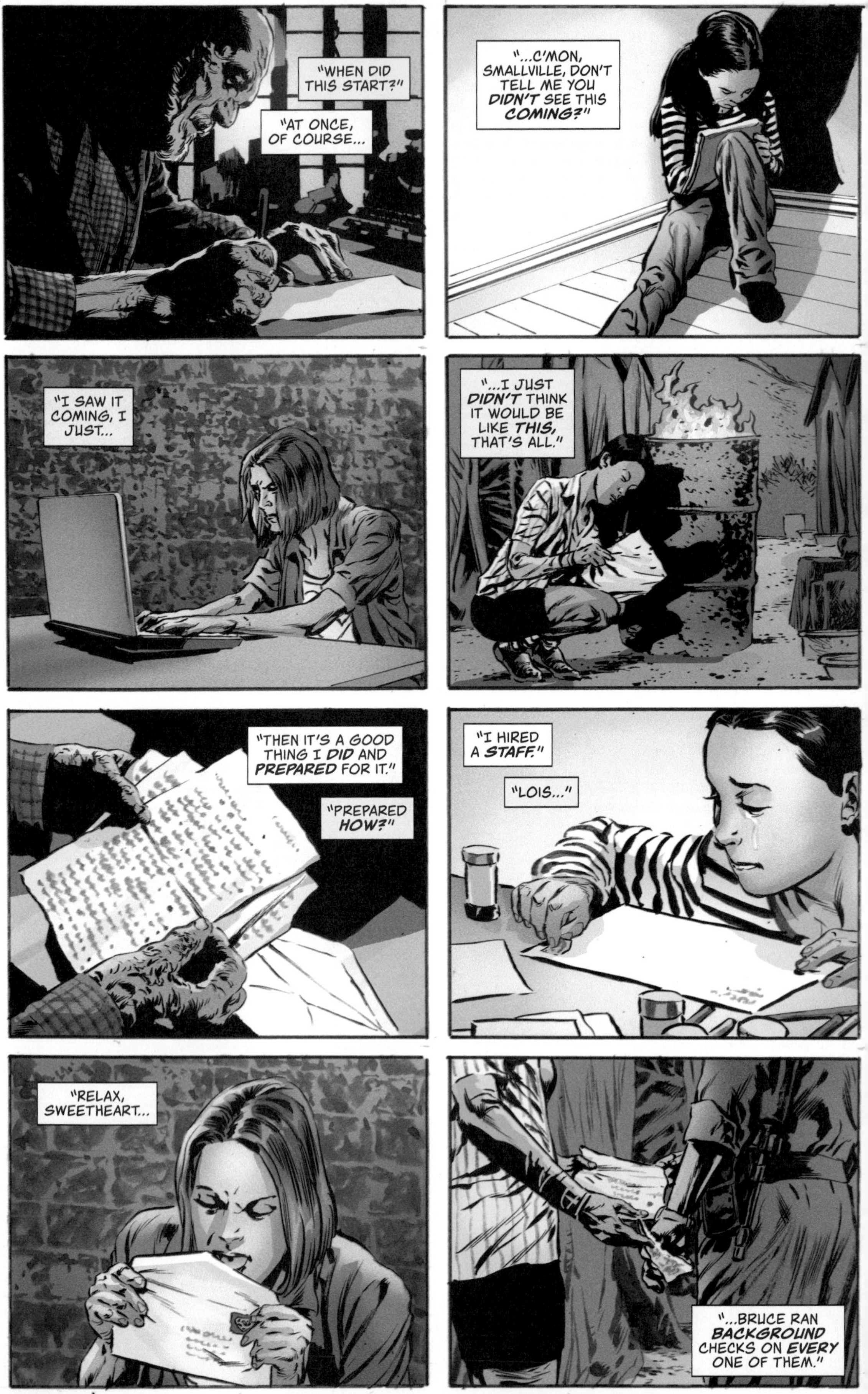
"WHEN DID THIS START?"
"AT ONCE, OF COURSE...
"...C'MON, SMALLVILLE, DON'T TELL ME YOU DIDN'T SEE THIS COMING?"
"I SAW IT COMING, I JUST...
"...I JUST DIDN'T THINK IT WOULD BE LIKE THIS, THAT'S ALL."
"THEN IT'S A GOOD THING I DID AND PREPARED FOR IT."
"PREPARED HOW?"
"I HIRED A STAFF."
"LOIS..."
"RELAX, SWEETHEART...
"...BRUCE RAN BACKGROUND CHECKS ON EVERY ONE OF THEM."

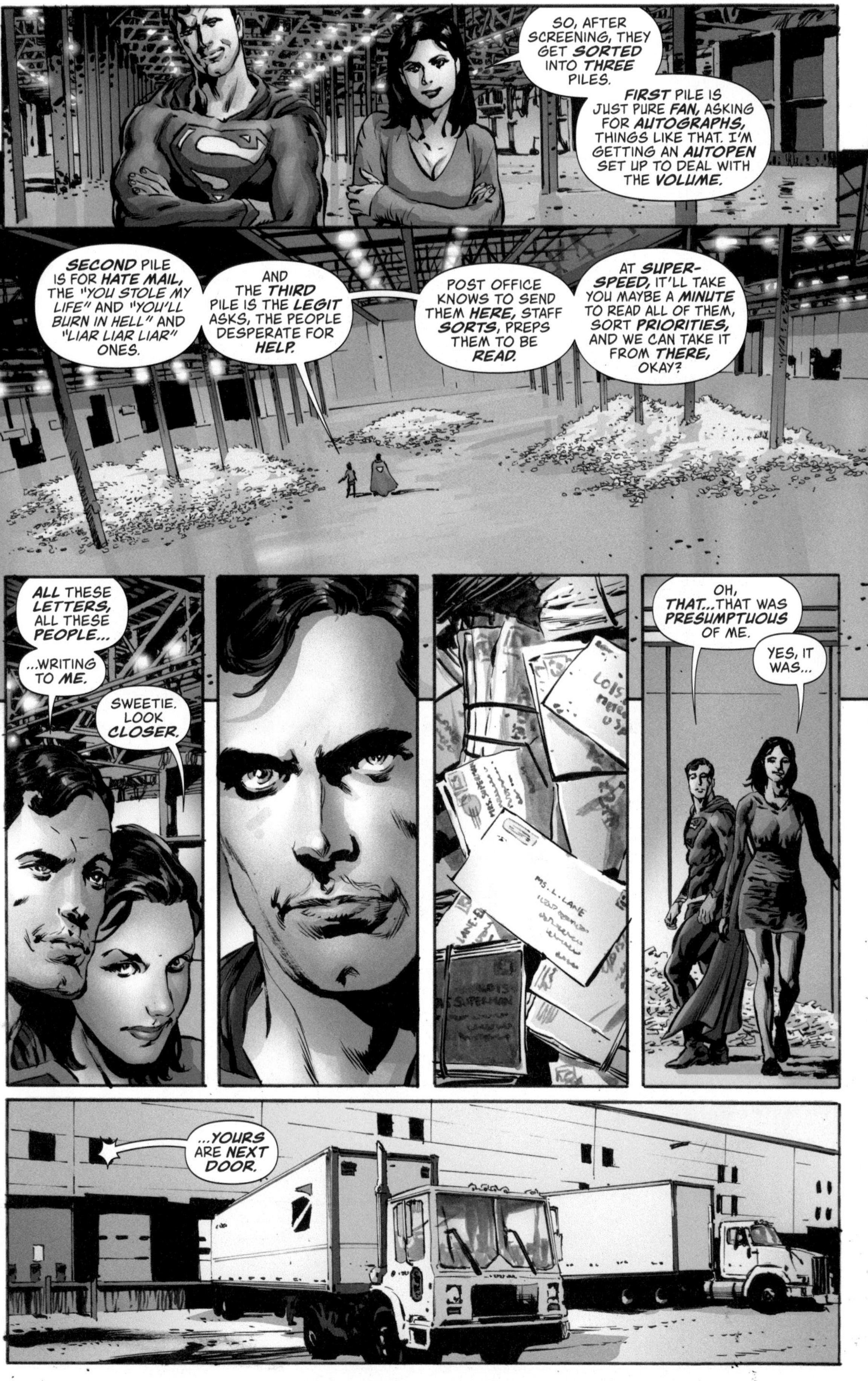
SO, AFTER SCREENING, THEY GET SORTED INTO THREE PILES.
FIRST PILE IS JUST PURE FAN, ASKING FOR AUTOGRAPHS, THINGS LIKE THAT. I'M GETTING AN AUTOPEN SET UP TO DEAL WITH THE VOLUME.
SECOND PILE IS FOR HATE MAIL, THE "YOU STOLE MY LIFE" AND "YOU'LL BURN IN HELL" AND "LIAR LIAR LIAR" ONES.
AND THE THIRD PILE IS THE LEGIT ASKS, THE PEOPLE DESPERATE FOR HELP.
POST OFFICE KNOWS TO SEND THEM HERE, STAFF SORTS, PREPS THEM TO BE READ.
AT SUPER-SPEED, IT'LL TAKE YOU MAYBE A MINUTE TO READ ALL OF THEM, SORT PRIORITIES, AND WE CAN TAKE IT FROM THERE, OKAY?
ALL THESE LETTERS, ALL THESE PEOPLE...
...WRITING TO ME.
SWEETIE. LOOK CLOSER.
OH, THAT...THAT WAS PRESUMPTUOUS OF ME.
YES, IT WAS...
...YOURS ARE NEXT DOOR.

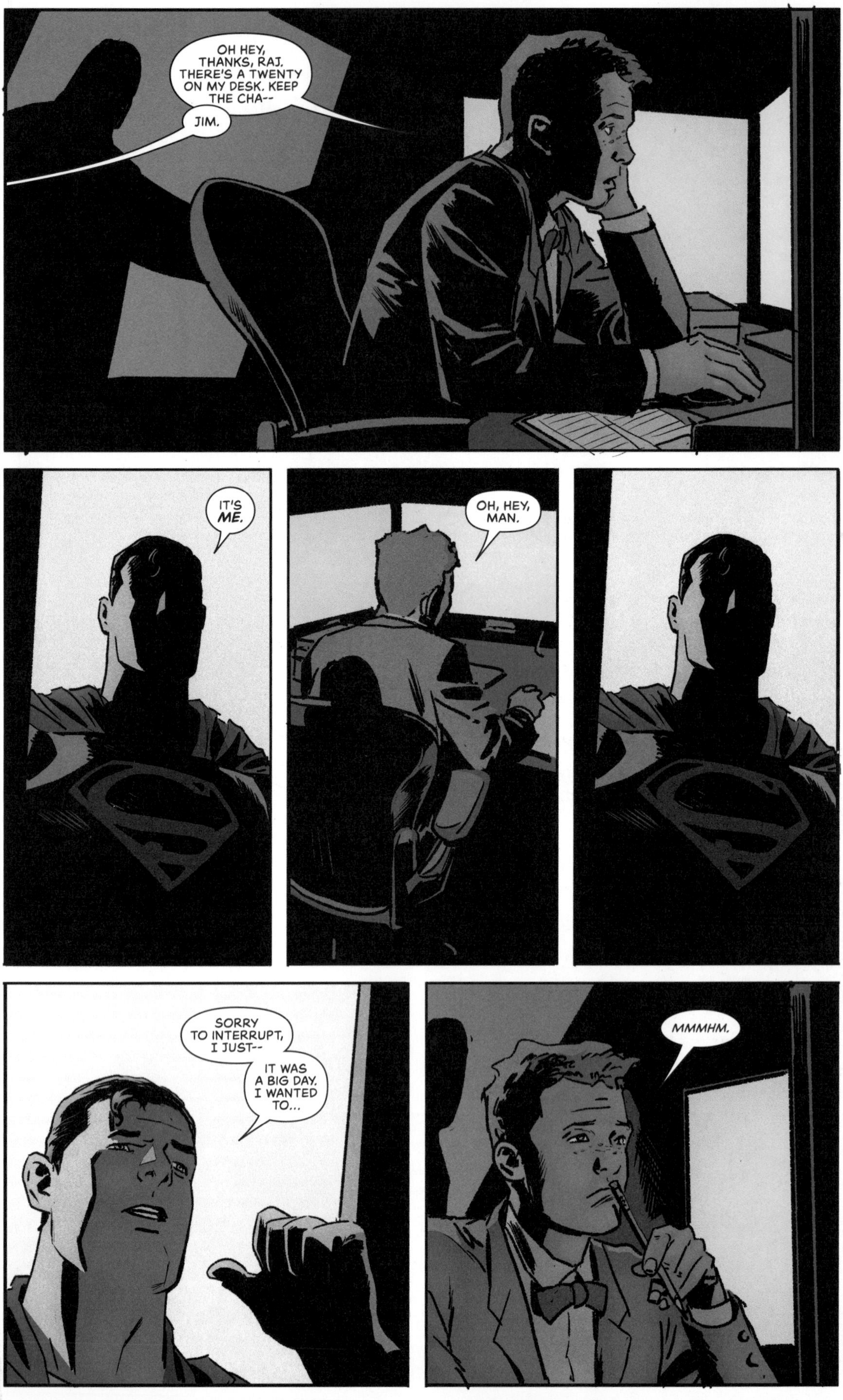
OH HEY, THANKS, RAJ. THERE'S A TWENTY ON MY DESK. KEEP THE CHA--
JIM.
IT'S *ME.*
OH, HEY, MAN.
SORRY TO INTERRUPT, I JUST--
IT WAS A BIG DAY. I WANTED TO...
MMMHM.

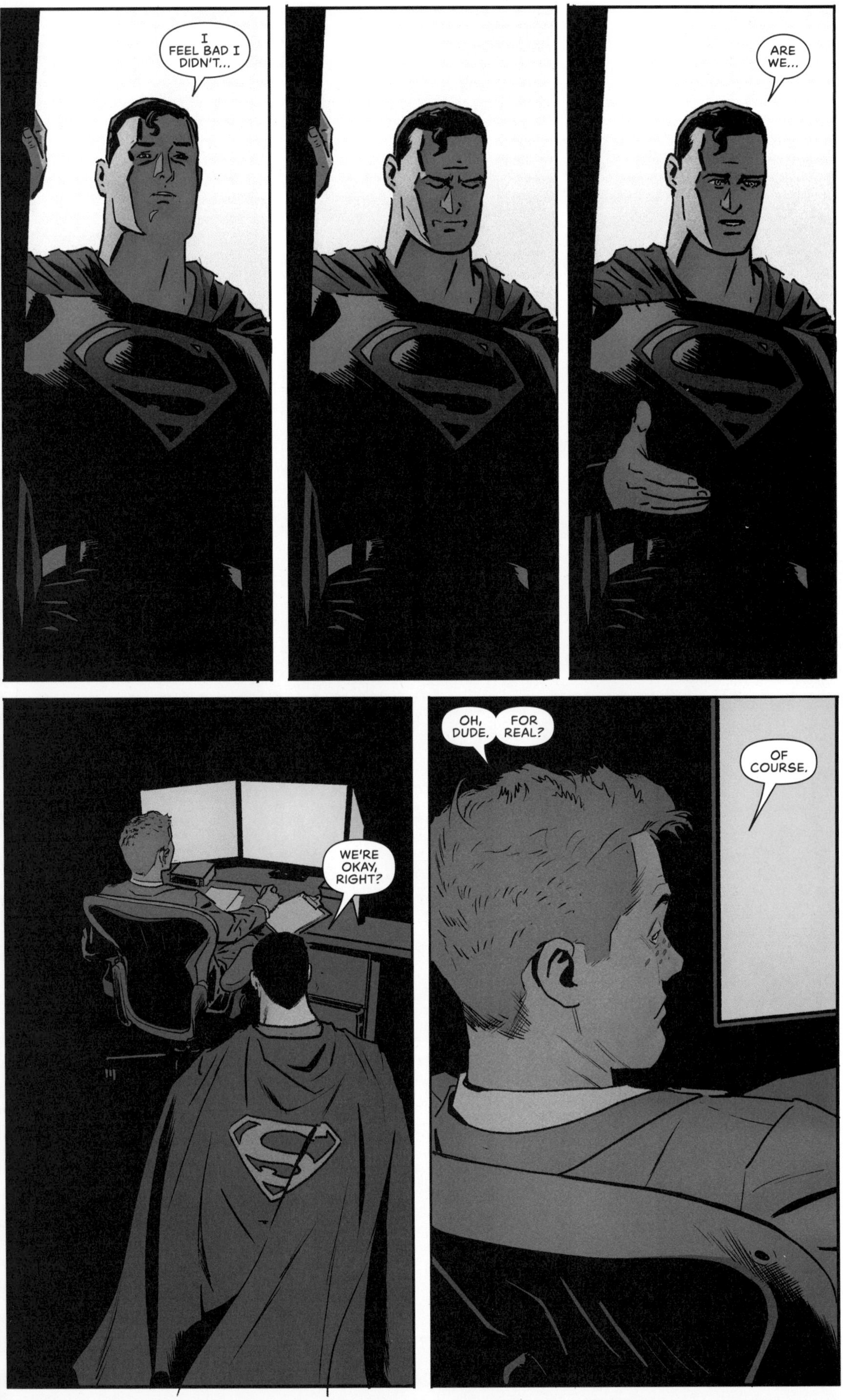
I FEEL BAD I DIDN'T...
ARE WE...
WE'RE OKAY, RIGHT?
OH, DUDE.
FOR REAL?
OF COURSE.

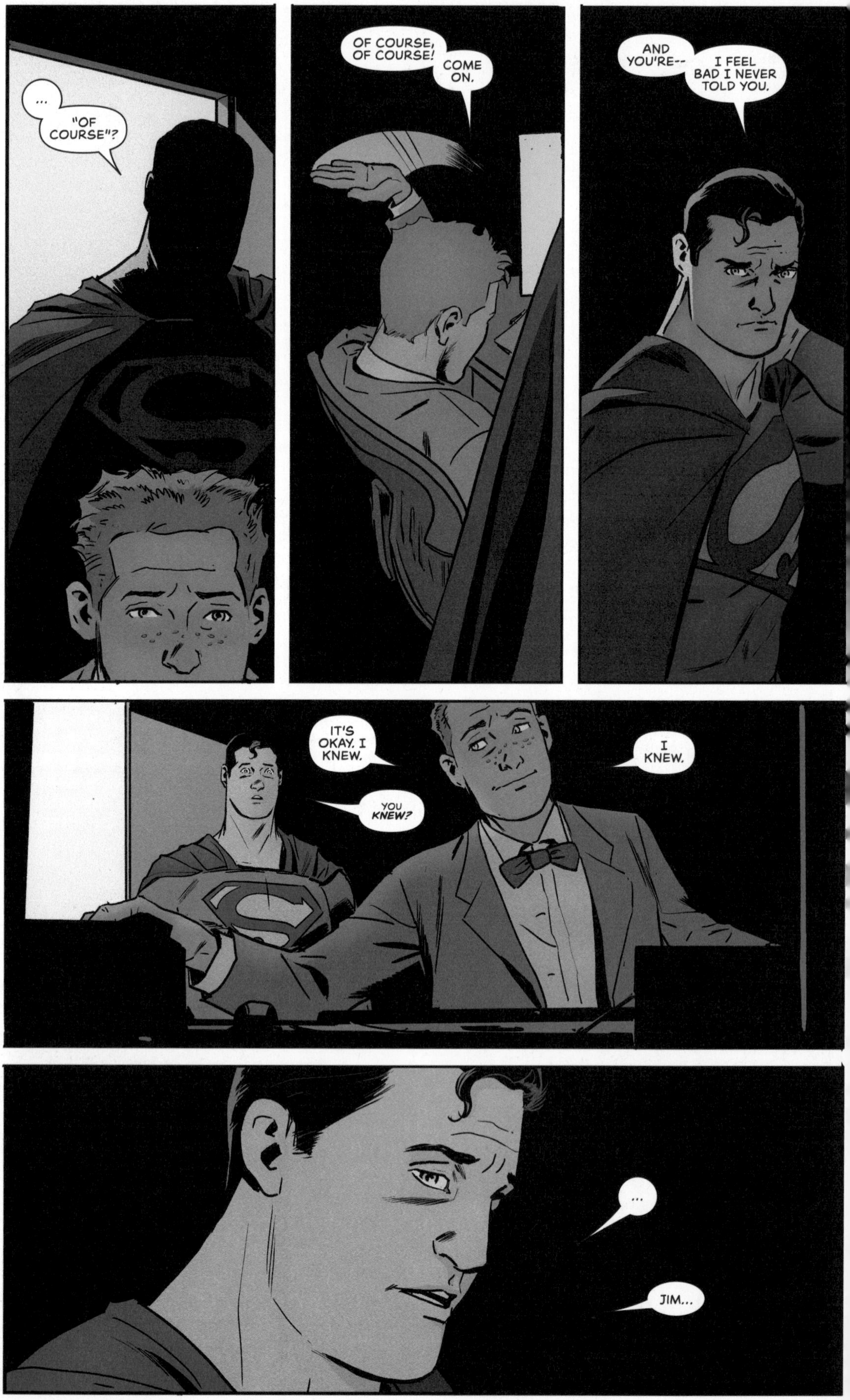
...
"OF COURSE"?
OF COURSE, OF COURSE!
COME ON.
AND YOU'RE--
I FEEL BAD I NEVER TOLD YOU.
IT'S OKAY. I KNEW.
YOU KNEW?
I KNEW.
...
JIM...

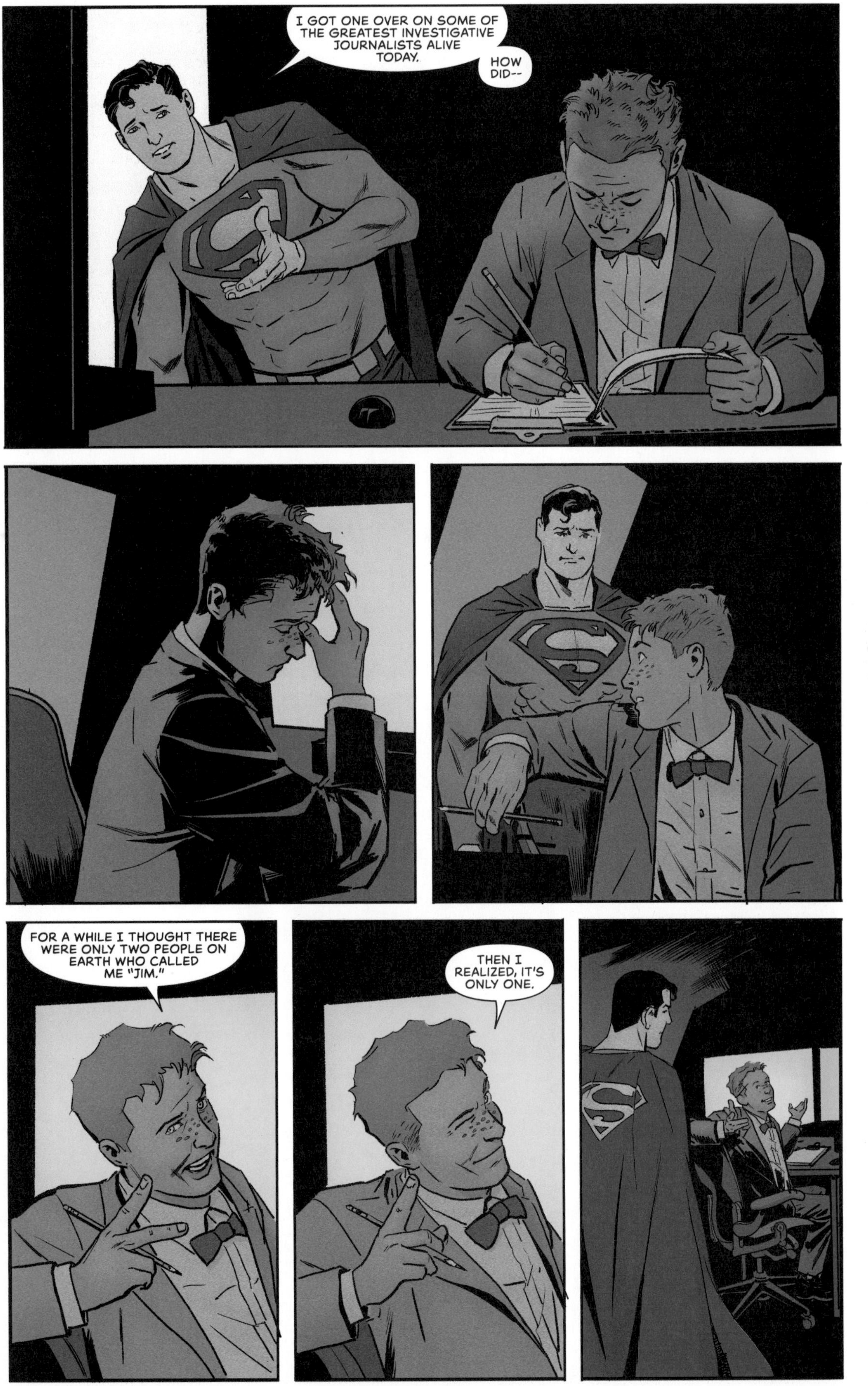
I GOT ONE OVER ON SOME OF THE GREATEST INVESTIGATIVE JOURNALISTS ALIVE TODAY.
HOW DID--
FOR A WHILE I THOUGHT THERE WERE ONLY TWO PEOPLE ON EARTH WHO CALLED ME "JIM."
THEN I REALIZED, IT'S ONLY ONE.

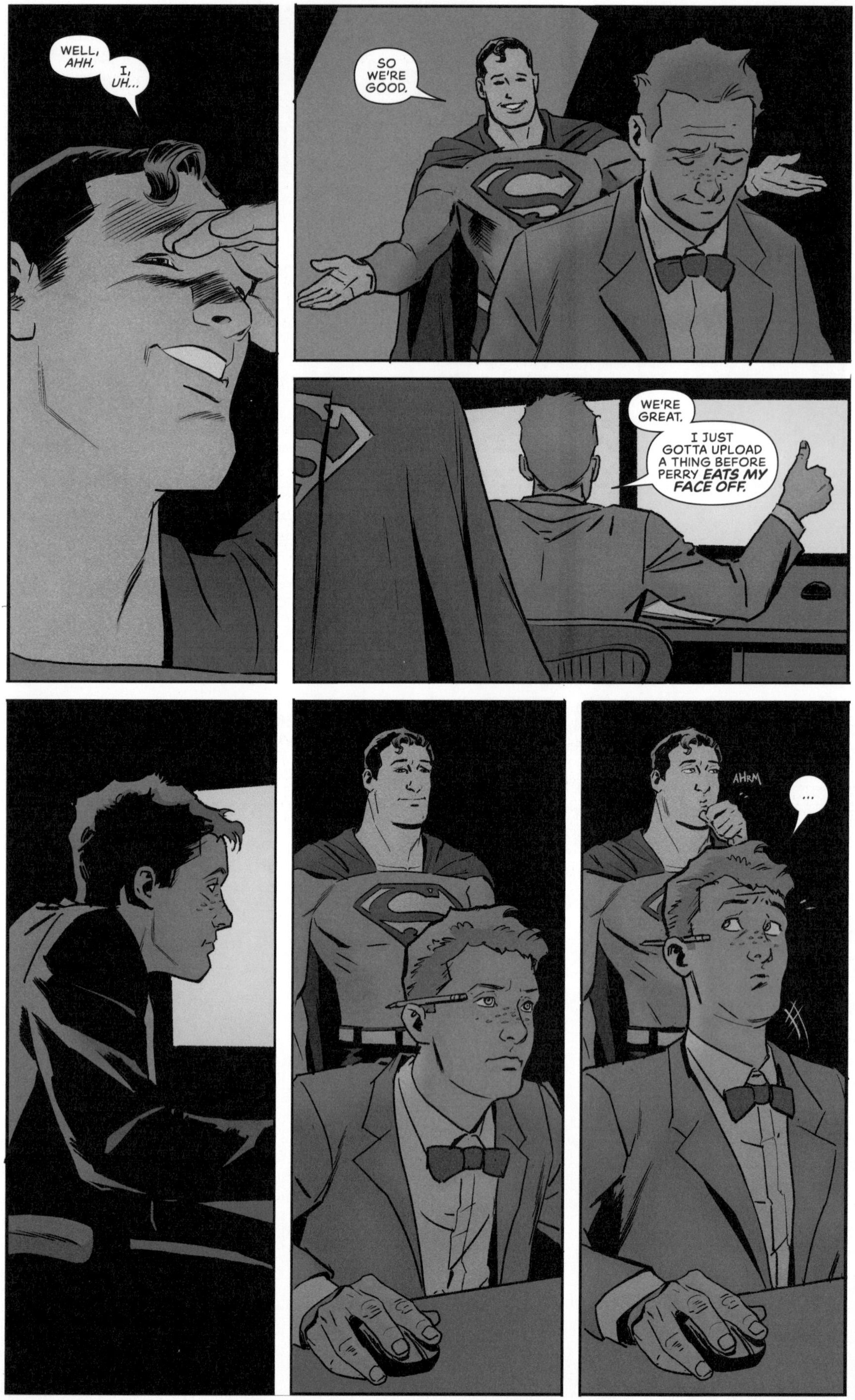
WELL, AHH.
I, UH...
SO WE'RE GOOD.
WE'RE GREAT.
I JUST GOTTA UPLOAD A THING BEFORE PERRY EATS MY FACE OFF.
AHRM
...

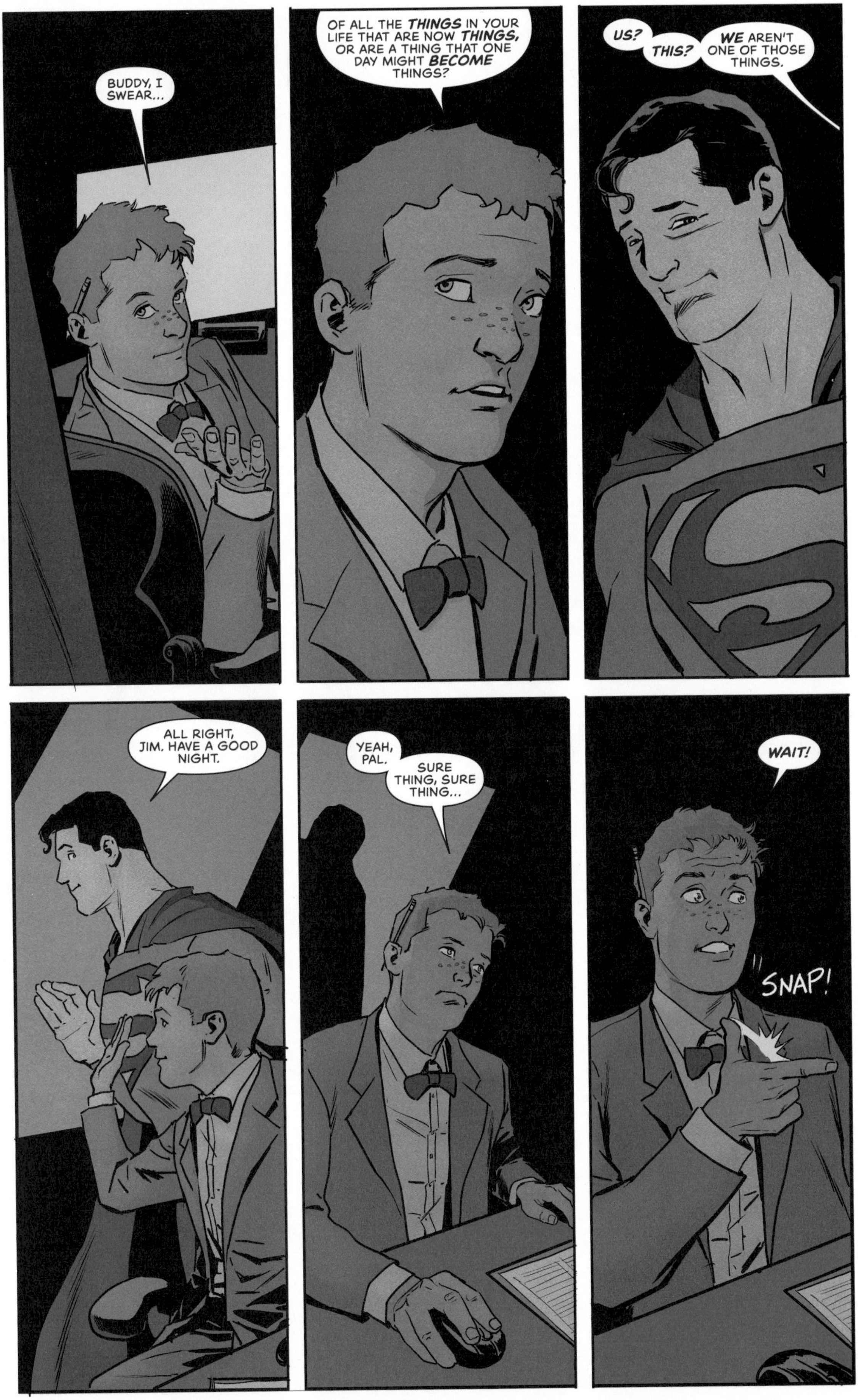
BUDDY, I SWEAR...
OF ALL THE THINGS IN YOUR LIFE THAT ARE NOW THINGS, OR ARE A THING THAT ONE DAY MIGHT BECOME THINGS?
US?
THIS?
WE AREN'T ONE OF THOSE THINGS.
ALL RIGHT, JIM. HAVE A GOOD NIGHT.
YEAH, PAL.
SURE THING, SURE THING...
WAIT!
SNAP!

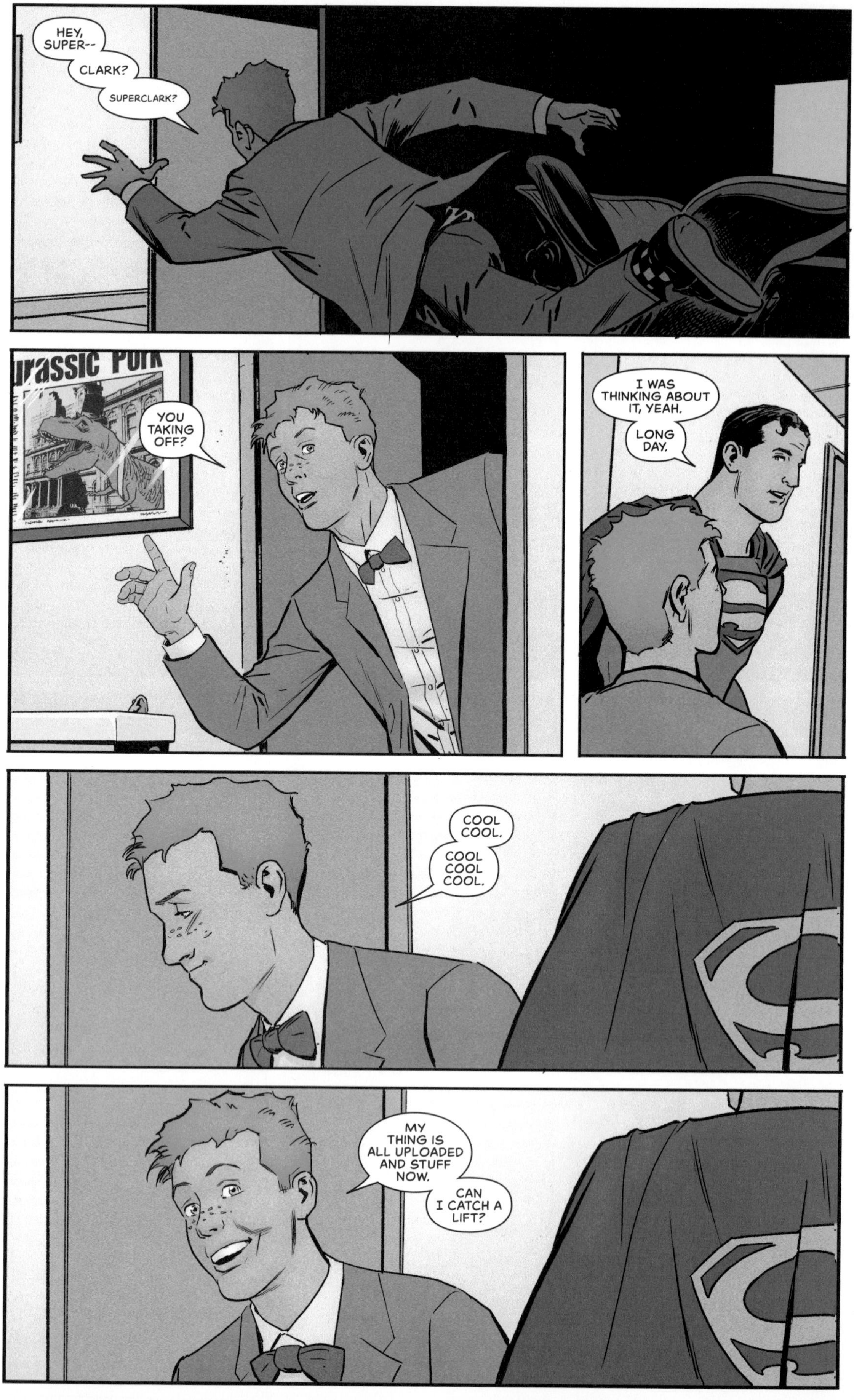
HEY, SUPER--
CLARK?
SUPERCLARK?
urassic Pork
YOU TAKING OFF?
I WAS THINKING ABOUT IT, YEAH.
LONG DAY.
COOL COOL.
COOL COOL COOL.
MY THING IS ALL UPLOADED AND STUFF NOW.
CAN I CATCH A LIFT?

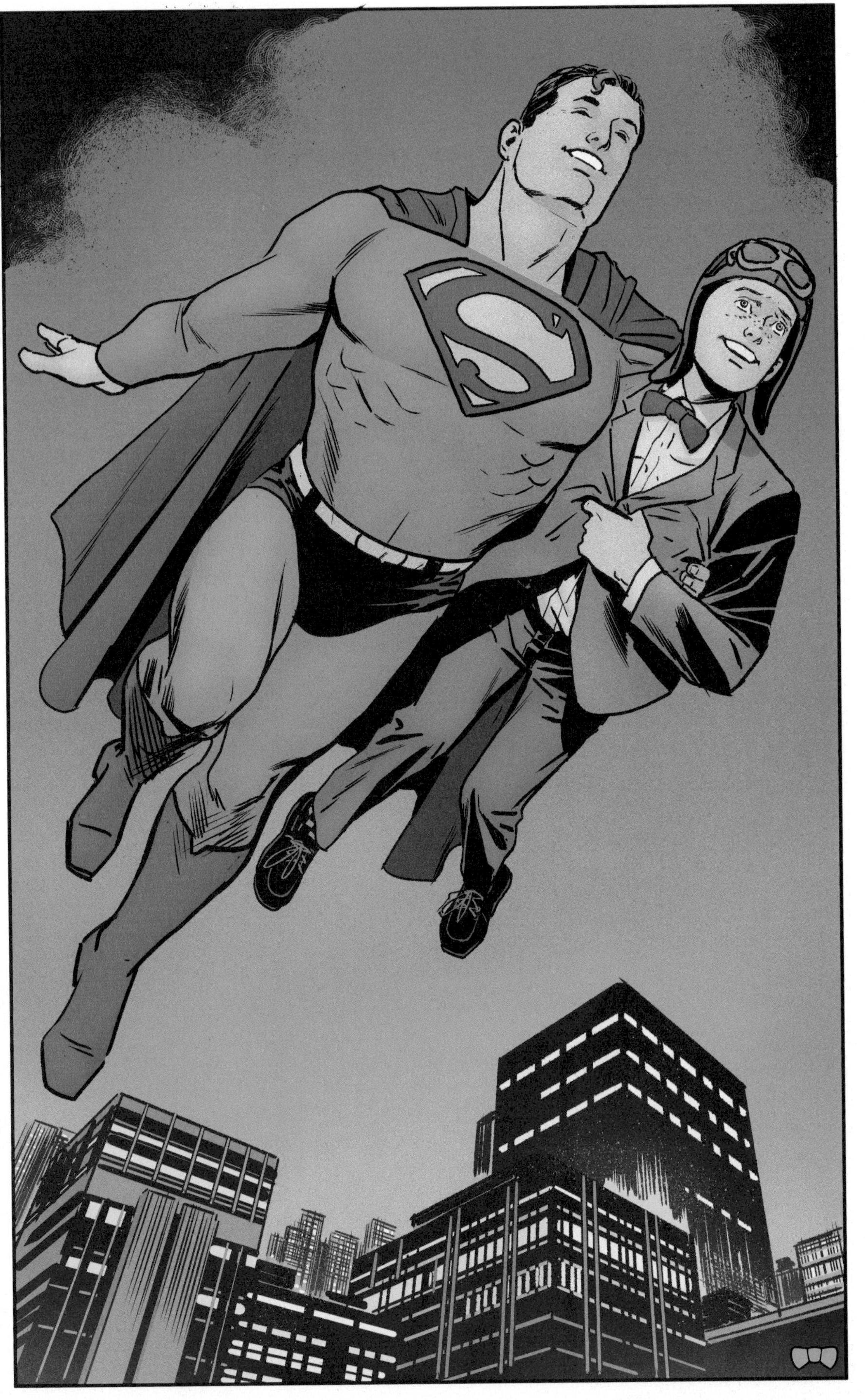

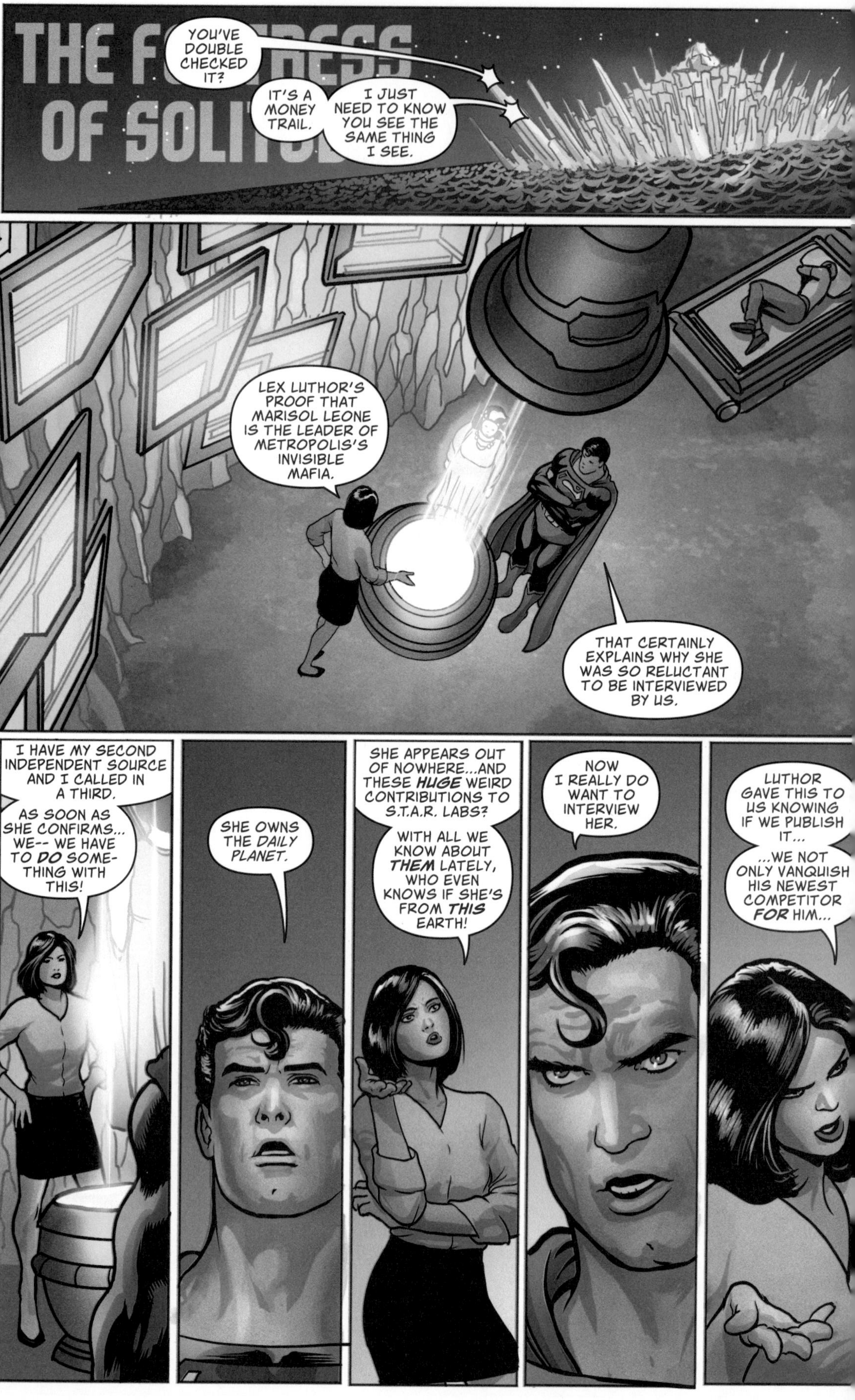

YOU'VE DOUBLE CHECKED IT?
IT'S A MONEY TRAIL.
I JUST NEED TO KNOW YOU SEE THE SAME THING I SEE.
LEX LUTHOR'S PROOF THAT MARISOL LEONE IS THE LEADER OF METROPOLIS'S INVISIBLE MAFIA.
THAT CERTAINLY EXPLAINS WHY SHE WAS SO RELUCTANT TO BE INTERVIEWED BY US.
I HAVE MY SECOND INDEPENDENT SOURCE AND I CALLED IN A THIRD.
AS SOON AS SHE CONFIRMS... WE-- WE HAVE TO *DO* SOMETHING WITH THIS!
SHE OWNS THE *DAILY PLANET*.
SHE APPEARS OUT OF NOWHERE...AND THESE *HUGE* WEIRD CONTRIBUTIONS TO S.T.A.R. LABS?
WITH ALL WE KNOW ABOUT *THEM* LATELY, WHO EVEN KNOWS IF SHE'S FROM *THIS* EARTH!
NOW I REALLY DO WANT TO INTERVIEW HER.
LUTHOR GAVE THIS TO US KNOWING IF WE PUBLISH IT...
...WE NOT ONLY VANQUISH HIS NEWEST COMPETITOR *FOR* HIM...

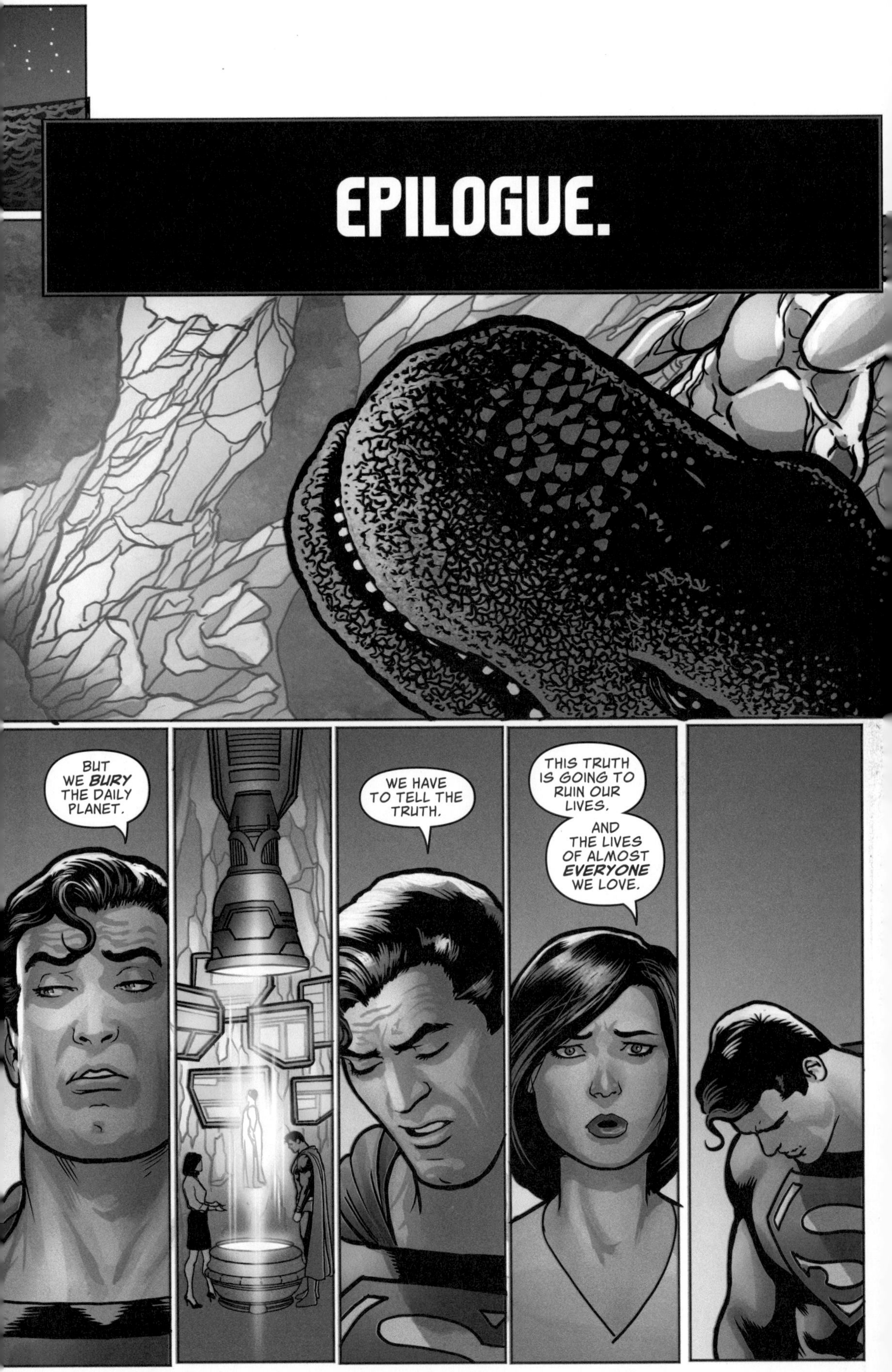
EPILOGUE.
BUT WE BURY THE DAILY PLANET.
WE HAVE TO TELL THE TRUTH.
THIS TRUTH IS GOING TO RUIN OUR LIVES.
AND THE LIVES OF ALMOST EVERYONE WE LOVE.

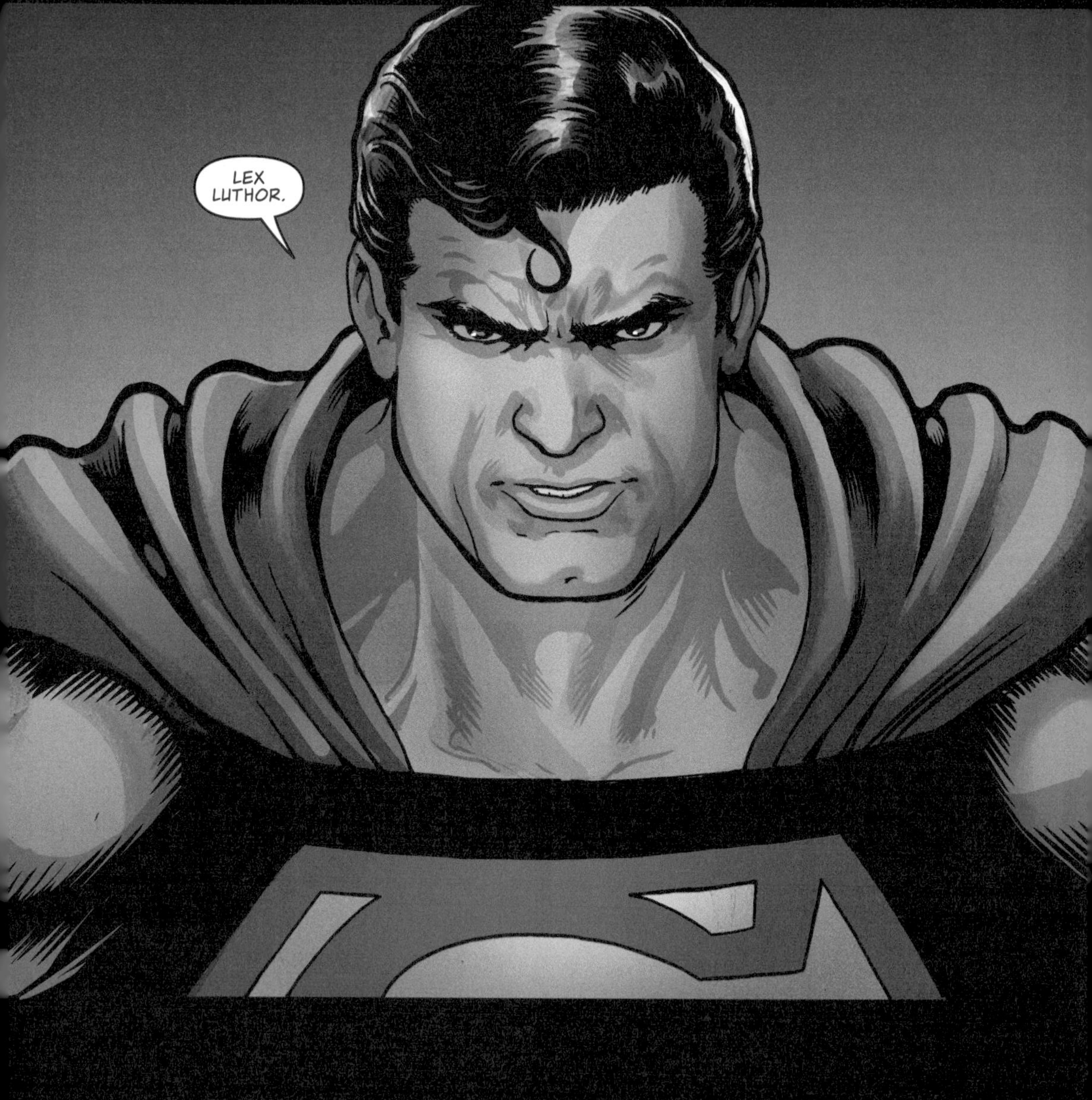
LEX LUTHOR.

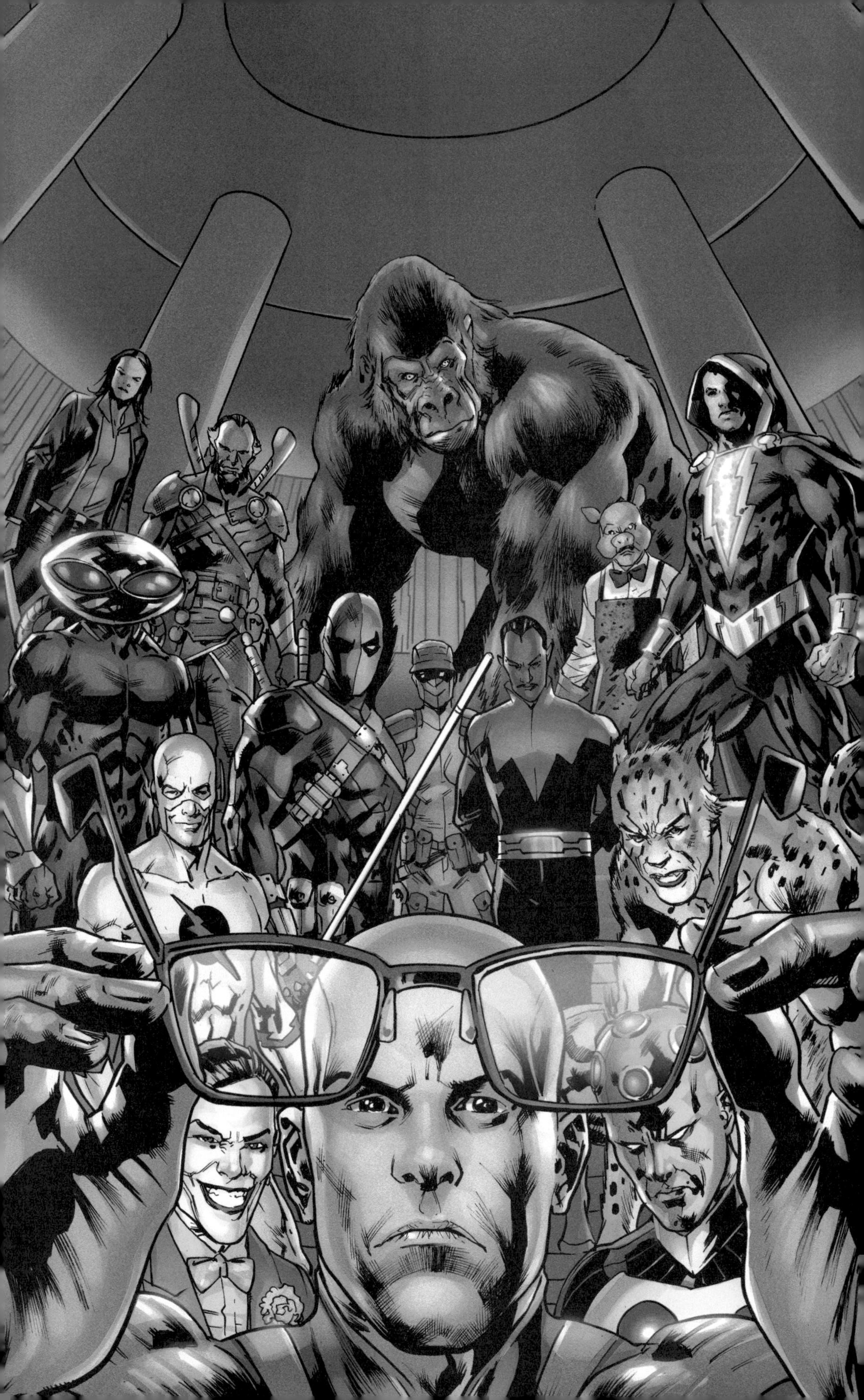

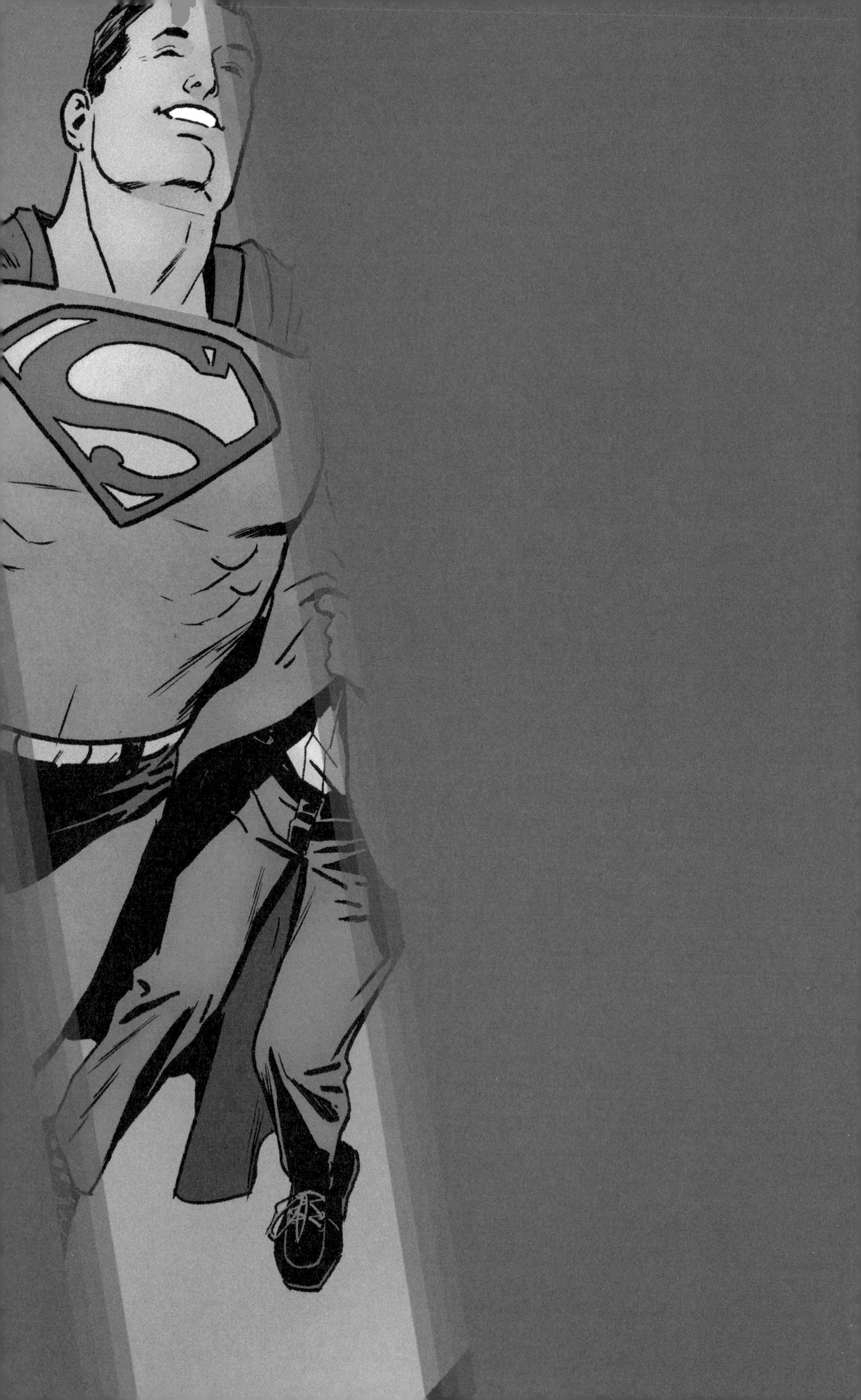

Clark Kent

told
the world
he is

DC Comics Proudly Presents *Superman: Villains*

Brian Michael Bendis, Matt Fraction, and Jody Houser
Writers

**Michael Gaydos, Riley Rossmo, Scott Godlewski, Bryan Hitch,
Cully Hamner, Steve Lieber, and Jim Mahfood**
Artists

**Michael Gaydos, Ivan Plascencia, Gabe Eltaeb, Alex Sinclair,
Dave McCaig, Nathan Fairbairn, and Jim Mahfood**
Colorists

Dave Sharpe, Clayton Cowles, Tom Napolitano, Troy Peteri, and Josh Reed
Letterers

Bryan Hitch and Alex Sinclair
Cover

Brittany Holzherr and Jamie S. Rich
Editors

SUPERMAN created by Jerry Siegel and Joe Shuster.
By special arrangement with the Jerry Siegel family.

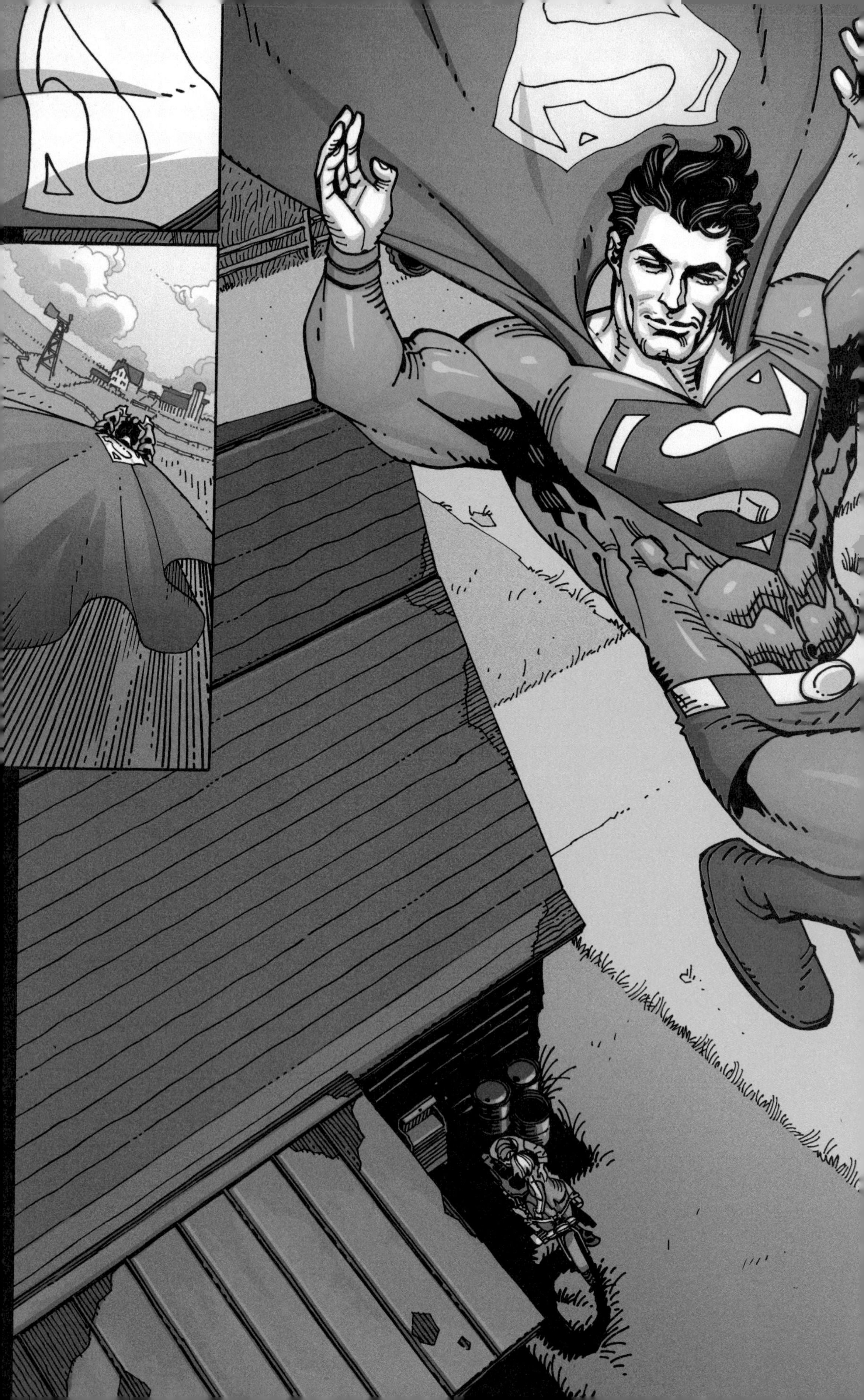

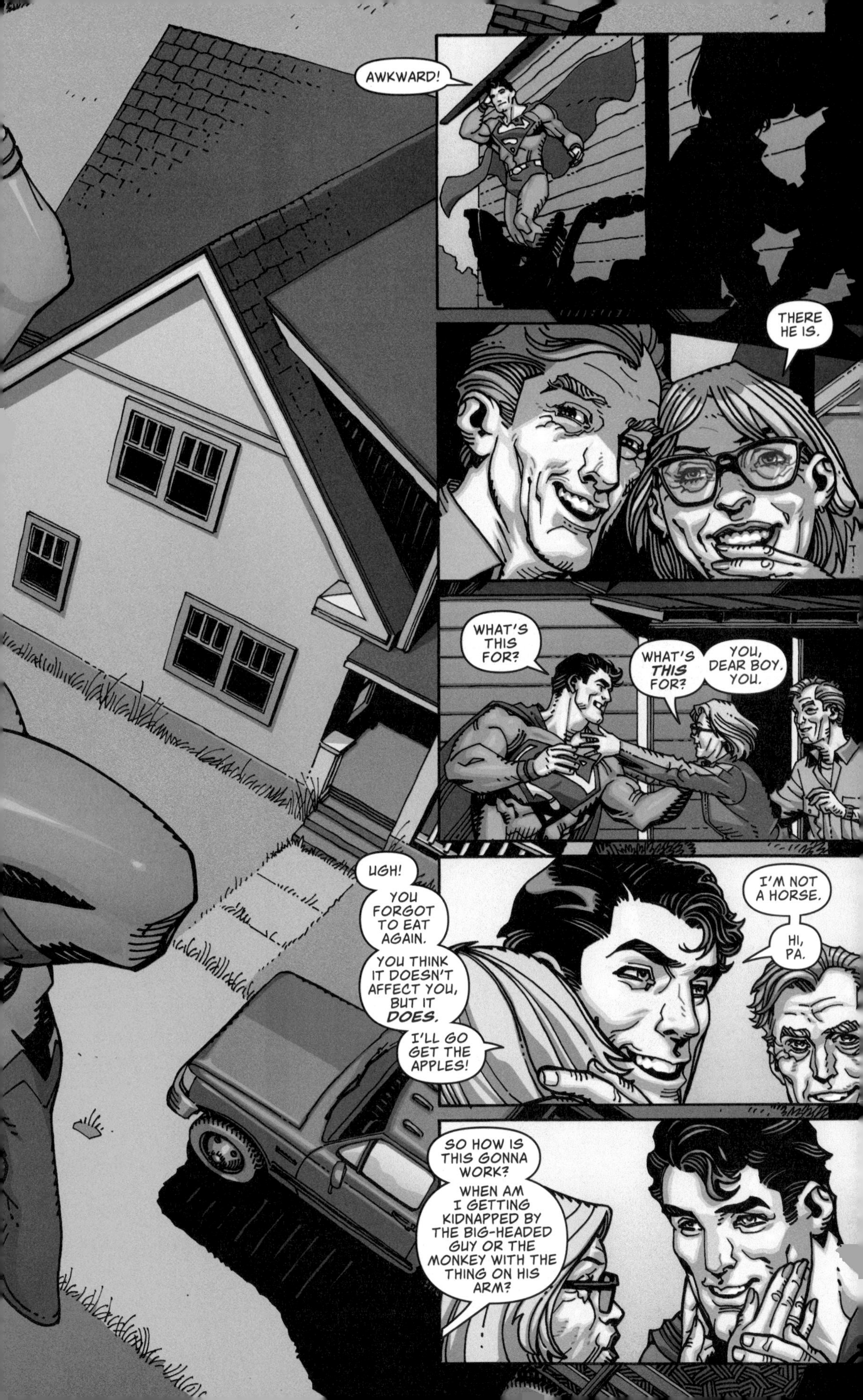
AWKWARD!
THERE HE IS.
WHAT'S THIS FOR?
WHAT'S *THIS* FOR?
YOU, DEAR BOY. YOU.
UGH!
YOU FORGOT TO EAT AGAIN.
YOU THINK IT DOESN'T AFFECT YOU, BUT IT *DOES.*
I'LL GO GET THE APPLES!
I'M NOT A HORSE.
HI, PA.
SO HOW IS THIS GONNA WORK?
WHEN AM I GETTING KIDNAPPED BY THE BIG-HEADED GUY OR THE MONKEY WITH THE THING ON HIS ARM?

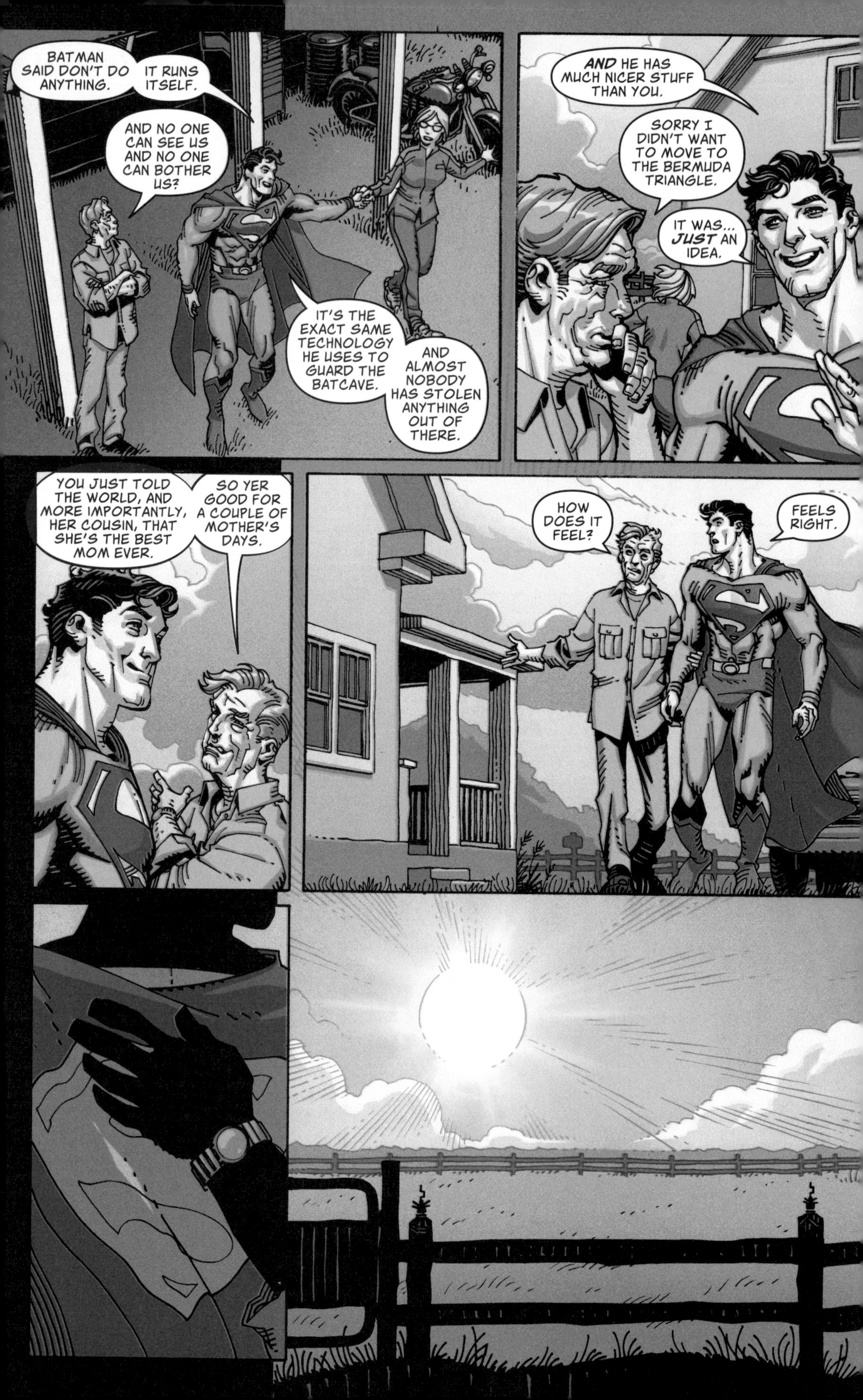
BATMAN SAID DON'T DO ANYTHING.
IT RUNS ITSELF.
AND NO ONE CAN SEE US AND NO ONE CAN BOTHER US?
IT'S THE EXACT SAME TECHNOLOGY HE USES TO GUARD THE BATCAVE.
AND ALMOST NOBODY HAS STOLEN ANYTHING OUT OF THERE.
AND HE HAS MUCH NICER STUFF THAN YOU.
SORRY I DIDN'T WANT TO MOVE TO THE BERMUDA TRIANGLE.
IT WAS... JUST AN IDEA.
YOU JUST TOLD THE WORLD, AND MORE IMPORTANTLY, HER COUSIN, THAT SHE'S THE BEST MOM EVER.
SO YER GOOD FOR A COUPLE OF MOTHER'S DAYS.
HOW DOES IT FEEL?
FEELS RIGHT.

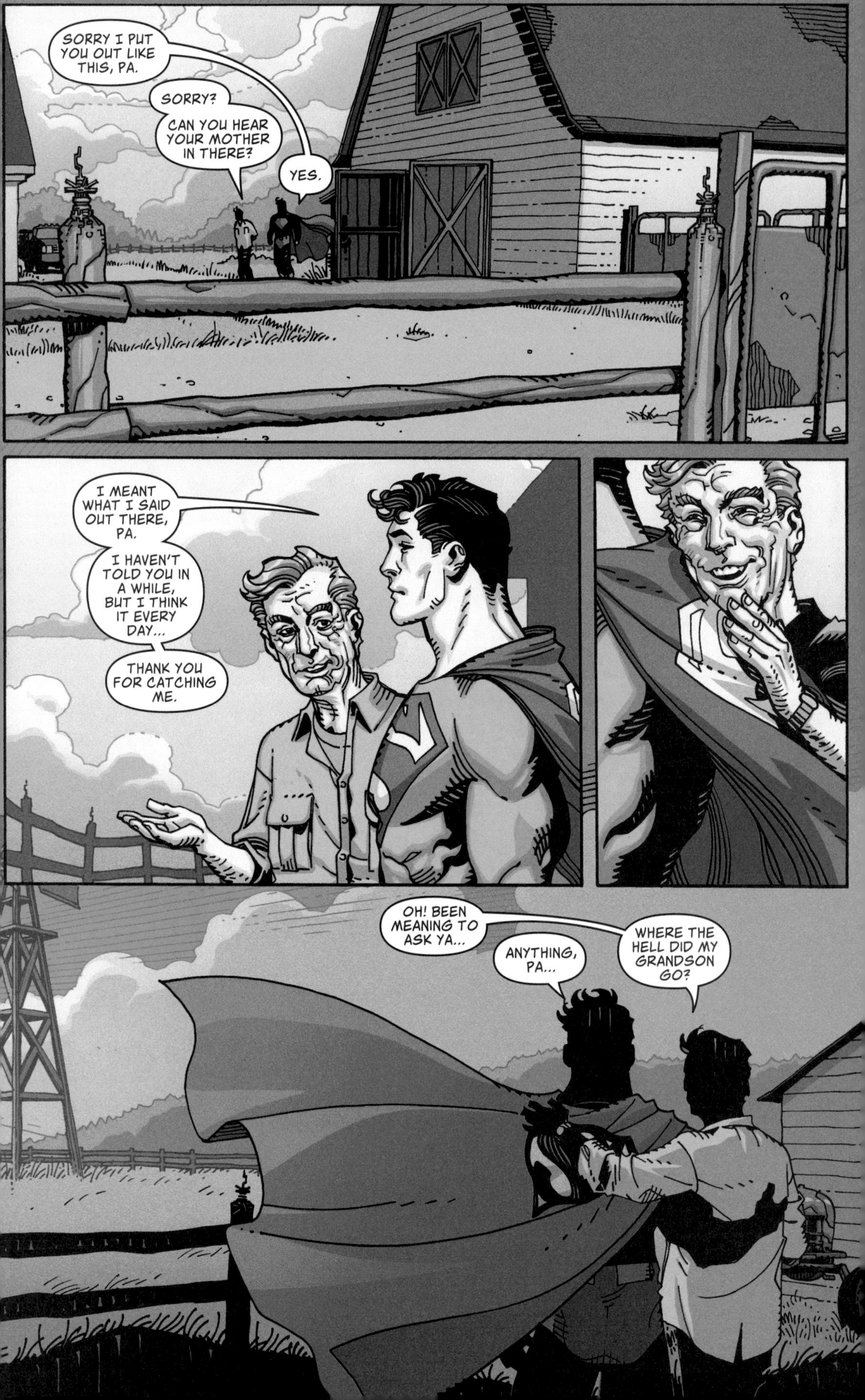
SORRY I PUT YOU OUT LIKE THIS, PA.
SORRY?
CAN YOU HEAR YOUR MOTHER IN THERE?
YES.
I MEANT WHAT I SAID OUT THERE, PA.
I HAVEN'T TOLD YOU IN A WHILE, BUT I THINK IT EVERY DAY...
THANK YOU FOR CATCHING ME.
OH! BEEN MEANING TO ASK YA...
ANYTHING, PA...
WHERE THE HELL DID MY GRANDSON GO?

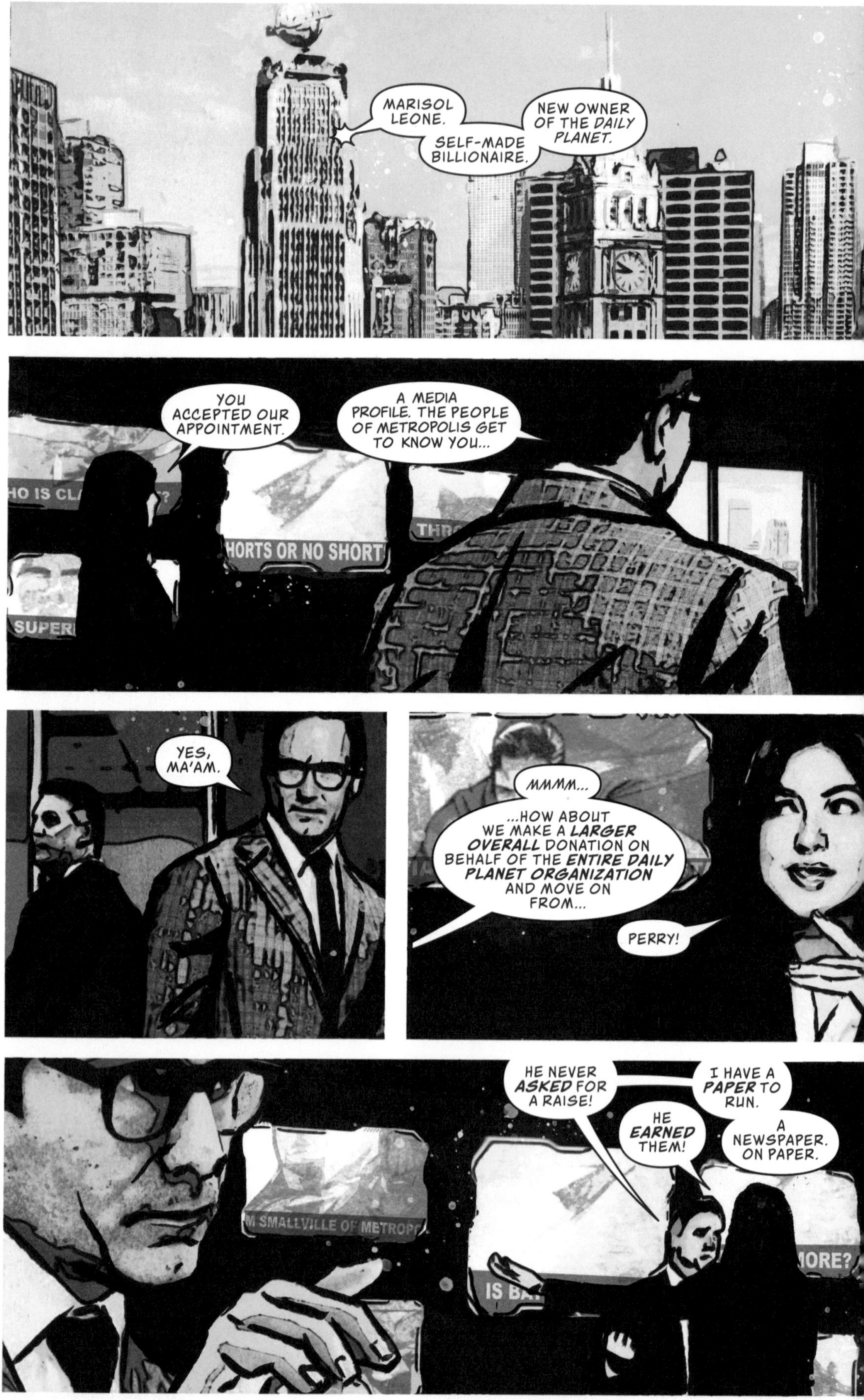
MARISOL LEONE.
SELF-MADE BILLIONAIRE.
NEW OWNER OF THE DAILY PLANET.
YOU ACCEPTED OUR APPOINTMENT.
A MEDIA PROFILE. THE PEOPLE OF METROPOLIS GET TO KNOW YOU...
YES, MA'AM.
MMMM...
...HOW ABOUT WE MAKE A LARGER OVERALL DONATION ON BEHALF OF THE ENTIRE DAILY PLANET ORGANIZATION AND MOVE ON FROM...
PERRY!
HE NEVER ASKED FOR A RAISE!
HE EARNED THEM!
I HAVE A PAPER TO RUN.
A NEWSPAPER. ON PAPER.

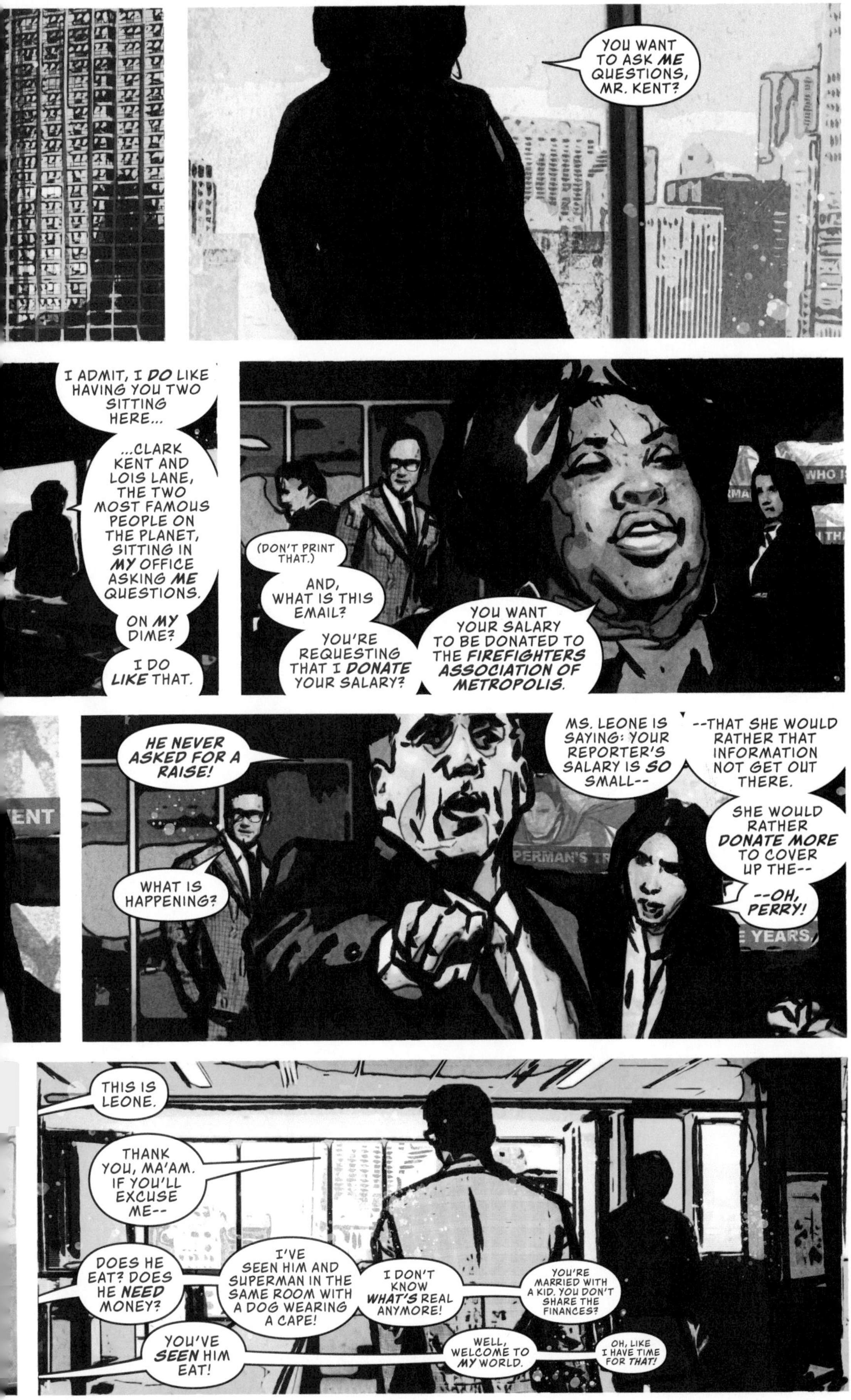
YOU WANT TO ASK ME QUESTIONS, MR. KENT?
I ADMIT, I DO LIKE HAVING YOU TWO SITTING HERE...
...CLARK KENT AND LOIS LANE, THE TWO MOST FAMOUS PEOPLE ON THE PLANET, SITTING IN MY OFFICE ASKING ME QUESTIONS.
ON MY DIME?
I DO LIKE THAT.
(DON'T PRINT THAT.)
AND, WHAT IS THIS EMAIL?
YOU'RE REQUESTING THAT I DONATE YOUR SALARY?
YOU WANT YOUR SALARY TO BE DONATED TO THE FIREFIGHTERS ASSOCIATION OF METROPOLIS.
HE NEVER ASKED FOR A RAISE!
WHAT IS HAPPENING?
MS. LEONE IS SAYING: YOUR REPORTER'S SALARY IS SO SMALL--
--THAT SHE WOULD RATHER THAT INFORMATION NOT GET OUT THERE.
SHE WOULD RATHER DONATE MORE TO COVER UP THE--
--OH, PERRY!
THIS IS LEONE.
THANK YOU, MA'AM. IF YOU'LL EXCUSE ME--
DOES HE EAT? DOES HE NEED MONEY?
YOU'VE SEEN HIM EAT!
I'VE SEEN HIM AND SUPERMAN IN THE SAME ROOM WITH A DOG WEARING A CAPE!
I DON'T KNOW WHAT'S REAL ANYMORE!
WELL, WELCOME TO MY WORLD.
YOU'RE MARRIED WITH A KID. YOU DON'T SHARE THE FINANCES?
OH, LIKE I HAVE TIME FOR THAT!

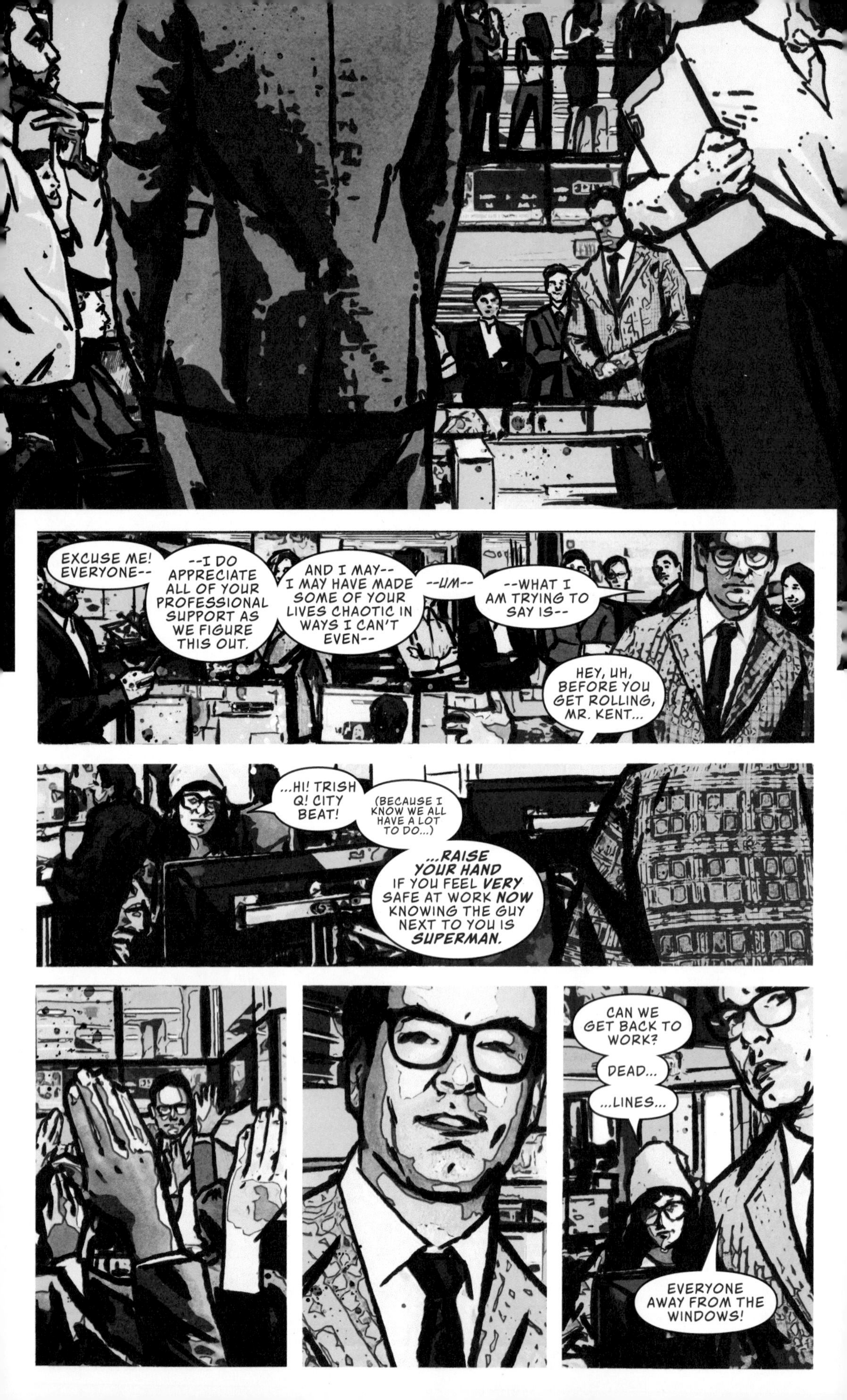

EXCUSE ME! EVERYONE--
--I DO APPRECIATE ALL OF YOUR PROFESSIONAL SUPPORT AS WE FIGURE THIS OUT.
AND I MAY-- I MAY HAVE MADE SOME OF YOUR LIVES CHAOTIC IN WAYS I CAN'T EVEN--
--UM--
--WHAT I AM TRYING TO SAY IS--
HEY, UH, BEFORE YOU GET ROLLING, MR. KENT...
...HI! TRISH Q! CITY BEAT!
(BECAUSE I KNOW WE ALL HAVE A LOT TO DO...)
...RAISE YOUR HAND IF YOU FEEL VERY SAFE AT WORK NOW KNOWING THE GUY NEXT TO YOU IS SUPERMAN.
CAN WE GET BACK TO WORK?
DEAD...
...LINES...
EVERYONE AWAY FROM THE WINDOWS!

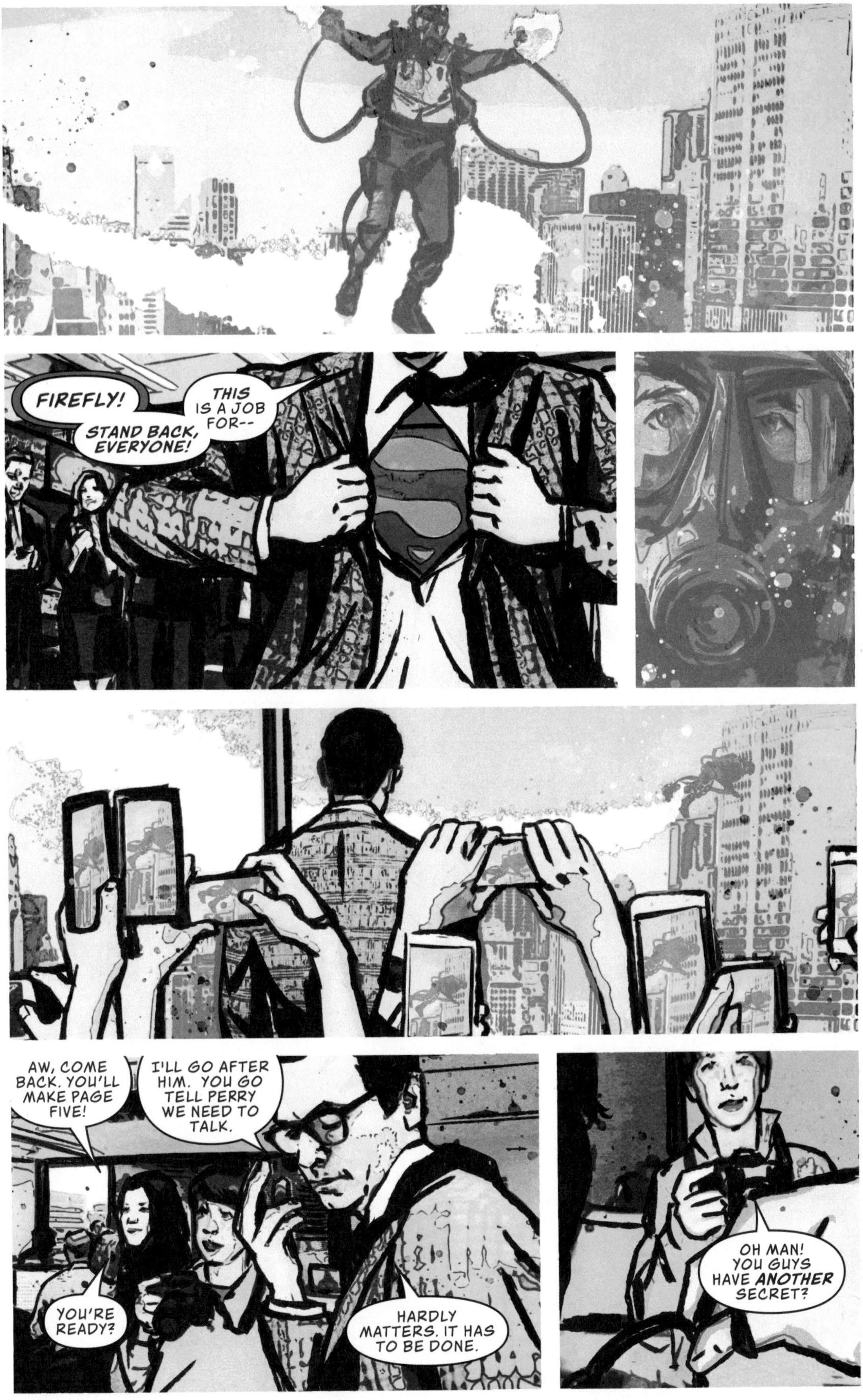
FIREFLY!
STAND BACK, EVERYONE!
THIS IS A JOB FOR--
AW, COME BACK. YOU'LL MAKE PAGE FIVE!
I'LL GO AFTER HIM. YOU GO TELL PERRY WE NEED TO TALK.
YOU'RE READY?
HARDLY MATTERS. IT HAS TO BE DONE.
OH MAN! YOU GUYS HAVE ANOTHER SECRET?

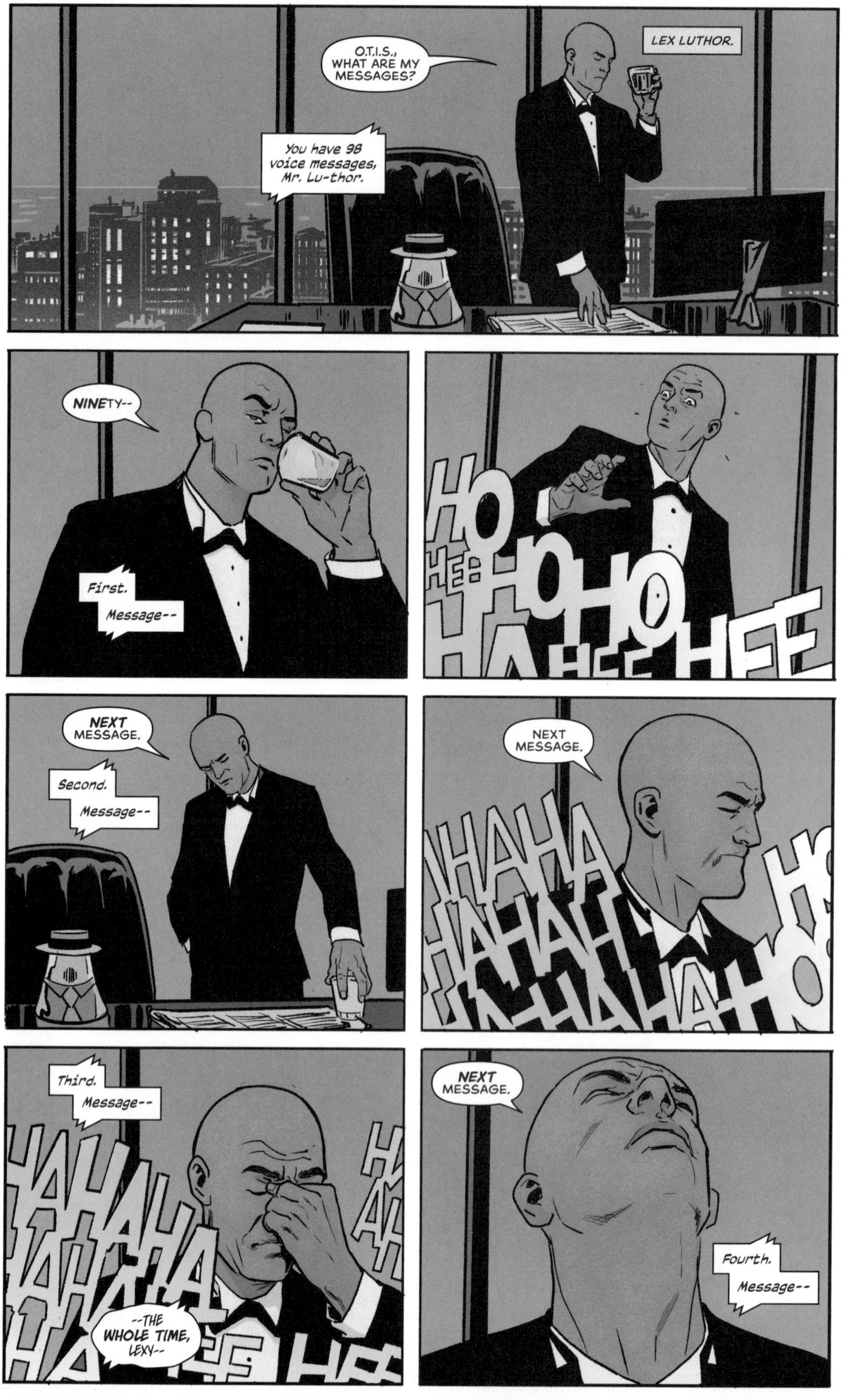
LEX LUTHOR.
O.T.I.S., WHAT ARE MY MESSAGES?
You have 98 voice messages, Mr. Lu-thor.
NINETY--
First. Message--
HO HO HO HEE HA HEE HEE
NEXT MESSAGE.
Second. Message--
NEXT MESSAGE.
HAHA HAHAHA HAHAHAHAHO HO
Third. Message--
HAHAHAHAHAHA HEE HEE
--THE WHOLE TIME, LEXY--
NEXT MESSAGE.
Fourth. Message--

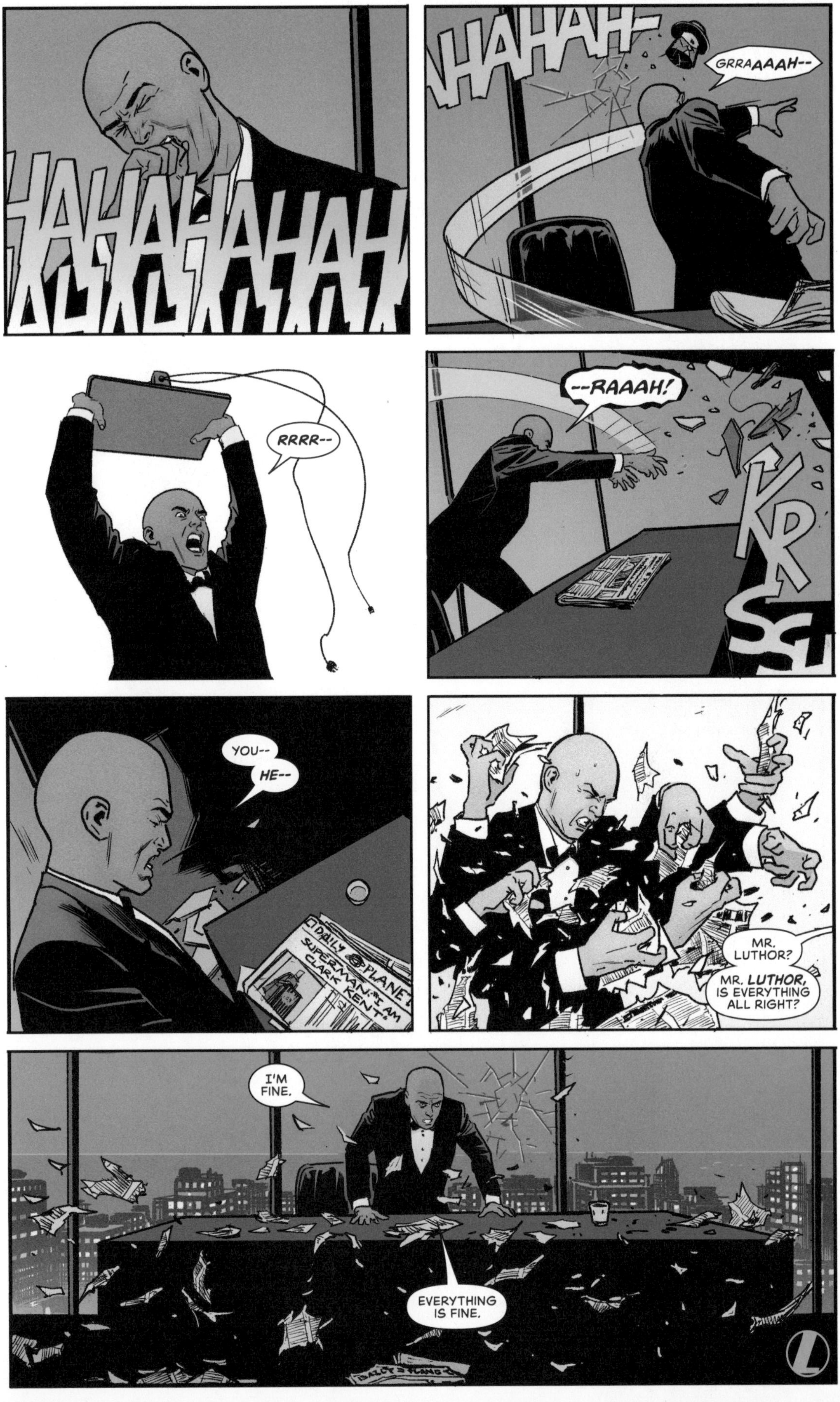
HAHAHAHAHAH
HAHAH-
GRRAAAAH--
RRRR--
--RAAAH!
KR
YOU--
HE--
DAILY PLANET
SUPERMAN: "I AM CLARK KENT."
MR. LUTHOR?
MR. LUTHOR, IS EVERYTHING ALL RIGHT?
I'M FINE.
EVERYTHING IS FINE.

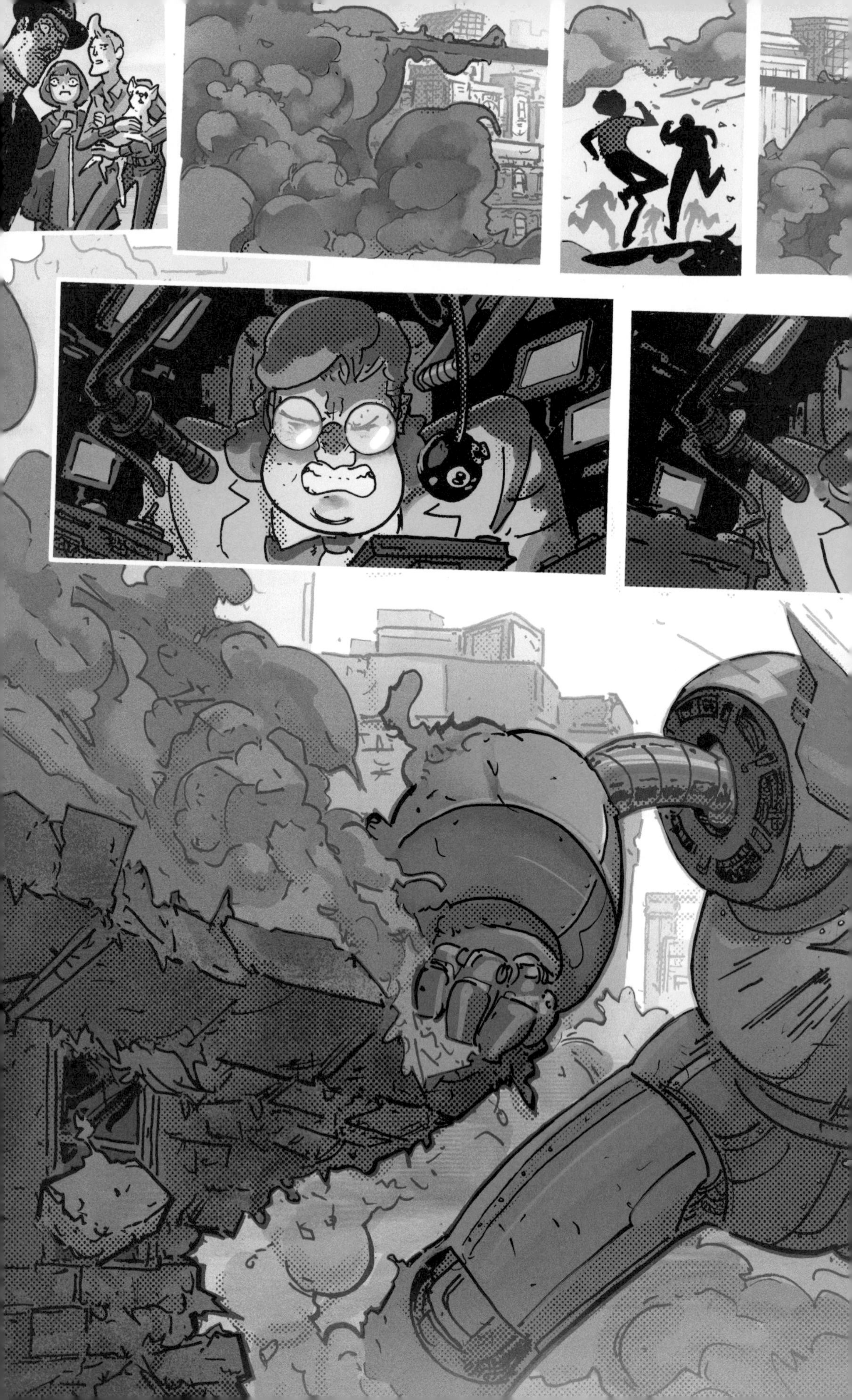

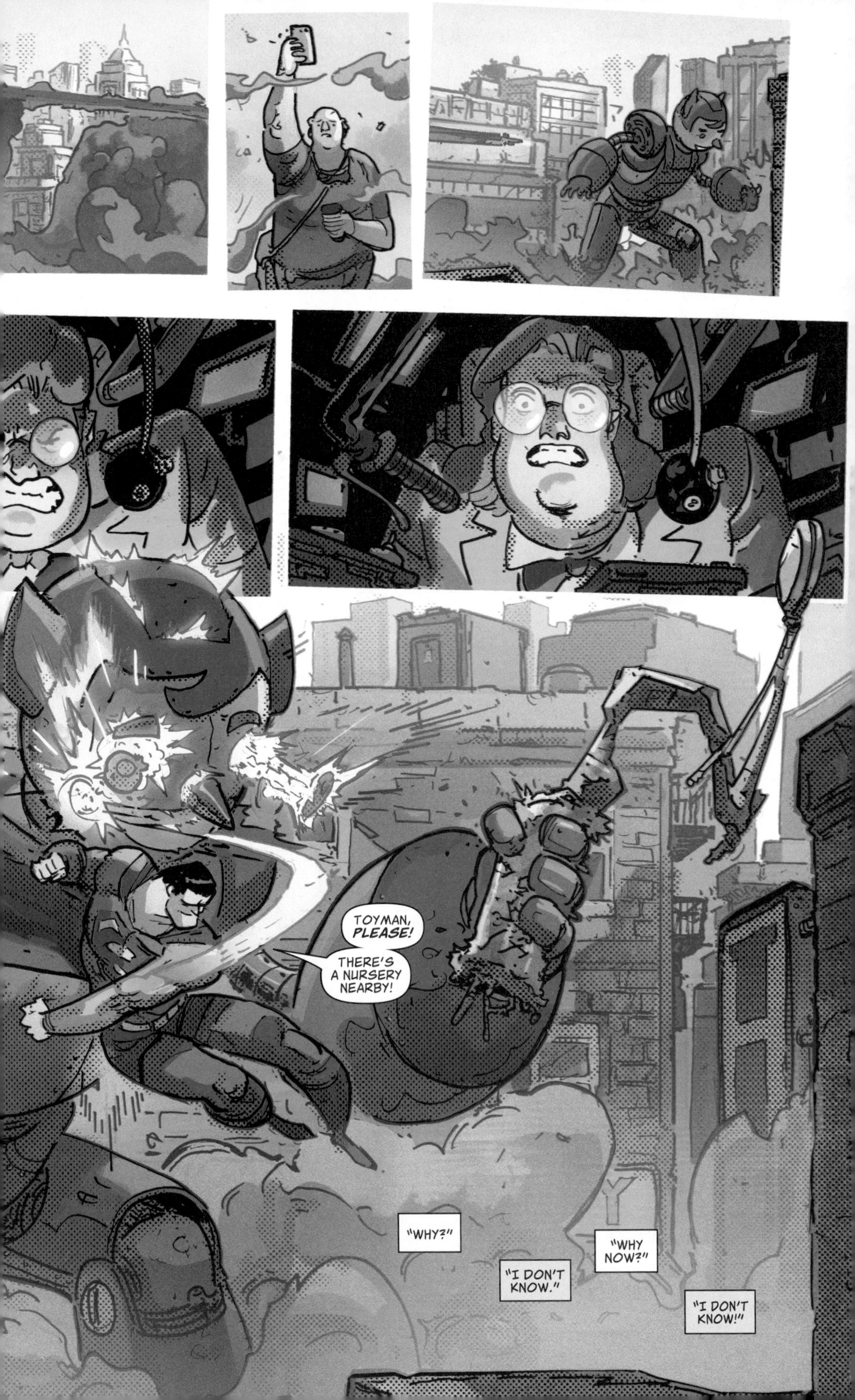
TOYMAN, PLEASE!
THERE'S A NURSERY NEARBY!
"WHY?"
"I DON'T KNOW."
"WHY NOW?"
"I DON'T KNOW!"

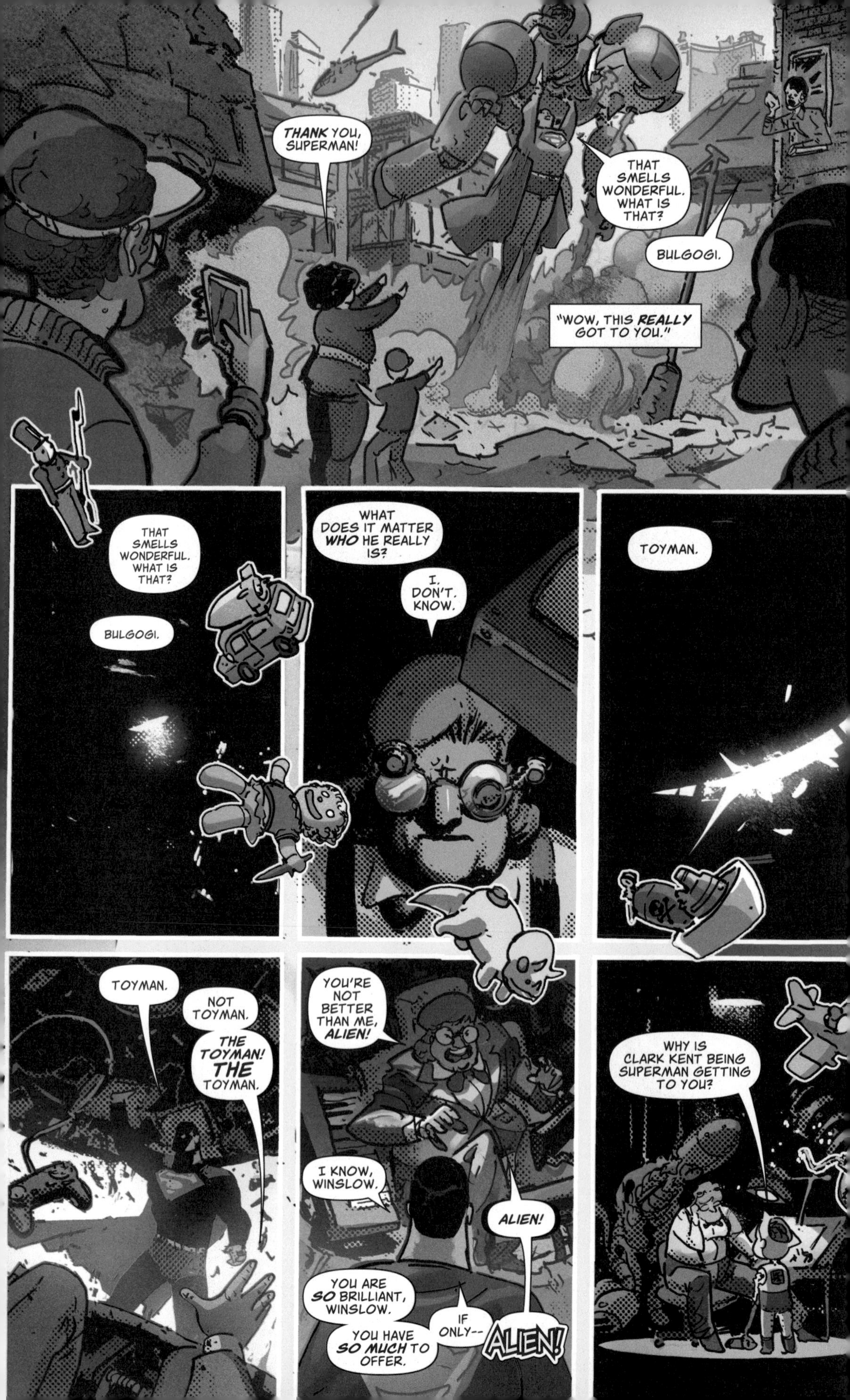
THANK YOU, SUPERMAN!
THAT SMELLS WONDERFUL. WHAT IS THAT?
BULGOGI.
"WOW, THIS REALLY GOT TO YOU."
THAT SMELLS WONDERFUL. WHAT IS THAT?
BULGOGI.
WHAT DOES IT MATTER WHO HE REALLY IS?
I. DON'T. KNOW.
TOYMAN.
TOYMAN.
NOT TOYMAN.
THE TOYMAN! THE TOYMAN.
YOU'RE NOT BETTER THAN ME, ALIEN!
I KNOW, WINSLOW.
ALIEN!
YOU ARE SO BRILLIANT, WINSLOW.
YOU HAVE SO MUCH TO OFFER.
IF ONLY--
ALIEN!
WHY IS CLARK KENT BEING SUPERMAN GETTING TO YOU?

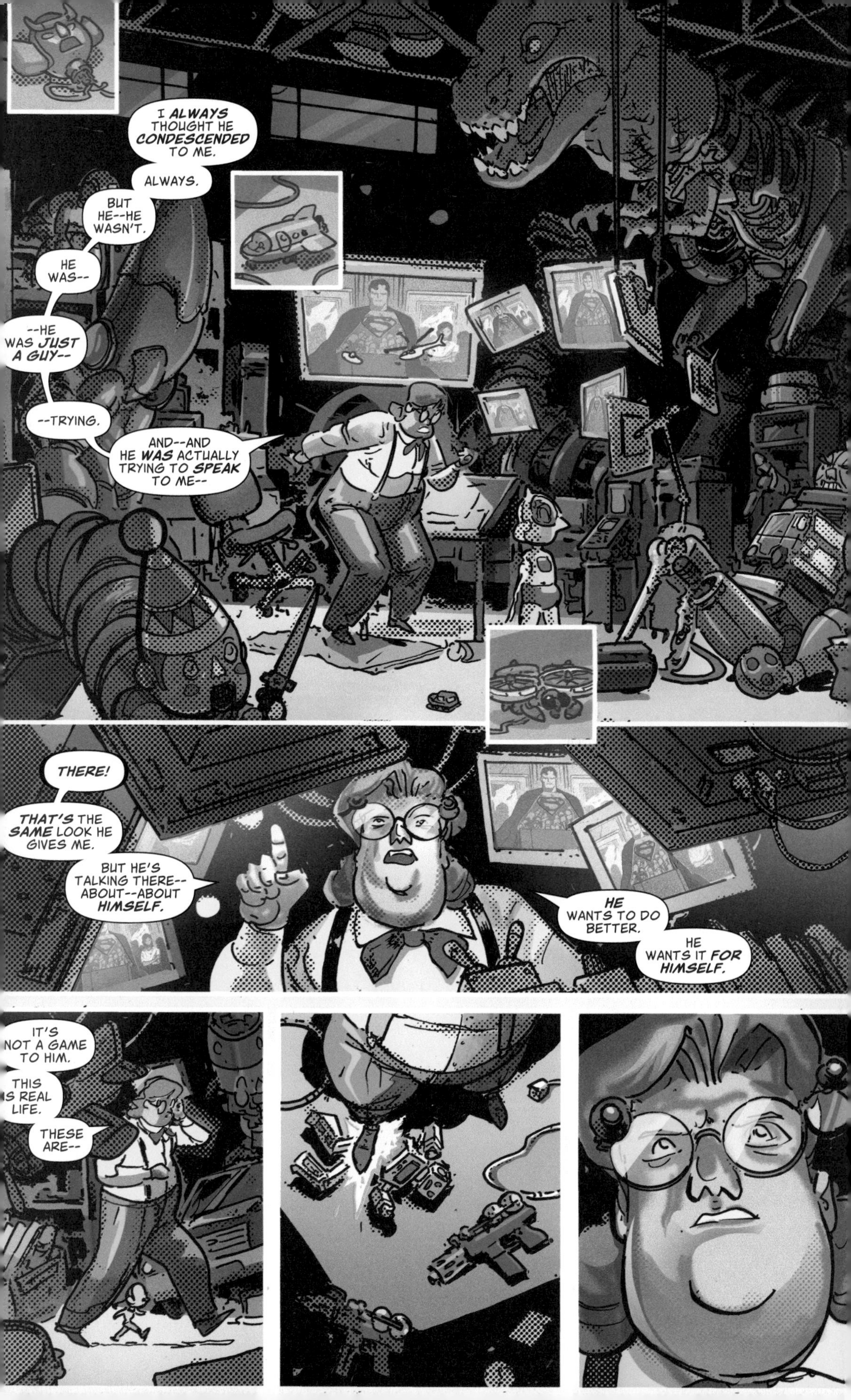

I ALWAYS THOUGHT HE CONDESCENDED TO ME.
ALWAYS.
BUT HE--HE WASN'T.
HE WAS--
--HE WAS JUST A GUY--
--TRYING.
AND--AND HE WAS ACTUALLY TRYING TO SPEAK TO ME--
THERE!
THAT'S THE SAME LOOK HE GIVES ME.
BUT HE'S TALKING THERE-- ABOUT--ABOUT HIMSELF.
HE WANTS TO DO BETTER.
HE WANTS IT FOR HIMSELF.
IT'S NOT A GAME TO HIM.
THIS S REAL LIFE.
THESE ARE--

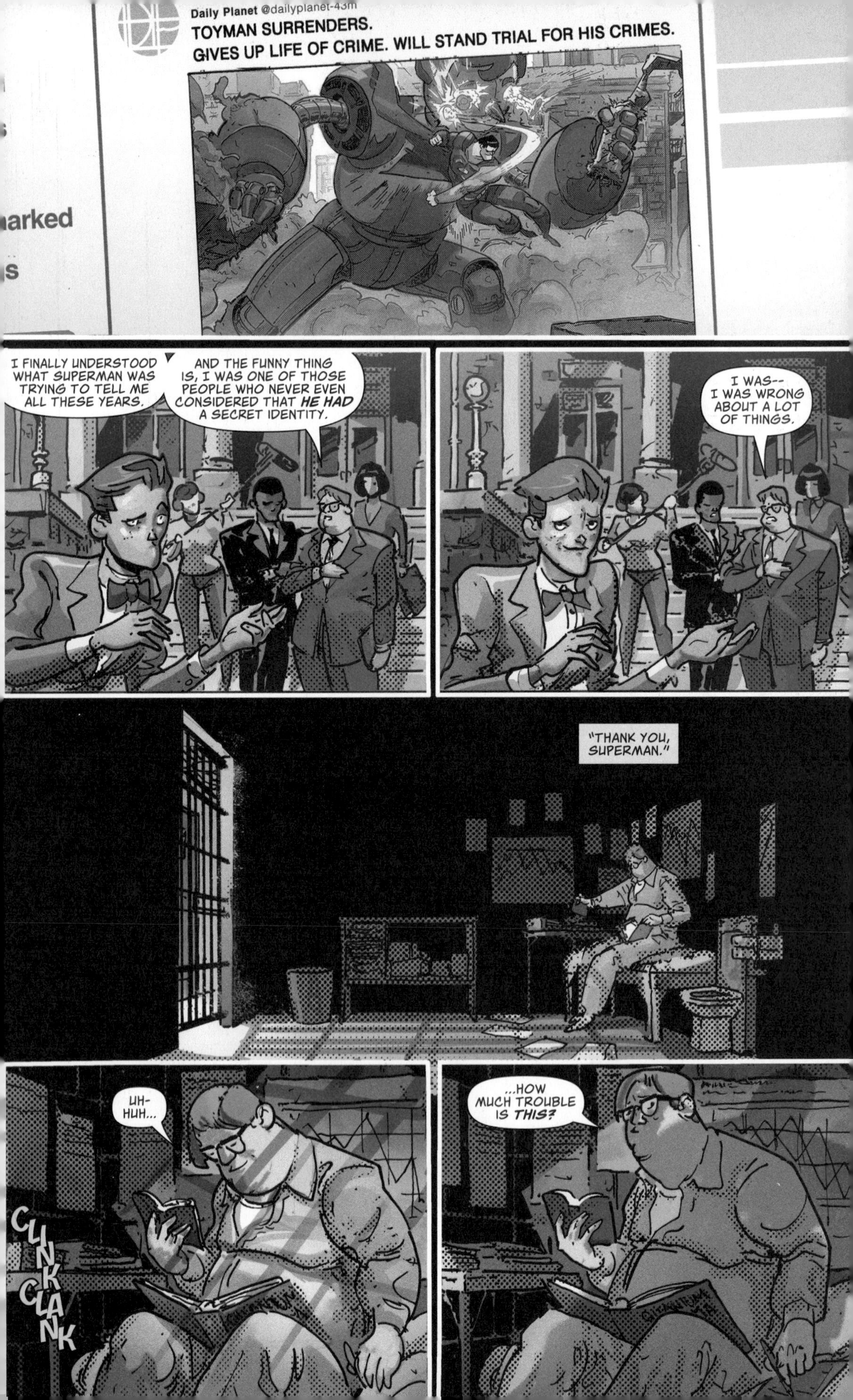

arked
s
Daily Planet @dailyplanet-43m
TOYMAN SURRENDERS.
GIVES UP LIFE OF CRIME. WILL STAND TRIAL FOR HIS CRIMES.
I FINALLY UNDERSTOOD WHAT SUPERMAN WAS TRYING TO TELL ME ALL THESE YEARS.
AND THE FUNNY THING IS, I WAS ONE OF THOSE PEOPLE WHO NEVER EVEN CONSIDERED THAT HE HAD A SECRET IDENTITY.
I WAS-- I WAS WRONG ABOUT A LOT OF THINGS.
"THANK YOU, SUPERMAN."
UH-HUH...
CLINK CLANK
...HOW MUCH TROUBLE IS THIS?

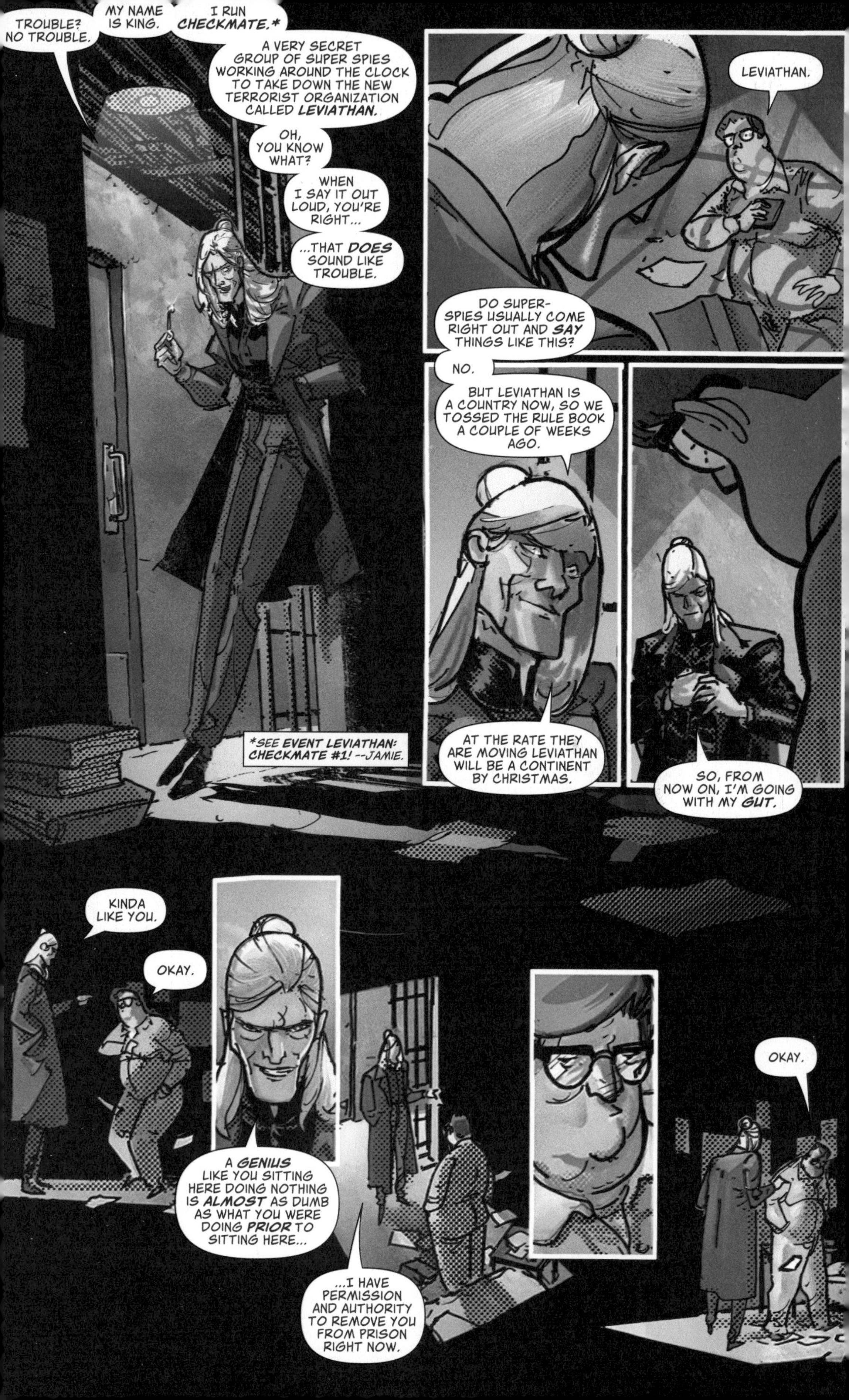
TROUBLE? NO TROUBLE.
MY NAME IS KING.
I RUN CHECKMATE.*
A VERY SECRET GROUP OF SUPER SPIES WORKING AROUND THE CLOCK TO TAKE DOWN THE NEW TERRORIST ORGANIZATION CALLED LEVIATHAN.
OH, YOU KNOW WHAT?
WHEN I SAY IT OUT LOUD, YOU'RE RIGHT...
...THAT DOES SOUND LIKE TROUBLE.
*SEE EVENT LEVIATHAN: CHECKMATE #1! --JAMIE.
LEVIATHAN.
DO SUPER-SPIES USUALLY COME RIGHT OUT AND SAY THINGS LIKE THIS?
NO.
BUT LEVIATHAN IS A COUNTRY NOW, SO WE TOSSED THE RULE BOOK A COUPLE OF WEEKS AGO.
AT THE RATE THEY ARE MOVING LEVIATHAN WILL BE A CONTINENT BY CHRISTMAS.
SO, FROM NOW ON, I'M GOING WITH MY GUT.
KINDA LIKE YOU.
OKAY.
A GENIUS LIKE YOU SITTING HERE DOING NOTHING IS ALMOST AS DUMB AS WHAT YOU WERE DOING PRIOR TO SITTING HERE...
...I HAVE PERMISSION AND AUTHORITY TO REMOVE YOU FROM PRISON RIGHT NOW.
OKAY.

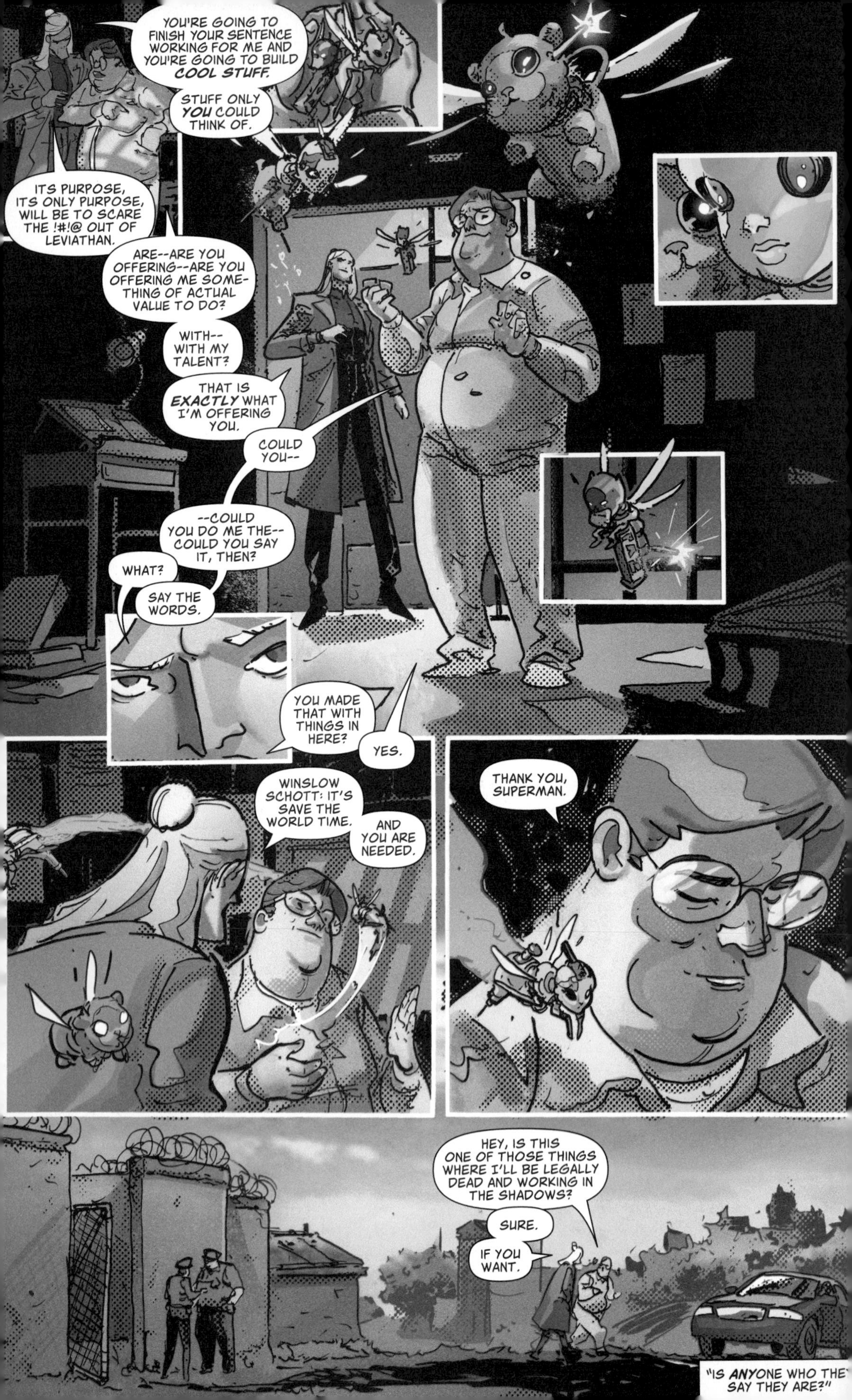

YOU'RE GOING TO FINISH YOUR SENTENCE WORKING FOR ME AND YOU'RE GOING TO BUILD COOL STUFF.
STUFF ONLY YOU COULD THINK OF.
ITS PURPOSE, ITS ONLY PURPOSE, WILL BE TO SCARE THE !#!@ OUT OF LEVIATHAN.
ARE--ARE YOU OFFERING--ARE YOU OFFERING ME SOME-THING OF ACTUAL VALUE TO DO?
WITH--WITH MY TALENT?
THAT IS EXACTLY WHAT I'M OFFERING YOU.
COULD YOU--
--COULD YOU DO ME THE--COULD YOU SAY IT, THEN?
WHAT?
SAY THE WORDS.
YOU MADE THAT WITH THINGS IN HERE?
YES.
WINSLOW SCHOTT: IT'S SAVE THE WORLD TIME.
AND YOU ARE NEEDED.
THANK YOU, SUPERMAN.
HEY, IS THIS ONE OF THOSE THINGS WHERE I'LL BE LEGALLY DEAD AND WORKING IN THE SHADOWS?
SURE.
IF YOU WANT.
"IS ANYONE WHO THE SAY THEY ARE?"

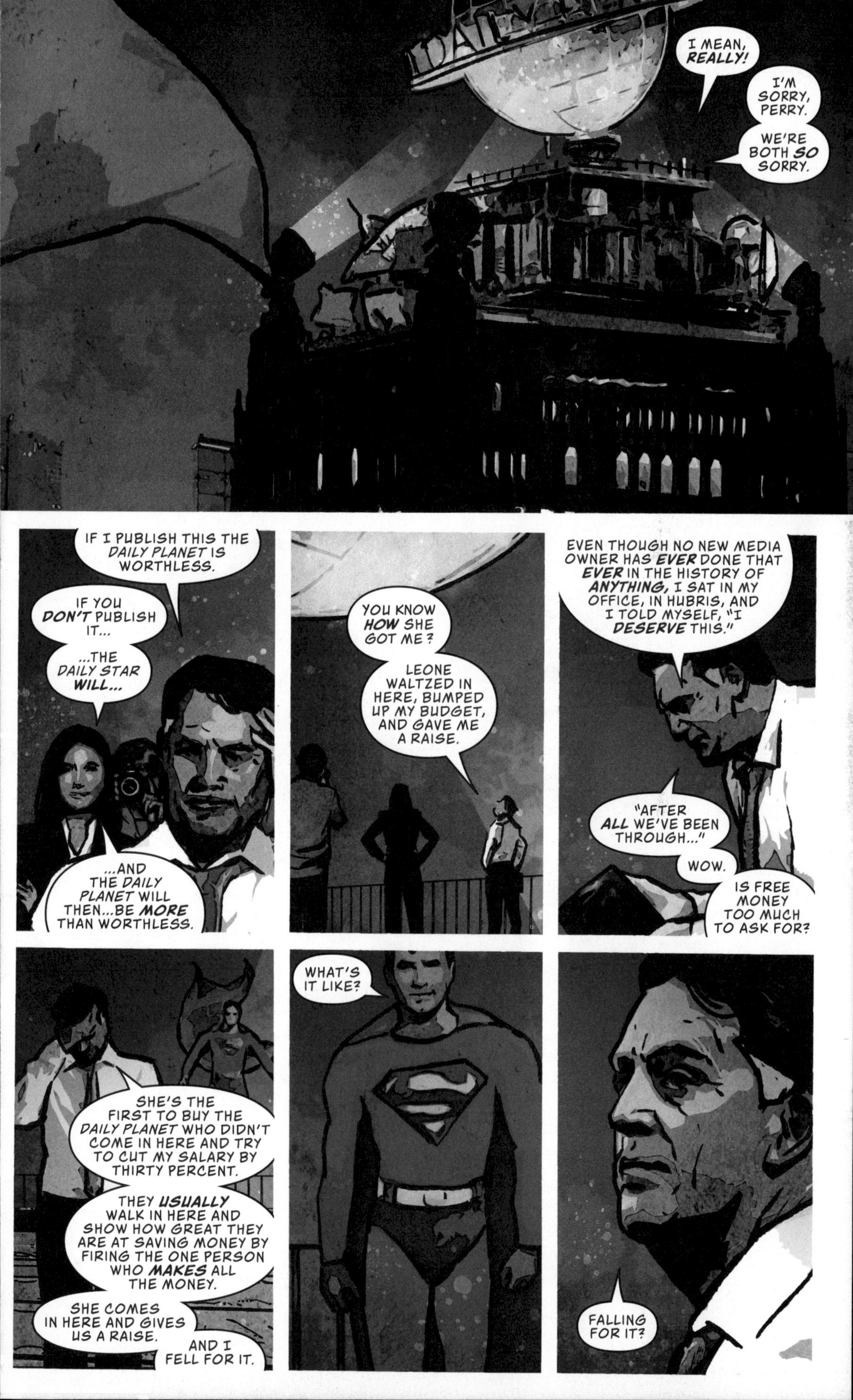
I MEAN, REALLY!
I'M SORRY, PERRY.
WE'RE BOTH SO SORRY.
IF I PUBLISH THIS THE DAILY PLANET IS WORTHLESS.
IF YOU DON'T PUBLISH IT...
...THE DAILY STAR WILL...
...AND THE DAILY PLANET WILL THEN...BE MORE THAN WORTHLESS.
YOU KNOW HOW SHE GOT ME?
LEONE WALTZED IN HERE, BUMPED UP MY BUDGET, AND GAVE ME A RAISE.
EVEN THOUGH NO NEW MEDIA OWNER HAS EVER DONE THAT EVER IN THE HISTORY OF ANYTHING, I SAT IN MY OFFICE, IN HUBRIS, AND I TOLD MYSELF, "I DESERVE THIS."
"AFTER ALL WE'VE BEEN THROUGH..."
WOW.
IS FREE MONEY TOO MUCH TO ASK FOR?
SHE'S THE FIRST TO BUY THE DAILY PLANET WHO DIDN'T COME IN HERE AND TRY TO CUT MY SALARY BY THIRTY PERCENT.
THEY USUALLY WALK IN HERE AND SHOW HOW GREAT THEY ARE AT SAVING MONEY BY FIRING THE ONE PERSON WHO MAKES ALL THE MONEY.
SHE COMES IN HERE AND GIVES US A RAISE.
AND I FELL FOR IT.
WHAT'S IT LIKE?
FALLING FOR IT?

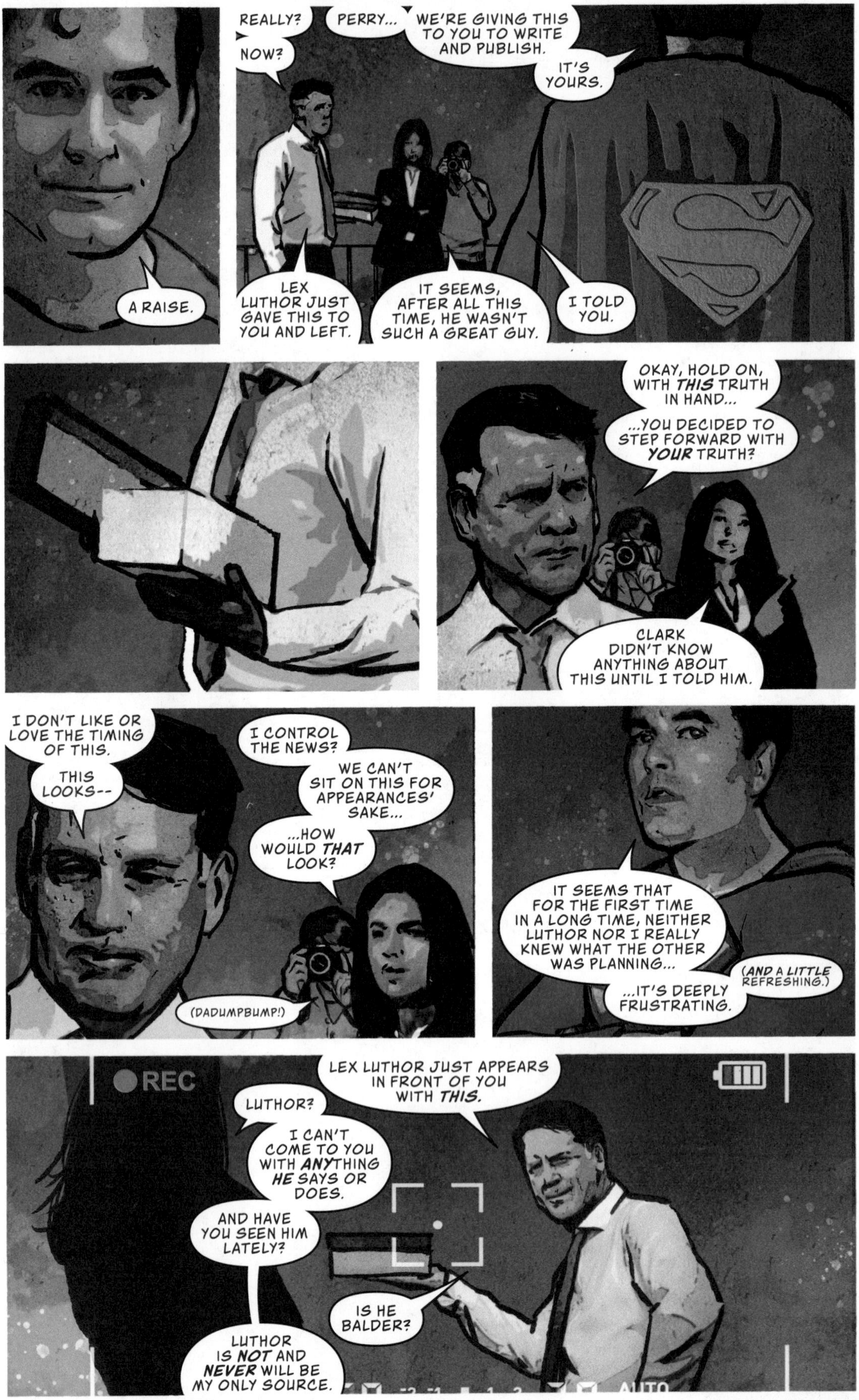
A RAISE.
REALLY?
NOW?
PERRY...
WE'RE GIVING THIS TO YOU TO WRITE AND PUBLISH.
IT'S YOURS.
LEX LUTHOR JUST GAVE THIS TO YOU AND LEFT.
IT SEEMS, AFTER ALL THIS TIME, HE WASN'T SUCH A GREAT GUY.
I TOLD YOU.
OKAY, HOLD ON, WITH *THIS* TRUTH IN HAND...
...YOU DECIDED TO STEP FORWARD WITH *YOUR* TRUTH?
CLARK DIDN'T KNOW ANYTHING ABOUT THIS UNTIL I TOLD HIM.
I DON'T LIKE OR LOVE THE TIMING OF THIS.
THIS LOOKS--
I CONTROL THE NEWS?
WE CAN'T SIT ON THIS FOR APPEARANCES' SAKE...
...HOW WOULD *THAT* LOOK?
(DADUMPBUMP!)
IT SEEMS THAT FOR THE FIRST TIME IN A LONG TIME, NEITHER LUTHOR NOR I REALLY KNEW WHAT THE OTHER WAS PLANNING...
...IT'S DEEPLY FRUSTRATING.
(*AND* A *LITTLE* REFRESHING.)
REC
LEX LUTHOR JUST APPEARS IN FRONT OF YOU WITH *THIS.*
LUTHOR?
I CAN'T COME TO YOU WITH *ANY*THING *HE* SAYS OR DOES.
AND HAVE YOU SEEN HIM LATELY?
IS HE BALDER?
LUTHOR IS *NOT* AND *NEVER* WILL BE MY ONLY SOURCE.
AUTO

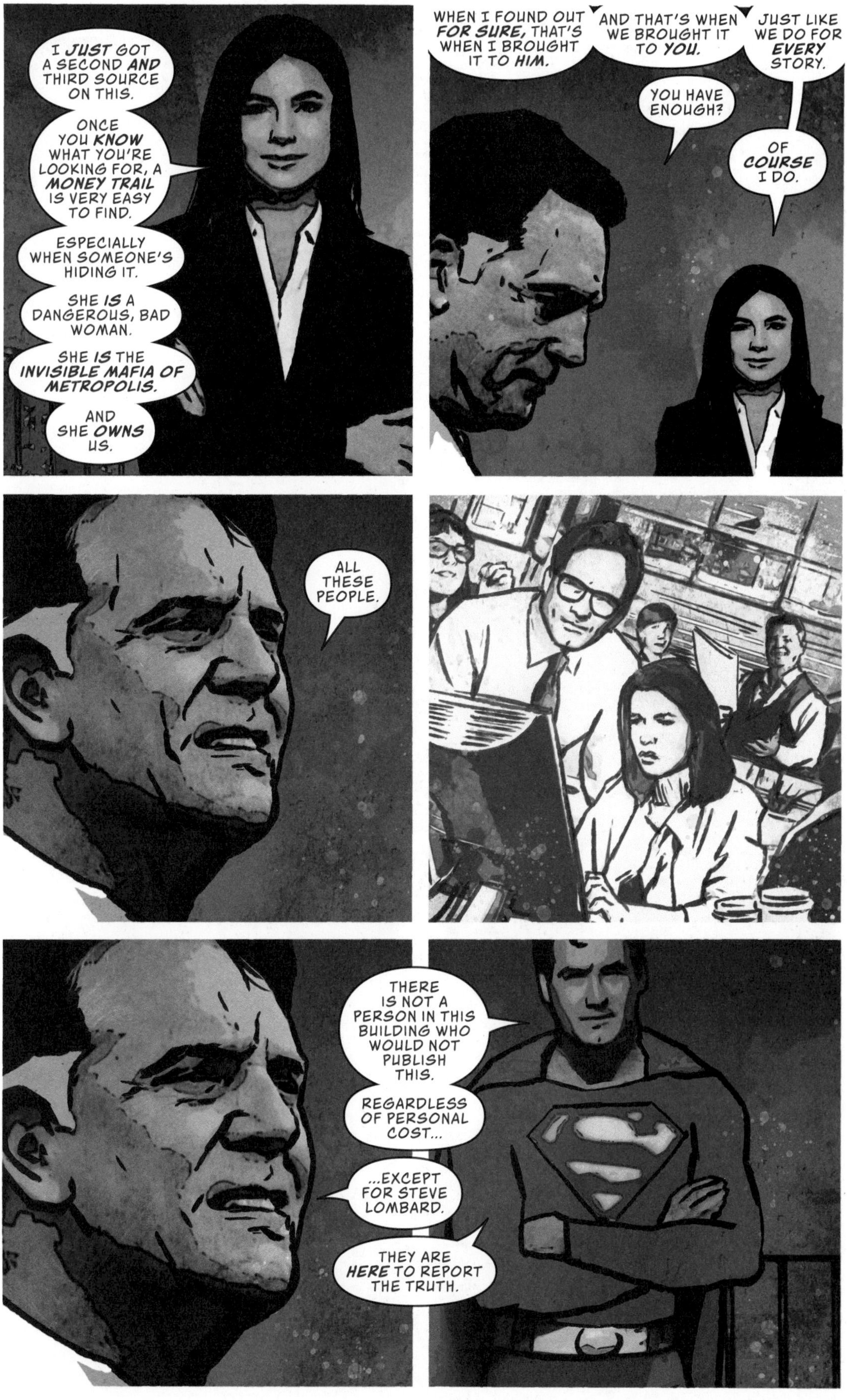
I JUST GOT A SECOND AND THIRD SOURCE ON THIS.
ONCE YOU KNOW WHAT YOU'RE LOOKING FOR, A MONEY TRAIL IS VERY EASY TO FIND.
ESPECIALLY WHEN SOMEONE'S HIDING IT.
SHE IS A DANGEROUS, BAD WOMAN.
SHE IS THE INVISIBLE MAFIA OF METROPOLIS.
AND SHE OWNS US.
WHEN I FOUND OUT FOR SURE, THAT'S WHEN I BROUGHT IT TO HIM.
AND THAT'S WHEN WE BROUGHT IT TO YOU.
JUST LIKE WE DO FOR EVERY STORY.
YOU HAVE ENOUGH?
OF COURSE I DO.
ALL THESE PEOPLE.
THERE IS NOT A PERSON IN THIS BUILDING WHO WOULD NOT PUBLISH THIS.
REGARDLESS OF PERSONAL COST...
...EXCEPT FOR STEVE LOMBARD.
THEY ARE HERE TO REPORT THE TRUTH.

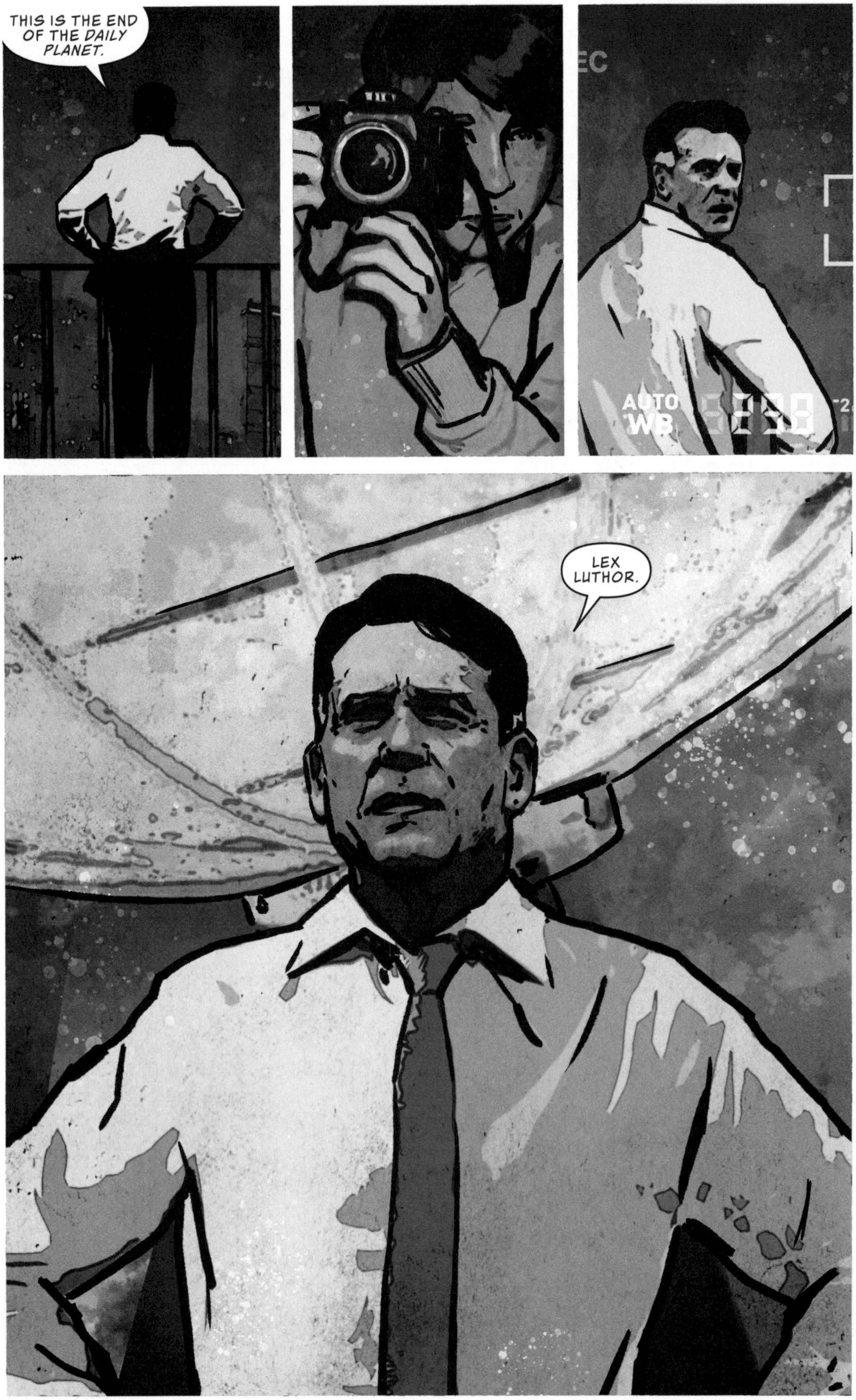
THIS IS THE END OF THE *DAILY PLANET.*
AUTO WB
LEX LUTHOR.

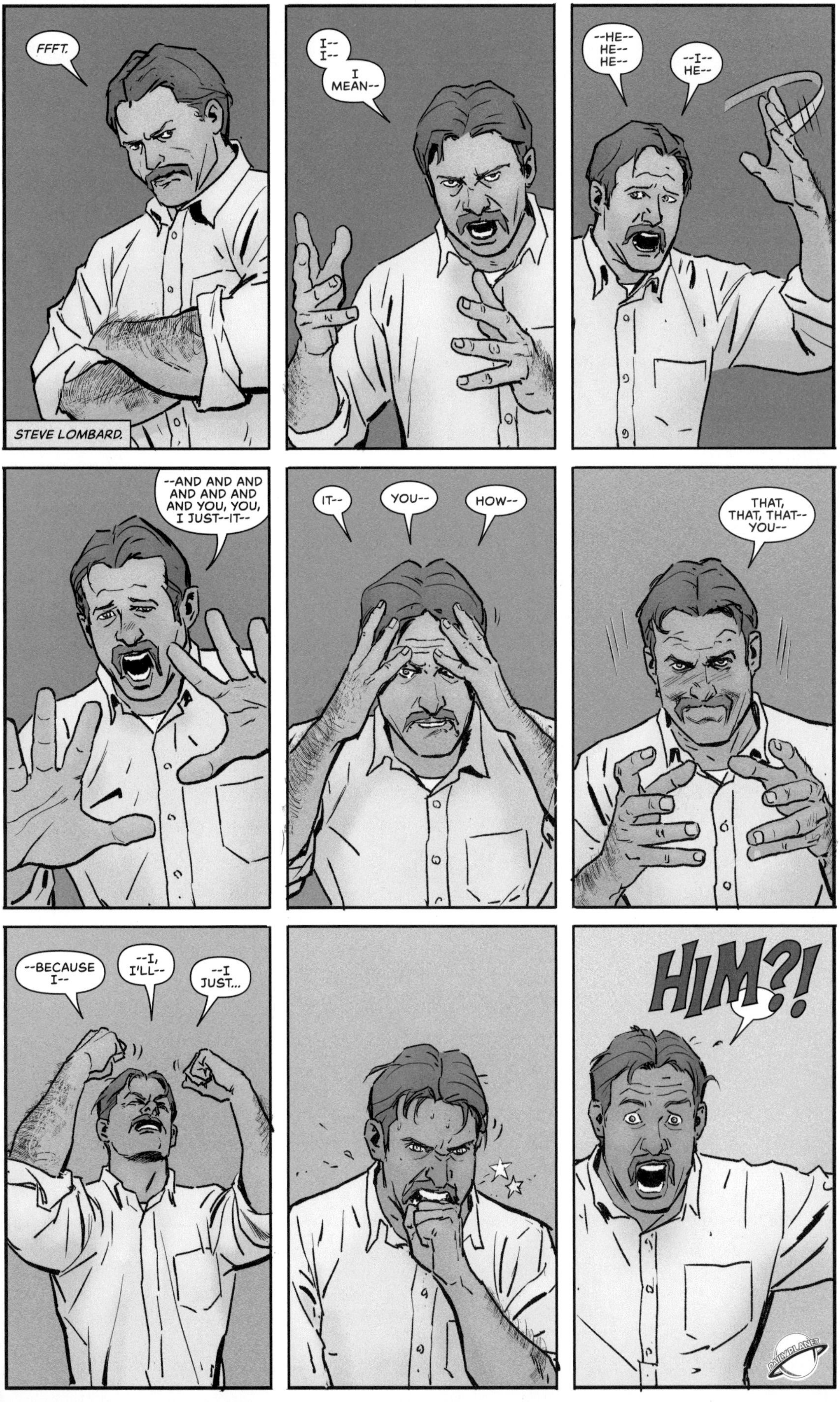
FFFT.
STEVE LOMBARD.
I--
I--
I MEAN--
--HE--
HE--
HE--
--I--
HE--
--AND AND AND
AND AND AND
AND YOU, YOU,
I JUST--IT--
IT--
YOU--
HOW--
THAT,
THAT, THAT--
YOU--
--BECAUSE
I--
--I,
I'LL--
--I
JUST...
HIM?!

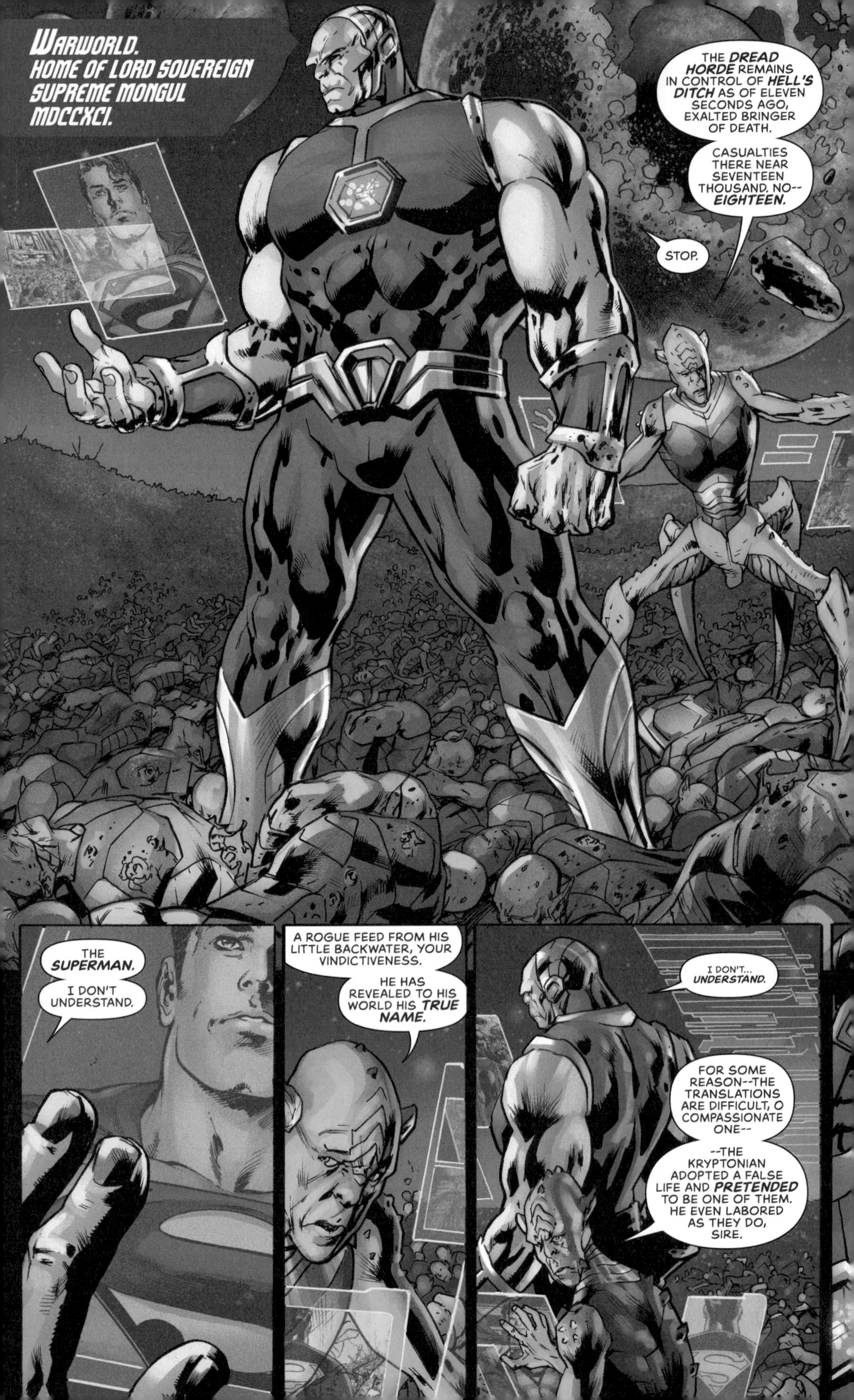
WARWORLD. HOME OF LORD SOVEREIGN SUPREME MONGUL MDCCXCI.
THE DREAD HORDE REMAINS IN CONTROL OF HELL'S DITCH AS OF ELEVEN SECONDS AGO, EXALTED BRINGER OF DEATH.
CASUALTIES THERE NEAR SEVENTEEN THOUSAND. NO-- EIGHTEEN.
STOP.
THE SUPERMAN.
I DON'T UNDERSTAND.
A ROGUE FEED FROM HIS LITTLE BACKWATER, YOUR VINDICTIVENESS.
HE HAS REVEALED TO HIS WORLD HIS TRUE NAME.
I DON'T... UNDERSTAND.
FOR SOME REASON--THE TRANSLATIONS ARE DIFFICULT, O COMPASSIONATE ONE--
--THE KRYPTONIAN ADOPTED A FALSE LIFE AND PRETENDED TO BE ONE OF THEM. HE EVEN LABORED AS THEY DO, SIRE.

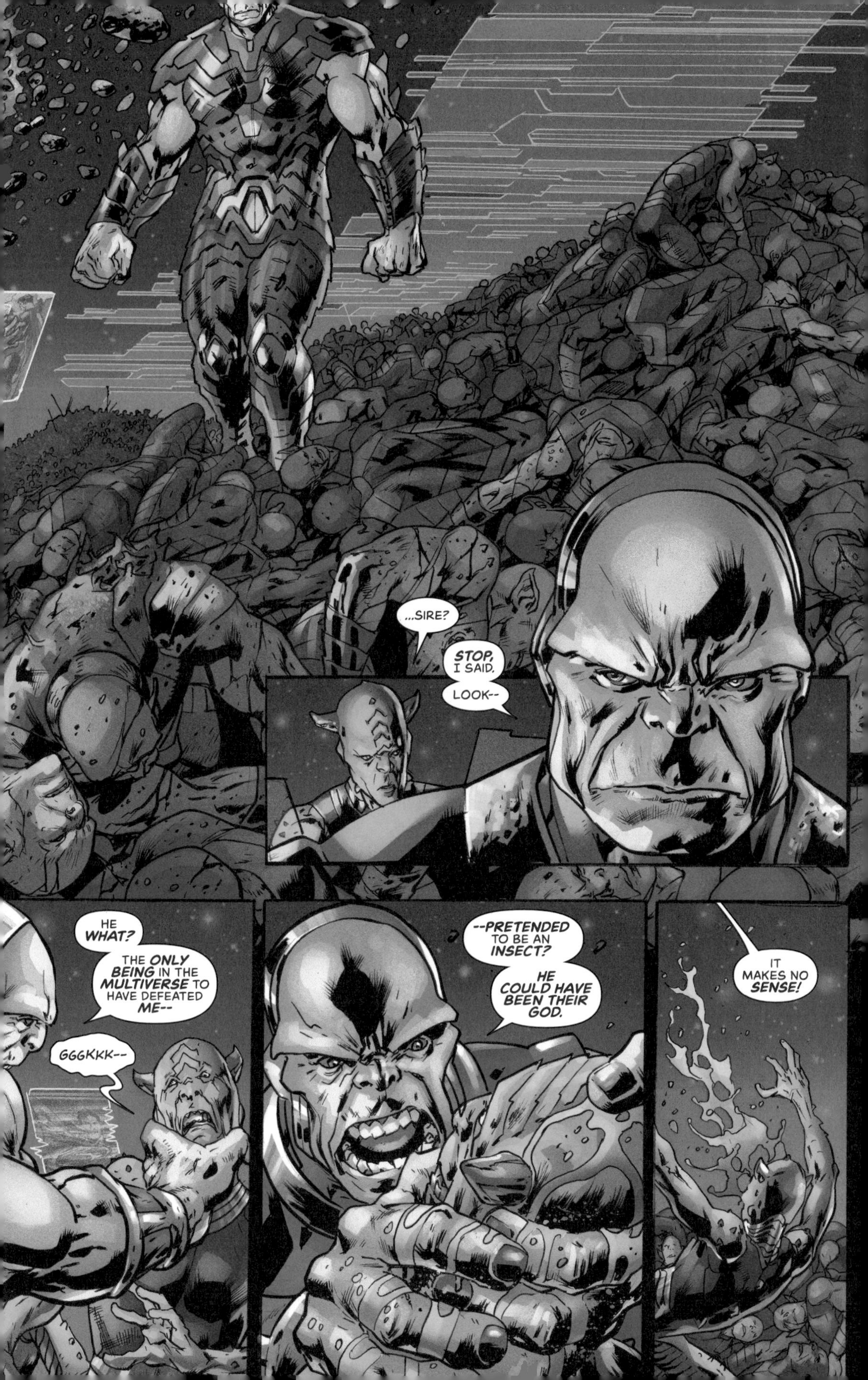
...SIRE?
STOP, I SAID.
LOOK--
HE WHAT?
THE ONLY BEING IN THE MULTIVERSE TO HAVE DEFEATED ME--
GGGKKK--
--PRETENDED TO BE AN INSECT?
HE COULD HAVE BEEN THEIR GOD.
IT MAKES NO SENSE!

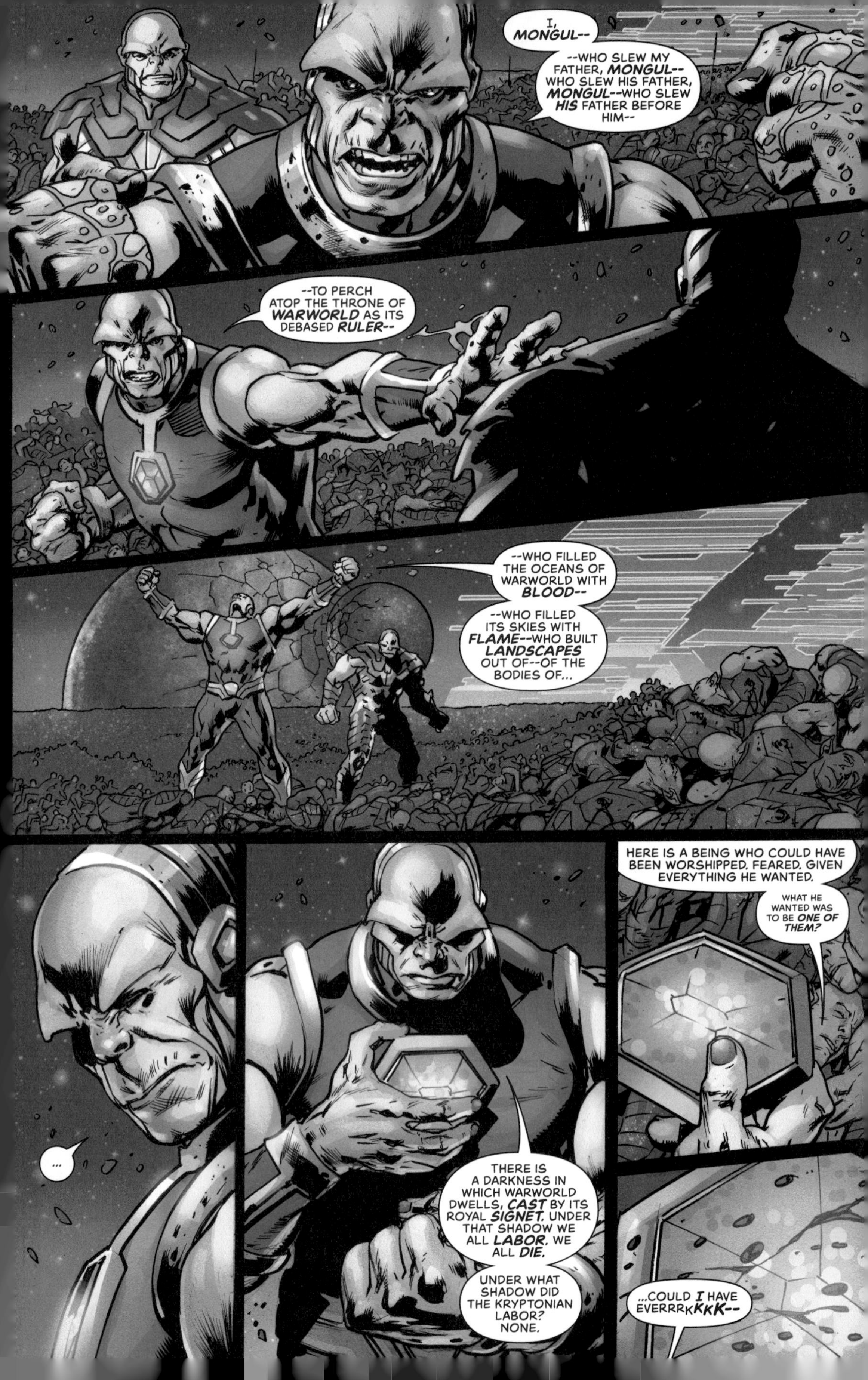
I, MONGUL--
--WHO SLEW MY FATHER, MONGUL--WHO SLEW HIS FATHER, MONGUL--WHO SLEW HIS FATHER BEFORE HIM--
--TO PERCH ATOP THE THRONE OF WARWORLD AS ITS DEBASED RULER--
--WHO FILLED THE OCEANS OF WARWORLD WITH BLOOD--
--WHO FILLED ITS SKIES WITH FLAME--WHO BUILT LANDSCAPES OUT OF--OF THE BODIES OF...
...
THERE IS A DARKNESS IN WHICH WARWORLD DWELLS, CAST BY ITS ROYAL SIGNET. UNDER THAT SHADOW WE ALL LABOR. WE ALL DIE.
UNDER WHAT SHADOW DID THE KRYPTONIAN LABOR? NONE.
HERE IS A BEING WHO COULD HAVE BEEN WORSHIPPED. FEARED. GIVEN EVERYTHING HE WANTED.
WHAT HE WANTED WAS TO BE ONE OF THEM?
...COULD I HAVE EVERRRKKKK--

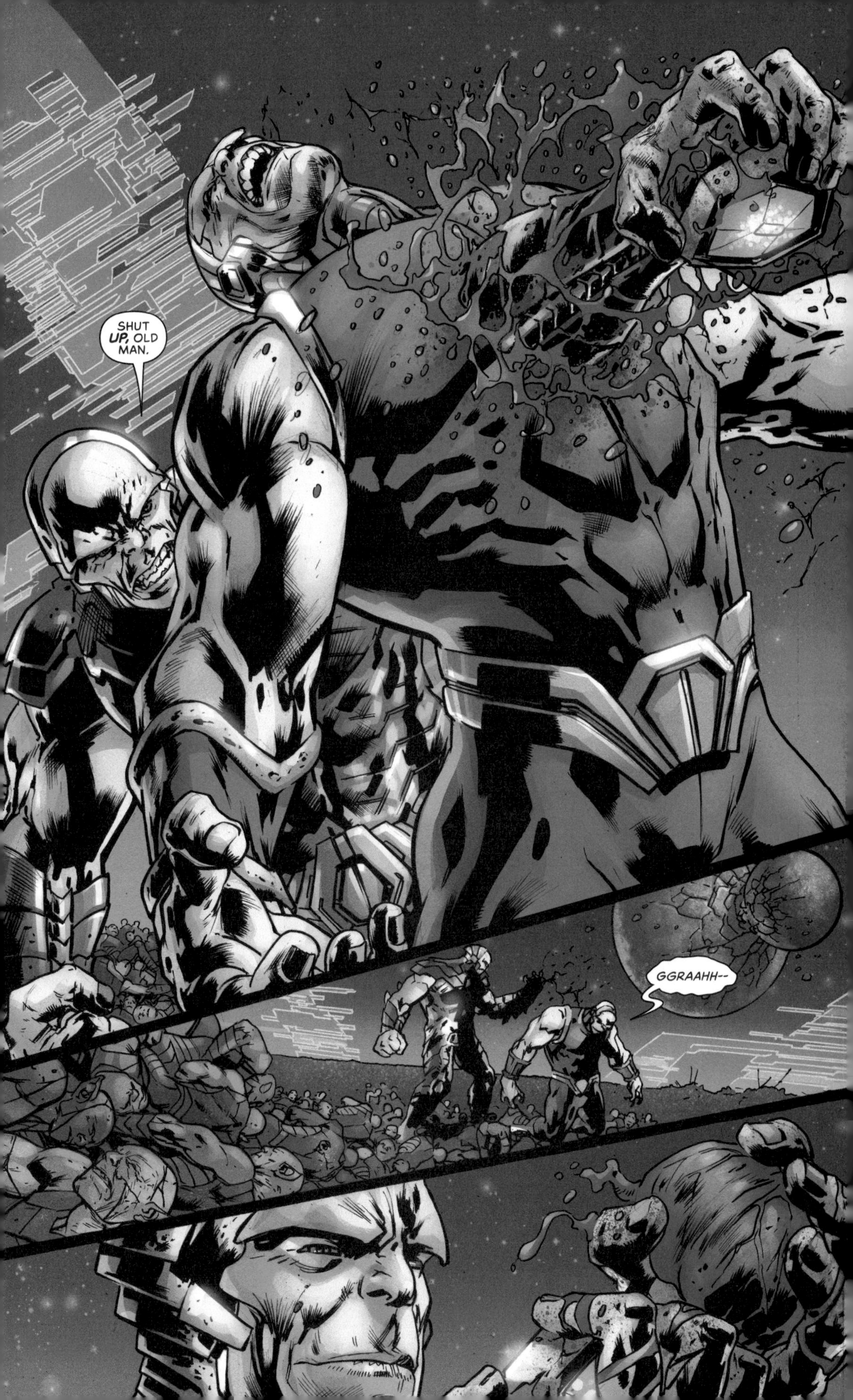
SHUT UP, OLD MAN.
GGRAAHH--

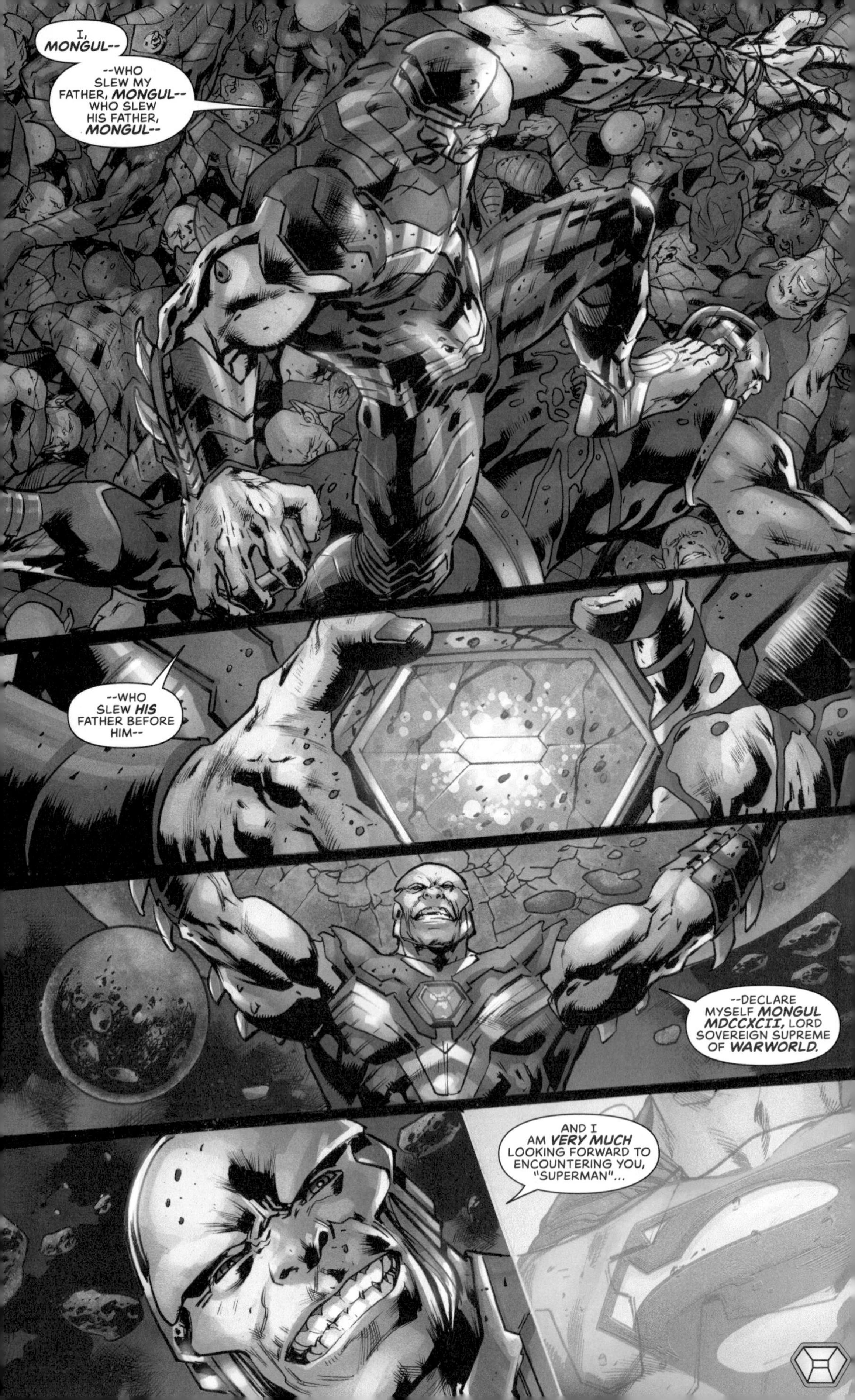
I, MONGUL--
--WHO SLEW MY FATHER, MONGUL-- WHO SLEW HIS FATHER, MONGUL--
--WHO SLEW HIS FATHER BEFORE HIM--
--DECLARE MYSELF MONGUL MDCCXCII, LORD SOVEREIGN SUPREME OF WARWORLD.
AND I AM VERY MUCH LOOKING FORWARD TO ENCOUNTERING YOU, "SUPERMAN"...

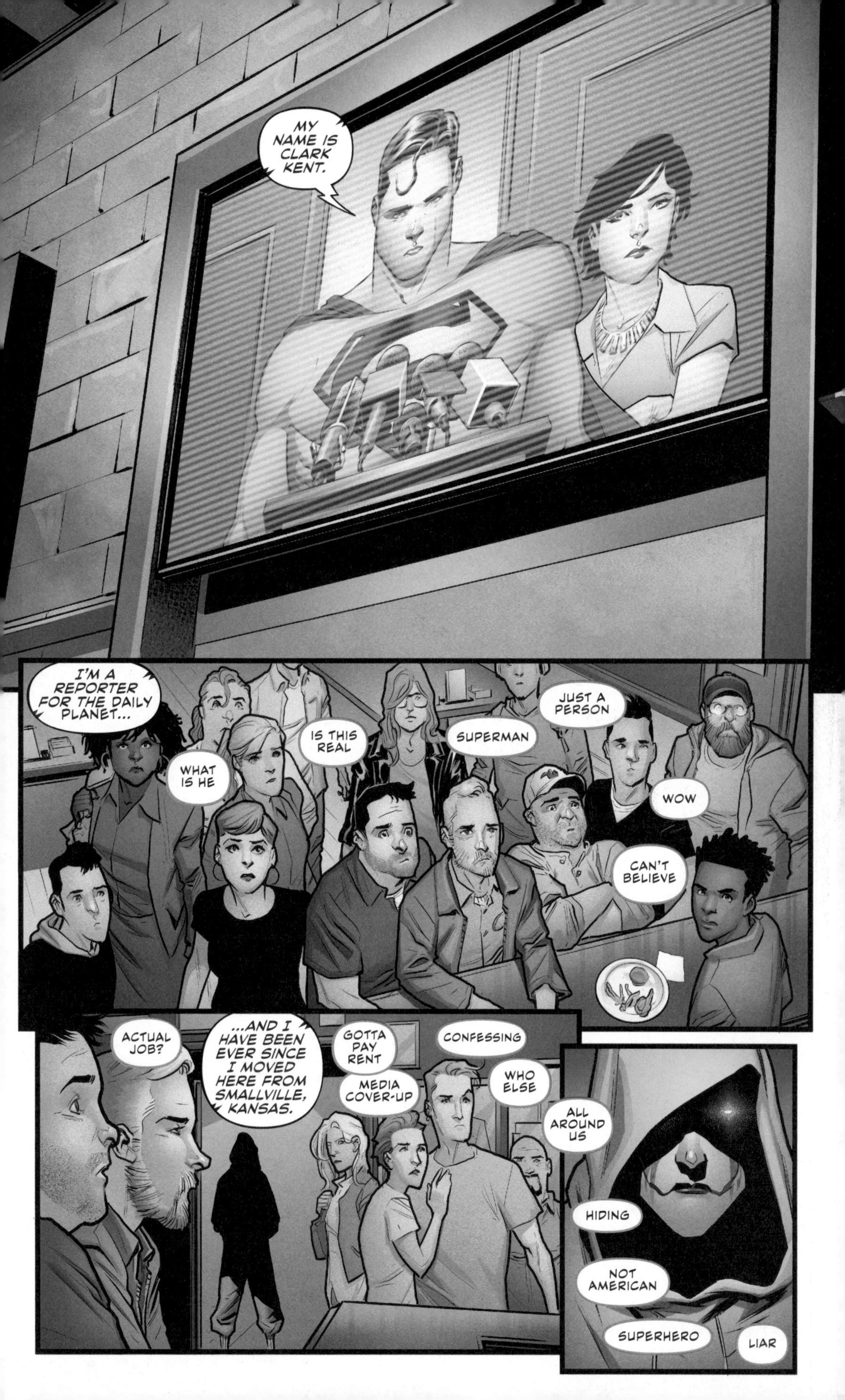
MY NAME IS CLARK KENT.
I'M A REPORTER FOR THE DAILY PLANET...
WHAT IS HE
IS THIS REAL
SUPERMAN
JUST A PERSON
WOW
CAN'T BELIEVE
ACTUAL JOB?
...AND I HAVE BEEN EVER SINCE I MOVED HERE FROM SMALLVILLE, KANSAS.
GOTTA PAY RENT
MEDIA COVER-UP
CONFESSING
WHO ELSE
ALL AROUND US
HIDING
NOT AMERICAN
SUPERHERO
LIAR

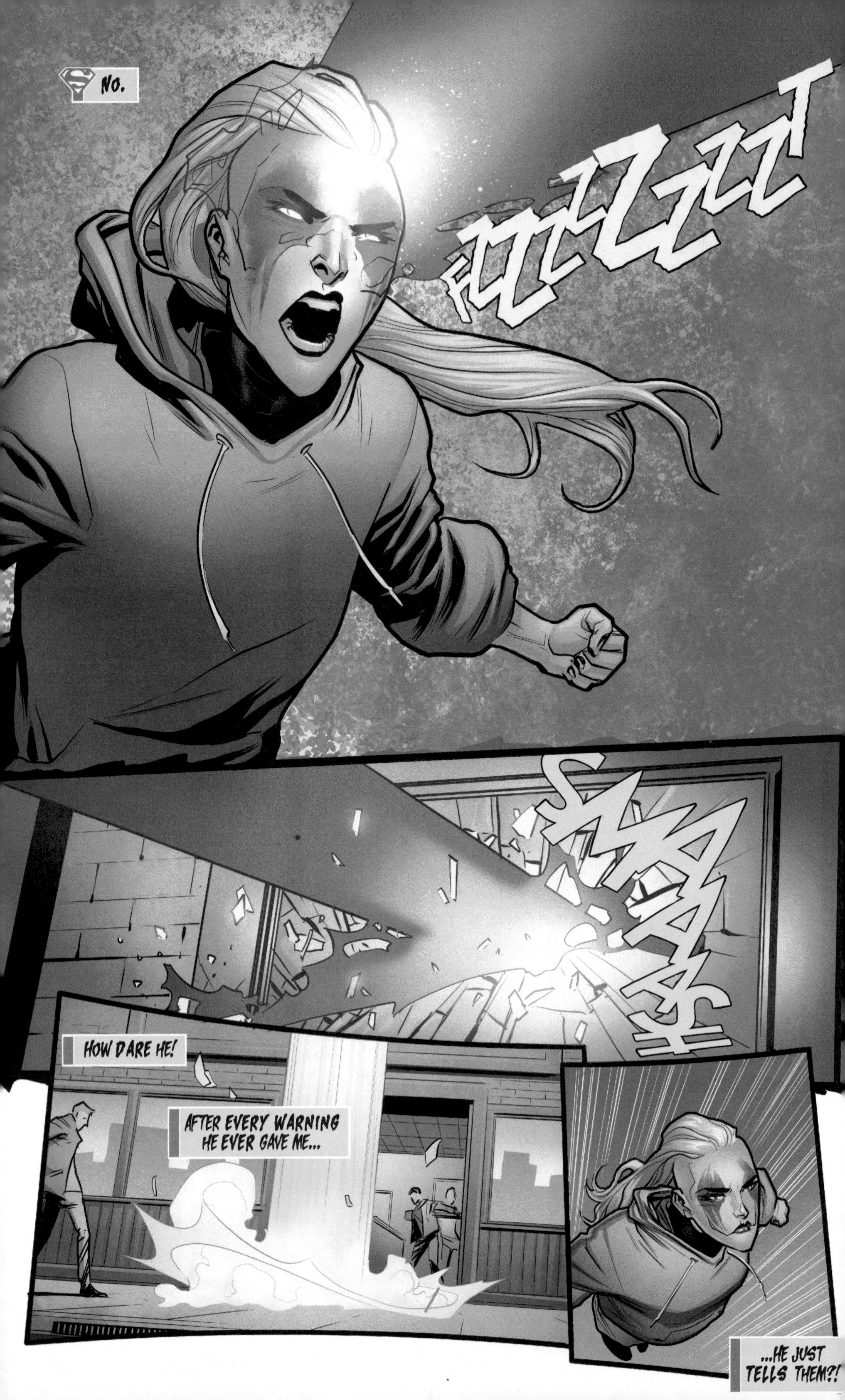

NO.
FZZZZZZZZT
SMASH
HOW DARE HE!
AFTER EVERY WARNING HE EVER GAVE ME...
...HE JUST TELLS THEM?!

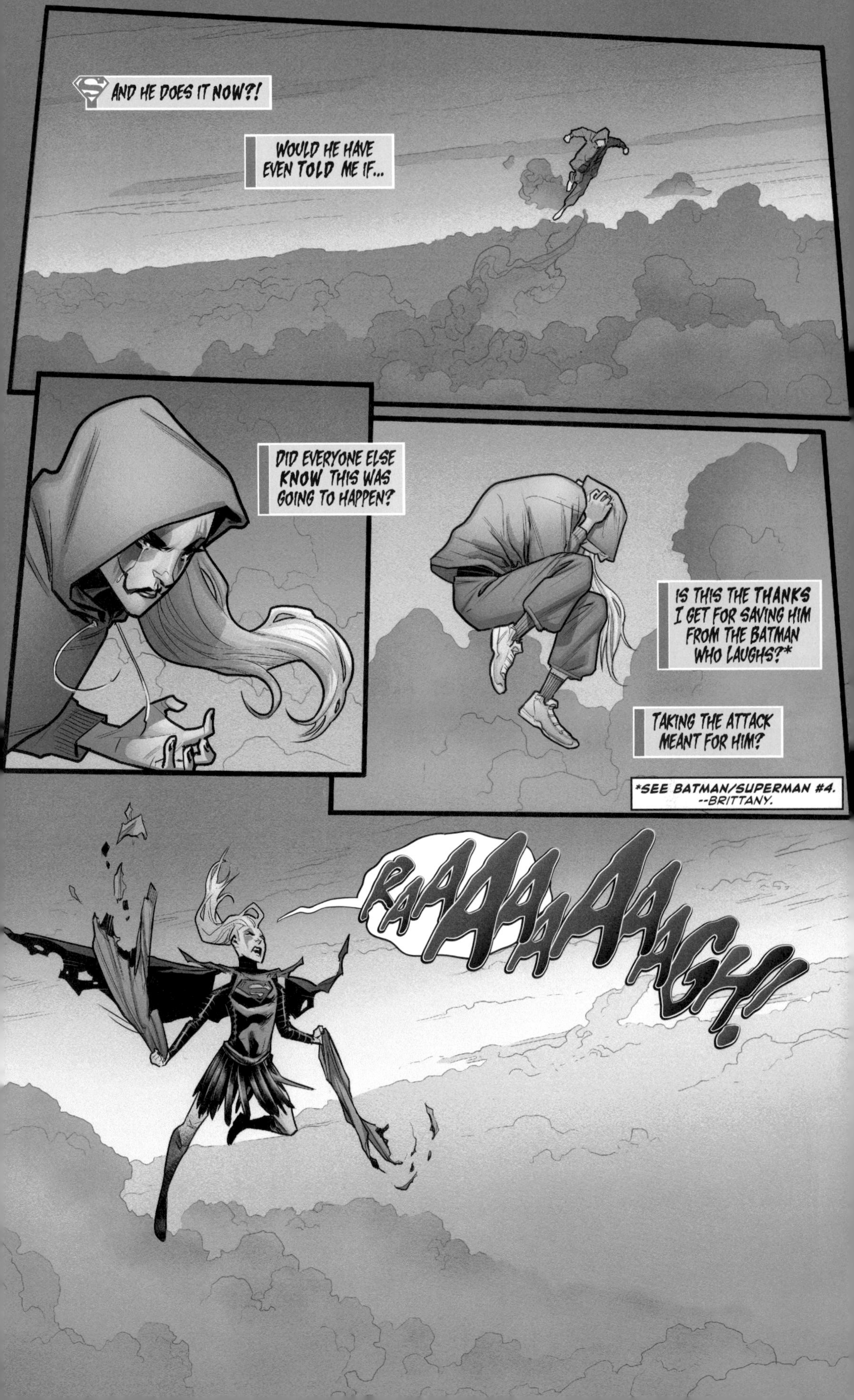
AND HE DOES IT NOW?!
WOULD HE HAVE EVEN TOLD ME IF...
DID EVERYONE ELSE KNOW THIS WAS GOING TO HAPPEN?
IS THIS THE THANKS I GET FOR SAVING HIM FROM THE BATMAN WHO LAUGHS?*
TAKING THE ATTACK MEANT FOR HIM?
*SEE BATMAN/SUPERMAN #4. --BRITTANY.
RAAAAAAAAGH!!

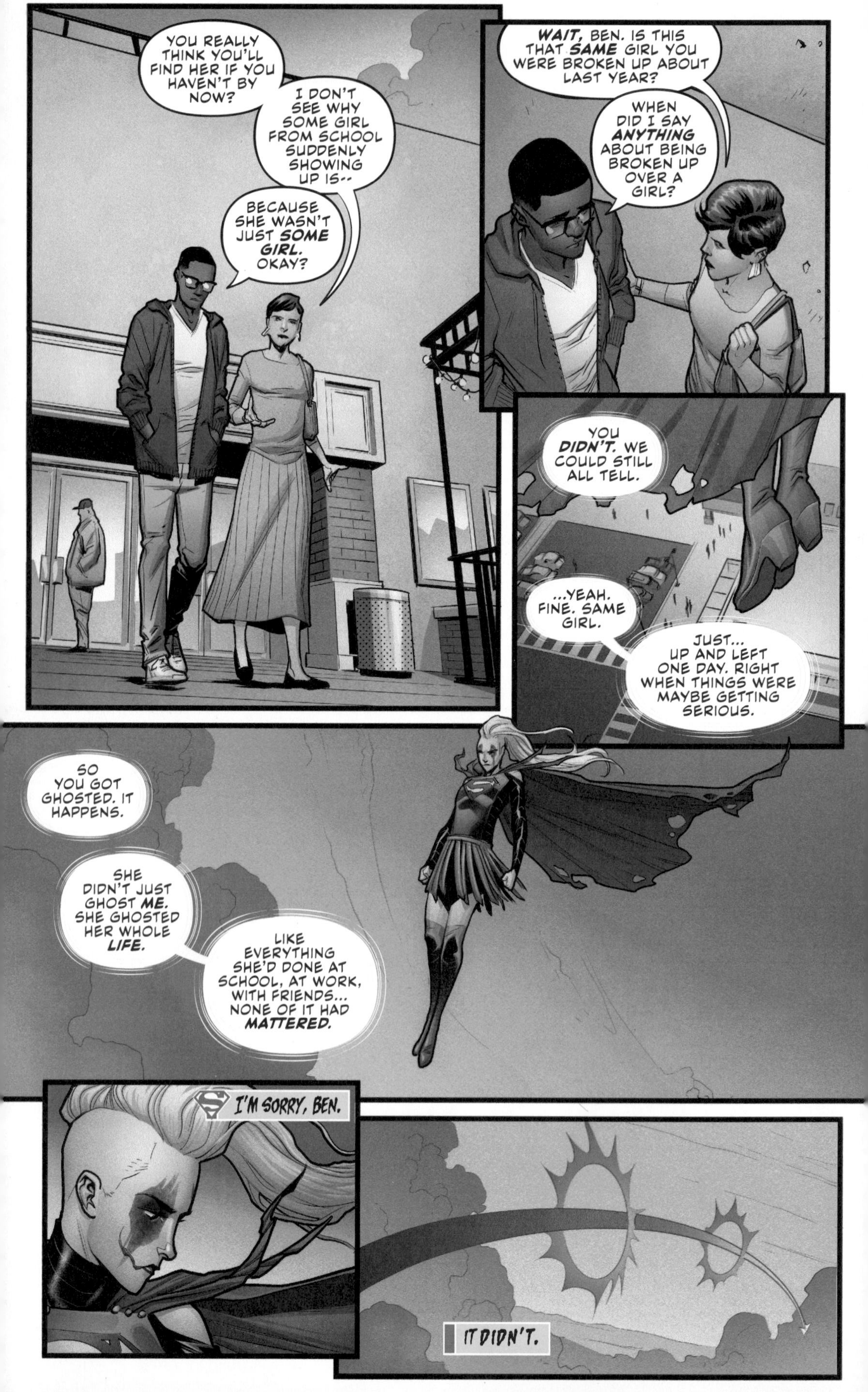
YOU REALLY THINK YOU'LL FIND HER IF YOU HAVEN'T BY NOW?
I DON'T SEE WHY SOME GIRL FROM SCHOOL SUDDENLY SHOWING UP IS--
BECAUSE SHE WASN'T JUST SOME GIRL. OKAY?
WAIT, BEN. IS THIS THAT SAME GIRL YOU WERE BROKEN UP ABOUT LAST YEAR?
WHEN DID I SAY ANYTHING ABOUT BEING BROKEN UP OVER A GIRL?
YOU DIDN'T. WE COULD STILL ALL TELL.
...YEAH. FINE. SAME GIRL.
JUST... UP AND LEFT ONE DAY. RIGHT WHEN THINGS WERE MAYBE GETTING SERIOUS.
SO YOU GOT GHOSTED. IT HAPPENS.
SHE DIDN'T JUST GHOST ME. SHE GHOSTED HER WHOLE LIFE.
LIKE EVERYTHING SHE'D DONE AT SCHOOL, AT WORK, WITH FRIENDS... NONE OF IT HAD MATTERED.
I'M SORRY, BEN.
IT DIDN'T.

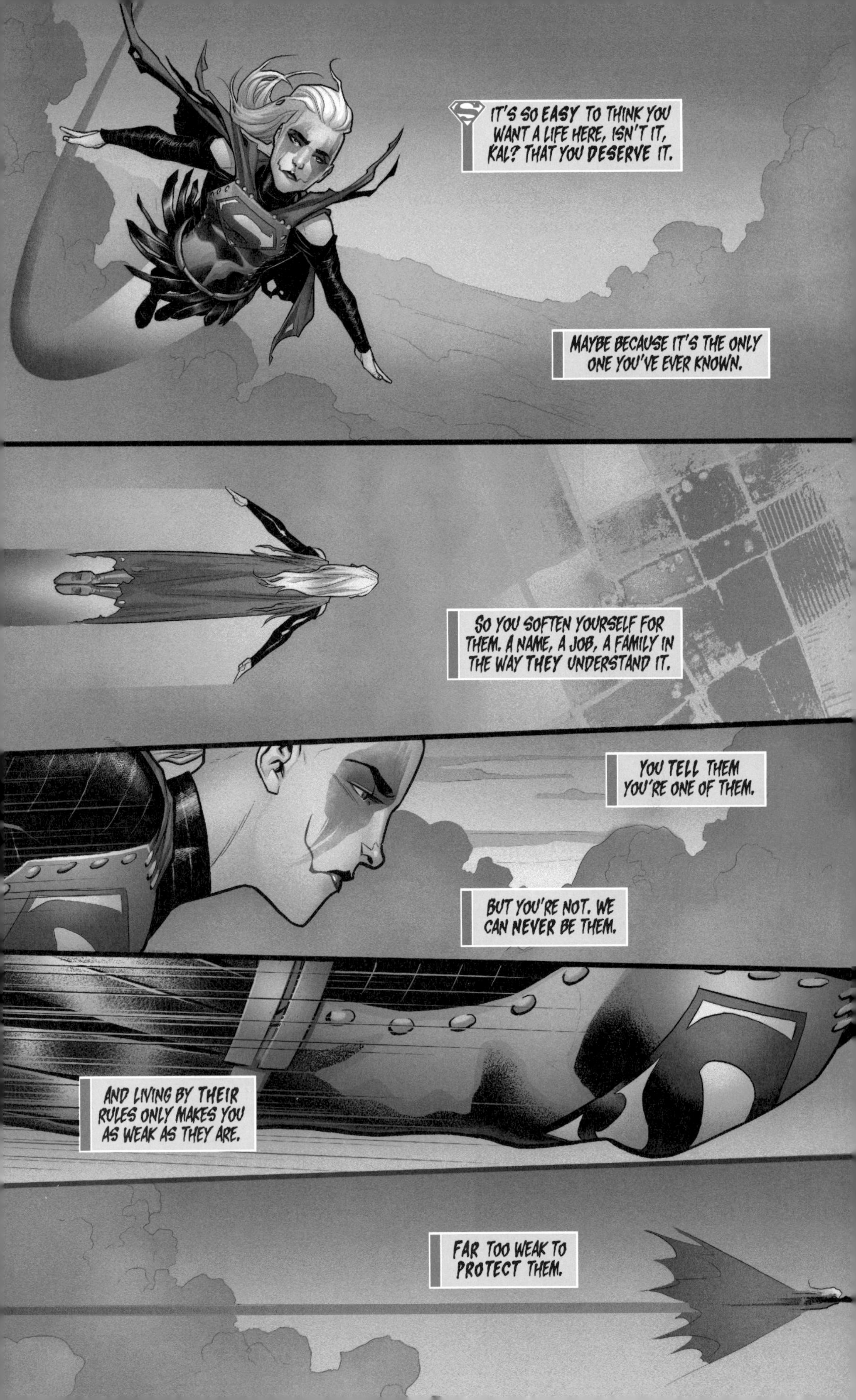
IT'S SO EASY TO THINK YOU WANT A LIFE HERE, ISN'T IT, KAL? THAT YOU DESERVE IT.
MAYBE BECAUSE IT'S THE ONLY ONE YOU'VE EVER KNOWN.
SO YOU SOFTEN YOURSELF FOR THEM. A NAME, A JOB, A FAMILY IN THE WAY THEY UNDERSTAND IT.
YOU TELL THEM YOU'RE ONE OF THEM.
BUT YOU'RE NOT. WE CAN NEVER BE THEM.
AND LIVING BY THEIR RULES ONLY MAKES YOU AS WEAK AS THEY ARE.
FAR TOO WEAK TO PROTECT THEM.

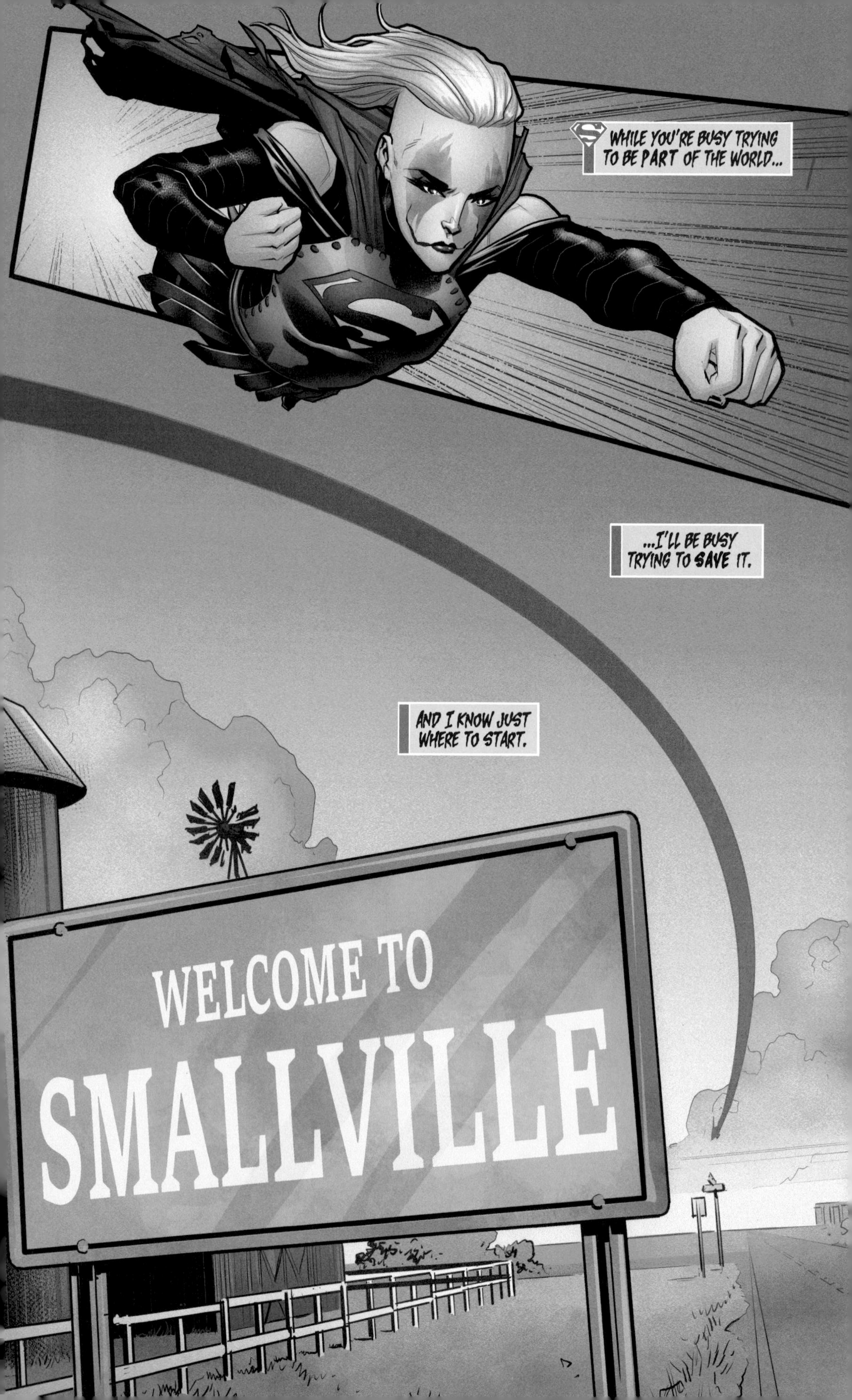
WHILE YOU'RE BUSY TRYING TO BE PART OF THE WORLD...
...I'LL BE BUSY TRYING TO SAVE IT.
AND I KNOW JUST WHERE TO START.
WELCOME TO
SMALLVILLE

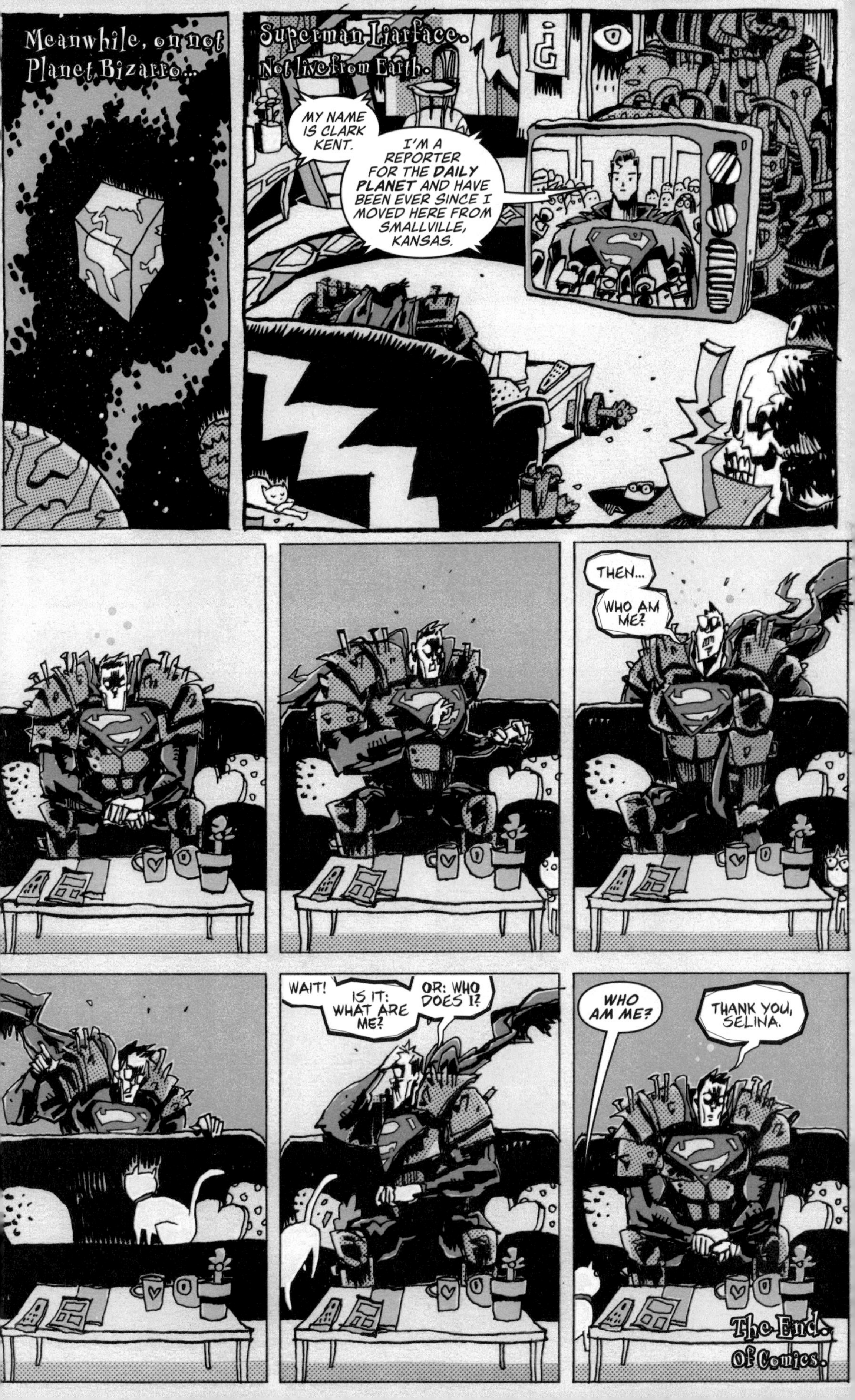
Meanwhile, on not Planet Bizarro...
Superman Liarface. Not live from Earth.
MY NAME IS CLARK KENT.
I'M A REPORTER FOR THE DAILY PLANET AND HAVE BEEN EVER SINCE I MOVED HERE FROM SMALLVILLE, KANSAS.
THEN...
WHO AM ME?
WAIT!
IS IT: WHAT ARE ME?
OR: WHO DOES I?
WHO AM ME?
THANK YOU, SELINA.
The End. Of Comics.

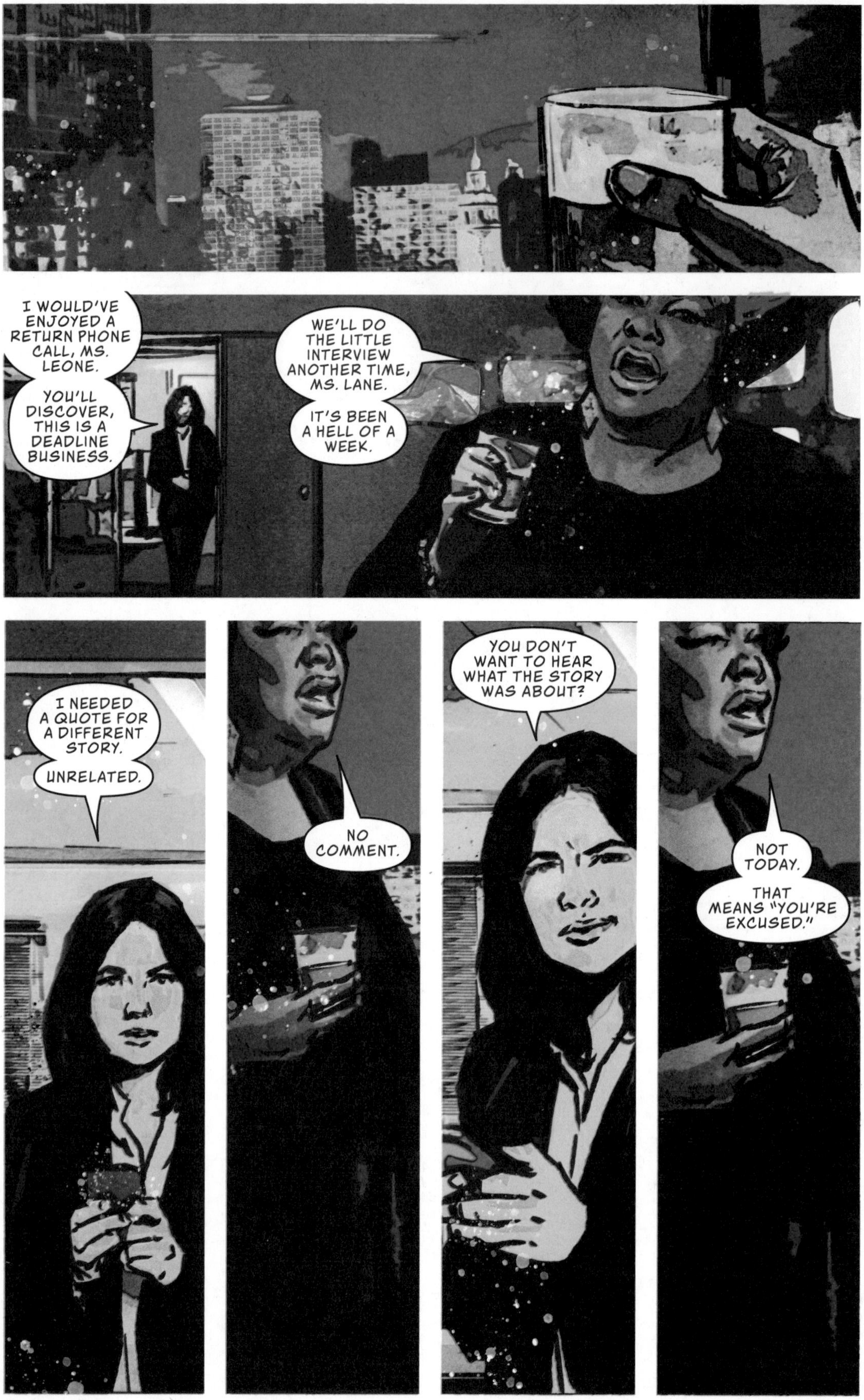
I WOULD'VE ENJOYED A RETURN PHONE CALL, MS. LEONE.
YOU'LL DISCOVER, THIS IS A DEADLINE BUSINESS.
WE'LL DO THE LITTLE INTERVIEW ANOTHER TIME, MS. LANE.
IT'S BEEN A HELL OF A WEEK.
I NEEDED A QUOTE FOR A DIFFERENT STORY.
UNRELATED.
NO COMMENT.
YOU DON'T WANT TO HEAR WHAT THE STORY WAS ABOUT?
NOT TODAY.
THAT MEANS "YOU'RE EXCUSED."

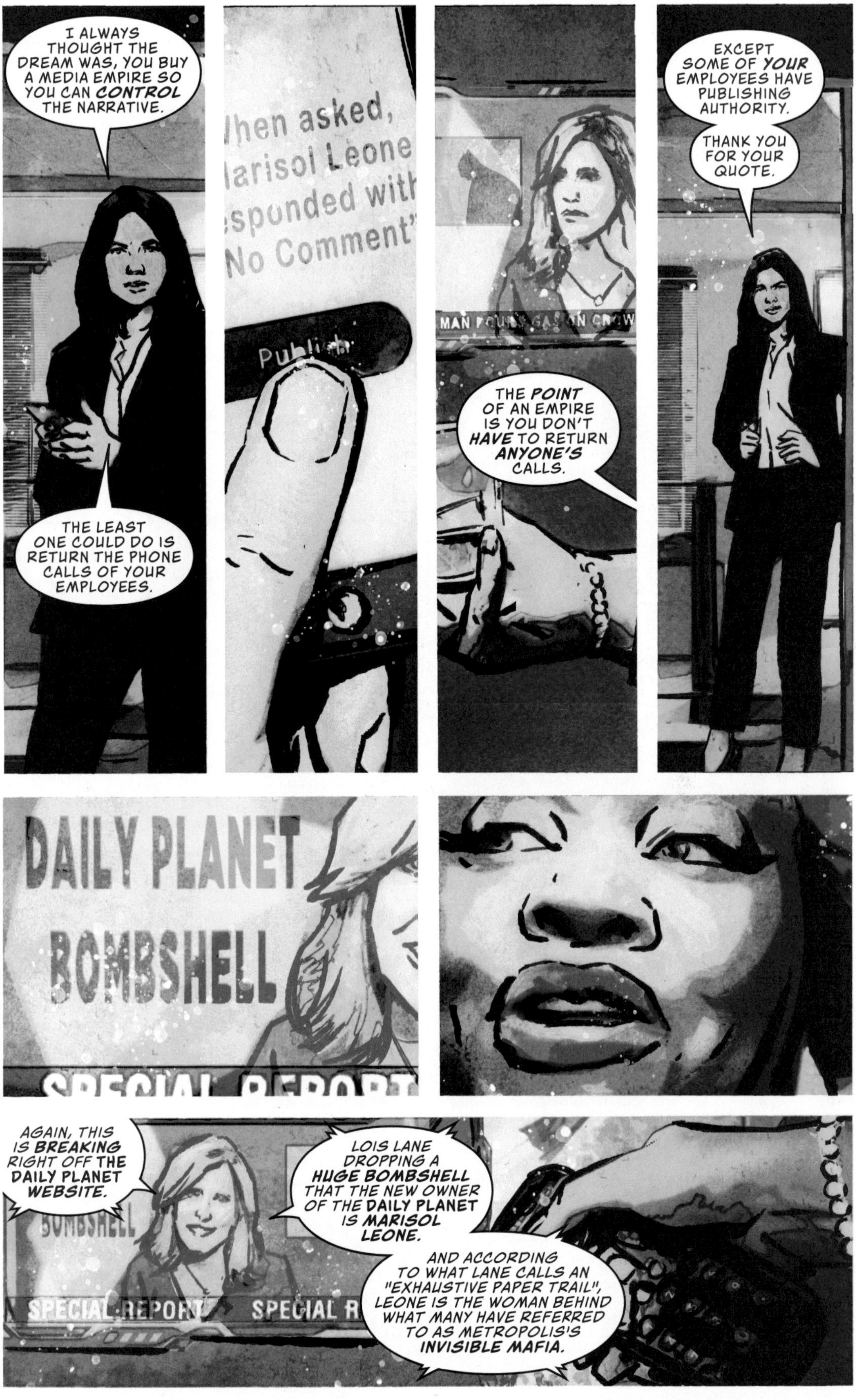
I ALWAYS THOUGHT THE DREAM WAS, YOU BUY A MEDIA EMPIRE SO YOU CAN *CONTROL* THE NARRATIVE.
THE LEAST ONE COULD DO IS RETURN THE PHONE CALLS OF YOUR EMPLOYEES.
hen asked,
arisol Leone
esponded with
No Comment"
THE *POINT* OF AN EMPIRE IS YOU DON'T *HAVE* TO RETURN *ANYONE'S* CALLS.
EXCEPT SOME OF *YOUR* EMPLOYEES HAVE PUBLISHING AUTHORITY.
THANK YOU FOR YOUR QUOTE.
DAILY PLANET
BOMBSHELL
*AGAIN, THIS IS **BREAKING** RIGHT OFF **THE DAILY PLANET WEBSITE.***
BOMBSHELL
SPECIAL REPORT
*LOIS LANE DROPPING A **HUGE BOMBSHELL** THAT THE NEW OWNER OF THE **DAILY PLANET** IS **MARISOL LEONE.***
*AND ACCORDING TO WHAT LANE CALLS AN "EXHAUSTIVE PAPER TRAIL", LEONE IS THE WOMAN BEHIND WHAT MANY HAVE REFERRED TO AS METROPOLIS'S **INVISIBLE MAFIA.***

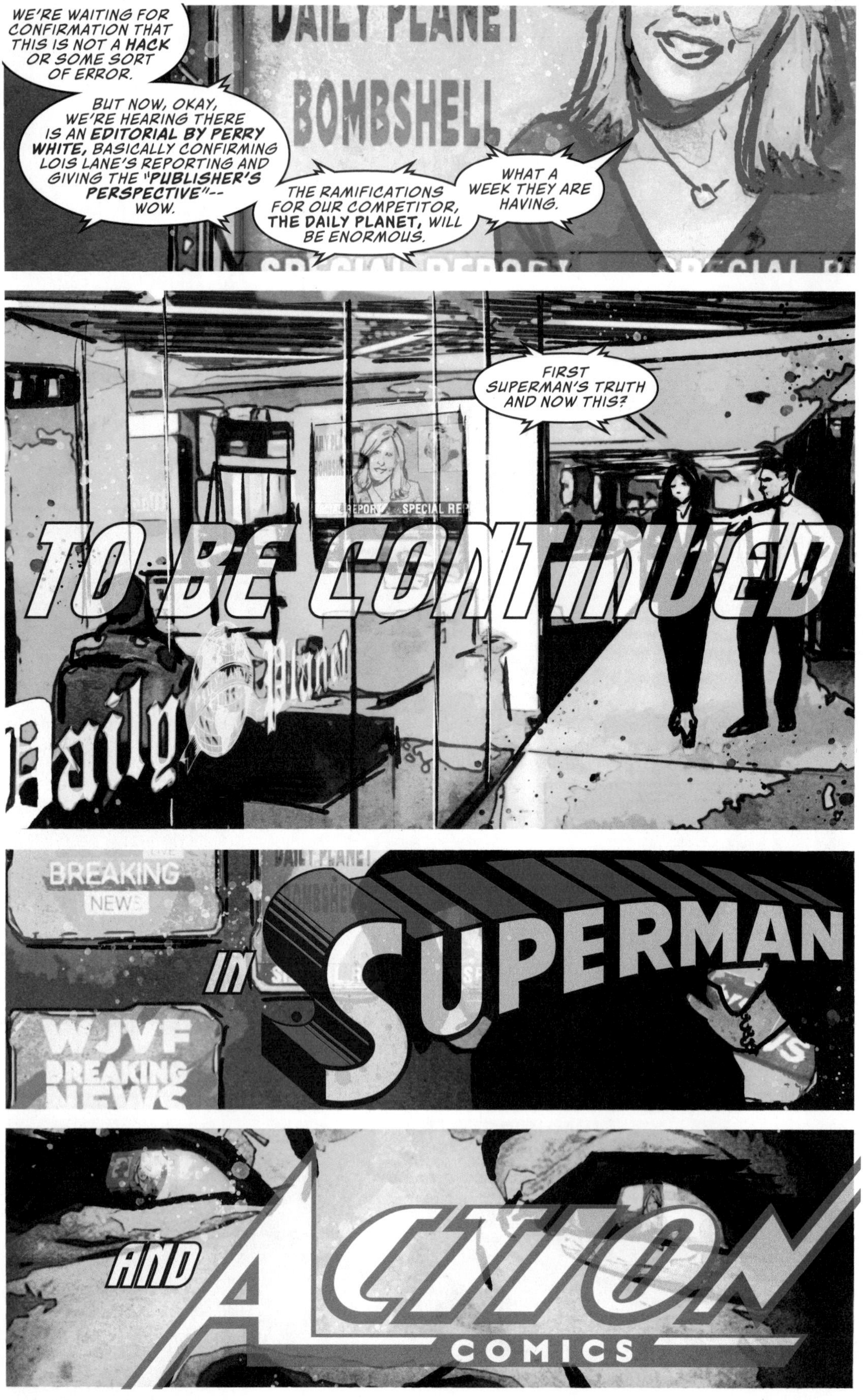
DAILY PLANET
BOMBSHELL
WE'RE WAITING FOR CONFIRMATION THAT THIS IS NOT A **HACK** OR SOME SORT OF ERROR.
BUT NOW, OKAY, WE'RE HEARING THERE IS AN **EDITORIAL BY PERRY WHITE,** BASICALLY CONFIRMING LOIS LANE'S REPORTING AND GIVING THE **"PUBLISHER'S PERSPECTIVE"**-- WOW.
THE RAMIFICATIONS FOR OUR COMPETITOR, **THE DAILY PLANET,** WILL BE ENORMOUS.
WHAT A WEEK THEY ARE HAVING.
FIRST SUPERMAN'S TRUTH AND NOW THIS?
TO BE CONTINUED
Daily Planet
BREAKING NEWS
WJVF BREAKING NEWS
IN SUPERMAN
AND ACTION COMICS

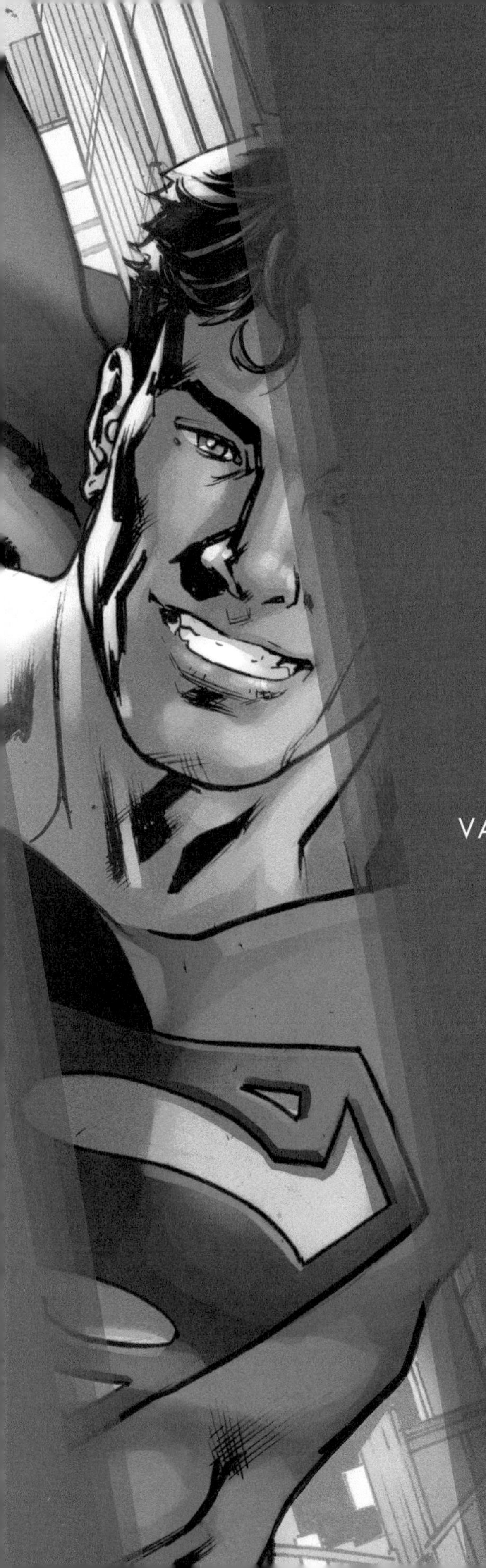

VARIANT COVER GALLERY

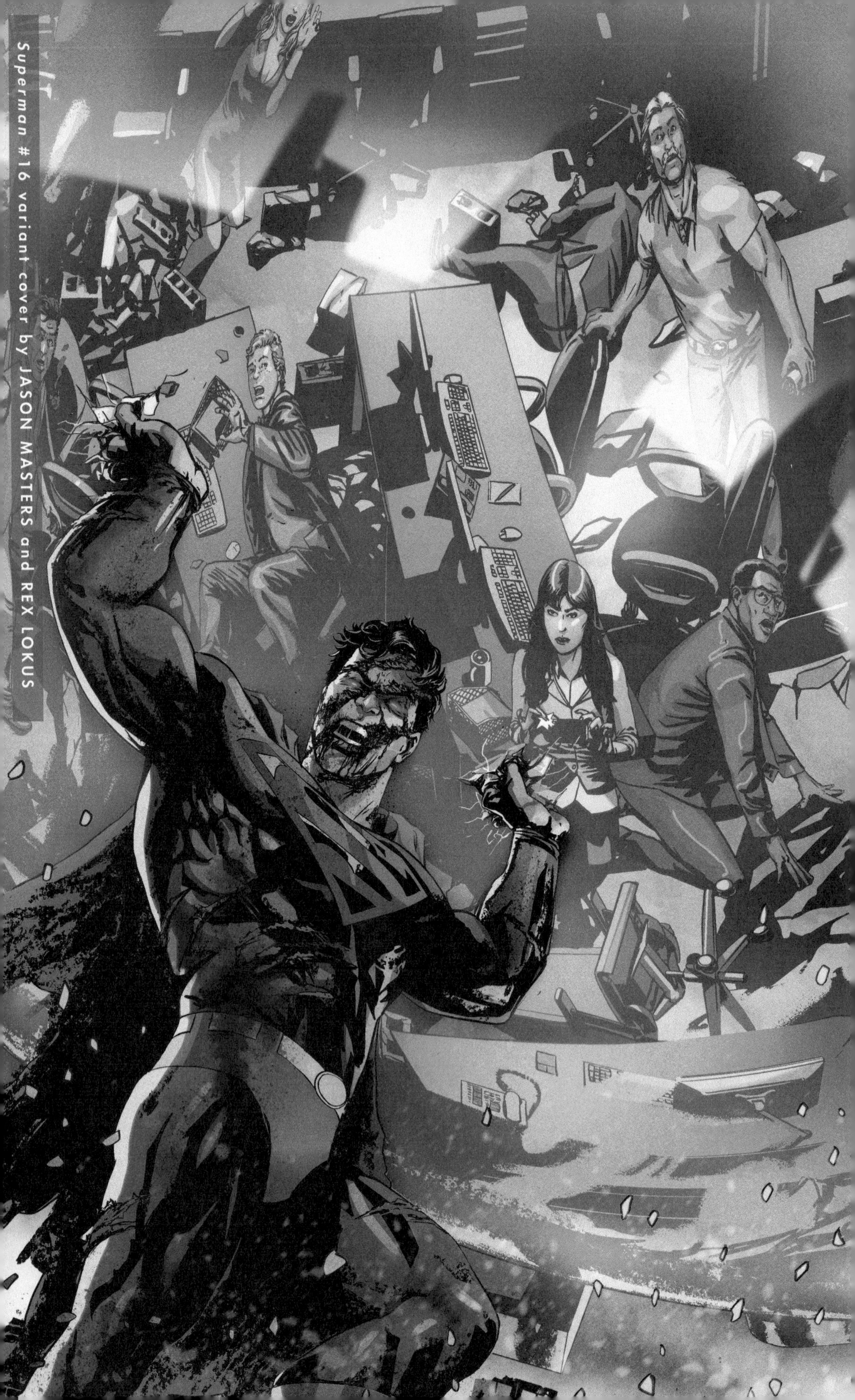

Superman #16 variant cover by JASON MASTERS and REX LOKUS

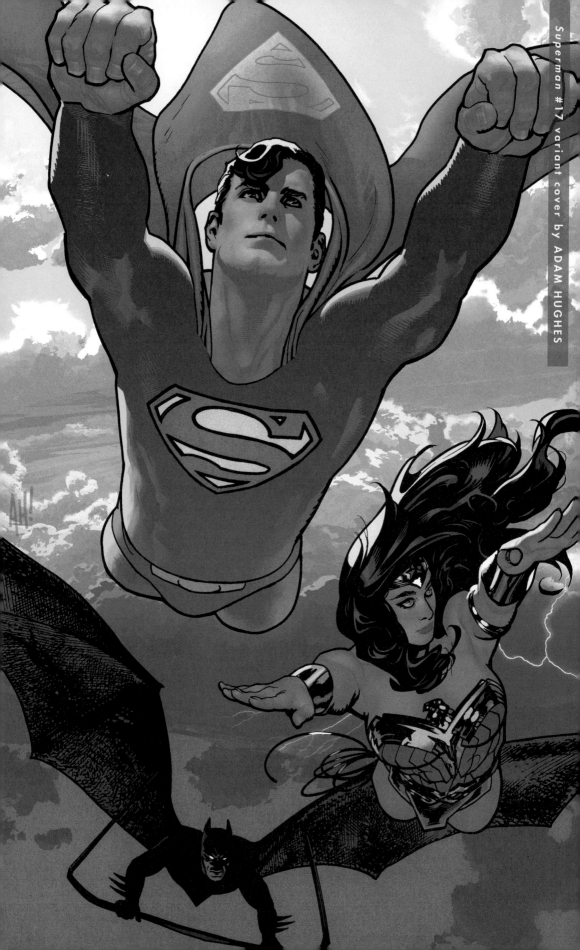
Superman #17 variant cover by ADAM HUGHES

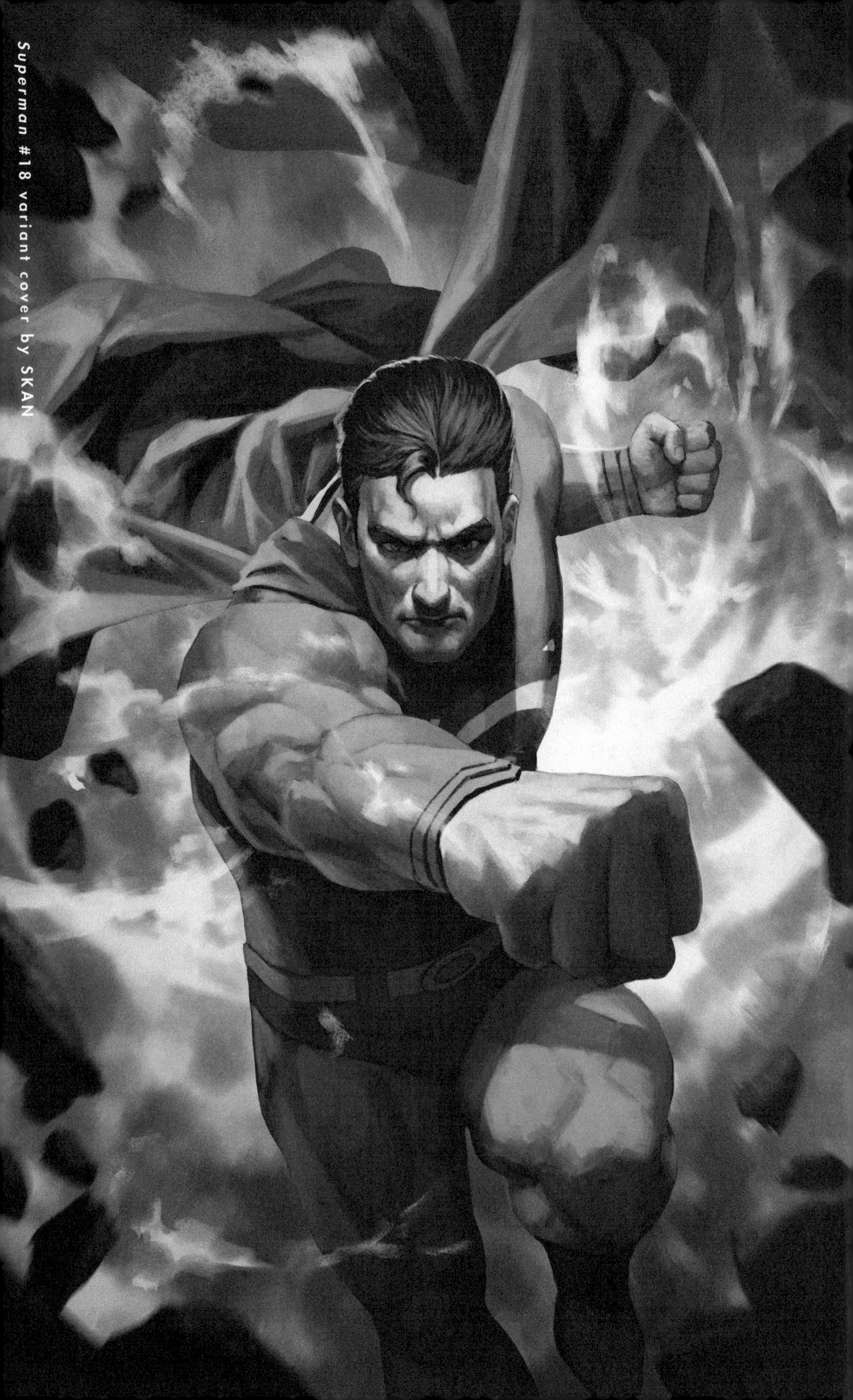

Superman #18 variant cover by SKAN

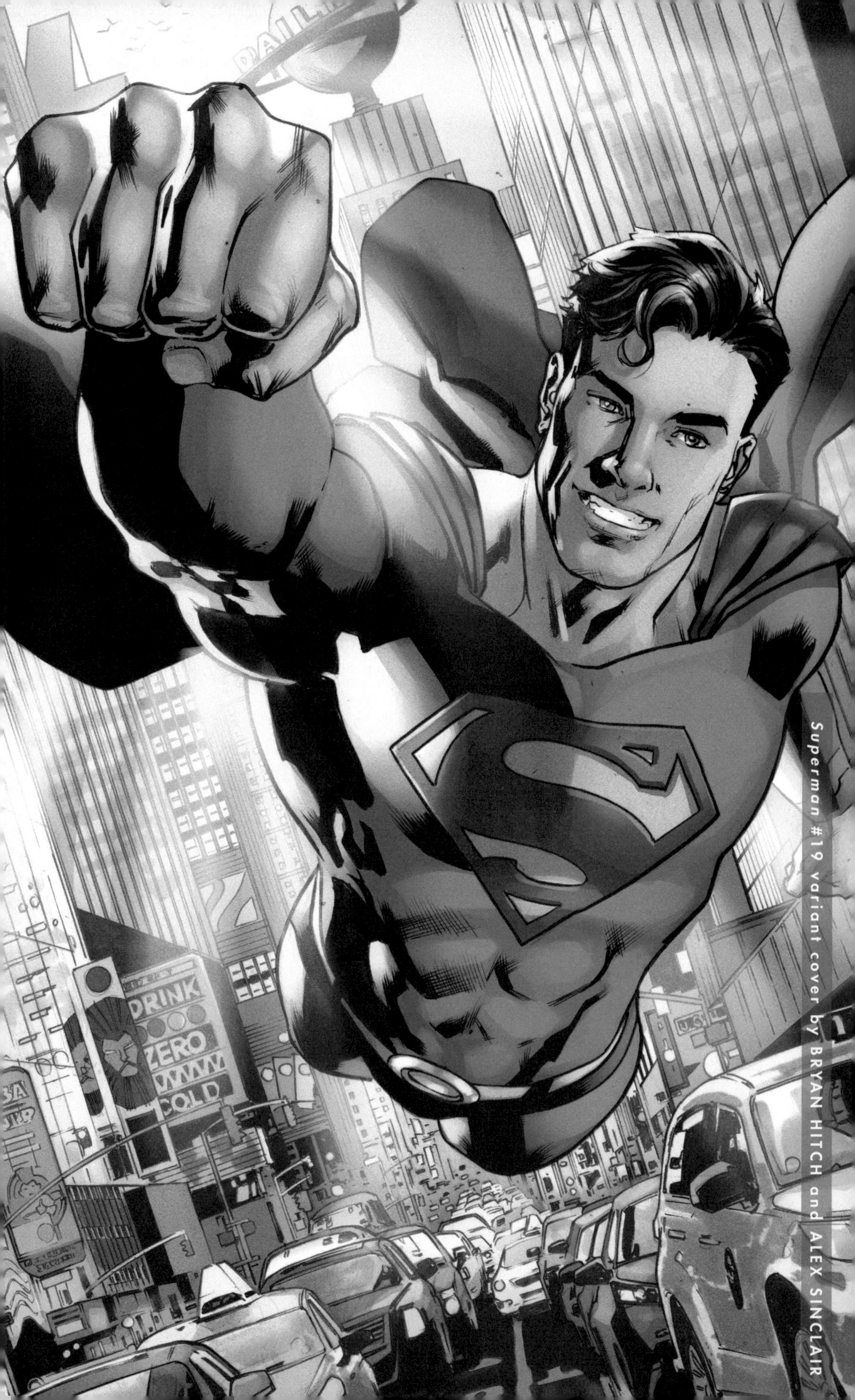
DRINK
ZERO
COLD

Superman #19 variant cover by BRYAN HITCH and ALEX SINCLAIR

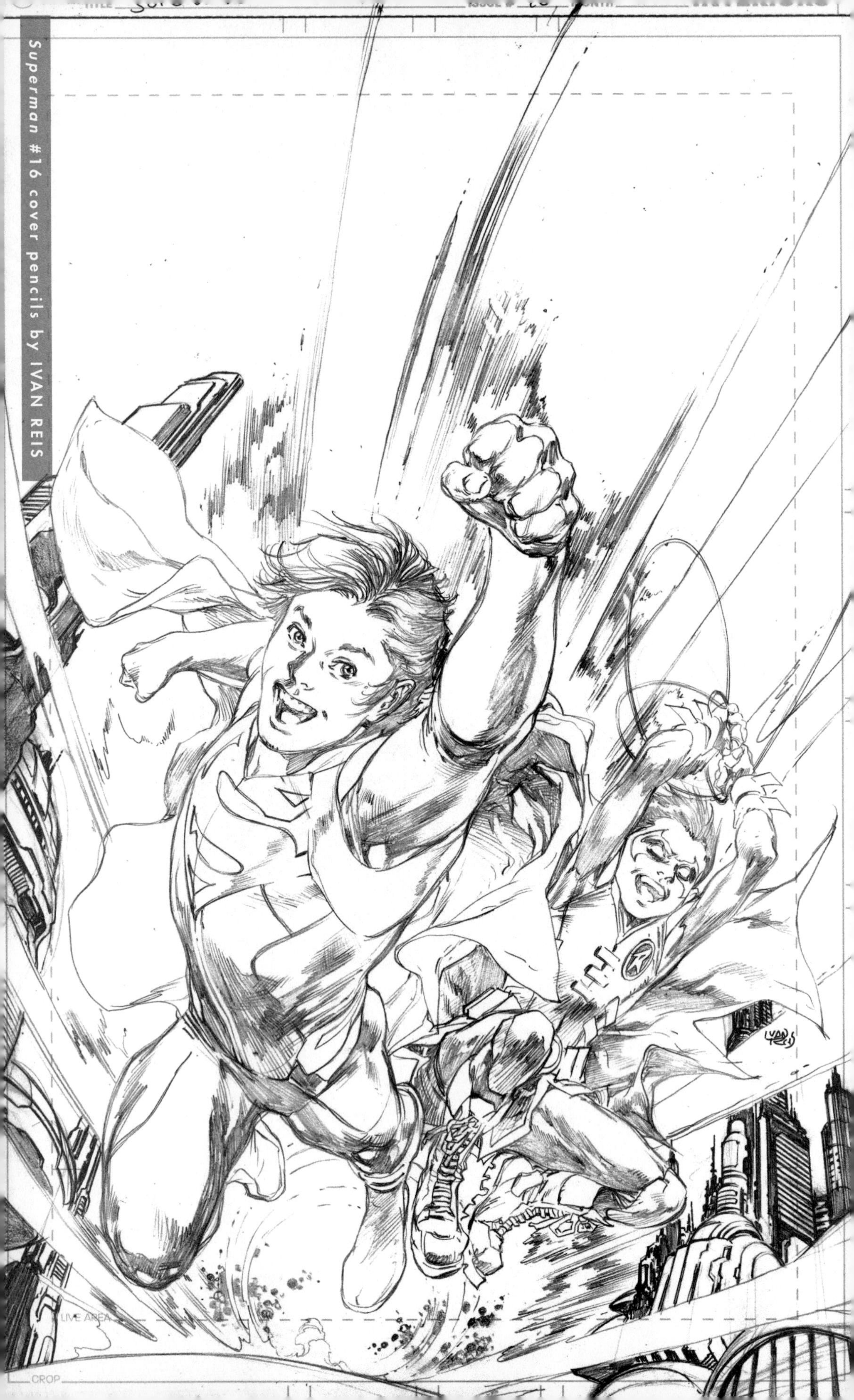

Superman #16 cover pencils by IVAN REIS

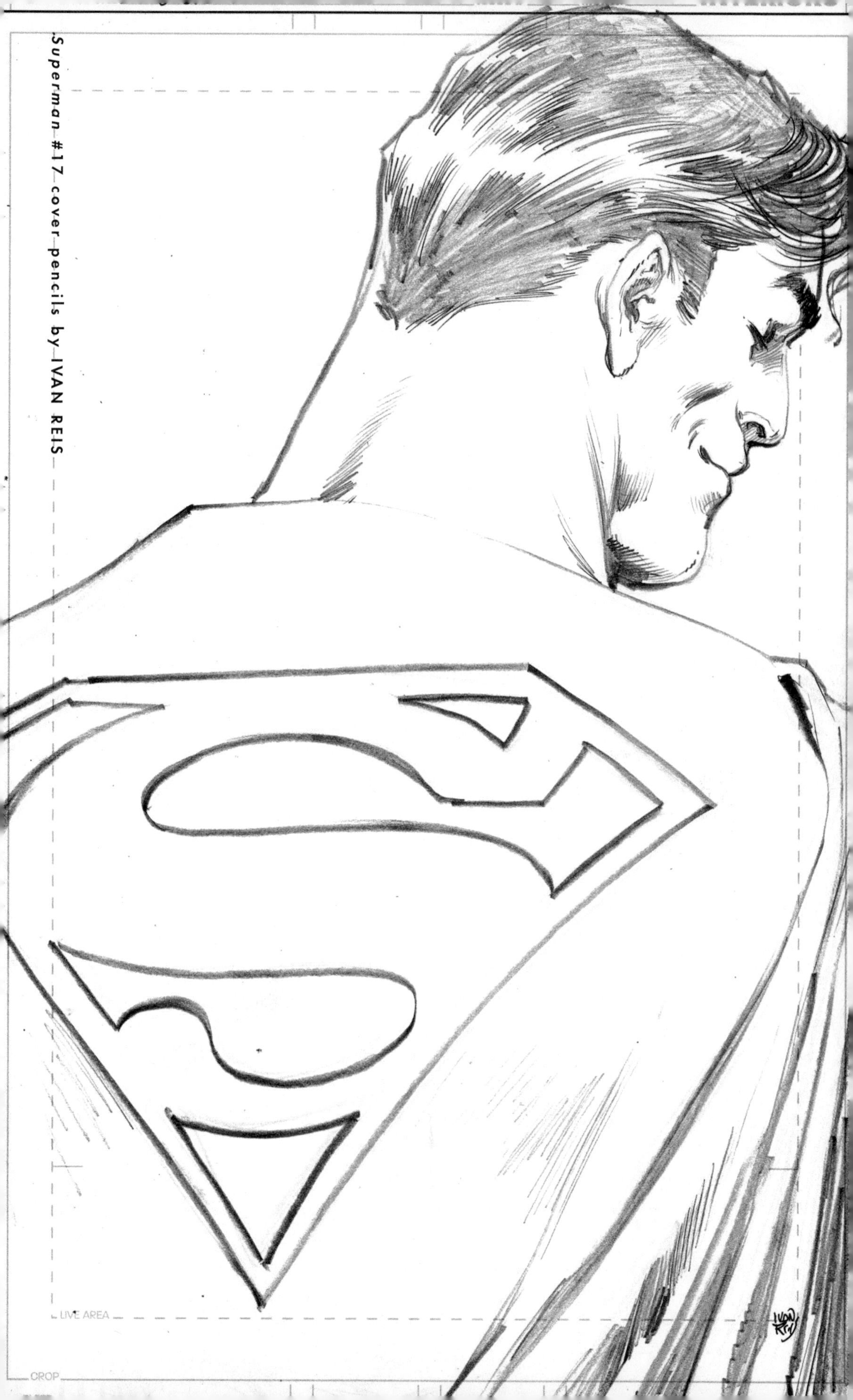
LIVE AREA
CROP

Superman #17 cover pencils by IVAN REIS

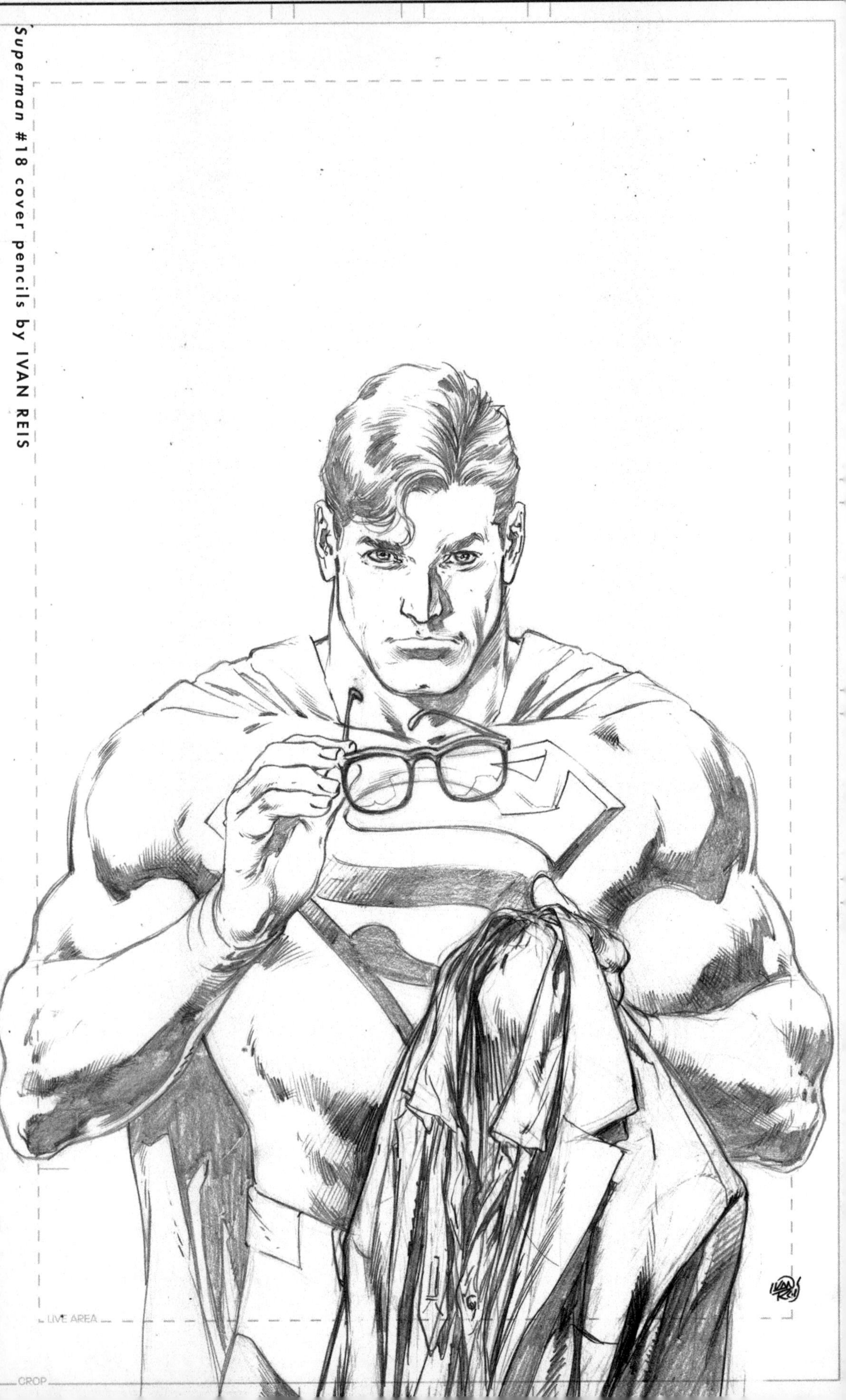
LIVE AREA
CROP

Superman #18 cover pencils by IVAN REIS

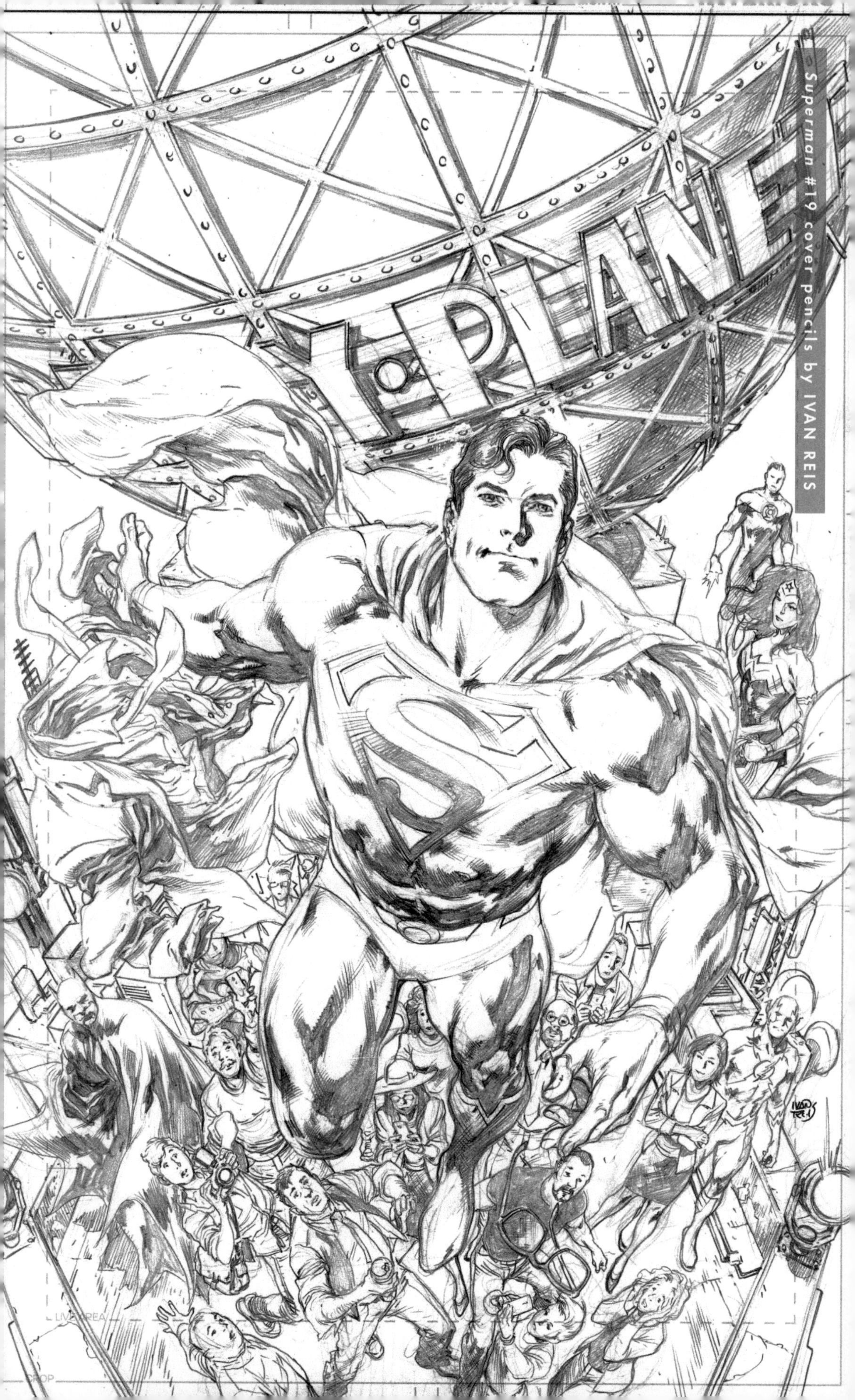
PLANE

Superman #19 cover pencils by IVAN REIS

"Genuinely great character work."
–POLYGON

"A compelling, character-focused start to the series."
–IGN

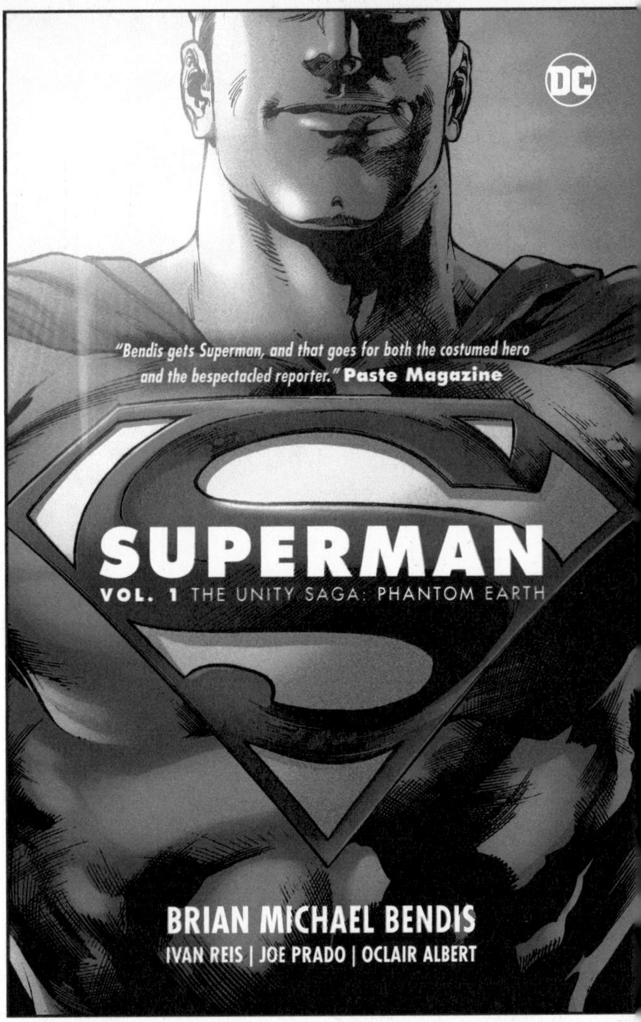
"Bendis gets Superman, and that goes for both the costumed hero and the bespectacled reporter." Paste Magazine
SUPERMAN
VOL. 1 THE UNITY SAGA: PHANTOM EARTH
BRIAN MICHAEL BENDIS
IVAN REIS | JOE PRADO | OCLAIR ALBERT

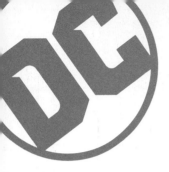

SUPERMAN

VOL. 1: THE UNITY SAGA: PHANTOM EARTH

BRIAN MICHAEL BENDIS AND IVAN REIS

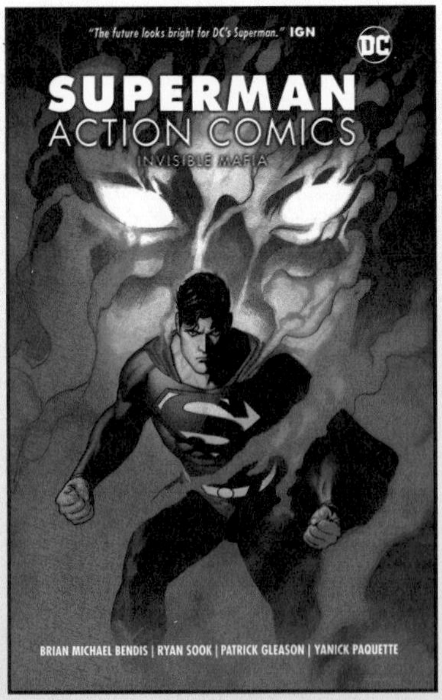
"The future looks bright for DC's Superman." IGN
SUPERMAN
ACTION COMICS
INVISIBLE MAFIA
BRIAN MICHAEL BENDIS | RYAN SOOK | PATRICK GLEASON | YANICK PAQUETTE

SUPERMAN: ACTION COMICS: INVISIBLE MAFIA

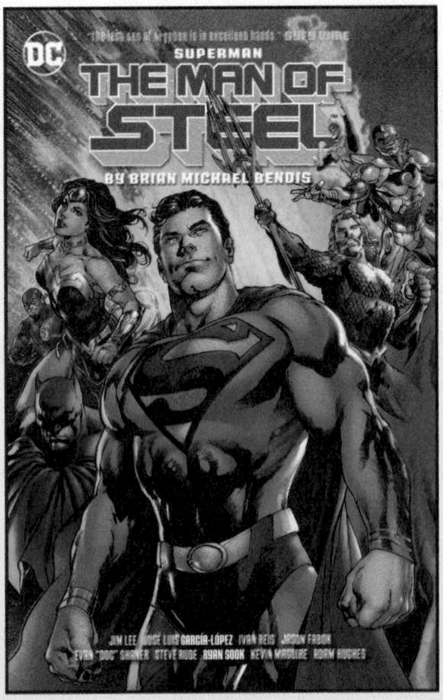
SUPERMAN
THE MAN OF STEEL
BY BRIAN MICHAEL BENDIS

SUPERMAN: THE MAN OF STEEL

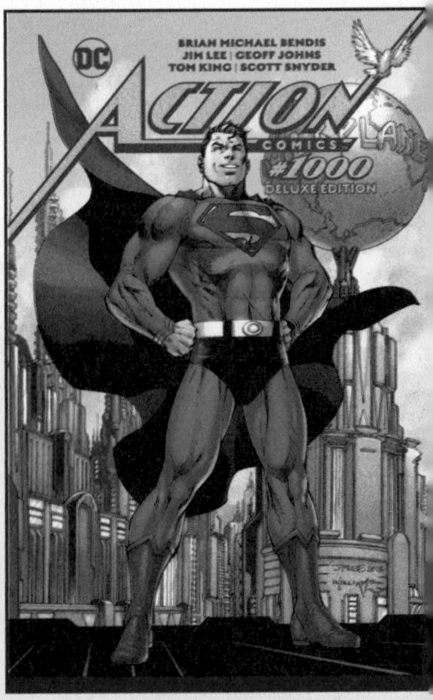
BRIAN MICHAEL BENDIS
JIM LEE | GEOFF JOHNS
TOM KING | SCOTT SNYDER
ACTION
COMICS
#1000
DELUXE EDITION

ACTION COMICS #1000: DELUXE EDITION

wherever comics and books are sold!